Oxford Studies in European Law

General Editors: Paul Craig and Gráinne de Búrca

EC MEMBERSHIP AND THE JUDICIALIZATION OF BRITISH POLITICS

EC Membership and the Judicialization of British Politics

DANNY NICOL

OXFORD
UNIVERSITY PRESS

OXFORD
UNIVERSITY PRESS

Great Clarendon Street, Oxford OX2 6DP

Oxford University Press is a department of the University of Oxford.
It furthers the University's objective of excellence in research, scholarship,
and education by publishing worldwide in

Oxford New York

Athens Auckland Bangkok Bogotá Buenos Aires Cape Town
Chennai Dar es Salaam Delhi Florence Hong Kong Istanbul Karachi
Kolkata Kuala Lumpur Madrid Melbourne Mexico City Mumbai Nairobi
Paris São Paulo Shanghai Singapore Taipei Tokyo Toronto Warsaw

with associated companies in Berlin Ibadan

Oxford is a registered trade mark of Oxford University Press
in the UK and in certain other countries

Published in the United States
by Oxford University Press Inc., New York

British Library Cataloguing in Publication Data

Data available

Library of Congress Cataloging in Publication Data
Nicol, Danny.
EC membership and the judicialization of British politics/Danny Nicol.
p. cm.—(Oxford studies in European Law)
Includes bibliographical references and index.
1. European Union—Great Britain. 2. Law and Politics. I. Title. II. Series.
KJE5092.G7N532001   341.242′2′0941—dc21   2001052062
ISBN 0–19–924779–X

1 3 5 7 9 10 8 6 4 2

Typeset in Janson
by Hope Services (Abingdon) Ltd
Printed in Great Britain
on acid-free paper by
T. J. International Ltd., Padstow, Cornwall

To Vladimir and Vera Derer

GENERAL EDITORS' PREFACE

Lawyers spend a considerable amount of their time looking at statutes. They interpret them, they attempt to divine what the legislator meant, and they assess the efficacy of the resulting instruments. This is a necessary part of the lawyers' stock in trade. It is an important exercise in its own right, whether the statute is dealing with a particular aspect of public law or private law.

It is all the more so when the statute has far-reaching implications for the constitutional structure of the state as a whole, such as the European Communities Act 1972, and the UK's entry into the European Economic Community. The legislation once enacted had to be interpreted and applied by the national courts, including notoriously difficult provisions such as section 2(4) of the Act. The courts would perforce have to make assumptions as to what Parliament meant when it passed the legislation as a whole, as well as the meaning to be attributed to specific provisions.

Danny Nicol's book provides us for the first time with an in-depth account of the Parliamentary proceedings that lay behind the UK's initial attempts to join the EEC, and focuses the spotlight on the debates that preceded the passage of the European Communities Act itself. It is a fascinating story. He shows the lack of consensus prevailing amongst Members of Parliament as to the constitutional impact on the UK of EEC membership. He reveals the imperfect understanding amongst the key players as to the importance and effect of doctrine propounded by the European Court of Justice. This doctrine, on issues such as direct effect and supremacy, was already well established when the UK debates on membership were held. The force of the principles propounded by the European Court of Justice, and the way in which they empowered national courts in their dealings with the executive and Parliament, were not fully appreciated by those engaged in the Westminster debates. The analysis of debates concerning human rights, and the passage of the 1998 Human Rights Act in the UK, provides a valuable comparison of the degree to which the legislature appreciated the constitutional import of its actions in these areas.

This book will be of interest to lawyers in general and to UK lawyers in particular, to those concerned with the legislative process, as well as to specialists concerned with the European Union.

November 2001   Paul Craig

Gráinne de Búrca

PREFACE

This is a book about Parliament. Written from the perspective of an academic lawyer, its object might crudely be characterized as examining what was in the mind of Parliament when it passed the European Communities Act 1972 and other statutes which have incorporated European law into our law. 'Crudely', because Parliament, being a collective body, does not possess a mind as such. Rather, my task was to assess how *widespread* and how *deep* were parliamentary understandings of the constitutional law implications of membership. The verbatim report of parliamentary debates in *Hansard* (and in the Irish parliamentary reports) provided the main material for this study, both plenary and committee debates being examined. In recent years analysis of parliamentary debates has been used by political scientists—Moon,[1] Lord,[2] and Garnett and Sherrington[3]—all, curiously, in the context of assessing House of Commons attitudes to the European Community in various respects.

My aim was to gain an insight into parliamentary understandings of the potential impact of Community jurisprudence on the legislative supremacy of Parliament. Here, examination of *Hansard* admittedly has its limitations. What parliamentarians *said* may not correspond with what they *knew* or *believed*. Doubtless some politicians deliberately did not say what they knew, so a certain caution is advisable. Nonetheless, examination of the parliamentary record remains the best methodology available. As Lord points out, content analysis of *Hansard* speeches, for all its methodological shortcomings, is better than sole reliance on randomly selected quotations.[4] Moreover it has the distinct advantage that 'however much MPs might wish to explain away their recorded views, they can never fully retract them'.[5] In contrast interviewing proved unreliable because of the inclination of interviewees to indulge in retrospective falsification. If, furthermore, one accepts Polsby's characterization of the British Parliament as an 'arena' legislature, then one ought to accord considerable importance to what was *said* and by *whom*.[6]

The study relied on both quantitative and qualitative analysis. Quantitatively, it was important to establish how many MPs appreciated that

---

[1] Moon (1985).   [2] Lord (1990).   [3] Garnett and Sherrington (1996).
[4] Lord (1992) 419–436.   [5] Garnett and Sherrington (1996) 387.
[6] Polsby (1990) 131.

the fundamental 'threat' to parliamentary sovereignty came not from the EC's political institutions but from the ECJ. Qualitatively, the speeches of those MPs who recognized the ECJ's potency were probed to assess the extent to which they realized that the ECJ's inroads into parliamentary sovereignty would be made via the intermediary of the British courts. At two stages in the research a numerical survey was undertaken of attacks by MPs on the various Community institutions. In practice, no doubt due to the polarized nature of the debate, there was no difficulty in distinguishing an 'attack' from something which fell short of an attack.

I will argue that this study raises critical questions about our governmental institutions and their legitimacy. Did parliamentarians realize that they were voting to place the British courts above the British Parliament? And should the courts, in interpreting the 1972 Act, be guided by what legislators *ought* to have understood, or by what they *actually* understood?

I would like to thank the City Solicitors' Educational Trust for funding the project. I would also like to thank: Paul Bernard, Jenny Deitches, Geoffrey Hand, Brigid Laffan, Jane Marriott, Finbarr Murphy, Philip Norton, David O'Keeffe, the late Richard Pitt, Jicca Smith, and Mark Wilde. I owe a special debt of gratitude to Ian Loveland. Above all I would like to thank my mother and my father for all their support.

D.A.N.

London
June 2001

CONTENTS

TABLE OF CASES

Introduction

The British Parliament could once make or unmake any law. Now, however, the United Kingdom courts only enforce the will of Parliament if it complies with the 'higher-order' law of the European Community. This book tells the story of how Parliament's legislative omnipotence came to be lost. It does so from the perspective of the parliamentarians themselves. It explores whether parliamentarians wittingly agreed to their relegation—examining what debate took place, how issues of parliamentary sovereignty were perceived, and how these perceptions evolved.

The narrative has a pervasive theme: the judicialization of politics in Britain. Law undeniably occupies a more central role in British politics than it did thirty years ago. Indeed, we have witnessed nothing short of the transformation of the British constitution from a constitution firmly based on politics to one increasingly based on law. The traditional UK constitutional model vested power overwhelmingly in the hands of the political actors, but this era has now drawn to a close. A combination of European Community membership, the robust growth of domestic judicial review, and the Human Rights Act has resulted in a major shift in power in favour of the courts. In particular, accession to the Community has proven the prime catalyst in the transformation of our public law, not least because it presented a wholesale challenge to the legislative supremacy of Parliament. The British judiciary's embrace of Community law has led to the demotion of Parliament into a legislature of limited competence.

The new constitutional settlement will undoubtedly generate an extensive literature assessing its impact and debating its merits and demerits. We can look forward to fierce debate between the supporters and detractors of the enhanced judicial role and the corresponding diminution of Parliament. The object of this book, however, is to investigate how we got here in the first place. Under the old constitutional arrangements Parliament was supreme:

under the new settlement its legislative power is significantly constrained. One might expect the relegation of the legislature to have met with considerable parliamentary resistance, or at least to have been subjected to vigorous debate. This book explores whether this was the case.

The convergence of the political and legal aspects of the constitution has profound implications. Gone are the days when every policy was potentially contestable at every general election. Ever-wider areas of legislative policy have been placed beyond the reach of a popular majority by the ever-growing law of the Community (and, arguably, of the European Convention on Human Rights), obedience to which is enforced by the British courts. The enormity of this constitutional transformation raises fundamental questions about the legitimacy of both parliamentary and judicial decision-making in this sphere.

The trend towards judicial activism has been extensively chronicled,[1] as has the executive's response.[2] However, the corresponding evolution of *parliamentary* attitudes has largely escaped analysis.[3] Yet it is surely valuable to chart the extent to which the 'legalization' of the political process has affected parliamentary discourse. The fact that Parliament now operates in the shadow of law[4] may reveal a shift in the behavioural role of MPs, exacting a greater consciousness of the restrictions placed upon them by the requirements of public law. Such information may furnish insights into the desirability of reform to integrate MPs further into the new constitution and help them adjust to their changed role. The book therefore examines the parliamentary debates relating to UK attempts to join the Community, to assess MPs' knowledge or ignorance of the legal implications of accession. It then goes on to analyse parliamentary approval of subsequent Treaty revisions (the Single European Act and the Maastricht Treaty), as well as the passage of the Human Rights Act 1998, to evaluate how MPs have acclimatized to the growing intrusion of law into the political sphere. The story ends in the late 1990s, by which time, it will be argued, parliamentary adaptation to the new constitutional order had been substantially achieved.

---

[1] See eg Griffith (1997) 326–333.   [2] See eg Woodhouse (1996), Loveland (1997).
[3] Rawlings, however, has analysed parliamentary reaction in the context of Maastricht ratification. See Rawlings (1994*a*).
[4] Ibid 255–256.

The judicialization of Britain

Until recently the UK was perceived as having a 'political constitution'.[5] As Griffith put it, the heart of the British constitution was that UK governments could take any action deemed necessary for the country's proper governance provided Parliament sanctioned the requisite legal changes.[6] This was because for some three hundred years the courts chose to adopt an essentially subordinate role *vis-à-vis* Parliament. They did so by formulating and loyally adhering to the doctrine of parliamentary sovereignty as the constitution's dominant legal principle. Parliamentary sovereignty means that the judiciary regard Parliament as the supreme lawmaker.[7] Under the doctrine the courts accept Parliament's right to make any law whatsoever. The role of the courts is to enforce each and every statute. It is not their place to question the validity of Acts of Parliament.[8] Furthermore since the loyalty of the courts is to the latest expression of Parliament's will, the courts will not permit earlier Parliaments to bind the present one.[9] This aspect of the doctrine preserved Parliament's status as a *continuously* sovereign institution: 'its unconfined sovereignty is created anew every time it meets, irrespective of what previous parliaments have enacted.'[10]

Since Acts of Parliament were the highest form of law, the judicial role was limited to applying and interpreting statute. Thus parliamentary sovereignty served to relegate the courts *vis-à-vis* the other organs of governance. The institutional beneficiaries of the doctrine were Parliament and government.

---

[5] Griffith (1979) 1–21. For a more recent view see Munro (1999) 8–14.

[6] Griffith (1979) 15.

[7] For a comprehensive exposition of the doctrine see Loveland (2000) ch 2.

[8] *British Railways Board v Pickin* [1974] AC 765, *Cheney v Conn* [1968] 1 All ER 779.

[9] *Ellen Street Estates Ltd v Minister of Health* [1934] 1 KB 590.

[10] Loveland (2000) 33. Opinion is, however, divided on one aspect of Parliament's inability to bind its successors. Supporters of the 'continuing' (or 'old') theory of parliamentary sovereignty maintain that Parliament cannot bind itself in any way whatsoever, whereas adherents to the 'self-embracing' (or 'new') school of sovereignty argue that Parliament can at least bind itself as to the *manner and form* by which future legislation is to be enacted. Some commentators argue that this distinction may prove relevant to the interpretation of the European Communities Act 1972 by the British courts (see eg Craig (1991) 251, Eekelaar (1997)). To other commentators such as Allan (1997) and Loveland (2000: 388–393), the 'continuing'/'self-embracing' distinction assumes less importance in explaining the UK courts' acceptance of the supremacy of Community law. In recent years there has been a welcome change of academic emphasis with more interest in the normative question of which version of parliamentary sovereignty *ought* to prevail, or indeed whether we ought to have parliamentary sovereignty at all (see especially Craig (1991)).

Parliamentary sovereignty obviously strengthened the power of Parliament, which was free to enact any law it liked without fear of judicial review. Above all, however, parliamentary sovereignty reinforced executive power. Since governments can generally push their legislation through Parliament, they could clothe their decisions in legality by inducing the legislature to enact them in statutory form. In his classic study of parliamentary sovereignty Dicey carefully distinguished *legal* sovereignty—the question of who has the right to make and unmake the supreme law of the land—from *political* sovereignty—the question of whose will prevails in the making of such legislation.[11] Certainly the government is the main political beneficiary of the legal doctrine of parliamentary sovereignty.[12]

The courts also limited their own power by adhering to the literal approach to statutory interpretation, whereby they eschewed judicial 'gap-filling' based on the invocation of legislative intention. Maverick judges who were overly creative in their construction of statute were liable to get their knuckles rapped by superior courts.[13] Judicial reluctance to manipulate the words used by the sovereign legislature served to strengthen the power of Parliament. The pre-eminence of the political actors over the courts was further reinforced by the fact that the constitution was based on a great deal of convention and little law.[14] Conventions—constitutional obligations obedience to which is secured despite the absence of judicial means of enforcement—dominate the constitution to such an extent that the very existence and role of Prime Minister and Cabinet are creatures of convention. Since no one can go to court to enforce conventions, their pre-eminence likewise served to keep the judiciary out of politics.

Judicial impotence *vis-à-vis* Parliament gave Members of Parliament little incentive to take much interest in court decisions. For MPs, the constitution

---

[11] Dicey (1959) 73.

[12] Dicey attributed political sovereignty to the electorate since 'the will of the electorate and certainly of the electorate in combination with the Lords and the Commons, is sure ultimately to prevail on all subjects to be determined by the British government . . . The electors can in the long run always enforce their will' (ibid 73). In fact although public opinion can have an influence— memorably the abolition of the community charge—the picture is not a consistent one. There can be formidable obstacles to the electors enforcing their will, not least the strength of consensuses formed by the political elite. Thus even 'in the long run' the electors have failed to enforce their will on the issue of the death penalty despite consistent opinion poll evidence pointing to public support for its reintroduction. Similarly neither main party favours restoring the link between pensions and average earnings despite some 70% opinion poll support for this policy.

[13] See eg Lord Simonds's criticism of Denning LJ in *Magor and St Mellons RDC v Newport Corpn* [1951] 2 All ER 839 at 841.

[14] See generally Dicey (1959), Marshall (1990).

was what happened. The courts operated only on the fringes of the political arena; the role of judicial review was 'sporadic and peripheral'.[15]

However, Parliament's supremacy was built on shaky foundations. The doctrine of parliamentary sovereignty is a doctrine whose fate lies in the hands of the courts. This fundamental point can be illustrated by considering the doctrine's historical genesis, the Glorious Revolution of 1688.[16] In the Glorious Revolution Parliament triumphed not over the courts but over the Crown. Subsequently, the courts understandably chose to side with Parliament by accepting its statutes as the supreme law of the land. Thus judicial obedience to statute *reflected* the ultimate *political* fact that Parliament was supreme over the executive, and that no one was supreme over Parliament.[17] The basic tenets of parliamentary sovereignty do not appear in the Bill of Rights 1689 nor in any other statute. Rather, Acts of Parliament were the highest form of law because the judges said they were. Parliamentary sovereignty was the gift of the courts; and what the courts have given, the courts could conceivably take back.

A change in the 'ultimate political fact' might prompt the courts to modify the legal doctrine or even abolish it. Parliament's 1971 decision to approve Community membership and its subsequent enactment of the European Communities Act 1972 could be taken to constitute such a change. In passing the Act, Parliament could be taken as having issued an invitation to the courts to reconsider parliamentary sovereignty in the light of membership. It would then be up to the courts whether to soldier on with unqualified parliamentary omnipotence, or else to create a massive exception to the parliamentary sovereignty doctrine in the Community law context. The aim of this book is to chronicle whether parliamentarians realized that this was what they were doing, and to examine how their constitutional understandings developed.

The profundity of the constitutional revolution underscores the importance of assessing political understanding of it. During the period covered by this book, the role of the courts was transformed. This transformation was gradual and step by step, but it was a transformation nonetheless. It was aided by a change in judicial personnel and, with it, attitudes. First, in the 1960s judges, emboldened by a dramatic change in the composition of the House of Lords, started taking a more interventionist approach to judicial review.[18] The Law Lords' new activism was intimately linked to their abandonment of the traditional literal technique of statutory interpretation in favour of a

---

[15] De Smith, Woolf, and Jowell (1995) p. vii.   [16] See Norton (1989).
[17] McLeod (1999) 79–83.   [18] Griffith (1993) ch 4.

more purposive approach. If the words of a statute took second place to judges' conception of the intention of the legislature, this would do much to liberate the courts from their past strictures. Although the expansion of judicial review primarily challenged the executive, it is arguable that judicial 'interpretation' of statute became so overly creative as to usurp the legislative function and present a challenge to the power of Parliament itself.[19] Secondly, British judges in the late 1980s and early 1990s fully embraced the opportunities offered to them to expand the judicial role by dint of UK membership of the Community. Community law doctrines had a far-reaching effect on judicial review generally[20] and on parliamentary sovereignty in particular. Within the scope of Community law, the British courts have now modified the doctrine of parliamentary sovereignty by making it 'the duty of a United Kingdom court, when delivering final judgment, to override *any rule of national law* found to be in conflict with any directly enforceable rule of Community law'.[21] Once again it should be emphasized that a different set of judges might have reacted differently to Community law.[22] Thirdly, in the 1990s a new generation of judges adopted a more vigorous approach to the protection of basic constitutional rights and this has now received the imprimatur of the legislature through the enactment of the Human Rights Act 1998. Although on a formal level the Act does not invite any further modification of the parliamentary sovereignty doctrine, the system of the Act will place immense pressure on legislators to amend or repeal statutory provisions which the courts deem incompatible with fundamental rights.

[19] eg *Padfield v Minister of Agriculture* [1968] AC 997 and *Anisminic v Foreign Compensation Commission* [1969] 2 AC 147. See the treatment of these cases by Loveland (2000) 410–411 and 69–71, Griffith (1993) 86 and 106, Griffith (1997) 105 and 108. On *Anisminic*, see Wade and Forsyth (2000) 707–710.

[20] Craig (1997*b*) 271–296.

[21] *Per* Lord Bridge, *R v Secretary of State for Transport, ex parte Factortame Ltd (No 2)* [1991] AC 603, 659 (emphasis added).

[22] Lord Bridge, who gave the forthright acceptance of the supremacy of Community law in *Factortame (No 2)* had also delivered a speech receptive to the future introduction of the principle of proportionality as a ground for (purely domestic) judicial review in *R v Secretary of State for the Home Department ex parte Brind* [1991] 1 AC 521. Neither of the two judges who expressed hostility to the introduction of proportionality as a ground of review in *Brind*, Lord Lowry and Lord Ackner, sat in *Factortame (No 2)*.

The pivotal role of EC membership: supremacy and direct effect

It would be mistaken, therefore, to attribute the public law revolution entirely to Community membership. Nonetheless, accession to the Community represented the decisive turning point. It constituted the strongest challenge to the political constitution because fundamental doctrines developed by the European Court of Justice (ECJ) conflicted directly with the legislative supremacy of Parliament. For this reason the question of parliamentary understandings of the legal impact of membership is the main (though not exclusive) focus of this book. The limitation of parliamentary sovereignty and the judicialization of politics are two inextricably linked issues. The fact that the voluminous 'supreme law of the land'—statute—was easily changeable by Parliament served to concentrate power in the hands of the politicians. As Richard Crossman put it, 'British politicians have no profound belief in natural law, largely because we have no written constitution or Supreme Court. If we don't like a law, we just change it.'[23] Once in the Community, however, the British courts might well choose to elevate the Treaty of Rome to the status of a new 'supreme law' unchangeable by Parliament, furnishing a ready yardstick by which the judiciary could assess the validity of statute.[24] Thus Community membership potentially opened up vast swathes of statute to judicial supervision. The decision to join the Community was a decision to switch from a politics-based model of governance to one firmly based on law.

This was because, early in the Community's life, the ECJ opted for a court-driven strategy to achieve the Treaty's aims. It chose to enlist national judiciaries in its efforts to ensure the uniform enforcement of Community rules. Its relentless 'directed use of judicial power'[25] involved empowering and obliging national judiciaries to prevent their national executives and legislatures from violating Community law.

---

[23] Mount (1993) 206.

[24] The EC Treaty can only be amended by unanimous agreement by the governments of the Member States, with the amendments ratified by the Member States each according to their respective constitutional requirements. The relevant provision is now embodied in Article 48 of the Treaty on European Union. (Since the period covered by this study predates the Amsterdam Treaty 1997, the book generally uses the pre-Amsterdam numbering of the Community Treaties.)

[25] Tridimas (1998) 11, 14.

First, in the celebrated *Van Gend en Loos* case in 1963,[26] the ECJ was asked by a Dutch customs tribunal whether Article 12 EEC (the 'standstill' provision prohibiting Member States from establishing new import duties or raising existing ones) was capable of giving rights to individuals which they could enforce in their national courts. This was a question of seminal importance. For, as even ECJ judges have acknowledged,[27] at first blush the Treaty of Rome looked like a mere international trade agreement, a compact between nations, which could in no way create enforceable rights for individuals.

On the issue of whether the ECJ had jurisdiction to hear the case, the Dutch and Belgian governments intervened to argue that the question of the internal effect of Community law within the Netherlands was a matter of Dutch constitutional law which fell outside the ECJ's remit. The ECJ tersely retorted that the question of what effect Article 12 had at the national level was a question of how Article 12 was to be interpreted. Since the issue was one of *Treaty interpretation*, the ECJ enjoyed jurisdiction under Article 177 of the Treaty. This holding was immensely important, since the ECJ was asserting that *it* would determine the internal effect of Community law within Member States.[28] At an even broader level, the ECJ's statement on jurisdiction set the stage for the wholesale use of the preliminary reference procedure to assess the compatibility of *national* measures with Community rules.

The ECJ went on to hold that Community law was indeed capable of creating rights for individuals which national courts and tribunals were obliged to protect—the doctrine of direct effect. Although it claimed some support for the creation of this doctrine from the text and system of the Treaty, its primary justification appeared to be that direct effect was necessary in order to achieve the objective of the Community, namely the establishment of a common market.

What was to be the status of such directly effective Community law rights in relation to incompatible national laws? The solution was only hinted at in *Van Gend en Loos*, where the ECJ characterized the new legal order which it had created as one in which 'the states have limited their sovereign rights, albeit in limited fields'. The following year, however, in *Costa v ENEL*, the ECJ established its doctrine of supremacy. It uncompromisingly declared

---

[26] Case 26/62 *NV Algemene Transport- en Expeditie Onderneming Van Gend en Loos v Nederlandse Administratie der Belastingen* [1963] ECR 1, [1963] CMLR 105.

[27] Koopmans (1983) 101.

[28] As such it furnished the jurisdictional basis not only for the doctrine of direct effect but for all the other doctrines—supremacy, indirect effect, State liability, effective remedies—which have done so much to bring about the uniform enforcement of Community law.

that Community law 'could not be overridden by domestic legal provisions, however framed'.[29] In the 1970 case of *Internationale Handelsgesellschaft* the ECJ spelt out the logic of this statement, holding that Community law prevailed even over national fundamental rights or the principles of a national constitutional structure.[30] Finally, in *Simmenthal*, decided in 1978, the ECJ made it clear that individuals had no need to appeal up to the highest court in each State for it to set aside incompatible national law. Rather, it was the duty of *every* court and tribunal in every Member State to enforce Community law in its entirety, and therefore to refuse to apply any conflicting national rule.[31] The ECJ in *Simmenthal* plainly envisaged a proactive role for the national courts in setting aside national legislation, for it instructed them to do so *if necessary of their own motion*, in other words, even if the need to refuse to apply national law had not been raised by the parties.

These decisions had an empowering effect both on the ECJ itself and on the national courts. In the case of the ECJ, supremacy and direct effect permitted the use of the preliminary reference procedure to assess the compatibility of national law with Community law. As Mancini has explained, although the EC Treaty does not permit ECJ review of national laws, it provided machinery which the ECJ has exploited to monitor the compatibility of national law with Community law. The ECJ achieved this through the expedient of pitching its rulings at a certain level of abstraction. Thus the ECJ has consistently declined to rule on whether national rule *A* is in violation of Community Regulation *B* or Directive *C*, but it has always been happy to indicate to what extent a *certain type* of national legislation can be regarded as violating that measure.[32] The ECJ's ingenious use of the preliminary reference procedure to explain to national courts the extent to which they would have to set aside national measures in favour of directly effective Community provisions elevated it to a status akin to that of a Supreme Court.

Direct effect and supremacy also empowered the national courts. The ECJ offered national courts the inducement of changing the balance of power in the Member States in favour of national judiciaries at the expense of national executives and legislatures. Weiler has argued that 'plain and simple judicial empowerment' was indispensable in recruiting the national courts and

---

[29] Case 6/64 *Flaminio Costa v ENEL* [1964] ECR 585, [1964] CMLR 425, 593.

[30] Case 11/70 *Internationale Handelsgesellschaft mbH v Einfuhr- und Vorratsstelle für Getriede und Futtermittel* [1970] ECR 1125, [1972] CMLR 255.

[31] Case 106/77 *Amministrazione delle Finanze dello Stato v Simmenthal SpA* [1978] ECR 629, [1978] 3 CMLR 263.

[32] Mancini (2000) 8–9.

tribunals as the ordinary courts of Community law.[33] Craig is critical of the customary portrayal of EC supremacy as representing a relative decline in national competence, arguing that although the *political* arm of national government is weakened, the *judicial* arm is strengthened.[34] Barav identifies a 'dramatic alteration in the constitutional status of the national judicial authorities' and ascribes this not wholly to the ECJ itself but also to 'continuous albeit discreet pressure exerted by the national courts, mainly through questions for preliminary rulings'.[35] Be that as it may, Community membership enhanced the power of all the courts and tribunals in the Member States. In countries where the constitution permitted judicial review of legislation, this was no longer to be the preserve of the Supreme or Constitutional Court. Rather, where national law was found to conflict with Community measures, all Member State courts were duty-bound to disregard the national law. However, Supreme or Constitutional courts did not go empty-handed either. They had been handed a new and expansive ground on which to invalidate domestic legislation.[36]

The shift in the balance of power in a country such as the United Kingdom, where the doctrine of parliamentary sovereignty traditionally made judicial review of primary legislation impermissible, was all the more stark. If the UK judiciary chose to embrace the ECJ's doctrines, then far from having to enforce every Act of Parliament, British courts and tribunals—whatever their rank in the legal hierarchy—would be empowered, indeed obliged, to disregard any statutes which in their opinion contravened Community law. This would constitute a most profound change to the UK's institutional balance.

Although the ECJ talked in terms of 'refusing to apply' national law—phrases such as 'setting aside', 'overriding', and 'disapplying' are also commonly used—there may be little difference between 'setting aside' and invalidation. Certainly the ECJ has always carefully maintained that invalidation is the preserve of the national courts. And it is true that there are contexts in which the national provision is rendered only partially impotent. For instance, national rules may be held to conflict with the free movement of goods when applied to products imported from other Member States and must therefore be disapplied in that context, but may remain perfectly valid in the context of the domestic product.[37] Furthermore, if the Community

---

[33] Weiler (1999) 192–197.   [34] Craig (1997*b*) 216.

[35] Barav (1994) 269.   [36] Nicol (1996) 579–581.

[37] eg the German beer purity rules in Case 178/84 *Commission v Germany* [1987] ECR 1227, [1988] 1 CMLR 780, the Italian requirement that pasta be made of durum wheat in Case 407/85 *Drei Glocken GmbH and Gertraude Kritzinger v USL Centro-Sud and Provincia autonoma di Bolzano* [1988] ECR 4233.

norm with which the national provision is incompatible is amended or repealed, the national provision—assuming it has not itself been repealed in the meantime—revives. There are, however, fields in which disapplication may mean much the same as invalidation, in that the national rule may be rendered ineffective in all contexts so long as the Community provision is in force. Typically this will occur in the growing number of policy areas in which Community law does not require the crossing of a frontier to trigger its application. Accordingly, for the ECJ to bestow upon every national court authority to 'refuse to apply' national law is in many cases a fig leaf for endowing that court with the power to strike down national law.[38]

EC membership thus presented a fundamental constitutional choice—between the (judicially self-imposed) doctrine of parliamentary sovereignty and the (ECJ-created) doctrines of supremacy and direct effect. It cannot be overemphasized that this choice was ultimately *a choice to be made by the British courts*. In the final analysis, it would be for the courts, presented with a case involving clear incompatibility between an EC provision and an Act of Parliament, to decide which prevailed. No attempt by Parliament to dictate in advance a desired outcome could relieve the judges of their dilemma. For even if Parliament at the time of accession signalled in the clearest terms its wish to abolish its own sovereignty, this was not Parliament's to give away. As the fundamental ground rule of the British constitution, parliamentary sovereignty is supposedly unalterable by Parliament. In addition, since one of the requirements of parliamentary sovereignty is that Parliament cannot be bound by its predecessors, it was an open question how the courts would react to a situation where Parliament on accession purported to accord supremacy to Community law over all future statutes, but later passed an Act contravening Community law. The question of whether the courts would abandon their long-standing loyalty to the Parliament of the day could only be resolved *by the courts themselves*, when obliged to decide a case which involved an irreconcilable clash between an Act of Parliament and Community law. At that point the British courts would have to opt either to uphold the traditional parliamentary sovereignty doctrine by enforcing the more recent statute, or else to accord primacy to Community law. Until such a case reached the courts, neither the continued survival of parliamentary sovereignty nor the successful establishment within the UK of the supremacy of Community law could be taken for granted.

---

[38] See De Witte (1999) 189–190, Nicol (1996) 586.

Legitimacy 1: parliamentary response

The incompatibility between parliamentary sovereignty and the supremacy of Community law raises acute questions relating to the constitutional understandings of British parliamentarians. Did MPs and peers appreciate that if they passed legislation inviting the courts to discard parliamentary sovereignty the courts might well go ahead and do just that? Did they grasp that their fate as a sovereign legislature rested in the hands of the judges? Did they realize that Community membership would endanger the dominance of politics over law?

The success or failure of parliamentarians to understand the potential of Community membership to effect a judicialization of the constitution has a vital bearing on Parliament's *legitimacy* as a law-making institution. In recent years Parliament's legitimacy crisis stemming from its 'growing irrelevance . . . to the main decisions affecting people's lives' has become increasingly acute.[39] Legitimacy is a concept with a range of meanings, and no attempt at an exhaustive review will be made here.[40] The rival conceptions have been neatly summarized in the description of legitimacy as containing 'both a social aspect, in terms of being rooted in popular consent, and a normative

---

[39] Riddell (2000) 19.

[40] Briefly, a fundamental division exists between Weber who defined legitimacy as the extent to which institutions are considered *by the public* to be right and proper (Weber (1968) 212–217) and Habermas who argued that *normative legitimizing principles* are required in order to assess an institution's 'right to rule' (Habermas (1973) 95–143). This distinction has been attributed to the gulf between the social scientist and the moral philosopher (Beetham (1991) 3–41), between the 'is' and the 'ought' (Habermas (1973) 102), and there is much to be said for Hyde's suggestion that these two very different concepts should be known by different names (Hyde (1983) n 45). It is of course open to commentators to choose between these contending definitions. Weber's conception of legitimacy is valuable in socio-political studies, where it is important to assess 'the capacity of the system to engender and maintain the belief that the existing political institutions are the most appropriate ones for the society' (Lipset (1960) 77). However, it is hard to disagree with Schaar's argument that such a definition, by trimming legitimacy of its normative content, has dissolved the concept into belief or opinion (Schaar (1984) 109). Being based purely on an empirical study of popular sentiment, the Weberian conception of legitimacy permits no assessment of whether such belief on the part of the public is motivated by 'good reasons' (Habermas (1979) 200). Thus the Nazi and Soviet totalitarian regimes would be regarded as legitimate. Weber's definition is inappropriate for the purposes of this study since, as Habermas argues, it demotes the academic commentator to an observer rather than a participant in the debate surrounding the political issues inherent in the study of legitimacy. To rest our interest in parliamentary informed consent merely on a survey of public opinion would be to adopt too narrow a focus. Our interest is rather in the *normative standing* of the power arrangements that the law validates.

aspect, in terms of the underlying values on which such consent is based'.[41] It is the normative aspect which concerns us here. In other words, we are interested in the criteria whereby one assesses an institution's (in this case, Parliament's) 'right to rule'. Such criteria are not universal but contentious and contestable. As Craig argues, they spring from a commentator's accompanying political background theory.[42] This book is therefore premised on the broader background thesis that envisages Parliament as at least fulfilling a serious participatory and deliberative role. Such a theory readily concedes that the political consequence of Parliament's legislative supremacy is a strengthened executive. However, it argues that executive dominance is *a matter of degree*, and that the power of government needs to be tempered by *participation, deliberation, and influence* by parliamentarians, not least in the context of fundamental constitutional change. A precondition to effective deliberation, however, is that parliamentarians should understand correctly the matters on which they legislate. This study is therefore based on the assumption that executive power needs to be offset by the pressure of *informed* debate in a representative assembly *which understands the legal implications of the measures on which it is voting*. To put it another way, Parliament should not make its decisions from a position of legal ignorance. The greater the enormity of the constitutional change legislators are asked to sanction, the greater should be their understanding of its implications.

Having opted for a version of legitimacy based on normative prescription, it is then necessary to arrive at 'a recognition of what *is* as the basis for bringing about what *ought* to be'.[43] If Parliament wielded no influence at all over government, then the question of whether or not parliamentarians enjoyed adequate understanding of legal issues would be irrelevant. We need therefore to consider the extent of Parliament's legitimization crisis.

It is widely acknowledged that Parliament's legitimacy, as measured by its meaningful participation and the importance attached by government to its deliberations, has been eroded. Commentators have often laid the blame at the door of executive omnipotence and Britain's First Past the Post electoral system. In particular the allegation that the power of the executive over the legislature is so overwhelming as to amount to 'elective dictatorship' has frequently been made. Bagehot considered that the main function of the House of Commons was as an electoral college, choosing the administration.[44] With the strengthening of the party system in the late nineteenth century, however,

---

[41] De Búrca (1996).   [42] Craig (1991) 218–223.   [43] Norton (1982) 110.
[44] Bagehot (1905) 130.

this function was lost, leading to doubts about the House's role.[45] The task of sustaining a government sat uneasily with the duty of holding it to account.[46] Dicey's normative justification for parliamentary sovereignty—that Parliament authentically represented the national will and controlled the executive in conformity with it[47]—swiftly disintegrated, and by 1931 Lloyd George was cheerfully conceding that 'the fact of the matter is that the House of Commons has no real effective and continuous control over the actions of the Executive'.[48]

Latterly Wade has argued that most legislation could more accurately be said to be enacted by government rather than Parliament, and has even suggested that some new body ought to be invented to give proper attention to legislation since Parliament is no longer willing or able to do so.[49] For Mackintosh, Parliament is merely one of the agencies through which government operates.[50] Similarly Harden and Lewis view Parliament as excluded from all but the final stages of policy-making.[51] Recent developments have merely underscored this long-standing constitutional reality. These include the growth of prime ministerial authoritarianism,[52] the elevation of appointed advisers[53] and corresponding downgrading of backbench opinion (whether in the form of departmental select committees[54] or parliamentary parties[55]), and the announcement of major policy initiatives to the media rather than to Parliament.[56] The increasing element of leadership control in both main parties over selection and reselection of parliamentary candidates has reinforced governmental domination of the legislature, since rather than the executive being accountable to the parliamentarians, parliamentarians are increasingly becoming accountable to the executive.[57] The increasingly obvious inability of Parliament to keep the executive accountable was reflected in Speaker Boothroyd's retirement statement:

---

[45] Norton (1982) 98.   [46] Nolan and Sedley (1997) 8.

[47] Dicey (1959) 70–76. See Craig (1991) 12–55.

[48] Quoted in LeMay (1964) 163. Contemporaneously Muir commented that '[o]ne of the chief causes of the failure of the House of Commons to exercise an effective control over Government is the dictatorship wielded by the Cabinet whenever it commands a majority, and, in particular, its practice of treating every serious criticism of the work of the Departments as an attack upon itself, to be resisted with the whole strength of its majority'. Muir (1930) 195.

[49] Wade (1980) 12–13.   [50] Mackintosh (1977) 129.

[51] Harden and Lewis (1986) 111.

[52] *The Times*, 8 February 1990, *Financial Times*, 24 July 1997, *Independent*, 1 May 1999.

[53] *Financial Times*, 6 May 1997, 3 June 1997.

[54] *The Times*, 7 October 1997, *Financial Times*, 15 July 1997.

[55] *Sunday Times*, 1 June 1997.   [56] *Financial Times*, 22 October 1997.

[57] *The Times*, 13 July 1997 (Labour); *The Times*, 7 October 1997 (Conservatives).

[T]he high reputation of Westminster abroad is not entirely reflected at home ... The level of cynicism about Parliament, and the accompanying alienation of many of the young from the democratic process, is troubling ... Let us make a start by remembering that the function of Parliament is to hold the Executive accountable. [HON. MEMBERS: 'Hear, hear'.] That is the role for which history has cast the Commons. It is the core task of Members ... It is in Parliament in the first instance that Ministers must explain and justify their policies.[58]

Some commentators argue that executive dominance has been reinforced by the First Past the Post electoral system under which the House of Commons is elected. First Past the Post has been seen by some as contributing to the establishment of 'an elective dictatorship based on minority rule'[59] since it 'puts a formidable premium upon party solidarity',[60] and damages the functional efficiency of the House of Commons in relation to its role in keeping the executive accountable.[61] This view is, however, contested. Supporters of the system argue that changing to a form of proportional representation would not result in some general increase in backbench influence but would ironically concentrate power *dis*proportionately in the hands of parties with the least electoral support.[62]

Nonetheless, it can be contended that executive power is not so overwhelming as to deprive Parliament of a role. Bagehot considered that the second most important function of the Commons, after electing the government, was an *informing* function: 'the function which belongs to it, and to the members of it, to bring before the nation the ideas, grievances and wishes of special classes.'[63] Likewise, for Muir writing in 1930, the *deliberative* role of the House was important:

Despite the omnipotence of a majority Cabinet, no Government dare make any important departure at home or abroad without publicly explaining and defending its action in the House of Commons ... Every Government ... however powerful, knows that it must publicly justify every important action that it takes, *and this must profoundly influence its policy* ... The debates on Government policy ... are perhaps the most valuable part of the House's work.[64]

---

[58] HC, 354, cols 1113–1114, 26 July 2000. See also the memoirs of John Major, where the former Prime Minister devotes his closing chapter (entitled 'The Empty House') to the decline of Parliament. He complains that 'too often we see judges in judicial reviews called upon to restrain the Executive, while at the same time the government thumbs its nose at a Parliament that is being bypassed, disregarded, treated as an irritation and "modernised" out of effectiveness'. Major (2000) 737–751.

[59] Hailsham (1978) 187–188.

[60] Finer (1975) 12–13.

[61] Blackburn (1995) 410–417.

[62] Hain (1986) 45.

[63] Bagehot (1905) 172.

[64] Muir (1930) 236 (emphasis added).

Moreover over the last thirty years there has been a rich academic literature supporting the view that Parliament has *reasserted* its legislative influence. The 1970–4 Parliament is widely seen as a turning point. Beer has talked in terms of a sudden breakdown in the 'Prussian discipline' which characterized parliamentary behaviour prior to the 1970s, linking this to a shift in backbench attitudes from 'deferential' to 'participant'.[65] Even before the 1970s, however, Butt's remarkable study identified significant backbench influence asserted in private rather than on the floor of the House, a view with which Jennings concurs.[66] Norton shows that, from the 1970–4 Parliament onwards, backbench assertiveness increasingly took the form of cross-voting. Between 1970 and 1984 the number of government defeats in both Houses exceeded 500, a level without precedent this century.[67] Norton argues that the more defeats there were, the more MPs appreciated the effect of cross-voting. Backbench deference was replaced with the expectation that MPs should participate in the country's governance.[68] This reflected a shift in the behavioural role of MPs in favour of Members who saw themselves primarily as advocates of specific policies.[69] Griffith's study of parliamentary scrutiny of government Bills also accepts that backbench impact on legislation is far from negligible.[70] Furthermore, during the 1980s backbenchers had an appreciable effect in influencing government *prior* to votes being taken, through the very threat of dissent.[71] Norton concludes that the growth of dissent dispelled the previously held assumption that every division was tantamount to a vote of confidence in the government. Thus, although cohesion remained a feature of parliamentary voting, this was not the cohesion of the pre-1970 era.[72] Parliament has thereby become a relatively more significant policy-influencing body, which has forced government to withdraw or modify measures, including some significant ones.[73] Furthermore, Baldwin has

---

[65] Beer (1982) 180–194.

[66] Butt (1967), Jennings (1961) 81 suggests that 'if any act of the Government threatens to lose votes, they [the backbenchers] will not vote against the Government in the lobbies but will complain to the Whips in the smoking room'. See also Herman (1972), Lynskey (1970), Strauss (1972).

[67] Norton (1985) 14.   [68] Ibid.   [69] Searing (1994), Norton (1997).

[70] Griffith (1974) 256.   [71] Norton (1985) 28.   [72] Ibid 41.

[73] Ibid. For instance, in the 1974–9 Parliament, backbenchers ensured the loss of the Scotland and Wales Bill, effectively wrecked the Dock Work Regulation Bill, and forced substantial changes to the 1977 and 1978 Finance Bills. In the 1979–83 Parliament, the government was forced under threat of defeat to withdraw the Local Government Finance Bill, the Iran (Temporary Measures) Bill, and proposals relating to charges for eye tests, reductions in the BBC's external services, and 'hotel' charges for patients in NHS hospitals. In the 1983–7 Parliament, despite the government's large majority, it felt obliged at the behest of backbenchers to amend the Rates Bill, the Police and Criminal Evidence Bill, and measures relating to EC milk production quotas and rate support grant.

identified a corresponding growth of independence in the House of Lords.[74] Similarly Munro suggests that the depiction of relations between Parliament and government has often been exaggerated. He argues that continuous public scrutiny through Parliament places pressure on all governments, regardless of their majorities.[75] Riddell has criticized the simplistic picture of 'the over-mighty executive and all-powerful whips', arguing that even the Blair government made concessions to its backbenchers.[76]

Despite the damage done to Parliament's legitimacy by executive dominance, legitimacy is not an all-or-nothing affair.[77] If one accepts Norton's thesis that Parliament does indeed hold a more than negligible sway over the executive,[78] or even Walkland's more modest characterization of Parliament as a vital 'communications medium for drawing public attention to issues',[79] it could be argued that Parliament might in part redeem itself if it were competent in dealing with the constitutional and legal issues which its deliberative role increasingly involves. It would not be altogether unreasonable to expect parliamentarians to understand such issues, in view of the fact that the House of Commons includes a sizeable number of lawyers—129 in the 1966–70 Parliament which first endorsed the UK's bid for EEC membership, 126 in the 1970–4 Parliament which passed the European Communities Act 1972.[80] The House of Lords included the Law Lords among its membership. The issues of legal understanding and informed consent are therefore a yardstick, albeit only one, against which the legitimacy of the legislature could be measured. Because of their constitutional importance, the decisions relating to membership of the European Community[81] and the subsequent major Treaty revisions constitute a suitable yardstick against which to measure the constitutional understandings of parliamentarians, as does the passage of the Human Rights Act. In particular we need to explore whether MPs and peers realized that by passing these measures they were voting to transform a political constitution to a more legally orientated one. If parliamentarians understood the implications of what they were doing, this would serve to enhance Parliament's legitimacy. Conversely if they largely failed to appreciate the legal significance of their actions, this undermines still further Parliament's

[74] Baldwin (1985) 96–113.

[75] Munro (1987) 208. He instances the large number of amendments to the Police and Criminal Evidence Act 1984. Despite the massive Conservative majority, the Act which was finally passed differed significantly from the original Bill.

[76] Riddell (2000) 18–19.   [77] Beetham (1991) 20.   [78] Norton (1990) 177–180.

[79] Walkland (1969) 69.   [80] Roth (1967), Roth and Kerby (1972).

[81] Ostensibly the Heath administration attached importance to informed consent by speaking in terms of eliciting the 'full-hearted consent of Parliament'. See Ch 3.

legitimacy claim. We will therefore examine whether Parliament attained an adequate ability to handle legal issues by the time of EC accession and, if not, whether it has since acquired one.

Legitimacy 2: judicial reasoning

Parliament is not the only organ of governance whose performance is subject to legitimacy challenges. Although Parliament may have invited the judiciary to do away with its own legislative omnipotence, it was the judges who accepted the invitation. As we shall see, in the *Factortame (No 2)* case in 1991 the House of Lords made it clear that directly effective Community law rights did indeed prevail over conflicting provisions of Acts of Parliament.[82] In so doing their Lordships have been accused of turning 'a blind eye to constitutional theory altogether'.[83] The 'crisis of legitimacy' surrounding *Factortame (No 2)* has been made all the more intense because it can be perceived as forming part and parcel of a more general shift of power in favour of the judiciary, the merits of which have been highly controversial.[84] The decision was preceded by the robust growth of judicial review in the 1980s and followed by the courts' development of common law fundamental rights in the 1990s, culminating in the enactment of the Human Rights Act 1998.

Judicial reasoning ought to be convincing at the best of times, but surely the more momentous the constitutional change involved in a decision, the more convincing the reasoning ought to be. This proposition should apply with particular force where the courts themselves are the institutional beneficiaries of the central principle being formulated. *Factortame (No 2)* brought about the end of three hundred years of apparently unchallengeable statutes. In a famous passage, Lord Bridge appeared to justify the constitutional change effected by the House of Lords' acceptance of the supremacy of Community law on the basis that Parliament had understood the legal consequences of Community membership:

If the supremacy within the European Community of Community law over the national law of Member States was not always inherent in the EEC Treaty it was certainly well established in the jurisprudence of the Court of Justice long before the United Kingdom joined the Community. Thus, whatever limitation of its sover-

---

[82]   *R v Secretary of State for Transport ex parte Factortame Ltd (No 2)* [1991] AC 603.
[83]   Wade (1996) 575.   [84]   See Ch 7.

eignty Parliament accepted when it enacted the European Communities Act 1972 was entirely voluntary.[85]

Certainly *the passage of the Act* was a voluntary action on Parliament's part, but whether *the limitation of sovereignty* was voluntary depends on whether the broad swathe of parliamentarians by and large comprehended the Act's sovereignty implications. In this context, the fact that the Act was passed by only eight votes in the Commons cannot be ignored. Lord Bridge's holding contrasts starkly with the view of Lady Thatcher, who, with the benefit of hindsight, has argued, 'most of us, including myself, paid insufficient regard to the issue of sovereignty in consideration of the case for joining the EEC at the beginning of the 1970s. . . . [T]here was a failure to grasp the true nature of the European Court and the relationship that would emerge between British law and Community law.'[86]

It is important to establish whether parliamentarians broadly understood the possible effect of Community membership on the domestic legal order, in which case the limitation of sovereignty would indeed have been 'entirely voluntary', or whether they largely failed to appreciate the constitutional consequences, in which case Parliament's self-restriction was unwitting. If the former were the case, then the reasoning in *Factortame (No 2)* would seem valid. If the latter were the case, then the courts will have to search elsewhere for reasons to justify their policy of according supremacy to Community law. Arguably they might find more convincing justifications by looking more deeply at Lord Bridge's underlying reasoning. Alternatively (and this will be my argument) they might find an even more compelling explanation by dwelling more broadly on the respective normative roles of political actors and courts in effecting constitutional change.

What should parliamentarians have known?

The narrative of this book explores the evolution of MPs' legal understandings chronologically. Chapter 2 examines the UK's first two attempts to join the Community. As regards the first attempt in 1961–3, parliamentarians were in no position to appreciate the legal implications of membership, since the landmark ECJ cases on supremacy and direct effect had not then been decided. However, by the second application in 1967, the two ECJ

---

[85] Ibid 658.   [86] Thatcher (1995) 497.

doctrines had been firmly established in *Van Gend en Loos* and *Costa v ENEL*, and one might assume that parliamentarians would recognize their significance.

One might also reasonably have expected MPs at this stage to have looked across the water to the United States of America. By 1967 there were obvious parallels between the pre-eminence of the ECJ within the Community constitutional order and the status of the US Supreme Court. Like the Supreme Court the ECJ could declare unlawful acts of both the central (Community) institutions and those of the states (the Member States) if it deemed them incompatible with the heavily entrenched constitution (the Treaty). Like the Supreme Court the ECJ sat at the very pinnacle of the institutional hierarchy. Just as the Supreme Court could invalidate Acts of Congress, so too measures adopted by the Community's political institutions, whatever their legal form, could be struck down by the ECJ if it deemed them incompatible with the Treaty. Furthermore in its early years the ECJ started to develop its own 'general principles of law' which it used as additional benchmarks to assess the constitutionality not only of Community acts but of Member State measures falling within the scope of application of the Treaty. From a British perspective, this change to a Supreme Court arrangement might have been considered desirable or undesirable, but either way it constituted a fundamental change in Britain's institutional balance which ought not to have been made without deliberation.

Chapter 3 examines the Heath White Paper on the constitutional implications of membership and analyses the October 1971 debate on the principle of membership. By then the ECJ had reinforced its supremacy jurisprudence by holding in *Internationale Handelsgesellschaft* that 'the validity of a Community measure or its effect within a Member State cannot be affected by allegations that it runs counter to either fundamental rights as formulated by the constitution of that State or the principles of a national constitutional structure'. Although the UK had no fundamental rights in the sense that everything can be changed by Parliament, it did possess principles of a national constitutional structure, notably the rules of parliamentary sovereignty. Even though the UK was not yet a Member State, the ECJ was clearly signalling that Community law must prevail over UK law notwithstanding parliamentary sovereignty. The implications of this judgment should also have been subjected to adequate parliamentary consideration.

Chapter 4 considers the scrutiny which MPs and peers accorded the European Communities Bill 1972. Sections 2(1), 2(4), and 3(1) of the Bill clearly aimed to import the ECJ's two doctrines into domestic law. All in all, the House of Commons spent 181½ hours considering the Bill.[87] The debate, and the Committee proceedings in particular, would have provided ample opportunity for MPs to dwell on the immutability or otherwise of parliamentary sovereignty.

Chapter 5 contrasts British parliamentary understandings of the constitutional implications of accession with those in Ireland, to establish the extent to which the state of knowledge of British parliamentarians might have been conditioned by the peripheral role of law in the pre-accession constitution. Whereas British MPs may have been concerned to preserve parliamentary sovereignty, it is possible that Irish TDs were no less anxious to safeguard the justiciable fundamental rights laid down in the constitution of Ireland. The comparative legal competence of the Oireachtas in relation to the potential power of both the ECJ and the national courts will be evaluated.

Chapters 6 and 7 trace the evolution of MPs' constitutional understandings through the major Treaty revisions, the Single European Act and the Maastricht Treaty. The expansion of Community competences meant that the supremacy and direct effect doctrines now applied to 'ever wider fields'[88] of activity. The reach of EC law was powerfully brought home to UK politicians by the *Working Time Directive*[89] case in 1996. Moreover any notion that parliamentary sovereignty was immutable was laid to rest by the *Factortame* and *EOC*[90] cases. Perhaps these cases made the British polity realize the impact of supremacy and direct effect in a way which foreign case law could not.

Chapter 8 is another 'comparison' chapter. It analyses the history of parliamentary debates on a Bill of Rights, culminating in the passage of the Human Rights Act 1998. It investigates whether the issues of parliamentary sovereignty and judicial power were clearer to MPs in the Bill of Rights context than in the Community context, and considers why this might have been the case.

Finally, Chapter 9 consolidates the issues and ideas developed above by putting forward answers to the questions which inspired this book. It contemplates whether constitutional reform might help remedy the shortcomings uncovered by this book and considers the wider implications of the study for scholars of both law and politics.

---

[87] Seaton and Winetrobe (1998) 45.

[88] Opinion 1/91 *Draft Agreement on the European Economic Area* [1991] ECR I–6079 para 21.

[89] Case C–84/94 *United Kingdom v Council* [1996] ECR I–5755, [1996] 3 CMLR 671.

[90] *R v Secretary of State for Employment, ex parte Equal Opportunities Commission* [1995] 1 AC 1.

Law and politics

Griffith was right to argue that a weakness in the study of law and the study of politics is that 'so often an intimate relationship is treated as no more than a chance meeting of two disparate disciplines' and that law and politics 'gain much mutual benefit when studied as one'.[91] The examination of the effect of political change on the courts, or (as in this book) the impact of legal change on politicians, contributes to the understanding of both disciplines. Earlier analyses of this genre have used parliamentary records to assess debates on the Community against *political* criteria such as issue anatomy and salience,[92] theories of foreign policy change,[93] and awareness of EC/EU political development.[94] This is the first time, however, that an analysis of parliamentary awareness of the *legal* consequences of membership spanning the period from the initial attempt to join to the aftermath of the *Working Time Directive* case has been attempted.[95] This book aims to contribute to the expanding field of legislative studies. It is also intended to add to the growing trend, especially in the Community law context, in favour of an interdisciplinary approach to legal scholarship, by illustrating the role that empirical studies can have in such scholarship. It is hoped that this book will make a worthwhile contribution in both respects.

[91] Griffith (1995) 3.   [92] Moon (1985) 1–4.   [93] Lord (1990) 1.
[94] Garnett and Sherrington (1996) 383–402.
[95] Rawlings (1994*a*) has usefully analysed aspects of House of Commons debate in the context of Maastricht ratification.

2

The United Kingdom's First Two Attempts to Join the EEC

This chapter examines parliamentary perceptions of the constitutional implications of membership at the time of Britain's first two ill-fated applications. When the first application was made the ECJ's seminal case law on supremacy and direct effect had yet to be decided, so MPs did not have much to go on beyond the supranationalism implicit in the Treaty itself. One would have been forgiven for assuming that the Community was merely another tile in the mosaic of *international* organizations which proliferated in the wake of the Second World War. By the second attempt, however, ECJ jurisprudence had fashioned the Community into an undeniably *supranational* legal entity. A question of particular interest, therefore, is whether this metamorphosis had a resonance on political consciousness. What impact did the ECJ's assertion of Community supremacy and judicial empowerment have on the terms of parliamentary debate?

The post-war drive towards European integration witnessed a trend in favour of entrusting dispute resolution to courts. The European Convention on Human Rights 1950 provided for a Court to 'ensure the observance of the engagements' undertaken by the Contracting States[1] and the European Coal and Steel Community Treaty 1951 set up a Court to ensure that 'in the interpretation and application of this Treaty . . . the law is observed'.[2] Doubtless 'once the Member States chose a division of powers regime specified in a controlling text and constituted an organ of third party dispute resolution . . . an institutional evolution was bound to occur'.[3] Nonetheless it seems unlikely that the original Member States anticipated that the European Court of Justice would play a prominent role in limiting national sovereignty. Shapiro

---

[1] Article 19 ECHR.   [2] Article 31 ECSC.   [3] Shapiro (1999) 340.

suggests that 'when the Member States opted for an ECJ, they thought that Luxembourg would be far closer to the Hague than the District of Columbia',[4] and Rasmussen considers it telling that the Treaty drafters eschewed the Italian and German models of US-inspired constitutional courts.[5] Indeed, the European Court of Human Rights' system of individual petition, with its focus on challenging Contracting States' actions, may have seemed a greater potential threat to national sovereignty.[6] Although the ECJ was early on seen as 'perhaps the most typically federal aspect' of the ECSC,[7] this was perceived largely in terms of the Court's role in preventing the *High Authority* from acting beyond its Treaty powers. Moreover the ECJ tended to interpret these powers narrowly.[8]

It was seemingly the power of the High Authority, not the Court, which deterred the 1950–1 Labour government from ECSC membership. According to Attlee, 'as a Government, we favoured every effort to effect greater European integration, such as . . . the setting up of the Coal and Steel Organisation . . . but we could not enter engagements to the full extent possible to the Continental powers'.[9] Attlee's administration considered itself 'unable to accept the views of the extreme federalists'.[10] It seemed, however, that for the Attlee government, any degree of supranationalism constituted 'extreme federalism', for it favoured strictly intergovernmental cooperation in limited fields. It opposed handing over 'the most vital economic forces of this country' to an authority 'that is utterly undemocratic and is responsible to nobody'.[11] Churchill used this reluctance as a stick to beat the government, yet on his return to No 10 his interest in integration vanished; along with most of his Cabinet and the bulk of the Foreign Office, he opposed closer economic and defence ties. The matter was hardly discussed in Cabinet.[12]

In 1955–6 the six ECSC Member States opened negotiations for the creation of a European Economic Community.[13] They resolved at a conference in Messina, Italy, to establish 'a united Europe, by the development of common institutions, the progressive fusion of national economies, the creation of a common market and the progressive harmonisation of . . . social policies'.

---

[4] Shapiro (1999) 330–331.   [5] Rasmussen (1986) 209.

[6] Robertson (1961) 184. This might explain Contracting States' initial reluctance to accept the ECHR's optional provisions. See Janis (1992*a*) 109.

[7] Haas (1958) 44. The same point is made by Mayne (1963) 22.   [8] Ibid 473.

[9] Attlee (1954) 173.   [10] Ibid.   [11] Attlee, HC, 477, col 472, 5 July 1950.

[12] Selsdon (1981) 413.

[13] West Germany, France, Italy, the Netherlands, Belgium, Luxembourg.

Of far greater practical importance was the conference's decision to appoint the Spaak Committee which drafted the EEC and Euratom Treaties.[14]

With the EEC's establishment in 1957, the expansion of the ECJ's jurisdiction must have seemed modest. For example, under the ECSC Treaty the Court could only deliver preliminary rulings on the validity of Community acts,[15] whereas under the EEC Treaty it could also give rulings on questions of interpretation.[16] Member States surely could not have predicted the way in which this innocuous-seeming change could be used to erode national sovereignty.[17] The EEC Treaty permitted natural persons,[18] not just undertakings and associations,[19] to challenge certain Community acts. But here again the focus was on keeping Community institutions within the limits of their powers.

Although invited to participate in the Spaak Committee's work, the British government had no intention of so doing. As Macmillan, then in Cabinet, explained, quite apart from the official belief that nothing would come of the negotiations, the weight of opinion in government, Opposition, and press was against membership. This was largely because UK obligations to the Commonwealth made it impossible for Britain to adhere to a tightly controlled supranational common market.[20] Under the Commonwealth preference system Britain gave largely free entry to raw materials and manufactures from Commonwealth countries and in return received favourable trade treatment from them. Joining the Community would subject Commonwealth imports to tariff barriers whilst EEC goods would enter the country free.[21] Reginald Maudling attributed the British attitude to the tradition of Commonwealth preference and our close links to the United States.[22] He considered that Britain's failure to recognize her historic decline led to the delusion that she could claim a leading place in the Community at the moment of her own choosing.[23]

There was, however, concern that UK trade would be harmed if British exports were excluded from the common market. On 7 February 1957, therefore, the government published a White Paper proposing the establishment of an industrial free trade area in Europe uniting the new EEC with the

---

[14] Camps (1993) 236, Mowat (1973) 143.   [15] Article 41 ECSC.
[16] Article 177 EEC.
[17] See the ECJ's rejection of the Belgian and Dutch governments' argument over jurisdiction in Case 26/62 *Van Gend en Loos* [1963] ECR 1, [1963] CMLR 105.
[18] Article 173 EEC.   [19] Article 33 ECSC.
[20] Macmillan (1971) 72–84.   [21] This possibility became known as 'reverse preferences'.
[22] Maudling (1978) 68–69.   [23] Ibid 232.

remaining countries in the Organization for European Economic Cooperation. The proposal, known as Plan G, envisaged that countries could decide their own *external* tariffs so that the UK could maintain Commonwealth preference. Despite initial enthusiasm from EEC Member States, the French government rejected Plan G in an official statement of 14 November 1958.[24]

Membership or association?

Rejection of Plan G left Britain with the option of applying for either EEC membership or associate status. Provisionally, to shield British trading interests and those of other non-EEC European countries from the common market, the UK joined the European Free Trade Area in November 1959. EFTA was established on classic intergovernmental lines, creating a free trade area in which member countries could determine their own external tariffs.[25]

Britain's relationship with the EEC was neglected at the 1959 general election.[26] Nonetheless, at Prime Minister's Questions on 16 May 1961, Macmillan disclosed that the issue of Community membership had 'been the subject of close study for a considerable time' by government departments. Hugh Gaitskell probed whether the government's object was some closer association falling short of membership, or whether it was thought that terms of entry could be secured that would nonetheless safeguard the positions of British agriculture, the Commonwealth, and the EFTA countries. The Premier replied that he hoped the Treaty could be amended and that Britain might be admitted as a full member subject to protocols or derogations. Thus Britain would form a partnership in Europe while fully carrying out her duties to the Commonwealth, EFTA, and her agricultural interests.[27]

Macmillan's aspiration to 'secure a real unity of the Western half of divided Europe'[28] faced three main obstacles. First, the interests of British farming (funded very differently from EEC countries) had to be safeguarded. Secondly, there was general concern that EEC membership would impinge too much on sovereignty. Thirdly, Commonwealth trade (and relations generally) was bound to suffer if the EEC customs union replaced

---

[24]   Maudling (1978) 457.

[25]   The other members were Denmark, Norway, Sweden, Switzerland, Austria, and Portugal.

[26]   Butler and Rose (1960) 71–72.   [27]   HC, 640, cols 1110–1114, 16 May 1961.

[28]   Macmillan (1973) 4.

Commonwealth preference. As regards the Conservative Party, Macmillan considered that 'certainly the Commonwealth aspects of the problem over-shadowed all others—politically, economically, and above all emotionally'.[29] It is noteworthy that at this stage the Commonwealth was a more important issue in Conservative eyes than concerns over sovereignty.

Accordingly Cabinet discussions concluded that Britain should seek membership on conditions which permitted Commonwealth exports to the UK to be maintained in the transitional period; and thereafter they should be restricted only if this would not damage essential Commonwealth interests. Also the Exchequer should remain free to support British farming. Ministers had a mandate to see if satisfactory arrangements could be negotiated; the government would then look at the 'package', and the Commonwealth would be kept informed throughout. On this basis the Cabinet unanimously agreed on 22 July 1961 to enter into negotiations with the Six to see if terms could be concluded on the basis of which the UK could join.

It is noteworthy that the common customs tariff, whereby imports from non-EEC countries received uniform treatment at the Community's external frontiers, was an essential ingredient of the common market; the agricultural policy was perhaps the Community's most important policy. Yet the British government clearly assumed that the existing Member States would countenance, at least to some degree, major 'opt-outs' for Britain from these regimes. This assumption that Britain could get a 'custom-built package' would not have appeared wholly unreasonable. The EEC was only five years old and the nature of its common market and policies were not set in stone. Furthermore the accession of new Member States was virgin territory; it could not be assumed that new members would simply be obliged to take on the entire *acquis communautaire* and, after all, Britain would be a major player. In any event, as a bargaining position it made sense to ask for what the government *wanted*, even if—in the nature of bargaining—it would ultimately have to settle for less.

The 1961 Commons debate on EEC membership

On 31 July 1961 Macmillan announced the application to the Commons.[30] British membership would be conditional on the terms being satisfactory to

[29] Ibid 6–7.   [30] HC, 645, cols 928–942, 31 July 1961.

'the Commonwealth interests',[31] to Britain's EFTA partners, and to the special needs of the UK (primarily agriculture). Parliament would then approve or reject the terms. Macmillan did not comment on sovereignty. However, he rejected the counter-proposal of applying for association with the Community, arguing that this would generate the same difficulties for the Commonwealth whilst depriving Britain of influence in Europe.

On 2 and 3 August, the House debated a government motion supporting the application.[32] Macmillan attacked the present division of Western Europe which detracted from its political strength and unity. The EEC's mass market offered a spur to British competitiveness and efficiency. The Premier played down the loss of sovereignty, seeking to draw a distinction between the 'economic' and the 'political'.[33] This distinction was nonsensical; the parties had often divided most sharply over economic policy, making the 'economic' intensely 'political'. Nonetheless the Butskellite consensus over the economic and social management of the 1950s/1960s 'affluent society' might have helped conceal this reality. Macmillan also emphasized that the Treaty did not deal with defence or foreign policy, but merely with trade and certain related social policy aspects.[34]

The Commonwealth issue loomed large. Macmillan stated that he would not have recommended applying for membership if he thought accession would injure the Commonwealth; rather, EEC membership would serve the Commonwealth best, since Britain in isolation was of little value to Commonwealth partners. All members of EFTA, he said, would coordinate their actions and remain united throughout the negotiations. Labour tabled an amendment that Britain should join 'only if this House gives its approval and if the conditions negotiated are generally acceptable to a Commonwealth Prime Ministers' Conference and accord with our obligations and pledges to other members of the European Free Trade Association'.

[31] Presumably this wording gave the UK government the final say on what was in the Commonwealth interests.

[32] HC, 645, cols 1480–1786.

[33] This appears part of a government strategy to downplay the extent to which EEC membership would constitute a new departure. For instance Heath, in his speech to the 1961 Conservative Conference, was careful to place Community membership in the context of other international bodies to which the UK already belonged: NATO, OECD, EFTA, the Council of Europe. See Campbell (1993) 124.

[34] HC, 645, col 1481.

Discussion of sovereignty

Overwhelmingly MPs had three main concerns: of the twenty-eight who spoke, twenty-six substantially addressed the sovereignty issue, twenty-seven the Commonwealth, and fourteen EFTA.

It was clear from this early debate that the pro- and anti-Marketeers had different conceptions of sovereignty. To put it another way, when they argued about sovereignty they were not arguing about the same thing. Anti-Market MPs perceived sovereignty in terms of *preservation of national choice over laws and policies*: 'the freedom of the people of this country to choose their fate and also not to be tied up in any political federation or union'[35] and 'a measure of independence . . . that we are not going to tie ourselves hand and foot to the six Governments of Europe exclusively'.[36] In contrast pro-Marketeers argued that sovereignty should be seen in terms of *effective control of the nation's destiny*, which, in a world dominated by superpowers, necessitated joining a larger unit.[37] They pointed out that it was not possible to reap the benefits of international cooperation of any variety without reducing national legislative freedom.[38] These differing conceptions of sovereignty did not, however, actually compete against each other. The protagonists tended not to subject the other side's notion of sovereignty to destructive analysis, and so the difference between the two conceptions was never really brought out into the open. The debate was characterized by each side simply reiterating its own conception of sovereignty rather than by critical dialogue.

Three themes emerge from the contributions of MPs hostile to membership. The first, and dominant, theme was that MPs focused their concern on the Community's *future* development. This would seem to suggest that the EEC *as it then stood* did not present too many sovereignty worries. Opposition Leader Hugh Gaitskell thought a directly elected Parliament would spell a federal Europe and wanted to know whether the EEC's basic structure could be modified as part of British entry.[39] (Like Macmillan, he clearly harboured hopes that the Community could be substantially changed to suit Britain.)

---

[35] Robin Turton, ibid, col 1689. [36] Manny Shinwell, ibid, col 1733.

[37] See eg Peter Smithers (Conservative, Winchester) (ibid, cols 1554–1556), Charles Pannell (Labour, Leeds West) (ibid, col 1706).

[38] See eg A Woodburn (Labour, Clackmannan) (ibid, col 1515), Sir Lionel Heald (Conservative, Chertsey) (ibid, col 1529), Edward Heath (ibid, col 1676), Duncan Sandys (ibid, col 1769).

[39] Ibid, cols 1494–1507.

Harold Wilson and ardent pro-Marketeer George Brown argued that the government should be more candid about the Treaty's ultimate goal of *political* federation.[40] These contributions seem to indicate a coordinated Labour frontbench campaign to highlight fears of a federal destiny.

Secondly, some MPs questioned whether membership was necessary to harvest the alleged economic benefits. Why, asked one, could a common market not be secured by mere international agreement?[41] Why, asked another, was it necessary to replace Britain's flexible, unwritten constitution which 'embodies the very spirit of our democracy' with a rigid, written Treaty?[42]

Thirdly, Labour MPs questioned whether adherence to the Treaty was compatible with a democratic socialist economic programme. In the only reference in the debate to the ECJ, William Blyton (Labour, Houghton-le-Spring) argued that membership would preclude the achievement of Labour's constitutional aims, since 'the Common Market has its own courts and its own judges which will decide issues which may be harmful to our own internal economy'. Others emphasized that the implementation of established Labour policies would require substantial Treaty amendment.[43] Labour pro-Marketeers retorted that social progress was more advanced in the Six than in Britain, and that the Treaty did not prevent public ownership.[44]

Labour's amendment was defeated by 318 to 209, and the government's motion was carried by 313 to 5 with Labour abstaining.

The Lords debate: constitutional and legal implications

When the matter came before the upper House on 2 August, the Lord Chancellor, Lord Dilhorne, indicated that the constitutional implications had been receiving consideration for some time. Though hampered by the Treaty's imprecise language, he and his legal team had concluded that some degree of supranational authority was implicit in it, though the 'pooling of

---

[40]   Ibid, cols 1758–1759.

[41]   Sir Derek Walker-Smith (Conservative, East Hertfordshire) ibid, cols 1507–1514.

[42]   Sir Lynn Ungoed-Thomas (Labour, Leicester NE) ibid, col 1576. Later a High Court judge, he upheld parliamentary sovereignty in *Cheney v Conn* [1968] 1 All ER 779.

[43]   Jennie Lee (Labour, Cannock) HC, 645, cols 1545–1552, Harold Wilson ibid, cols 1657–1658.

[44]   See eg Roy Jenkins (ibid, cols 1585–1590), Charles Pannell (ibid, col 1714).

authority' was strictly limited to the Community's fields of activity. Thus membership would have a negligible effect on criminal procedure, land law, contract, and tort. Nor would it affect the laws of the welfare state or deprive Parliament of the power to nationalize industries.

I venture to suggest that the vast majority of men and women in this country will never directly feel the impact of the Community-made law at all. In the conduct of their daily lives they will have no need to have regard to any of the provisions of that law; nor are they at all likely ever to be affected by an administrative action of one of the Community institutions. With few exceptions, the obligations under the Community law will fall directly only on industrial and commercial concerns, long-distance carriers, and persons or firms engaged in the export of agricultural products.[45]

The Community institutions were vested with powers to enact legislation which overrode those of national authorities and which were incapable of challenge in national courts.[46]

Regulations would have to be given effect to in our law as they stand. Should they conflict with existing Statute or Case Law they would override it. . . . *In any subsequent legislation of our own we should have to take good care that it did not conflict with any Community regulations or directives* . . . So, my Lords, to the extent I have mentioned, in the case of both regulations and directives, the legislative function of Parliament would have to give way to that of the Council and the Commission.[47]

Clearly, therefore, Lord Dilhorne considered that Community membership would still be subject to the full rigours of parliamentary sovereignty. He assumed that Community law would be vulnerable to implied and express repeal by subsequent statute, and so Parliament would have to 'take good care' to legislate in conformity with it. The legislative supremacy of Parliament was perceived as resilient and immutable.

Lord Dilhorne noted that British courts would be called upon to enforce Community legislation and ECJ judgments. He did not envisage that much use would be made of the preliminary reference procedure, since 'we could take steps, within our own system, to see to it that there would be consistent and expert interpretation of the Community law so that the need for

[45] HL, 243, cols 419–420, 2 August 1962 (emphasis added). Later at col 425 he reiterated: 'the exercise of all the powers to which I have referred is confined to a limited field—the free flow of goods and services, and the free exercise of work and skills throughout the Community. Community law operates only in these fields, or in matters directly related to them.'

[46] A curious view, since Article 177 EEC permitted national courts to make preliminary references to the ECJ on the validity of Community secondary legislation.

[47] HL, 243, col 420 (emphasis added).

reference will rarely arise in courts of first instance'.[48] Moreover, British involvement in drawing up future Community instruments would reduce the problems caused by differences in drafting style, legal conceptions, and interpretative technique.

The *ultimate* sovereignty of Parliament would remain, since the Act required to incorporate the Treaties could be repealed, like any other. However, in international law, this could only be justified in exceptional circumstances; the Treaty was concluded for an unlimited period with no provision for its termination; if withdrawal took place without justification and without the approval of the other Member States, it would breach Britain's international obligations. It is interesting that Lord Dilhorne perceived EEC arrangements as dependent on international law, rather than viewing Community law as *sui generis*.[49]

It is interesting that even though Lord Dilhorne's statement focused on the legal implications, he sidelined the role of the ECJ. He talked in terms of Parliament's legislative function having to 'give way' to that of the Council and the Commission, but not to the decisions of the ECJ. He predicted that the Council would not readily override national interests, but did not consider whether the ECJ would take the same attitude. He insisted that recourse to the preliminary references procedure would be exceptional. The ECJ's federalizing potential, judicial lawmaking, and relentlessly teleological approach to interpretation could not be appreciated at this early stage.

Academic reaction

Analyses by academic lawyers at the time shared Lord Dilhorne's confidence that parliamentary sovereignty would survive Community membership unscathed. They accepted its durability unquestioningly. Thus Keenan saw no way of preventing British courts from enforcing inconsistent legislation passed inadvertently by Parliament.[50] An interpretation Act might provide that the incorporating statute could only be repealed by express words, but this would appear to have no effect, since the Court of Appeal in *Ellen Street Estates v Minister of Health* had confirmed that no words of a previous statute

[48] HL, 243, col 422.
[49] Parliamentary sovereignty means that statute prevails over UK international obligations. See *Mortensen v Peters* (1906) 14 SLT 227.
[50] Keenan (1962).

could inhibit the power of Parliament to change the law through implied repeal.[51] The only consolation was that judges would be reluctant to construe legislation so as to create inconsistency. Thompson and Marsh took precisely the same position with regard to parliamentary sovereignty.[52]

Party and Commonwealth reaction

Questions of sovereignty were nonetheless pivotal to Labour's rejection of membership in autumn 1962. On 9 September Gaitskell issued a statement opposing entry on the terms emerging from the negotiations. At Labour's Conference he made an emotional attack on entry on Macmillan's terms; the EEC's creators sought a federation which would mean 'the end of a thousand years of history' with Britain 'a mere province'.[53] Once again he appeared to place the emphasis on the Community's future development.

He also attacked the Common Agricultural Policy as 'one of the most devastating pieces of protectionism ever invented' and described the treatment of the Commonwealth as 'odious'. Tony Benn commented that Gaitskell projected EEC supporters as traitors to the Commonwealth and extremists.[54] Labour's Conference approved a National Executive Committee statement opposing entry on existing terms, laying down five essential conditions for entry, but allowing for further negotiations. The five conditions consisted of the government's three (satisfactory terms on the Commonwealth, EFTA, and UK agricultural interests) supplemented with safeguards for economic planning and an independent foreign policy.[55] It is interesting that controversy over sovereignty focused on questions of *scope* rather than issues of enforceability and effectiveness. For Gaitskell, plainly, the Community was only acceptable if its supranational decision-making was restricted to *very* limited fields. Labour's scepticism made it harder for the government to claim that Britain wholeheartedly endorsed Community membership.

The following day a Conference of Commonwealth Prime Ministers met in London. This meeting 'showed the great perturbation felt by most Commonwealth countries about the likely terms of Britain's entry'.[56] Macmillan recorded '[a] broadside attack on us, led by Diefenbaker on the first day. . . . Menzies wound up the first day with a very able and *very*

51 [1934] 1 KB 590.
53 Williams (1979) 734.
55 *The Times*, 19 February 1962.
52 Thompson and Marsh (1962).
54 Benn (1987) 1.
56 Wilson (1971) 94.

damaging speech. Holyoake said New Zealand would be ruined.'[57] There was better news for Macmillan on 11 October when the Conservative Conference overwhelmingly rejected an anti-EEC amendment.[58]

The negotiations and the first French veto

The early 1960s were marked by an increasing governmental willingness to accept existing Community arrangements. In September 1960 Edward Heath, the Lord Privy Seal charged with conducting the negotiations, had told the Council of Europe that 'for Britain to sign the Treaty of Rome in its present form would be impossible'.[59] However, by February 1961 he had informed the Western European Union that provided the Six could accommodate British difficulties over agriculture and the Commonwealth, Britain would 'consider' reducing Commonwealth preferences and imposing a common external tariff on non-EFTA and non-Commonwealth countries. Yet despite increasing British readiness to compromise, negotiations were protracted. First, the need to acclimatize public opinion to the idea of entry meant the UK could not simply sign the Treaty of Rome. Secondly, it was necessary to secure the best possible deal for the Commonwealth. Thus by January 1963, terms for some 2,500 products had been agreed, with less than thirty still outstanding.[60] Quite apart from this, the French representatives— to the exasperation of the Five—spun out the negotiations.[61] Thus Macmillan already perceived de Gaulle, not Parliament, as the impediment to British membership.

Sure enough, at an Élysée press conference on 14 January 1963, de Gaulle effectively vetoed British membership. Britain, he pronounced, was insular, maritime, and bound up by her diverse trade. UK accession would completely alter the whole set of relationships that had been drawn up between the Six. Indeed Britain could only be accommodated within a very different

---

[57] The Canadian, Australian, and New Zealand Prime Ministers respectively. Macmillan (1973) 131. There was particular concern about New Zealand because it was uniquely dependent upon export of dairy products to the UK and it feared that the common customs tariff and Common Agricultural Policy would have a devastating effect on trade.

[58] Macmillan (1973) 137.   [59] *The Times*, 28 September 1960.

[60] Campbell (1993) 125. These negotiations earned Heath the sobriquet 'Grocer Heath'.

[61] For instance the French negotiators presented a completely new set of proposals on temperate foodstuffs at the end of July 1962, widely seen as a move to prevent agreement being reached before the summer break on 4 August.

Atlantic community under American domination, not the strictly European construct which France sought. In short, Britain would need to transform herself to become part of the European Community, 'without restriction and without reservation'.[62] The President proposed that before Britain could join, she needed to stop claiming that her agriculture should be privileged, abandon her EFTA undertakings, and adopt a 'truly common tariff' by surrendering Commonwealth preferences.[63] As a sop, de Gaulle suggested Britain could at least have an association agreement with the EEC.

In public the government maintained a brave face. Deputy Premier R A Butler announced that it was 'business as usual' and Macmillan stated that European unity should remain the government's aim.[64] However, the Prime Minister recorded in his diary that 'all our policies at home and abroad are in ruins . . . European unity is no more; French domination of Europe is a new and alarming feature . . . We have lost everything, except our courage and determination.'[65] The Opposition's response was muted by Hugh Gaitskell's death five days after the veto; however, Labour appeared more open-minded to alternatives to Community membership. Harold Wilson stated that no one in the House welcomed the French position and suggested it was time to establish an Atlantic economic and political alliance. George Brown proposed a Commonwealth economic conference. The press were hostile to de Gaulle, the *Guardian* arguing that 'in effect he was asking not merely that Britain cease to demand the Rome Treaty plus, but that she should accept the Rome Treaty minus'; *The Times* noting that 'shock and disapproval seem to have been the chief reactions to President de Gaulle's press conference among France's partners in the Common Market'.[66]

On 29 January 1963 the Commission formally notified Heath that Britain's application had been rejected by France and negotiations were therefore terminated.

Van Gend and *Costa* ignored

Seven days after the formal end of negotiations, the ECJ delivered its seminal judgment in *Van Gend en Loos*.[67] The case involved an attempt by a Dutch

[62] Lacouture (1985) 358.
[63] *Guardian*, 15 January 1963.
[64] *The Times*, 16 January 1963, *Guardian*, 22 January 1963.
[65] Macmillan (1973) 366.
[66] *Guardian*, 15 January 1963, *The Times*, 16 January 1963.
[67] Case 26/62 *NV Algemene Transport- en Expeditie Onderneming van Gend en Loos v Nederlandse Administratie der Belastingen* [1963] ECR 1, [1963] CMLR 105.

company to enforce an article of the Treaty of Rome before a national tribunal.

The Dutch and Belgian governments intervened to argue that the ECJ had no jurisdiction to decide the case. The status and effect of the Treaty within the Kingdom of the Netherlands was, they maintained, a matter of *Dutch* constitutional law. The ECJ tersely retorted that the issue was in fact a question of Treaty interpretation—was the Treaty provision in question to be construed as giving rights to individuals at the national level? By taking jurisdiction to answer the question the ECJ boldly asserted the competence to determine the enforceability of Community norms within the Member States' own legal systems, thereby setting Community law apart from international law.

As to the substance of the case, the ECJ held on the level of general principle that Community law was capable of conferring rights upon individuals which the national courts and tribunals must protect. It justified this holding on the grounds that *'the spirit, the general scheme and the wording'* of the Treaty dictated this result. By the *spirit* of the Treaty, the ECJ seemed to be referring to its objective. The ECJ considered that since the Treaty's aim was to create a common market, this in itself suggested that direct effect was necessary. This was 'confirmed' by the Treaty preamble which talked in terms of creating 'an ever closer union between the *peoples* of Europe'. The Treaty's establishment of lawmaking institutions furnished further evidence that Community law was designed to give rights to individuals. As for the *general scheme* of the Treaty, the ECJ considered that Article 177 (now 234) EC confirmed that the States had acknowledged that Community law conferred nationally enforceable rights. Having examined the spirit and system of the Treaty, the ECJ without more ado concluded that the Community constituted a new legal order conferring rights on individuals. Significantly the ECJ reserved its detailed examination of the *wording* for the question of whether specifically Article 12 EEC, the Treaty article at issue, produced direct effect. Thus not only was the 'wording' relegated to third on the ECJ's list of three, but, in addition, it was only relevant to the 'micro-decision' on whether the Treaty article in question was directly effective. The 'macro-decision' as to whether Community law was capable of giving rights to individuals at all had been based on arguments relating to the Treaty's aims and system, without extensive textual analysis.

The German, Dutch, and Belgian governments intervened to argue that the Treaty explicitly laid down procedures to ensure Community law was respected. These were specifically the provisions in Article 169 whereby the

Commission could bring enforcement proceedings against Member States and the procedure whereby Member States could sue other Member States under Article 170. The three governments argued that these were intended to be the exclusive means of ensuring the Treaty was obeyed. This was the enforcement machinery to which they had 'signed up' when they acceded to the Treaty. Accordingly there was no room for a direct effect doctrine. The ECJ retorted that it saw no need why these means of enforcement should be mutually exclusive: the vigilance of individuals would complement the diligence of the Commission and the Member States.

It is telling that three of the six Member States argued against establishing the direct effect doctrine. Thus the ECJ was strikingly unconcerned with the original intent of the contracting parties when they agreed the Treaty of Rome. It was guided instead with what *ought* to have been the intentions of the founding States, given that they had set themselves the lofty ambition of turning their continent into a single market.

The importance of *Van Gend* can scarcely be overstated. It transformed an entity which appeared to all intents and purposes to be an international trade organization into a supranational one. The ECJ had assumed control of the status and enforceability of EC law within the Member States.

Van Gend did not deal squarely with the question of what happened when a Community norm clashed with a national law, although the ECJ had talked in terms of the Community limiting the sovereign right of Member States, albeit within limited fields. A year and a half later, however, the ECJ uncompromisingly declared in *Costa v ENEL* that such directly effective Community law rights prevailed over national law—the supremacy doctrine.[68] Again its justificatory arguments were primarily teleological rather than textual. It emphasized that the Treaty had created its own legal system which involved the transfer of powers from the States to the Community. Furthermore the Community's programme of integration, combined with the terms and spirit of the Treaty, meant that the force of Community law could not vary from State to State. The ECJ dwelt on only one Treaty provision: Article 189, which stipulated that regulations 'shall be binding' and 'directly applicable in all Member States'. This, the Court argued, confirmed that Community law was supreme. In fact Article 189 constitutes a particularly weak supremacy clause. In the first place, the ECJ's argument is that all Community law overrides incompatible national law, yet the argument relating to Article 189 only concerns regulations. (Indeed, regulations are not the

---

[68] Case 6/64 *Flaminio Costa v ENEL* [1964] ECR 585, [1964] CMLR 425.

supreme form of Community law; Treaty provisions are.) Secondly, Article 189 fell short of expressly stating that regulations prevail over national measures. Its stipulation that regulations 'shall be binding' could just as easily have been interpreted as applying purely on the international law plane. All in all, the Treaty contains nothing equivalent to the unequivocal supremacy clauses which typify the constitutions of federal countries. And yet the ECJ held that Community law prevailed over any national law 'however framed'—sending a clear signal to national legislatures that they could not override Community law by any form of words.

What was the reaction to these legal landmarks in Britain? *Van Gend en Loos* and *Costa v ENEL* were not reported in any form in the British daily press. In contrast, newspapers did give prominence to the *political* stagnation preceding both judgments—the de Gaulle veto in the case of *Van Gend*, and an unspectacular conclusion to the de Gaulle–Erhard talks on European political union in the case of *Costa*. Thus the Community's judicial transformation from international organization to *sui generis*, proto-federal entity went unreported. Since the judgments were unpublicized they could have no effect on domestic political discourse.

As for the legal world, the *Common Market Law Review* was established in 1963 and carried a case note on *Van Gend* as well as an article on the case by Judge Donner. But domestic law journals and practitioner periodicals allowed the landmark cases to pass without comment. There was no mention of them in the *Modern Law Review*, *Law Quarterly Review*, *Cambridge Law Journal*, or even *Public Law*. The *Solicitors' Journal* of 1963, 1964, and 1965 merely contained a handful of articles on EEC competition law. Other UK jurisdictions also ignored the new case law, neither the *Juridical Review* nor the *Scottish Law Gazette* nor the *Northern Ireland Legal Quarterly* carrying any relevant material. The lack of interest in the Community's legal evolution was also reflected in legal education; even in 1972 Professor Lasok lamented the fragmentary teaching of Community law with 'no full-blooded courses having been established on an appreciable scale'.[69] One might draw the conclusion that British lawyers suffered from a lamentable degree of parochialism.

---

[69] Lasok (1972) 83.

Labour's change of heart

Labour's 1964 manifesto scarcely mentioned the EEC and indeed devoted a whole section to boosting *Commonwealth* trade.[70] The issue was not prominent in the election campaign,[71] and did not loom large during the course of the 1964–6 Labour government, though anti-Marketeers were aware of constant pressure 'not only on the part of officials but also of George Brown' to revise government policy in favour of membership.[72]

At first, Wilson hoped for some 'middle way' between EFTA and EEC membership. On 24–5 April 1965, taking the view that Europe 'could not continue as Sixes and Sevens', he convened a meeting of European democratic socialist leaders. Mindful that the EEC 'was consolidating its economic union and raising stiffer and stiffer barriers against the rest of Europe and the world', he put forward several possible solutions. One was integration of the two economic blocs. A second was that some EFTA countries could join the EEC whilst others could associate with it. A third possibility was a low-tariff or free trade area of the Thirteen with the Six maintaining 'the *totality* of their economic integration' and the Seven preserving 'their *several independent constitutions* within a relatively loose free-trade area'.[73] It is significant that, in contrast to Macmillan's efforts to distinguish the 'economic' from the 'political', Wilson was prepared (at least in private) to counterpose economic integration to constitutional independence.

Labour's 1966 election manifesto proposed that 'Britain should be ready to enter Europe' with appropriate safeguards, this commitment having been endorsed by the Party's National Executive Committee with only five votes against. The issue loomed large during the general election, the Conservatives wanting Britain to 'take the first favourable opportunity' of joining. Wilson accused Heath of 'rolling on his back like a spaniel at any kind of gesture from the French'; Heath argued that such remarks amounted to a flat refusal to join.[74] However, with Labour's re-election the pledge was reiterated in the Queen's Speech: the government 'would be ready to enter the European Economic Community provided essential British and Commonwealth interests were safeguarded'.

In May 1966 Wilson initiated an EFTA Prime Ministers' Conference to consider future relations with the Community. It issued a communiqué

70 *The Times* Guide to the House of Commons 1964, 268–278.
71 Butler and King (1965) 131–132.   72 Douglas Jay quoted in Castle (1984), 33.
73 Wilson (1971) 96–97 (emphasis added).   74 Butler and King (1966) 63, 88, 92, and 111.

resolving to initiate discussions between the EEC and EFTA with a view to seeking closer cooperation and pursuing joint policies to promote trade, economic expansion, and social welfare.[75] Accordingly the EFTA Council was charged with facilitating contacts with the EEC. As hope of such an accommodation faded, Wilson's position on EEC membership became ambivalent:

he was so apt to say different things to different people and to conceal his real feelings that it is impossible to chart the course of his thinking with any confidence, but the first two years of his government seem to have been marked by a gradual and reluctant acceptance of the impossibility of finding a halfway house and his recognition of the fact that, if this were true, Britain's future would be safest as part of the EEC.[76]

He informed Tony Benn that he did not favour membership and feared being isolated and forced to join by a Cabinet dominated by pro-Marketeers.[77] However, on 23 October 1966 Wilson held a Chequers meeting of ministers to discuss EEC entry and on 10 November he made a Commons statement (endorsed, line by line, by Cabinet) disclosing that the government had reviewed all aspects of British relations with the EEC, including the issues of EFTA and the Commonwealth. In the light of this, it was the government's clear intention to enter the EEC 'if our essential British and Commonwealth interests can be safeguarded'. The government also convened in December 1966 another EFTA conference where it induced the EFTA countries to go along with Britain abandoning her obligations under the London Agreement whereby all the EFTA countries would join the Community together, either as Members or Associates.

Wilson's and Foreign Secretary George Brown's tour of EEC capitals (January–February 1967) was ostensibly intended to assess whether British and Commonwealth interests could be safeguarded inside the Community. The real objective was to test de Gaulle's stance.[78] Wilson promised the Italians that 'we were prepared to accept the Treaty of Rome and not to seek such amendments or revisions as would fundamentally alter its character'.[79] The meeting with de Gaulle, however, was delphic; the President mused that Britain could not join without changing the Community's fundamental character, and so some other means of British participation might be found: either

---

[75] Wilson (1971) 147.

[76] Ziegler (1993) 240. Wilson's other biographer, Pimlott, reaches the same conclusion but records that 'some believed that Wilson was . . . Machiavellian, and only wanted to make the attempt in order to show that it could not succeed' (Pimlott (1992) 438).

[77] Benn (1987) 392.   [78] Spanier (1972) 6.   [79] Wilson (1971) 421.

'something entirely new' or association. Wilson made it clear that there was 'no solution in these alternatives'.[80]

From March to May 1967 Wilson launched several detailed Cabinet discussions on each aspect of Community membership, which produced (without any resignations) a decision to apply for membership. The Parliamentary Labour Party also supported British entry by a clear majority. On 2 May Wilson announced the fresh application to the Commons.

The Commons Debate on the White Paper

On 8 May 1967 the House debated the White Paper *Membership of the European Communities*.[80] Wilson announced that, provided certain problems could be resolved, 'we shall be ready to accept the Treaty with only such adjustments as are necessary and consequential on the accession of a new member'.[81] This statement underscored Labour's volte-face. Gone was the talk of Treaty revision to safeguard Commonwealth trade or permit socialist economic policies. Some difficulties, Wilson opined, were best settled inside the EEC—an evolving, dynamic entity—rather than by waiting outside another five years to see how it would develop. Most of Wilson's lengthy speech was devoted to the economic benefits—he predicted a profound improvement in British industry, boosting confidence, growth, and research and development. As for the Commonwealth, he argued that the House had accepted five years previously that British entry meant a common external tariff and the end of Commonwealth preference. This was a spurious claim, since the House had taken no vote on membership in 1962 and so had not 'accepted' anything. Moreover Macmillan had not made it clear that Commonwealth preference would have to go. Wilson pledged that the government would seek associate status for Commonwealth countries and a special arrangement for New Zealand.

On sovereignty, echoing without explicitly mentioning *Costa v ENEL*,[82] Wilson noted that Community membership involved vesting legislative and judicial powers, in certain fields, in the Community institutions and consequently limiting the ordinary exercise of national powers; Parliament would therefore have to refrain from passing inconsistent legislation.[83] So like Lord Dilhorne five years earlier, Wilson presented compliance with Community

---

[80] Wilson (1971) 430–437.   [81] Cmnd 3269.
[82] HC, 746, col 1062, 8 May 1967.   [83] Case 6/64; [1964] ECR 585.

law as a matter of parliamentary goodwill. Also like Dilhorne he emphasized the narrowness of the Community's scope:

Community law is mainly concerned with industrial and commercial activities, with corporate bodies rather than private individuals. By far the greater part of our domestic law would remain unchanged after entry. . . . The main effect of Community law on our existing law is in the realms of commerce, Customs, restrictive practices and immigration and the operation of the steel, coal and nuclear energy industries.[84]

It is ironic that this was the position which Macmillan had taken and which Wilson had derided six years earlier.

Wilson argued that restraints on Parliament's legislative freedom were by no means unprecedented; he instanced the UN Charter, NATO, GATT, and EFTA. This was misleading, since he failed to mention how the enforcement of Community rules by the national courts established in *Van Gend* set the EEC apart from these purely international organizations. Somewhat cryptically he noted that the constitutional and legal implications had to be assessed in the light of 'the way in which the Member States have been applying Community law, taking full account of realities prevailing in the Member States' and that this had 'greatly reassured us about the implications for Britain'.[85] Seemingly this suggests that existing EEC countries were slipshod in their compliance with Community norms, and that Britain could follow suit. This governmental perception was reflected in George Brown's memoirs:

[o]ne of the things that had always worried people was what Britain might commit herself to by adhering to the Treaty of Rome, but I'd long ago discovered that the Treaty of Rome, like the Bible, takes account of any possible sin, provides the antidote and thereby offers ways and means of obtaining sanctity afterwards. On our tour of Europe the Prime Minister also learned this. We found that other people bound by the Treaty of Rome had managed to provide for all their private troubles, and it was pretty obvious that we could provide for ours, even within the terms of the Treaty.[86]

Opposition Leader Edward Heath noted that the three main parties now favoured Community membership. He mocked Labour's retreat from its position that British membership would necessitate significant Treaty revision. The government now accepted the Treaty, the Common Agricultural Policy, the levy system, the common tariff, the loss of preferences, and the creation of reverse preferences. Furthermore the London Agreement had been abandoned. Wilson had accepted nearly all the 'humiliating' terms he had once condemned Heath for approving. The Liberals wholeheartedly

---

[84] HC, 746, col 1087.   [85] Ibid, col 1088.   [86] Brown (1972) 221.

backed membership; Plaid Cymru were opposed but would have supported membership had Wales been given independence; the Ulster Unionists (still allied to the Conservatives) were split.[87]

Analysis of MPs' contributions reveals less emphasis on the Commonwealth than in 1961, twenty-three out of the fifty-one MPs discussing it, others (including the Chancellor and First Secretary) giving it only a fleeting mention. This reflects the perception that the Commonwealth was a lesser issue, partly because Commonwealth countries were becoming reconciled to the inevitability of Britain's Community membership, partly because of dwindling British esteem for the Commonwealth owing to the problems of South Africa and Rhodesia.[88]

Discussion of sovereignty

In the debate no MP referred specifically to *Van Gend* or *Costa*. Moreover no MP pointed out that the obligation to comply with Community law was now not merely a matter of international comity but a duty to be enforced by *British* courts and tribunals. Many of the comments about constitutional implications were wildly inaccurate. For example the abdication of sovereignty involved in EEC membership was likened to that involved in membership of the UN, GATT, and NATO;[89] the Treaty was characterized as 'mostly a statement of aims and principles, rather than a code of positive law';[90] MPs assured themselves that 'the essentials of the whole law of this country are not touched in any way by the Treaty'.[91]

A recurrent theme was that the Treaty of Rome was now to be accepted unconditionally, save for transitional arrangements and those amendments consequential on enlargement.[92] This was resented by Labour anti-Marketeers, who wanted the government to stand by the five 'Gaitskell

---

[87] There were no Scottish Nationalists in the 1966–70 Parliament.

[88] Pimlott (1992) records that Wilson's personal attachment to the Commonwealth 'lost much of its gloss, largely because of strained relations over UDI. Bit by bit the future was looking more European and the reasons for not jumping on the EC bandwagon were diminishing' (435). Miller (1974) comments that 'to some extent, the urge to "enter Europe" represented a conscious turning away from the Commonwealth on the part of large sections of the British élite' (338).

[89] Percy Grieve (Conservative, Solihull) HC, 746, col 1600, 10 May 1967, James Griffiths (Labour, Llanelly) ibid, col 1131.

[90] Sir David Renton (Conservative, Huntingdonshire) ibid, col 1369, 9 May 1967.

[91] Sir Lionel Heald (Conservative, Chertsey) ibid, col 1546, 10 May 1967.

[92] eg John Rankin ibid, col 1563.

conditions'. These MPs tended to focus on loss of control of the economy (notably planning, state aids, and regional policy) whereas Conservative anti-Marketeers objected more generally to the erosion of parliamentary sovereignty.[93] Thus socialists promoted a more *ends-orientated* conception of sovereignty whereas Tories valued the preservation of national freedom of *choice*.

Once again a pervasive focus was the *future* development of the Community. The question was whether the Community would develop into a federation. Members seemed oblivious to the federalizing effect of the ECJ's *existing* case law. The Conservative frontbench position was surprisingly candid. Heath wanted deep integration. He considered that the logical consequence of a common market was to move to a single currency. He also favoured a common defence policy with France and Britain holding the nuclear deterrent 'in trust' for the other EEC countries. More broadly he wanted to create an entity in which politicians thought in terms of Europe and the interests of Europe.[94] Reginald Maudling, closing the debate for the Opposition, believed that

to get the full benefit of the advantages that scale can bring one wants not merely the suppression of tariffs but such things as a common company law, a common taxation basis, a common commercial law—all the things that exist in an economic union . . . We shall finish up, if we enter, with a common currency, a common reserve system, and common policies on the pressure of demand, because there cannot be a free movement of goods, labour and capital unless we work on this basis. This is not part of the Treaty of Rome. It is part of the sheer logic of economic cooperation.[95]

He concluded that 'if we try to argue between theoretical federation or the theory of the *Europe des états*, we would not cope with the real problems, which are . . . coming up every day in economics and in politics'.[96] Similarly First Secretary Michael Stewart, summing up for the government, asked himself whether EEC membership would lead to some kind of federal prison, but reasoned that the political institutions of Europe had yet to be worked out.[97] Wilson himself, emphasizing the 'characteristically cautious and practical' way in which the Community then operated, contended that

---

[93] Contrast eg the contributions of Michael Foot (ibid, cols 1117–1118) and Stan Orme (Labour, Salford West) (ibid, col 1338) with those of Sir Derek Walker-Smith (ibid, cols 1618–1619) and Michael Clark Hutchinson (Conservative, Edinburgh South) (ibid, cols 1567–1568).

[94] Ibid, cols 1282–1300, 9 May 1967.

[95] Ibid, cols 1629–1634, 10 May 1967.

[96] Ibid, col 1634.

[97] Ibid, col 1643.

[T]he federal momentum towards a supra-national Europe in which all issues of foreign and defence policy, for example, would be settled by majority voting, *for the time at least*, has died away. . . . Parliament's decision must be based not so much on what might ultimately evolve, but on the existing working of the Community . . . For the immediately foreseeable future, British public opinion would not contemplate any *rapid* move to a federal Europe.[98]

Wilson's qualified assurances were unlikely to mollify doubters. Moreover, the 'dying away' of federal momentum was scarcely applicable to the ECJ, yet this went unmentioned. Federalism was thus seen purely in political, not legal, terms.

The House approved the Statement by 488 to 62. Thirty-five dissenters and 51 abstainers were Labour—nearly a quarter of the parliamentary party. Nonetheless Wilson was able to boast that the majority constituted the largest on a major issue since the development of modern party alignments, both main parties having imposed a three-line whip.

Why the Labour volte-face? Why was the party which had sought to attach the most conditions to EEC membership now prepared to stomach the unamended Treaty? Wilson may have wished to counter the Conservatives, who had once again started pushing EEC membership when Heath became leader.[99] He may also have believed the Community would foster his 1960s economic panacea, technology.[100] Perhaps more convincing is Tony Benn's explanation, attributing Wilson's conversion to the search for a solution to Labour's inability to engineer economic revival.

Those of us who favoured the application were not too worried about the conditions because we were a defeated Cabinet. Going back to the war, we had tried as a Labour Government to solve the country's economic problems and we had left in a balance of payments crisis in 1951. The Tories had tried and had left in a balance of payments crisis in 1964. We had tried and had had to put the brakes on in 1966, and we were now looking for solutions to our problems from outside and somehow we were persuaded that the Common Market was the way of making progress.[101]

Lack of confidence in British governments 'going it alone' was echoed by several contributors to the Commons debate. Some argued that Britain's failure since 1945 to achieve economic growth necessitated finding a place in a wider

---

[98] Ibid, col 1093, 8 May 1967 (emphases added). The point was reinforced by the speech of Foreign Secretary George Brown at col 1506.

[99] Beloff (1968) sums up his contribution as moving the Conservative Party away from its pro-American bias (which had inspired the first French veto) in favour of a new effort to join the EEC.

[100] Robins (1979) 47–51.   [101] Benn (1987) 496 (diary entry for 30 April 1967).

community.[102] Others argued that not just economic disappointments but Britain's subordinate international role (as exemplified by her abandonment by the USA over Suez) meant that joining a larger entity was her only chance of playing a world role.[103] On the other side of the divide, Ronald Bell (Conservative, Buckinghamshire South) argued forcefully that divesting control of economic affairs to a larger organization could be used by governments to evade accountability for their stewardship of the country's economy.[104]

However, the Commons debate reveals that the political benefit of membership—Britain's enhanced influence on the world stage—seemed more important to some MPs than the (more questionable) economic advantages. This was explicitly stated in the speeches of George Brown (Foreign Secretary),[105] Sir Alec Douglas-Home (Shadow Foreign Secretary),[106] Gilbert Longdon (Conservative, Hertfordshire SW),[107] and John Hall (Conservative, Wycombe).[108]

The Lords debate on the White Paper

Debate in the House of Lords gave the Lord Chancellor, Lord Gardiner, the opportunity to comment on the legal implications of membership. His Lordship did not mention *Van Gend* or *Costa*, but stated that membership involved a transfer of legislative and judicial powers in certain fields to the Community institutions and a corresponding limitation of the exercise of national powers in these fields.

Community law . . . would override our national law so far as it was inconsistent with it. Under the British constitutional doctrine of Parliamentary sovereignty no Parliament can preclude its successors from changing the law. It is, however, implicit in acceptance of the Treaties that the United Kingdom would not only accept exist-

---

[102] James Griffiths (Labour, Llanelly) HC, 746, cols 1125–1126, 8 May 1967.

[103] Robert Maxwell (Labour, Buckingham) ibid, col 1605, 10 May 1967.

[104] Ibid, cols 1385–1386, 9 May 1967. '[w]hen an incomes policy begins to get a bit sticky, people begin to look for other ways of solving the problem. This is not a great step forward; it is a step sideways. Solving economic problems . . . with universal adult suffrage is no joke, and the temptation to shift some of the problems to some of the institutions in Brussels, which are more insulated from democratic pressures, is very great. Not all Administrations are strong enough to resist.'

[105] Ibid, col 1516, 10 May 1967.

[106] Ibid, col 1103, 8 May 1967.

[107] Ibid, col 1144.

[108] Ibid, col 1561, 10 May 1967.

ing Community law but would also refrain from enacting future legislation inconsistent with Community law. Such a restraint on our legislative system would not be unprecedented. Our legislation often takes account—has to take account—of treaty obligations.[109]

It is remarkable that Lord Gardiner started by stating that Community law would 'override' UK law, only immediately to contradict this statement by making it clear that EEC law would remain subject to the full rigours of parliamentary sovereignty. Thus all in all Lord Gardiner's analysis was very similar to that of Lord Dilhorne, taking no account of the way in which the ECJ's two landmark cases had rearranged the Community's constitutional architecture during the intervening period.

Accepting that in theory there was no constitutional means to prevent future Parliaments enacting incompatible legislation, Lord Gardiner nonetheless regarded it as an 'unprofitable academic exercise' to speculate on a future Parliament *expressly* legislating in conflict with Community law. Risk of *inadvertent* contradiction could not be ruled out; but British participation in lawmaking would reduce the likelihood of incompatibility. Like Lord Dilhorne before him, Lord Gardiner clearly saw EEC law as vulnerable to both express and implied repeal. Thus the primacy of Community law was to be at the mercy of parliamentary comity. It would appear that Lord Gardiner was so convinced of the resilience of parliamentary sovereignty in the face of the ECJ doctrines that he felt no need to argue in the alternative about the possible reactions of the British courts to direct effect and supremacy.

As to the scope of Community law, Lord Gardiner repeated the mantra that Community law would have no effect on most areas of law, approving Lord Dilhorne's view five years earlier that the vast majority of people would never directly feel the impact of Community law at all.[110] Abysmally, he only mentioned the ECJ in the context of assisting British courts on questions of interpretation, and assessing the validity of any executive or legislative act of a *Community* institution.

---

109   HL, 282, col 1202, 8 May 1967.

110   Ibid, col 1203. 'Nothing in the Treaties would, for example, touch our criminal law, the onus of proof or the presumption of innocence, matrimonial law, law of inheritance, land law, law of tort or its Scottish equivalent, law of contract (save in relation to restrictive practices), the relation of landlord and tenant, housing, or town and country planning. Nor would there be any reason to expect the creation of future Community law in these fields without the agreement of the United Kingdom, since any enlargement of the powers of the Community to create new law would need . . . unanimous consent of all the members.'

The second White Paper

A second White Paper, *Legal and Constitutional Implications of United Kingdom Membership of the European Communities*, was published after the parliamentary debates.[111] Yet again it did not explicitly mention *Van Gend* or *Costa*. These cases undoubtedly had some influence on the issues raised in the White Paper. However, the way in which it dealt with these issues was not entirely satisfactory.

The White Paper presented a confused picture. First it stated that there was nothing novel in the notion of direct effect;[112] what *was* novel about the Treaty was the power conferred on Community institutions to (*a*) issue subordinate instruments and (*b*) administer and enforce Community law subject to ECJ control. Substantial and complex legislation would be needed both to give effect to existing legislation and to make provision for the reception into domestic law of Treaty provisions and directly applicable Community instruments, including those coming into force after accession. The unprecedented constitutional innovation would lie in the acceptance in advance as part of the law of future Community provisions. Further, this directly effective Community law was *'designed'* to prevail over domestic law. The Act incorporating Community law into British law would therefore have to do this so as to override conflicting existing national law. Moreover within the fields occupied by Community law Parliament would have to *refrain* from passing fresh inconsistent legislation.

Once again this appears to play down the effect of *Costa* in precluding national legislatures from passing such legislation, since the domestic courts are obliged to accord priority to the conflicting Community provision. Instead the White Paper again likened the loss of sovereignty to membership of the UN, ECHR, and GATT.

However, having gone along with the traditional British government line of equating Community law with international law, the White Paper highlighted that directly effective Community law provisions 'would fall to be considered by the United Kingdom courts and would present them with problems of interpretation *and questions of the relationship between the*

---

[111] Cmnd 3301.

[112] Such provisions were 'by no means unknown to the law of the United Kingdom', occurring in various Conventions relating to carriage by air or by sea and to the regulation of sea fisheries (para 3). The White Paper failed, however, to pick up on the ECJ's 'novel' self-proclaimed power to determine which Community provisions enjoyed direct effect.

Community law and our ordinary national law' (emphasis added).[113] This statement seems to indicate, albeit in a heavily veiled way, that government legal
advisers were finally entertaining doubts as to whether parliamentary
omnipotence was everlasting. They were also showing some inkling that the
doctrine's fate lay in judicial hands. However, this sat unhappily with the earlier paragraphs which spoke in terms of Parliament 'refraining' from passing
conflicting legislation.

The White Paper then offered the reassurance that Community legislative
powers were limited by the Treaties to mainly economic objectives and that
overwhelmingly domestic law would remain unchanged. It repeated
Wilson's formulation that directly effective Community law conferred rights
not obligations on individuals in their private capacities, and that in so far as
obligations were imposed, they were imposed on industrial and commercial
activities. There was therefore no reason to think basic rights and liberties of
individuals would be weakened or destroyed.

The White Paper also displayed an incomplete appreciation of the impact
of *Van Gend en Loos*. It stated that the main responsibility for enforcing
Community law lay with the Commission or High Authority. The role of
preliminary references was presented purely in terms of clarifying
Community provisions. The post-*Van Gend* role of Article 177 in assessing
the compatibility of *national* measures with Community law was unmentioned.

Academic reaction

Academic lawyers now sought ways of reconciling parliamentary sovereignty
with the supremacy of Community law. Martin suggested that since the sovereignty doctrine admits of *actual* limitations though not *legal* ones, the
answer lay in the development of a constitutional convention that Parliament
would not use its power to legislate contrary to Community law.[114] In contrast Mitchell took an altogether more radical stance. He criticized the White
Paper for glossing over the sovereignty issue. He considered ambiguous the
notion that Parliament 'would have to refrain from passing inconsistent legislation': 'refraining can be a matter of courtesy, of comity, or of obligation.'
He doubted whether parliamentary sovereignty existed at all in the form in

---

[113] Para 25.   [114] Martin (1968–9).

which it was generally expressed, and therefore saw no insuperable difficulties in fitting membership into the UK constitutional framework. He emphasized that British courts had become too deferential to governmental *and parliamentary* activity, whereas the Community system relied heavily upon courts for its development and evolution.[115]

The velvet veto

The brooding presence of de Gaulle continued to hang like a cloud over the fate of the application. On 16 May 1967 the President held a press conference at which he denied there was any question of a veto. It was simply a matter of finding out whether British membership was possible within the EEC framework or whether to wait until Britain had 'undergone a profound transformation'. Specifically he objected to the position of sterling and Britain's ability to cope with a switch from cheap Commonwealth food to dearer EEC food. He suggested three alternatives: the destruction of the Community in favour of 'a totally new edifice' (but this contained the risk of Atlantic domination); association of Britain and EFTA partners; or simply to wait for internal and external British developments. This speech was dubbed 'the velvet veto' by the British press.

The 1967 Labour Conference debate

At Labour's 1967 Conference the Transport and General Workers' Union, Labour's largest affiliate, moved a resolution calling upon the government to insist on proper safeguards for British agricultural interests, maintain the right to plan the economy, and consider alternative policies in consultation with the Commonwealth and Britain's other trading associates. Frank Cousins, moving, argued that these issues should be resolved before entry rather than taking 'on good faith the intentions of a capitalist system dominated mainly by right-wing governments in Europe'.[116] The General and Municipal Workers moved a resolution welcoming the decision to apply for EEC membership. Its proponents argued that in fact membership would lay

---

[115] Mitchell (1967–8). See also Mitchell (1960–1) 348–350 and Mitchell (1968) ch 4.
[116] Report of the Sixty-Sixth Annual Conference of the Labour Party (Scarborough, 1967) 271.

the foundations for a socialist Europe. Winding up for the National Executive, George Brown said the government could find nothing fundamentally objectionable about the Treaty of Rome: 'there is . . . no requirement to keep on saying we want the freedom to plan the economy. They are planning theirs. They have been going ahead . . . faster than we have.'[117] He added that a federal Europe, widely predicted in the early 1960s, had not transpired, and by joining the Community Britain would be better placed to influence its destiny. The TGWU resolution was defeated by 3.5 million to 2.5 million votes; the GMW resolution was carried by 3.3 million to 2.6 million. It is interesting to note once again the value-laden conception of sovereignty advanced by the Labour Left; what was important was not the right to make or unmake any law *per se*, but rather the right to enact a planned socialist economy.

The real veto

On 18 November the Wilson government devalued the pound and ten days later de Gaulle issued 'the most resounding *"Non"* to any question of British entry'. The President pronounced that for Britain to join, a profound transformation must take place.[118] He strongly wished 'England' to 'choose and accomplish the immense effort which would transform her'. As things stood, the British economy was incompatible with Europe, its currency too weak, its trade and budget deficits too large.[119] Wilson issued a point-by-point rejoinder—with no illusions that this would sway the President. The French simply refused to allow the Community to open negotiations. However, the British application remained on the table.

EEC and parliamentary sovereignty: conclusion

In this early phase British politicians really had no awareness of the possible legal implications of Community membership. Some of the blame needs to be laid at the door of Whitehall. The remarkable similarity between the Macmillan and Wilson White Papers indicates that *Van Gend* and *Costa* had

---

[117] Ibid 285. 'They' refers to the EEC Member States.
[118] Wilson (1971) 594.   [119] Cook (1984) 391.

strikingly little impact on governmental thinking. In particular the 1967 White Paper did not serve legislators well. It failed to draw their attention to the incompatibility between the doctrines of parliamentary sovereignty and EEC law supremacy. It ought to have flagged up far more clearly to MPs the possibility that the courts might eventually modify parliamentary sovereignty in response to EEC membership.

This failure on the part of government was coupled with MPs' inability to see things in legal terms. Both government and Parliament thought in political rather than legal terms and this affected their perception of sovereignty. The result was that legislators did not comprehend how parliamentary sovereignty would be affected nor did they understand that in sanctioning Community membership they would in all likelihood be changing the institutional balance within the British constitution in favour of the courts.

Parliamentary reaction to *Padfield, Conway*, and *Anisminic*

At this point we must digress from the EEC issue to consider parliamentary reaction to a purely domestic judicial development of great moment. The year 1968 witnessed something of a judicial review revolution. *Padfield v Minister of Agriculture*,[120] *Anisminic v Foreign Compensation Commission*,[121] and *Conway v Rimmer*[122] represented significant judicial inroads into executive and (arguably) parliamentary power—the same inter-institutional issues that ought to have been raised by EEC membership in the wake of *Van Gend* and *Costa*.

The *Padfield* case centred on the interpretation of a provision of the Agricultural Marketing Act 1958. Under this statute the Minister could refer complaints about the milk marketing scheme to a committee of investigation 'if the Minister in any case so directs'. Milk producers in south-east England complained that the milk pricing regime was unfair to them, but the Minister declined to refer their complaint on the grounds that it raised 'wide issues', calling into question the entire nationwide pricing system. The House of Lords rejected the Minister's argument that he enjoyed an *unfettered* discretion as to whether to refer complaints. As Lord Upjohn put it,

First, the adjective nowhere appears in section 19, it is an unauthorised gloss by the Minister. Secondly, even if the section did contain that adjective I doubt if it would

---

[120] [1968] AC 997.   [121] [1969] 2 AC 147.   [122] [1968] AC 910.

make any difference in law to his powers. . . . [T]he use of that adjective, even in an Act of Parliament, can do nothing to unfetter the control which the judiciary has over the executive, namely that in exercising their powers the latter must act lawfully and that is a matter to be determined by looking at the Act and its scope and object in conferring a discretion upon the Minister rather than from the use of an adjective.[123]

This seemed to suggest that the courts, by using the purposive approach to interpretation, could deny the 'sovereign' Parliament the right to insulate ministers from judicial scrutiny. Lord Morris of Borth-Y-Gest, dissenting, argued that if Parliament *had* intended the Minister to refer every serious complaint, it could have easily imposed such a duty in plain terms.[124]

In *Anisminic* a company complained that the Foreign Compensation Commission (FCC) had, in deciding its claim for compensation, misconstrued the governing statute, the Foreign Compensation Act 1950. However, the Act also contained an 'ouster clause', a provision seeking to remove the FCC's decision-making from judicial scrutiny. This provision stipulated that 'determinations' of the FCC were not to be questioned in any court of law.

Their Lordships reasoned that if the FCC had trespassed beyond its circumscribed area of inquiry, then the purported 'determination' would be no determination at all but a nullity, and so the ouster provision could be circumvented. Furthermore, the majority held that the FCC had indeed fallen outside its permitted ambit. For although admittedly the FCC had had jurisdiction to *embark* on the decision-making process relating to Anisminic's claim, it had fallen outside its jurisdiction by making an error of law *during* its inquiry.

Lord Morris again dissented. Sure enough, he argued, the courts could intervene if the FCC had started on an inquiry which was outside its allotted territory. But where Parliament had elected to refer issues of law as well as of fact to a tribunal for its determination, then the ouster clause rendered such decision-making unchallengeable. It evidently weighed heavily with Lord Morris that Parliament had clearly *intended* to secure finality of decision-making. In contrast, the majority, having embraced purposivism in *Padfield*, seemingly eschewed it in *Anisminic*, choosing instead to accord priority to a strong interpretative obligation in favour of the right of access to the courts.

The majority's reasoning would appear to render ouster clauses ineffective whenever public decision-makers commit errors of law. Indeed the House would presumably have adopted exactly the same position in respect of judicial scrutiny of the FCC's decision *had the ouster clause not existed*. The courts

[123] At 1060G.   [124] At 1038D.

would still have been willing to review for error of law, and unwilling to examine whether, having made no such error, the tribunal had come to a 'right' or 'wrong' decision.[125] The impotence of ouster provisions sits unhappily with Parliament's vaunted right to make or unmake any law.[126]

Conway v Rimmer involved less of a challenge to Parliament's legislative supremacy and more of a challenge to executive power. The Home Secretary objected to the disclosure of documents in a case in which a former probationary police constable was suing his former superintendent for malicious prosecution. It was accepted that these documents might well be crucial for proving the plaintiff's case, since they were reports about him made during his probationary period by the defendant. The House held that in the event of disputes over whether documents should be withheld in judicial proceedings, the task of balancing the public interest in disclosure with the public interest in non-disclosure must be undertaken *by the courts*. Previously, the courts had treated as conclusive a minister's statement as to whether information should be withheld.[127]

The controversy generated by these decisions is illustrated by the writings of academic commentators. For Griffith, writing from a socialist perspective, the holding in *Padfield*, that the statutory wording 'if in any case the Minister so directs' produced a discretion in which the courts could interfere, constituted a great 'curtailment of Ministerial power'[128] and a blurring of the earlier distinction between matters which fell under ministerial discretion and those which came under judicial competence.[129] The treatment of the ouster clause in *Anisminic* constituted an 'extreme case of judicial interference with the powers of public authorities'.[130] In arguing that the House of Lords in *Padfield* and *Anisminic* was 'biting into the red meat of statutory powers', Griffith appears to suggest that the court was taking such liberties with statutory interpretation as to violate parliamentary sovereignty.[131] The decision in *Conway* that the courts, not the executive, had the final say on whether evidence in cases should be withheld in the public interest represented a 'dramatic assertion by the judiciary of their right to override the view of Ministers on what was or was not in the public interest . . . [I]t is not clear why judges rather than Ministers should have the final decision in such matters.'[132]

---

[125] Since Parliament had enacted no appeal procedure.

[126] As Craig puts it, such provisions 'could, therefore, only immunise from attack errors of law within jurisdiction, and this concept has itself now largely ceased to exist'. Craig (1999*b*) 813.

[127] *Duncan v Cammell Laird & Co Ltd* [1942] AC 624.   [128] Griffith (1993) 86.

[129] Griffith (1997) 105.   [130] Ibid 108.

[131] Griffith (1993) 106.   [132] Ibid 85.

Loveland, writing from a more centre-left political position, suggests that *Padfield* and *Anisminic* represent extreme examples of the courts paying little heed to conventional understandings about the relationship between Parliament and judiciary.[133] Even the more traditionalist Wade and Forsyth characterize *Anisminic* as an example of the courts rebelling against Parliament.[134]

MPs, however, failed to pick up on the common theme of enhanced judicial power. Parliamentary comment was sparse and in all three cases MPs were supportive of the plaintiffs. For example the sole reference to *Padfield* was a written question to Agriculture Minister Fred Peart from Terence Boston (Conservative, Faversham) asking what action the Minister proposed to take on Mr Padfield's complaint in the wake of the House of Lords judgment. Peart replied that he was directing the Committee of Investigation to consider the complaint and report to him.[135] The epilogue was that the Committee upheld the complaint, but the Minister rejected the Committee's findings.[136] The issues in *Conway* were raised when Sir Derek Walker-Smith asked Wilson whether in the light of the judgment government departments would minimize their claims of Crown privilege. The Prime Minister agreed that such claims should be kept to an absolute minimum.[137]

It was *Anisminic*, though, which attracted most debate, because the judgment neatly coincided with the passage through Parliament of the Foreign Compensation Bill 1969. In the light of *Anisminic* the government introduced a new Clause 2(4) to enable the Crown by Order in Council to confer power on the Foreign Compensation Commission to determine any question as to the interpretation of the provisions under which it acted. The debate contained no backbench criticism of *Anisminic*, despite the Law Lords' apparent violation of parliamentary sovereignty. Indeed those MPs who spoke in the relevant Committee debate paid no attention to the government's argument that the effect of the judgment was contrary to Parliament's intention in passing the original ouster clause.[138] Instead they criticized the new clause as 'a travesty of justice'[139] since 'no tribunal should be free to make this kind of mistake without being subject to appeal'.[140] Criticism intensified in the Lords where judges lined up to attack the new

---

[133] Loveland (2000) 66–71, 409–411.
[134] Wade and Forsyth (2000) 706–710.
[135] HC, 759, col 182w, 22 February 1968.
[136] HC, 780, cols 46–47w, 31 March 1969.
[137] HC, 761, cols 1156–1157, 26 March 1968.
[138] HC, 776, col 570, 22 January 1969 (Foreign Minister William Whitlock) and HL, 299, col 18, 4 February 1969 (Foreign Under-Secretary Lord Chalfont).
[139] HC, 776, col 579, 22 January 1969 (R J Maxwell-Hyslop (Conservative, Tiverton)).
[140] Ibid, col 576 (Sir John Foster (Conservative, Northwich)).

ouster clause. Lord Denning[141] and Lord Wilberforce[142] argued that the supervisory powers of the courts must be preserved to safeguard the rule of law. In Committee Viscount Dilhorne proposed an amendment to permit an appeal to the Court of Appeal *on jurisdictional matters only*, and despite government opposition this was carried by 55 to 32. Yet the way in which the House of Lords in *Anisminic* had expanded the concept of 'jurisdiction' was not discussed. Nor was there any debate on the principle of whether the courts should respect Parliament's right to preclude judicial supervision by enacting ouster clauses.[143] Only the Lord Chancellor was critical of the judgment, tersely arguing that the three Law Lords who formed the majority had achieved their result by 'a play on words'.[144] When the Bill returned to the Commons the government, mindful of the criticism they had attracted, introduced a new clause broadly conforming to the Lords amendment.[145]

A curious feature of the debate was the government's insistence throughout that there was no governmental interest in the matter.[146] Yet the executive is the chief political beneficiary of parliamentary sovereignty and would stand to lose by its limitation. Instead, inasmuch as parliamentarians perceived a constitutional principle, it was access to justice. A concerted defence of the conflicting principle, parliamentary sovereignty, was strikingly absent. The political actors seemed to view each of these cases in isolation from each other. They were unable to consider the jurisprudential developments at the appropriate level of generality, and were therefore unable to grasp the implications. The lack of awareness of parliamentarians of their domestic judicial review 'revolution' neatly mirrors their treatment of the EEC. MPs were blind to the effect that key judicial decisions would have on the UK's institutional balance. The courts were not seen as a threat to Parliament and parliamentary sovereignty was not perceived as relating to Parliament's relationship with the courts.

[141] HL, 299, col 54, 4 February 1969.

[142] Ibid, cols 56–57. He complained that the ink was hardly dry on the Law Lords' judgments before the clause was introduced.

[143] Indeed it was Lord Wilberforce who appealed to parliamentary sovereignty, by arguing that giving power to the courts to determine questions of jurisdiction would keep the FCC within the ambit intended by Parliament. Ibid, cols 648–649, 13 February 1969.

[144] Ibid, col 44, 4 February 1969.

[145] HC, 782, col 1736, 1 May 1969 (Sir Arthur Irvine SG), section 3, Foreign Compensation Act 1969.

[146] Lord Gardiner LC: 'I agree that it is a non-Party political question, a matter of opinion' (HL, 299, col 643, 13 February 1969). Sir Arthur Irvine SG: 'the Government have nothing to gain or lose whether the solution of this matter is to leave the law as it stood after the House of Lords' judgment, to adhere to the subsection inserted on Report in this House or to adopt some middle course' (HC, 782, col 1736, 1 May 1969).

3

The 1971 White Paper and the Vote on the Principle of Entry

In 1961 and 1967 Parliament had merely been asked to approve the opening of negotiations. Accession was still a fairly distant prospect and the terms were unknown, and it is conceivable that these factors contributed to MPs' constitutional naïveté. There was little reason to place the consequences for parliamentary sovereignty under the microscope if membership was not imminent. The third, successful, attempt to join the Community would leave MPs no such excuses.[1]

On 30 June 1970 negotiations commenced under the new Heath government. The Community had set as its negotiating principle that 'the solution of any problems of adjustment which may arise must be sought in the establishment of transitional measures and not in changes to existing rules'.[2] Accordingly negotiations were premised on total acceptance of the Treaty and existing Community policies, with discussions focusing on transitional periods.[3] Acceptance of the Treaty plainly also encompassed acceptance of the ECJ's *interpretation* of the Treaty, including the doctrines of supremacy and direct effect. These constitutional fundamentals were therefore non-negotiable and did not feature in the bargaining process. Small wonder, then, that Sir Con O'Neill, the British delegation's leading civil servant, felt obliged to conclude that the negotiations were peripheral and secondary: what mattered, he recalled, was getting into the Community, and

---

[1] On a *formal* level, the Heath negotiations formed part of the second, 1967, application, since following de Gaulle's veto, although the French delegation had refused to agree to the opening of negotiations, the British application remained on the Council's agenda. The reality of the situation, however, was that no serious progress was made in the ensuing sixteen months (O'Neill (2000) 11).

[2] Ibid 21.

[3] Ibid 18.

the negotiations were only concerned with securing that objective at an acceptable price.[4]

Heath announced that the parliamentary debate on entry would be divided into three parts: an 'expository and exploratory' debate on the White Paper before the summer recess; a vote 'in principle' when Parliament reconvened to decide whether Britain should join; and 'substantial' consequential legislation which Parliament would consider during the 1971–2 Session.[5]

There was disagreement as to the relative political importance of the latter two debates.[6] Heath regarded the 'vote in principle' as seminal, presenting the legislation as mere implementation of that decision. Enoch Powell considered the first vote solely preliminary, since the function of the House was to take decisions not on hypothetical or general matters but on specific legislation. Perhaps the most realistic assessment came from Jenkins: 'a good majority [on the vote in principle] we regarded as necessary to provide a momentum for the difficult further stages on the road to entry.'[7]

The White Paper: 'no erosion of essential national sovereignty'

The government published its White Paper *The United Kingdom and the European Communities*[8] in July 1971. It addressed questions of sovereignty but, like its 1967 predecessor, it fudged them. It asserted that, as the Community had developed, '[t]he interests of each Member State have been preserved and promoted, as well as the interests of the Community as a whole'.[9] The document did not tackle the question of what happened when these interests conflicted. *Costa* and *Van Gend* were, as usual, not mentioned.

Like its predecessor, too, the White Paper contained statements on sovereignty which sat uncomfortably with each other. On the one hand it envisaged the expansion of Community competences beyond existing spheres. The Community, it avowed, clearly intended to coordinate foreign policies and make progress towards economic and monetary union. The document argued that British participation in these ventures was the only way to achieve superpower status. On the other hand it argued that the EEC was no federa-

---

[4] O'Neill (2000) 355.   [5] Annex C of Cmnd 4715, 44–45.

[6] From a *legal* standpoint, in view of the dualist nature of the British constitution, the passage of the legislation was the significant debate.

[7] Jenkins (1991) 329.   [8] Cmnd 4715, 7 July 1971.   [9] Ibid, para 16.

tion but a Community of great and established nations. This was reflected in the Luxembourg Accords. Moreover,

Like any other treaty, the Treaty of Rome commits its signatories to support agreed aims; but the commitment represents the voluntary undertaking of a sovereign state to observe policies which it has helped to form. *There is no question of any erosion of essential national sovereignty*; what is proposed is a sharing and an enlargement of individual national sovereignties in the general interest.[10] (Emphases added.)

The document claimed that, as things stood, the Community's institutions were 'purely economic'. The EEC Treaty was concluded for an unlimited period with no mechanism for withdrawal. However, the Community system rested ultimately on the continuing consent of Member States and their Parliaments. The English and Scottish legal systems would remain intact. Certain Treaty provisions and secondary legislation (on commercial, economic, and closely related matters) would be included in our law, but the common law would remain the basis of the legal system, and British courts would continue to operate as at present. All the essential features of our law would remain, 'including the safeguards for individual freedom such as trial by jury and *habeas corpus* and the principles that a man is innocent until proved guilty, as well as the law of contract and tort (and its Scottish equivalent), the law of landlord and tenant, family law, nationality law and land law'.[11]

Several objections to these assertions could be advanced. First, as the ECJ had emphasized in *Van Gend*, the Treaty of Rome was not 'like any other treaty'. It had created its own legal order. Secondly, the claim that membership would involve no loss of 'essential' sovereignty was nonsensical, since the distinction between matters of 'essential' and 'non-essential' sovereignty is incapable of objective differentiation but is a matter of political opinion. The distance between the parties expanded in the early 1970s, the Heath government professing to abandon Butskellism in favour of its right-wing 'Selsdon Man' approach, whereas the Labour Party Conference was poised to adopt its most left-wing programme ever.[12] As we shall see, Labour MPs became preoccupied with whether the Treaty's state aids provisions would lead to the Commission vetoing regional assistance to the North, Scotland, and Wales. To them, potential obstructions to regional policy would indeed infringe essential sovereignty, whereas some Conservatives might relish such a

---

[10] Ibid, para 29.   [11] Ibid, para 31.

[12] *Labour's Programme 1973* included the commitment to nationalize at least one top company in each of the twenty-five major sectors of the economy.

limitation,[13] or at least view it with equanimity. The same could be said of value added tax, lately introduced in the face of fierce Labour opposition. In any case, the Six's ambitious new goals of common foreign policies and monetary union were surely matters which a wide range of people might view as constituting part of 'essential sovereignty'. Thirdly, it was an open question whether ECJ jurisprudence would leave the English legal system 'intact'. If one accepts that the dominant constitutional doctrine in English law is parliamentary sovereignty, it was perfectly possible that, once in the EEC, English courts might consider themselves obliged to disapply this doctrine in the Community context in compliance with the ECJ's supremacy principle. If so, then British courts would not be continuing 'to operate as at present'. More broadly the White Paper had emphasized the importance of continuing consent on the part of national parliaments but had failed to highlight the extent to which the Community system was based on the continuing cooperation of national courts. Fourthly, the emphasis on the Community's 'purely economic' character yet again draws a questionable distinction between economics and politics. Certainly in the early 1970s, many of the key political differences between the parties were over economic policy.

The White Paper was imbued with the pro-Marketeers' conception of sovereignty: Britain's ability to achieve desired goals, rather than the preservation of Britain's national legislative choice. This conception was reflected in the fact that the document did not even consider as an option the possibility of the country 'going it alone'. Instead it emphasized that there existed no alternative grouping of countries offering the same possibilities. Any North Atlantic grouping would be US dominated; the Commonwealth now lacked the necessary cohesion and British trade with it had declined sharply, just as trade with the Community had rapidly increased. The document warned that a decision *not* to join would mean that 'we should have renounced an imperial past and rejected a European future . . . [British] power to influence the Communities would steadily diminish, while the Communities' powers to affect our future would as steadily increase'.[14] The concluding rallying cry was printed in bold: 'every choice involves challenge as well as opportunity. Her Majesty's Government are convinced that the right decision for us is to accept the challenge, seize the opportunity and join the European Communities.'[15]

---

[13] eg Norman Tebbit shared Heath's belief that entry into a common market governed by the strict Treaty provisions forbidding state subsidies would force industry to look to itself, rather than the state, for solutions (Tebbit (1988) 94).

[14] Cmnd 4715, para 64.   [15] Ibid, para 66.

The debate on the White Paper: 'essential sovereignty' and 'real influence'

The White Paper was debated on 21–6 July. It came under attack from anti-Marketeers and pro-Marketeers alike. There were two prongs to the back-bench attack. First, the propagandist tone of the document as a whole was thought inappropriate for a White Paper.[16] It read too much like a party political manifesto.[17] Secondly, the claim that membership involved no 'erosion of essential national sovereignty' was regarded as at best thin and at worst downright deceitful.[18] MPs tended not to go into detail as to why precisely they objected to the 'essential sovereignty' claim, but it seems clear that most had in mind that the *scope* of Community rules would be wider than the government claimed. Only Sir Edward du Cann (Conservative, Taunton) raised obliquely the question of *enforceability*. He characterized the 'essential sovereignty' argument as a gross exaggeration, though 'Professor Dicey, whose work I was obliged to read *ad nauseam* at University, would have had a stronger word for it'. Neither could he accept that the English and Scottish legal systems would survive intact.[19]

The pro-Marketeers who lined up to attack the White Paper clearly wanted Parliament and people to go into the Community far more aware of the sovereignty implications.[20] No doubt they thought that the EEC cause would be better served by a feisty promotion of the pro-Marketeers' conception of sovereignty. Perhaps like the *Guardian* they found the White Paper overly timid: 'the idea of a dynamic political union does not appear. Instead, the Government paints a cautious picture designed not to frighten wavering Conservative backbenchers.'[21]

---

[16] Alf Morris (Labour, Manchester Wythenshawe) HC, 821, col 1543, 21 July 1971, Philip Whitehead (Labour, Derby South) ibid, col 1670, 22 July 1971.

[17] Harold Wilson ibid, col 1495, 21 July 1971.

[18] Neil Martin (Conservative, Banbury) HC, 821, col 1508, 21 July 1971; Sir Edward du Cann ibid, col 1763, 22 July 1971; Neil McBride (Labour, Swansea East) ibid, col 1563, 21 July 1971; Alf Morris (Labour, Manchester Wythenshawe) ibid, col 1543, 21 July 1971; Kenneth Clarke (Conservative, Rushcliffe) ibid, col 1779, 22 July 1971; Sir Geoffrey de Freitas (Labour, Kettering) HC, 822, col 91, 26 July 1971.

[19] HC, 821, col 1763, 22 July 1971.

[20] They were Dick Douglas (Labour, Clackmannan and East Stirlingshire) HC, 821, col 1933, 23 July 1971; Philip Whitehead (Labour, Derby South) ibid, col 1670, 22 July 1971; Kenneth Clarke (Conservative, Rushcliffe) ibid, col 1779, 22 July 1971; Sir Geoffrey de Freitas (Labour, Kettering) HC, 822, col 91, 26 July 1971.

[21] *Guardian*, 8 July 1971.

Even those EEC supporters who had no criticism of the White Paper made no attempt to defend the 'essential sovereignty' argument. Pro-Marketeer after pro-Marketeer strikingly omitted even a token mention of it. Rather than maintaining that the Community's ambit was modest, they presented the prospect of a progressive reduction in Britain's ability to control events (both economic and foreign policy) unless she tied herself to a larger entity. Even Edward Heath did not bother with the 'essential sovereignty' argument, contending instead that the foremost 'question of principle' was how Britain could continue to exert a strong and constant influence in the world.[22] Nor did the 'essential sovereignty' argument feature in Heath's television broadcast on the day the White Paper was published,[23] nor in his speech to a laudatory Conservative Central Council the following week.[24] Similarly his chief negotiator Geoffrey Rippon ignored the 'essential sovereignty' point.[25]

Labour pro-Marketeers adopted much the same position. Roy Jenkins, dismissing fears for parliamentary sovereignty as 'detailed constitutional points', thought EEC membership would not involve major invasions of sovereignty. However, he spent far more of his speech discussing how Britain could increase her *influence* and *control* over decisions which affected her, since 'if we delude ourselves by thinking that we can cling to the shadow of sovereignty, as a result we shall have less and not more influence on what really happens to us'.[26] By way of illustration he related how, as British Chancellor attending crisis meetings of the Group of Ten, all the non-EEC countries—even the USA—had been obliged to wait (once more than ten hours) for the ministers of the Six to meet together before any decisions could be taken. Other Labour pro-Marketeers argued that membership would lead to greater control of multinational companies[27] and to higher growth, enabling greater redistribution of wealth.[28] They also appealed to Labour's commitment to internationalism.[29]

---

[22] HC, 821, col 1467, 21 July 1971.

[23] *The Times*, 9 July 1971.

[24] Ibid, 15 July 1971.

[25] HC, 821, col 1592, 21 July 1971.

[26] Ibid, col 1704, 22 July 1971. This was Jenkins's final parliamentary intervention before the policy decision of the Labour Party Conference obliged him, as Deputy Party Leader, to muzzle his views.

[27] John Smith (Labour, Lanarkshire North) argued against the notion of a wholly theoretical national sovereignty which could be flouted by the economic power of international companies, and maintained that the institutions which could control them were in the EEC. HC, 822, cols 129–130, 26 July 1971. See similarly Tam Dalyell ibid, cols 834–835, 26 July 1971.

[28] See eg Dick Taverne (Labour, Lincoln) (HC, 822, cols 139–142, 26 July 1971) and Robert Sheldon (Labour, Ashton-under-Lyne) (HC, 821, cols 1755–1760, 22 July 1971).

[29] See eg Alan Fitch (Labour, Wigan) (HC, 822, cols 112–115, 26 July 1971), who saw the Community as a prelude to world unity and world government.

To rub in the government's 'real influence' argument, ministers lined up to emphasize Britain's decline, present and prospective, outside the Community. Foreign Secretary Sir Alec Douglas-Home (who perceived sovereignty in terms of 'the reality of power and influence') portrayed Britain as weak and in decline. The only way to influence events in the context of the new superpowers was for the 'middle-powers of Europe' to act together.[30] Chancellor Anthony Barber warned of slow growth outside the Community, with Britain increasingly overshadowed both economically and politically by a stronger, richer Europe.[31]

Thus for the pro-Marketeers sovereignty was certainly not about the preservation of legislative choice but about the attainment of economic and foreign policy strength. There was little analysis of whether Britain or the Community would be the beneficiary of the 'real influence' to which they repeatedly referred. Britain's voice would, after all, be diluted in Council by the other Member States. Perhaps the issue was not so much 'influence' as the ability to achieve *predetermined* goals which formed part of a pro-Marketeer consensus. These goals would seem to include improved economic performance within the context of a market-based mixed economy and a more powerful role on the world stage. Thus the pro-Marketeer vision of sovereignty was distinctly teleological.

An anti-socialist constitution?

There were no objections from Conservatives that the Treaty might foist socially progressive policies on the UK, but much criticism from Labour MPs that it formed a politically biased constitution. There were fears that nationalization of manufacturing sectors might breach Article 92 on state aids.[32] Some saw the Treaty as prohibiting a whole raft of progressive measures, thereby rendering radical opposition unconstitutional.[33] The Left's conception of sovereignty thus involved the electorate being able to choose between a capitalist government and one which would seek to undermine the capitalist nature of society. It was no less *aims driven* than that adopted by the Left's pro-EEC opponents. Sovereignty was worth having so that voters were free to eschew capitalism and embrace socialism.

[30] Ibid, col 1709, 22 July 1971.   [31] HC, 822, col 51, 26 July 1971.
[32] Stan Orme (Labour, Salford West) HC, 821, col 1787, 22 July 1971.
[33] R T Paget (Labour, Northampton) ibid, cols 1719–1720, 22 July 1971. He instanced redistributive taxation, quotas, controls, subsidies, and penalties to influence commercial decisions.

Direct effect ignored

In four days of debate just two MPs touched on the subject of the ECJ, and both disregarded the empowering effect of *Van Gend* and *Costa* on the national courts. Thus R T Paget (Labour, Northampton) noted that Britain's unwritten constitution, which enabled Parliament to change every law, would be swapped for

a series of constitutional laws above us, which we cannot change. As we make laws here we shall have to bear in mind all the time that those laws are subject to review by a court at Brussels [*sic*] which may declare them unconstitutional *vis-à-vis* the European constitution, and order us to revoke them. . . . This is a pretty rigid constitution.[34]

Michael Clark Hutchinson (Conservative, Edinburgh South) also perceived the ECJ alone as the villain of the piece:

Then there is the Community Court. It has wide powers which are likely to grow. Its opinions can be sought on numerous cases, and its rulings can and do affect not only companies but individuals. Disputes involving individuals or organisations in the United Kingdom should be settled in London or Edinburgh and not in Luxembourg. . . . That is one of the things that sovereignty is about.[35]

This argument seems based on a purely nationalistic assumption that British disputes should be settled by British courts, and does not touch on the relationship between courts and Parliament.

The run-up to the vote on principle

With the debate on the White Paper ending without a division, attention focused on how MPs would vote in October.

Conservatives in the country were relatively united in support of the Community. The Party Conference voted by 2,474 to 324 for membership on the terms secured by the government, an eight-to-one majority.[36] In contrast, however, Conservative MPs were not so compliant: in 1970, forty-four

---

[34] R T Paget (Labour, Northampton) col 1718, 22 July 1971.
[35] HC, 822, cols 110–111, 26 July 1971.
[36] *The Times*, 14 October 1971.

had signed a Commons early day motion opposing membership, and by 1971 the government's majority was below thirty.[37]

Labour was divided into three camps: those who strongly supported entry and were not deterred by the terms;[38] those who opposed membership *simpliciter*;[39] and those, like Wilson, who did not wish to commit Labour against membership on principle, but realized that 'entry on Tory terms' had to be opposed to preserve Party unity.[40] The issue was made even more emotive due to the widespread view within the Party that the Heath government was the most reactionary for decades, bent on reversing the post-war consensus, and that accordingly any action to shorten its life would be welcomed. Wilson recognized that Labour support for entry would be unacceptable both to the majority of the parliamentary party and to the Party in the country and would be seen as shoring up the government. Yet outright opposition to membership would force the passionately pro-EEC wing (unofficially led by Roy Jenkins) out of the Party. The effect was to focus debate between the two front benches artificially on the terms.

On 17 July 1971, the Labour Party Conference met in special session to debate the issue.[41] No vote was taken at the Conference, but it gave Wilson a platform to clarify Labour objections.[42] These seemed based overwhelmingly on economic concerns (balance of payments, capital movements) and substantive areas of Community policy (treatment of Commonwealth sugar producers and New Zealand) rather than on constitutional considerations. There was some suggestion, however, that the Treaty would be biased against the Left since he also expressed anxiety over the Treaty's effect on regional policy and suggested that the Conservatives wanted a common market to depress labour costs, since Conservative European policy was simply 'one more dimension to the policies that they have been pursuing at home'.[43] He added that he would not be deflected from recommending the course he

[37] Shepherd (1996) 413.

[38] This group included those who left the Party in 1981 to form the SDP but also loyalists such as Roy Hattersley and Philip Whitehead, as well as the Parliamentary Labour Party's Chairman, Douglas Houghton.

[39] This group included the Labour Left but also a large number of anti-EEC right-wingers such as Peter Shore and Douglas Jay.

[40] This group also included James Callaghan and Denis Healey.

[41] *The Times*, 9 July 1971, Jenkins (1991) 325.

[42] The arrangement was that the NEC on 28 July 1971 would pass a resolution on Labour's attitude to entry on the government's terms. This text would then be sent to affiliated organizations which could submit amendments to it. These would be debated at the normal Annual Conference in October which would determine Labour's definitive position.

[43] *Report of the Seventieth Annual Conference of the Labour Party 1971*, 359.

believed right for Britain, nor from doing all in his power to maintain Party unity.[44]

On 28 July Labour's NEC voted to oppose 'entry into the Common Market on the terms negotiated by the Conservative Government' and invited 'the Parliamentary Labour Party . . . to unite wholeheartedly in voting against the Government's policy'. This was endorsed by the October Annual Conference by 5,073,000 to 1,032,000. James Callaghan, summing up for the executive, stated that it was the Party's job on 28 October to get the Tories out of office, and that therefore Labour MPs should unite on this issue and accept the Party's verdict. At the Conference, rumour was rife that Wilson had agreed with Jenkins that pro-Marketeers could vote with the government on 28 October provided they voted against the government consistently thereafter.[45] Wilson vigorously denied this.

The Liberal Party wholeheartedly favoured membership, boasting a record of consistent support for the EEC since its inception. The Liberal Conference had earlier overwhelmingly endorsed entry on the government's terms.[46] The Scottish National Party opposed not just the terms but the principle of membership, arguing it would adversely affect Scotland as a development area and would make decision-making even more remote.[47] Ulster Unionists were split, some supporting the government, others rejecting membership on grounds of Northern Ireland's economic interests or the desire to maintain parliamentary sovereignty.[48] The nationalists (Bernadette Devlin and Gerry Fitt) also opposed membership though they did not speak in the debate. No Plaid Cymru MPs had been elected to the 1970 Parliament.

Debate on the principle of membership

The six-day Commons debate commenced on 21 October. The motion was 'that this House approves Her Majesty's Government's decision of principle to join the European Communities on the basis of the arrangements which have been negotiated'.

---

[44] *Report of the Seventieth Annual Conference of the Labour Party 1971*, 359.
[45] *Guardian*, 6 October 1971, *The Times*, 7 October 1971, Jay (1980) 457–458.
[46] *Guardian*, 18 September 1971.
[47] See eg Donald Stewart HC, 821, cols 1928–1931, 23 July 1971.
[48] Stanley McMaster (Belfast East) HC, 823, col 1575, 26 October 1971, James Molyneaux (Antrim South) ibid, col 1799, 27 October 1971.

Initially Heath was determined to impose a three-line whip on Conservative MPs. However, Francis Pym, then Chief Whip, calculated that a free vote would not increase the Tory rebel vote beyond 30–40, but would pressurize the Opposition to follow suit, liberating Labour pro-Marketeers to vote for entry.[49] In fact the Parliamentary Labour Party voted by 140 to 111 for a whipped vote. Nonetheless, Jenkins considered the Conservative free vote 'a bold and skilful tactical ploy, for [Heath] had more to gain from us than to lose from his own side'.[50]

Legal sovereignty versus real influence

The debate saw further differentiation between either side's competing conceptions of sovereignty. This time, pro-Marketeers explicitly sought to draw a distinction between legal sovereignty and political power, belittling the former. Thus David Waddington argued:

In a sense, entry involves a surrender of sovereignty. It involves this Parliament deciding that, in certain closely defined areas, it will act only in agreement with its fellow members. But . . . a country may have complete legal sovereignty, complete power to pass whatever laws it wishes in an attempt to control every kind of activity of its citizens, and yet be so weak as to be incapable of protecting its people from military, economic, or other action taken by other countries. Conversely, another country may sacrifice quite a lot of its legal sovereignty and yet, by acting in partnership with others, be able to exercise very much more power and give greater protection to its citizens than it ever could and did before that sacrifice was made.[51]

Conservative and Labour pro-Marketeers alike criticized their opponents for clinging to a purely legalistic conception of sovereignty.[52] The important fact was that there was no way Britain had the same power to guide her destiny as she had enjoyed in 1900 or 1945.[53] On the Labour side, pro-Marketeers instanced runs on sterling, failure to secure economic objectives, and

---

[49] Indeed William Rodgers had written personally to Heath begging him to allow a free vote, arguing that this would maximize his majority since Labour pro-Europeans easily outnumbered Conservative antis. Campbell (1993) 400.

[50] Jenkins (1991) 329, Campbell (1993) 402, Kitzinger (1973) 187–188.

[51] HC, 823, col 1438, 25 October 1971.

[52] John Selwyn-Gummer ibid, col 2024, 27 October 1971, John Mackintosh (Berwick & East Lothian) ibid, cols 2020–2021, 27 October 1971. David Owen praises the latter speech as 'a lucid demolition of the nineteenth-century concept of sovereignty' (Owen (1991) 184).

[53] HC, 823, col 2024, 27 October 1971.

Britain's low standing in international affairs.[54] For instance Charles Pannell (Labour, Leeds West) argued that Labour's housing programme had been scuppered by a surrender of sovereignty to international bankers, and that its foreign policy had been characterized by an abdication of sovereignty to President Johnson over Vietnam.[55]

The assertion that Community membership would make a stark difference to Britain's influence, and that therefore the decision on whether or not to join was of fundamental importance, was made by both the Prime Minister and Chancellor.[56] This surely drove the final nail into the coffin of the 'essential sovereignty' argument. As Michael Foot put it, it was strange indeed to insist that Europe would make momentous decisions at the same time as claiming that there was no erosion of essential sovereignty.[57]

An executive coup—but not a judicial one?

For their part anti-Marketeers added a new argument to their armoury. They pointed to the loss of accountability of ministers to Parliament resulting from membership. Conservative Sir Derek Walker-Smith argued:

We are asked by the White Paper to say that entry will involve no sacrifice of essential sovereignty. Of course it depends on what is meant by 'essential'—not essential, perhaps, if only the Executive matters, if Members of Parliament are to be seen and not heard, to acquiesce and not decide; not essential, perhaps, if one believes in elitism . . . For those who believe that Parliament still has a function as the elected representatives of a free people . . . the sacrifice is essential indeed.[58]

Elystan Morgan (Labour, Cardigan) pointed out that the Commission, not the Council, had jurisdiction over state aids under Article 92.[59] For him, this

---

[54] Robert Maclennan ibid, col 1966, 26 October 1971; John Mackintosh ibid, cols 2020–2021, 27 October 1971.

[55] Ibid, cols 1285–1292, 25 October 1971.

[56] Heath: 'I do not think that any Prime Minister has stood at this Box in time of peace and asked the House to take a positive decision of such importance as I am asking it to take tonight.' Ibid, col 2202, 28 October 1971. Barber: 'Whatever the divisions of opinion in the country, in the House and inside the parties themselves, there is one thing on which we can all agree. It is that the choice before us is great; indeed, probably the greatest peace-time issue which has to be decided in this country in this generation.' Ibid, col 1736, 27 October 1971.

[57] Ibid, col 1257, 25 October 1971.   [58] Ibid, cols 2134–2135, 28 October 1971.

[59] Trade and Industry Secretary John Davies argued that, although the Commission could reproach a country for its state aid measures, 'nothing prevents the country concerned from

typified the transfer of sovereignty to unaccountable bureaucracies.[60] Labour's William Molloy (Ealing North) predicted that membership would lead to ministers refusing to answer parliamentary questions on the grounds that the relevant issues were now matters for the Commission, Council, or ECJ.[61] Anthony Buck (Conservative, Colchester) retorted that the ECJ had no power to impose sanctions and had a very limited jurisdiction. He complained of scurrilous propaganda exaggerating the ECJ's possible impact on British affairs.[62]

Overall there was sparse comment on the ECJ considering its centrality in the Community's constitutional architecture. Only one other MP mentioned it in the six days of debate. Goronwy Roberts (Labour, Caernarvon) laconically remarked that the reality of the Community's structure was 'a bureaucratic Commission which runs the show backed by the sanction of a supreme court on the American model'.[63] This comparison overestimated the role of enforcement proceedings and failed to spell out the prospect, implicit in *Van Gend* and *Costa*, of litigants going before the British courts to have statutory provisions set aside. It also projected the image of the ECJ as the mere enforcer of Commission decisions, rather than a force for integration in its own right. It is telling that the only MPs to criticize the ECJ linked it to the growth of *executive* power (domestic and European) rather than pinpointing the likely increase in *judicial* power as a discrete constitutional development. There was seemingly no inkling whatsoever of the way in which Community membership would shift power to the national courts.

There was also a comment by Elystan Morgan (Labour, Cardigan) quoting Bebr's *Modern Law Review* article[64] to the effect that the Treaty created its own legal order resulting from a transfer of power from States to the Community. Yet not only did Morgan fail to mention the ECJ, but Bebr devoted a whole section to the impact of the supremacy doctrine *on the municipal courts* and Morgan failed to pick up on this.

The neglect of the enhanced role which UK courts would enjoy in enforcing Community law suggests that parliamentarians continued to treat parliamentary sovereignty as concerned solely with Parliament's powers in relation to EC institutions, not with the relationship between Parliament and courts. *Van Gend* and *Costa* were not explicitly mentioned, and nor was the new case

---

raising the matter within the Council of Ministers . . . we cannot be overridden on a matter of basic national interest'. Eric Heffer heckled: 'Read Article 93.' Ibid, col 1858, 27 October 1971.

[60] Ibid, col 1431, 25 October 1971.   [61] Ibid, cols 2156–2157, 28 October 1971.
[62] Ibid.   [63] Ibid, col 1555, 26 October 1971.   [64] Bebr (1971).

Internationale Handelsgesellschaft,[65] which established that the validity of a Community measure could not be affected by allegations that it ran counter to *inter alia* the principles of a national constitutional structure—in the UK's case, surely, the doctrine of parliamentary sovereignty.

Division in pro-Market camp

The debate exposed for the first time the 'marriage of convenience' between two groups of parliamentarians who united in support of EEC membership but differed sharply as to how the Community should develop. Peter Hardy (Labour, Rother Valley) identified a split between those pro-Marketeers who denied that entry would lead to political federation, and those who took the opposite view.[66] This disagreement was also highlighted by Jasper More (Conservative, Ludlow) who lampooned pro-Marketeers as being divided between the 'Band of Hope', who wanted 'European baptism by total immersion—a united federal Government, common foreign policy, the lot', and 'the Unity of Oddfellows', 'who insist on things like the veto, national identity and so on'.[67]

The speeches of pro-Marketeers suggest some foundation for this. Some expressly stated that they did not seek a European superpower or a US-style arrangement.[68] Others wanted Britain to act as a restraining influence on federalization within the Community or asserted that they would have opposed entry had they thought it would mean federation.[69]

In contrast, other pro-Marketeers were disarmingly candid about their support for a federal United States of Europe with democratic institutions.[70] Some expressed a desire to extend the Community's ambit to the whole range of foreign relations and defence.[71] Indeed Heath himself spoke of the decision vitally affecting the world's balance of forces and of Europe taking over

[65] Case 11/70 [1970] ECR 1125, [1972] CMLR 255.

[66] HC, 823, cols 1044–1045, 21 October 1971.

[67] Ibid, col 1294, 25 October 1971. John Sutcliffe (Conservative, Middlesborough West) made much the same point at cols 1396–1397, 25 October 1971.

[68] David Owen ibid, col 1633, 26 October 1971, Sir John Rodgers (Conservative, Sevenoaks) ibid, col 1412, 25 October 1971.

[69] Peter Trew (Conservative, Dartford) ibid, cols 1305–1306 (25 October 1971), John Biggs-Davison (Conservative, Chigwell) ibid, col 1995 (27 October 1971).

[70] John Pardoe ibid, col 1652 (26 October 1971). Jeremy Thorpe ibid, col 2127 (28 October 1971).

[71] Duncan Sandys ibid, col 2177 (28 October 1971).

her own defence commitments.[72] Labour spokespersons pointed out the contradiction between Heath's support for the Luxembourg Compromise and his insistence that Britain would play its full part in the Werner plan which, if implemented, would destroy what remained of Parliament's sovereignty, since the logic of economic and monetary union was federalism.[73]

The division between federalist and non-federalist pro-Marketeers was reflected in their writings. Duncan Sandys expressed support for a 'maximalist' approach to Community membership in a book published by the European Movement,[74] whereas David Owen in his memoirs attacked with hindsight the 'closet federalism' of Heath and Jenkins, observing that 'an uneasy truce was reached in British politics to postpone serious discussions on this question until Britain was firmly embedded within the European Community'.[75]

State aids and regional policy

Controversy over the Treaty's lack of political neutrality markedly intensified. Once again this was confined to Labour's ranks; there was no feeling among Conservatives that the Treaty would impose unwanted social costs on the UK. Indeed, Social Services Secretary Sir Keith Joseph applauded Article 117, which enjoins the Member States to harmonize 'upwards' their national living, working, and employment conditions. He argued that 'in the wider sphere of social policy, nothing but good can come from closer association and collaboration with our neighbours. We share the same problems and the same purposes.'[76]

However, on the Labour side the Treaty was denounced as capitalist[77] by Labour MPs Raphael Tuck (Watford),[78] Jim Sillars (South Ayrshire),[79]

[72] Ibid, col 2203 (28 October 1971).

[73] Barbara Castle ibid, col 1848 (27 October 1971), James Callaghan ibid, col 2199 (28 October 1971). The Werner plan, a Community-commissioned report of bankers and financial experts chaired by the Luxembourg Prime Minister, proposed economic and monetary union, with a 'centre of decision for economic policy' at Community level, able to influence national budgets, and responsible for changes in the external parity of the Community bloc of currencies, or single currency.

[74] Rippon et al (1971) 106–110.   [75] Owen (1991) 177.

[76] HC, 823, col 1112, 22 October 1971.

[77] It must be borne in mind that at the time the Labour Party in the country, disenchanted with the 1964–70 government's record, was moving in favour of policies involving greater governmental control of the economy.

[78] HC, 823, col 1577, 26 October 1971.   [79] Ibid, col 1673, 26 October 1971.

Gavin Strang (Edinburgh East),[80] Hugh Jenkins (Putney),[81] Roy Hughes (Newport),[82] and Les Huckfield (Nuneaton).[83] Concern over the politically loaded nature of the Treaty was closely related to anxiety over the fate of UK regional policy.[84] These worries were not confined to Labour MPs, but were shared by some Conservatives and Ulster Unionists.[85] The response of pro-Marketeers was that in practice Member States were permitted dynamic regional policies.[86] Moreover the Community's potential to boost economic growth would have a knock-on beneficial effect on the regions.[87]

Criticism of the Treaty's politically biased character extended to fiscal policy. Labour MPs argued that it was impossible to be pro-EEC but anti-VAT,[88] that Parliament would lose its ability substantially to alter the balance between direct and indirect taxation,[89] and that Parliament and the British people would have less power to protest over VAT than Hampden had to protest about ship money.[90]

---

[80] HC, 823, col 1735, 27 October 1971.   [81] Ibid, col 1906, 27 October 1971.

[82] Ibid, col 1920, 27 October 1971.   [83] Ibid, col 1955, 27 October 1971.

[84] Stanley Clinton Davis (Labour, Hackney Central) (ibid, col 1483, 26 October 1971) considered that Article 92 seriously impaired the ability to plan the economy, making movement towards democratic socialism impermissible. George Thomas (Labour, Cardiff West) (ibid, cols 1596–1599, 26 October 1971) alleged that the Commission could and did modify Member State regional policy, and that the government had capitulated by failing to negotiate safeguards.

[85] Teddy Taylor (ibid, cols 1525–1526, 26 October 1971) claimed that the Commission had recently vetoed regional aid to Trieste, despite the existence of a million unemployed in Italy. He thought Britain's Industrial Development Certificate system, whereby the government controlled industrial location, would be rendered ineffective in a single market where firms could choose to set up in France rather than Glasgow. Stanley McMaster (Ulster Unionist, Belfast East) (ibid, cols 1525–1526, 26 October 1971) wanted a protocol attached to the Treaty exempting the UK's disadvantaged regions from Articles 92 and 93. The same demand was also made by Ronald King Murray (Labour, Edinburgh Leith) (ibid, col 1010, 21 October 1971).

[86] See eg William Rodgers (ibid, col 948, 21 October 1971) and Richard Hornby (Conservative, Tonbridge) (ibid, col 969, 21 October 1971).

[87] See eg Carol Johnson (Labour, Lewisham South) (ibid, col 1171, 22 October 1971), David Steel (ibid, col 972, 21 October 1971), and Sir Keith Joseph (ibid, col 1113, 22 October 1971).

[88] Geoffrey Rhodes (Labour, Newcastle East) ibid, col 1875, 27 October 1971.

[89] Dr John Gilbert (Labour, Dudley) ibid, cols 2137–2138, 28 October 1971.

[90] Michael Foot ibid, col 1259, 25 October 1971. Presumably Foot was making the point that recourse to British institutions would be of no avail to either MPs or citizens since the matter would lie beyond the powers of Parliament.

The legitimacy of the government's mandate

Anti-Marketeers voiced doubts as to whether the government had a mandate for entry. The Conservative manifesto pledged to 'negotiate, no more, no less'. Moreover Heath in May 1970 had promised Britain would only join with 'the full-hearted consent of Parliament and people'. Michael Foot was scathing: '"The people" got lopped off that formula fairly early on. . . . Then we were left only with the "full-hearted consent of the British Parliament". Instead of "full-hearted", perhaps "half-hearted" has been substituted.'[91] Calling for a general election on the issue, Denis Healey remarked that not only had the people been denied a vote, but the belated promise of a free vote was humbug, with 150 ministers and parliamentary private secretaries obliged to support the government. Indeed, the Chancellor and Leader of the House had announced on radio that the government would resign if defeated on the issue.[92]

Government spokesmen dismissed these arguments tersely. Sir Alec Douglas-Home retorted that the commitment to 'negotiate, no more, no less' clearly meant that if the government were successful in negotiations, Britain would join. In closing the debate, Heath was blunt. 'I have always made it plain to the British people that consent to this course would be given by Parliament—[HON. MEMBERS: "Resign".]—Parliament is the Parliament of all the people.'[93] The question of legitimacy becomes intense if Parliament's decision to join were considered irreversible. The consensus was that withdrawal would be constitutionally effortless but politically difficult. Harold Wilson referred to the doctrine that Parliament could not bind its successors, seemingly threatening to use this as a bargaining chip in renegotiations. However, he subsequently rather spoilt the effect by denying that he had withdrawal in mind, threatening instead to 'work it as the French did after 1958', in other words a policy of complete national self-interest. Angus Maude (Conservative, Stratford-upon-Avon),[94] Richard Crawshaw (Labour, Liverpool Toxteth),[95] Carol Mather (Conservative, Esher),[96] and Donald Stewart (SNP, Western Isles)[97] all expressed the view that it was practical, not constitutional, considerations which would make withdrawal difficult.

[91] Ibid, col 1265, 25 October 1971.
[92] Ibid, cols 938–940, 21 October 1971.
[93] Ibid, col 2212, 28 October 1971.
[94] Ibid, col 1816, 27 October 1971.
[95] Ibid, col 1931, 27 October 1971.
[96] Ibid, col 1918, 27 October 1971.
[97] Ibid, col 1993, 27 October 1971.

Labour faced a legitimacy crisis of its own. There was disagreement over whether Labour MPs should be bound by Conference policy. William Rodgers considered that MPs could not be expected to go meekly through the division lobby with their tails between their legs; he wanted freedom to vote in favour of entry, just as he would defend to the last the right of his anti-Market colleagues to vote against.[98] Roy Hattersley considered that the country would not admire a group of men (*sic*) who, having constantly campaigned for membership in the national interest, did not have the courage to vote in conformity with that view; his duty, as reflected in Burke's writings, was to use his judgment and then courageously to apply that judgment.[99] In contrast Norman Atkinson (Tottenham) asserted that it was the duty of all Labour MPs to accept Conference policy decisions.[100]

The outcome

The Jenkinsites, marshalled by William Rodgers, kept in close contact with the government Whips Office throughout this period. As Jim Prior recorded: 'all through this anxious time we made great efforts privately to keep Roy Jenkins and his group informed, and they in turn advised us on what was possible ... The work was well rewarded as in the major vote on the principle of entry we had a majority of 112.'[101] The result (Ayes 356, Noes 244) was considered by the press to be 'well above expectation'[102] and 'very much larger than had been expected'.[103] Sixty-nine Labour MPs had voted for entry, with 20 abstaining; 39 Conservatives opposed entry, with 2 abstaining. The pro-Marketeers were jubilant, the antis not downcast because they thought they could still defeat the enabling legislation, the Jenkinsites having vowed to support the government no further.

---

[98]   Michael Foot ibid, cols 946–947, 21 October 1971.

[99]   Ibid, cols 1805–1806, 27 October 1971.

[100]   Ibid, col 1771, 27 October 1971. Two years later left-wing rank and file members established the Campaign for Labour Party Democracy to make Conference policy decisions binding on the Parliamentary Labour Party.

[101]   Prior (1986) 86.

[102]   *Guardian*, 29 October 1971.

[103]   *The Times*, 29 October 1971.

Conclusion

The House of Commons had taken its policy decision by a decisive majority with little indication that MPs understood that compliance with Community law would not be a matter of self-denying ordinance nor of international comity but of legal compulsion enforced by the domestic courts. The 1971 White Paper had done nothing to clarify this point for MPs. Its statement that the domestic legal order would 'remain intact' was more likely to mislead.

It was of course arguable at the time that parliamentary sovereignty might preclude the full force of *Van Gend* and *Costa* applying in the UK. The British courts might stick to their traditional loyalty to enforce the latest expression of Parliament's will, irrespective of whether this conflicted with directly effective Community law. What was significant was that this point was not even discussed. The striking feature was the lack of concern over the legal implications, particularly the respective institutional positions of the courts and Parliament. Legislators showed great interest in what Parliament would no longer be able to do—both in general terms (eg the 'essential sovereignty' argument) and specifically (eg state aids)—but very little interest in the effectiveness or otherwise of the Community's compliance machinery, and its impact on British constitutional arrangements. In a nutshell no one perceived parliamentary sovereignty in terms of the power of the UK courts.

Whilst one might expect pro-Marketeers to play down the possibility of a shift in power from Parliament to courts, the lack of anti-Marketeer comment suggests a more deep-seated reason for MPs' lack of constitutional awareness. Perhaps the most convincing explanation is the constitutional milieu in which parliamentarians functioned. During the preceding sixty years the courts had not only respected the doctrine of parliamentary sovereignty but had (at least until the late 1960s) adopted a restrained attitude to judicial review. The fact that the judiciary had for so long operated only on the fringes of the political arena meant that for parliamentarians the world of public law was alien territory. They were accustomed to working within a politics-based constitution largely untouched by legal concerns. Their inability to appreciate the likelihood that Community membership would entail a shift in power from Parliament to the judges stemmed in no small measure from their unfamiliarity with having to grapple with legal doctrines.

4

The Passage of the European Communities Bill

If one were looking for reasons to excuse MPs' lack of constitutional under-standing of the EEC's impact on parliamentary sovereignty, one might find it in the *generalized* nature of the debate. Until 1972 MPs had concentrated on the broad political and economic pros and cons of membership. It is arguable that, once MPs' minds were focused on *specific legal provisions* rather than the wider picture, this might have made them more aware that they might be vot-ing for a major shift in the institutional balance between Parliament and courts. In particular a Committee stage, involving discrete consideration of each constitutional aspect, ought to have given MPs ample scope to dwell on the sovereignty implications.

As with the previous chapters, our focus must be on government as much as on backbenchers. We have seen that Whitehall had thus far failed to fur-nish Parliament with an accurate picture of the likely constitutional implica-tions of membership. Would governmental portrayal of the legal effects of accession be any more satisfactory when the progress of the European Communities Bill obliged ministers to elucidate each and every provision? Since government largely controls the parliamentary agenda, we must also assess the adequacy of consideration of the constitutional issues that was permitted.

The legislative problem 1: experience in the Six

The UK had an advantage over the original Six in that the supremacy doc-trine was well established by the time of accession. MPs might have looked to the Continent to furnish some indication as to whether the doctrine would be accepted in the British courts. Although only the UK constitution had as its dominant characteristic the legislative supremacy of its Parliament, there were obstacles to Community law supremacy in the Six. For instance in France no court had power to declare legislation invalid, whereas the German and Italian constitutions contained human rights provisions which took precedence over all other forms of legislation, and might well be held to prevail over Community law. Had the doctrine of EEC law supremacy failed to take root in the legal systems of the Six, it would have been reasonable to suppose that the doctrine would fare no better in the UK.

In some Member States, acceptance of the ECJ's supremacy doctrine was facilitated by the constitution's (or the courts') adherence to a monist rather than a dualist approach to international law. Under a monist system, domestic courts apply international treaties as such, as soon as they are ratified; whereas under a dualist system, the national legislature must pass legislation to implement the treaty obligations, whereupon national courts will enforce treaty provisions only to the extent that they now form part of national law. In Belgium it was not clear whether the State was monist or dualist; the constitution contained no provision that would settle any conflict between a rule of international law and national law.[1] But in 1971 the Belgian Cour de Cassation adopted the monist approach. In *Le Ski*[2] it affirmed the supremacy of Community law over national law *and* asserted that it was the duty of the judge dealing with the case to 'set aside the application'[3] of conflicting domestic provisions.[4] Significantly the Cour de Cassation declined to affirm the Cour d'Appel's holding that the Belgian Parliament retained the right to legislate contrary to Community law by express enactment.[5] There appeared to be no resistance to the supremacy of Community law in the Netherlands[6] and Luxembourg[7]—also monist jurisdictions.

---

[1] Ganshof van der Meersch (1983) 74.

[2] *Minister for Economic Affairs v SA Fromagerie Franco-Suisse 'Le Ski'*, judgment of 21 May 1971 [1972] CMLR 330.

[3] The Court distinguished this from invalidation (para 14). The judge merely deprives the national law of effect. Thus if the Community provision is repealed, the incompatible national provision revives (Ganshof van der Meersch (1983) 86).

[4] *'Le Ski'* (n 2 above) 373 (para 12).   [5] Judgment of 4 March 1970, [1970] CMLR 219.

[6] The primacy of international law over domestic law was firmly established in Dutch law by the time of accession. This priority was spelt out in Article 94 of the constitution. In the early years of membership academic debate focused not on whether EEC law was supreme but on whether this (generally accepted) supremacy derived from Article 94 or from the Treaty of Rome itself (Chorus et al (1991) 315).

[7] Article 49*bis* of the Grand Duchy's constitution states that 'l'exercice d'attributions réservées

In Germany the Federal Constitutional Court in *Lütticke*[8] had declared that the German courts were obliged to apply Community provisions and that these displaced conflicting national law. The Court also held that it was not competent to determine whether a norm of ordinary municipal law was incompatible with a provision of Community law since this was a matter for the first instance courts. Importantly, the Court's reaction to the *Internationale Handelsgesellschaft* preliminary ruling, in effect carving out an exception to *Lütticke*, was not delivered until May 1974.[9] Thus the supremacy principle appeared to be accepted by the German courts prior to UK accession.

Italian law at this stage also appeared to respect the primacy of Community law. When *Costa v ENEL* returned from the ECJ, the Guidice Conciliatore of Milan dutifully refused to apply the conflicting Italian provisions 'because they are unlawful *vis-à-vis* the Community system to which the Italian system is bound to apply itself'.[10] It was not until *Frontini* in December 1973 that the Italian courts' acceptance of Community law supremacy was called into question.[11]

In France the Cour de Cassation (Criminal Chamber) had accepted the supremacy of Community law in *Ramel*,[12] on the grounds that Article 55 of the French Constitution 1958 gave treaties a higher legal status than municipal laws. Only the French Conseil d'État, in *Semoules*,[13] declined, without any statement of principle, to accord primacy to a Community regulation over a French *ordonnance*. It seemingly accepted the French government's view that the administrative court's constitutional role was the subordinate one of applying statutes and that it could not alter its institutional position by its mere will.[14]

To sum up, at the time of the Bill's passage, the Member State courts seemed broadly to have accepted the supremacy doctrine with the rogue

---

par la Constitution au pouvoirs législatif, exécutif et judiciaire peut être temporairement dévolu par traité à des institutions de droit international'. This provision, introduced on accession, appears to establish that the legislation of Community institutions may override that of domestic institutions subject to Luxembourg's 'ultimate' right to leave the Community.

[8] *Alfons Lütticke GmbH*, judgment of 9 June 1971, 31 BVerfGE 145 (in German).

[9] [1974] 2 CMLR 540.   [10] Judgment of 4 May 1966.

[11] [1974] 2 CMLR 372.

[12] *Administration des Contributions Indirectes et Comité Interprofessionnel des Vins Doux Naturels v Ramel*, judgment of 22 October 1970, [1971] CMLR 315.

[13] *Syndicat Général de Fabricates de Semoules de France*, judgment of 1 March 1968, [1970] CMLR 395.

[14] Ibid 404–405.

exception of the Conseil d'État. The cases restricting the application of the doctrine in Germany and Italy were yet to be decided.

The legislative problem 2: pre-Bill academic critiques

Whatever the view taken of the supremacy doctrine in the Six, there was intense academic and judicial controversy as to its application to the United Kingdom even before the Bill's publication. While continental jurists such as Bebr[15] and Pescatore[16] sought to clarify the direct effect and supremacy doctrines for the benefit of a British legal readership, British scholars disagreed over their impact on parliamentary sovereignty. Not all academics assumed that *Van Gend* and *Costa* could apply in the UK. Perhaps the wisest words were those of de Smith, that there were 'no sure means of predicting the constitutional impact on the United Kingdom of admission to such an association'.[17] Accordingly de Smith himself hedged his bets. He suggested that, assuming that it was correct that Parliament could not bind its successors, apparent discrepancies between Community law and municipal law would often be reconcilable with the aid of presumptions of legislative intent. However, if cases of inconsistency became frequent, and if the ECJ's supremacy principle became consolidated throughout the Member States, this would strengthen the case for reformulating the parliamentary sovereignty doctrine. The lack of an accepted procedure for changing the basic rule of the constitution did not render that rule unchangeable, though judicial acceptance of such a change might not be readily forthcoming.

Conversely H W R Wade found it hard to envisage the judges choosing to abandon their deeply held allegiance to the Parliament of the day.[18] He thought a European Communities (Annual) Act would be required, enabling Parliament to reassert each year the supremacy of Community law and resolving any intervening conflicts. Alternatively a provision could be inserted into every statute making that Act subject to Community law.

It is difficult to see why Wade felt so sure of judicial intransigence. He had, after all, observed in his seminal 1955 article 'The Legal Basis of Sovereignty' that 'the seat of sovereign power is not to be discovered by looking at Acts of any Parliament but by looking at the courts and discovering to whom they

---

[15] Bebr (1971). Gerhard Bebr was Legal Adviser to the Commission.
[16] Pescatore (1970). Pierre Pescatore was an ECJ judge.   [17] De Smith (1971).
[18] Wade (1972).

give their obedience'.[19] The position he took in 1972 is hard to understand in view of the disagreement between Lords Diplock and Denning over where the 'seat of sovereign power' lay. Lord Diplock wrote extra-judicially that parliamentary sovereignty would be unaffected by EEC membership; the courts would give effect to any subsequent conflicting statute. Parliament's compliance with Community law would rest entirely on voluntary abstinence, a matter of politics, not law.[20] Yet Lord Denning MR in *Blackburn v Attorney General*[21] in 1971 had stated *obiter* that whether Parliament would be able lawfully to withdraw from the Community remained an open question. One could extrapolate from this that a fortiori whether Parliament could 'lawfully' legislate contrary to Community law whilst remaining in the EEC would also be an open question.

The Treaty of Accession

Negotiations had not in fact been completed by the time the 'vote in principle' was taken on 28 October 1971. Most significantly, arrangements for UK accession to the Common Fisheries Policy were only announced to the House on 13 December. Anti-Marketeers were outraged both at the substance of the fishing agreement and at the fact that the House had been obliged to agree to membership in ignorance of it.[22] Harold Wilson accused the government of deliberately postponing the question of fisheries until after the debate.[23] It is ironic, in view of the fact that debate had focused on 'the terms', that one of the most controversial terms of membership had not by then been resolved.

Quite apart from the fishing agreement, however, there was a controversy of even greater constitutional moment: the vote on 28 October had been taken without the Treaty of Accession being published. Furthermore, Heath intended signing the Treaty of Accession without Parliament seeing, let alone discussing, its contents. Accordingly Labour used an Opposition Day to table a motion obliging the government to publish the Treaty and hold a Commons debate on it before Heath signed it, in recognition of its 'unique character'.[24] To this the government tabled an amendment 'that, [since]

---

[19] Wade (1955) 196. [20] Diplock (1972).

[21] [1971] 2 All ER 1380. [22] Jay (1980) 462.

[23] HC, 828, col 64, 13 December 1971. He claimed a rumour to this effect had emanated from Brussels sources, not from the government.

[24] HC, 829, col 678, 20 January 1972.

under international law the Treaty of Accession to the European Communities would not become operative until ratified, this House approves the intention of Her Majesty's Government to lay before the House the full and agreed English text of the Treaty when signed and the Government's proposals for the legislation required for its implementation'.[25]

It was common ground that as a matter of both constitutional law and convention, there was normally no requirement for a government to disclose a treaty's contents before signature. The Opposition's case was built solely on the unique nature of the Accession Treaty and Treaty of Rome. The argument ran that, since these treaties involved far-reaching obligations, and since Parliament stood to lose so many powers, the government should show sensitivity to the House's feelings rather than adopt an overly legalistic and formalistic position.[26] MPs could have put a more forceful case had they adopted an argument based on *Van Gend* that the EEC Treaty was not an international agreement at all but rather an embryonic constitution. Their lack of legal awareness meant that they perceived the Treaty as simply a *far-reaching* international agreement.

The government was unmoved. Geoffrey Rippon, Heath's chief negotiator,[27] reminded MPs that treaty-making power resided in the Crown; it was for Parliament to put treaties into effect within the United Kingdom by amending domestic law. The existing arrangements struck the proper balance between the government's responsibility to conduct foreign affairs effectively and Parliament's right to be informed. Both Rippon and Sir Geoffrey Howe SG emphasized that Parliament had never before been brought so closely into the process of treaty-making. The substance of the Accession Treaty was well known, since the government had taken exceptional care to keep the House informed.[28]

The government amendment was carried by 298 votes to 277, and the resolution as amended was carried by 296 to 276.[29]

---

[25] Ibid, col 695, 20 January 1972.

[26] Peter Shore ibid, col 681, 20 January 1972, Ronald King Murray ibid, col 719, 20 January 1972, Jo Grimond ibid, col 707, 20 January 1972.

[27] And Chancellor of the Duchy of Lancaster.

[28] Rippon: HC, 829, col 704, 20 January 1972; Howe: ibid, col 797, 20 January 1972.

[29] Ibid, cols 798–799, 20 January 1972. On *Panorama* the same night, Heath himself dismissed the twenty-one-vote majority against Labour's motion as 'really a bogus thing, a phoney thing', insisting that the October vote was 'the decisive one . . . That is what Parliament really thinks about coming into the Community' (Campbell (1993) 437).

The form of the Bill

There was considerable parliamentary speculation as to the nature of the implementing legislation in advance of its publication. It had been widely assumed that accession would necessitate a 'Bill of a Thousand Clauses', writing every Treaty provision and piece of secondary legislation into domestic law and repealing and amending conflicting UK legislation. The parliamentary debates of 1971 confirm that MPs of both parties had shared this assumption.[30] At Labour's Common Market Conference in July 1971, Michael Foot had threatened that the Opposition would obstruct 'the mountain of legislation' which would be required.[31]

In the immediate run-up to the Bill's publication, however, government supporters started to argue for a shorter Bill. Sir John Foster (Conservative, Northwich) went so far as to argue for a one-clause Bill, with eight weeks' discussion. He counselled against placing the Treaty texts in the legislation; statute lent itself to the House's amending procedure and the Treaty could not be amended.[32] Howe noted Foster's suggestion with interest but considered it inappropriate for him at that stage to anticipate the form of the legislation.

My hon. Friend is wrong, however, when he argues as a matter of principle that the legislation to implement a treaty allows no scope for amendment, because the House will be familiar with much legislation implementing other treaties of more or less importance in the past, all of which has been capable of amendment, dependent upon the way in which the Government of the day chooses to implement the treaty obligations.[33]

The government did little to disabuse most Members of their belief that the implementing measure would consist of a 'Bill of a Thousand Clauses' until on 25 January 1972—just five days after Howe's refusal to be drawn on the matter—it presented for First Reading a Bill of only twelve clauses, the

---

[30] See eg Peter Mills (Conservative, Torrington) (HC, 821, col 1872, 23 July 1971), William Ross (Labour, Kilmarnock) (HC, 823, col 1489, 26 October 1971).

[31] *Report of the Seventieth Annual Conference of the Labour Party*, 431, 17 July 1971.

[32] HC, 829, col 716, 20 January 1972. Roland Moyle (Labour, Lewisham North) thought Foster was wrong; since Parliament was sovereign it could insist that the Treaty be amended, and if the Six would not accept that position, 'it's the Government's hard luck': ibid, col 769, 20 January 1972.

[33] Ibid, col 794, 20 January 1972. But Howe stonewalled an intervention from Arthur Lewis (Labour, Lewisham West) as to whether 'the House' (*sic*) would be able to amend the Community Treaties.

first three of which formed the essential constitutional provisions.[34] The Opposition denounced the Bill as a 'lawyers' conjuring trick', threatening 'innumerable amendments to build into the Bill all the explicit amendments that the Government . . . edited out'.[35]

At Business Questions two days later, two distinct grievances emerged from the Bill's opponents. First, they objected to the concept of Community law automatically becoming British law in the absence of a full legislative process.[36] Secondly, they considered that the Bill's terseness hindered proper discussion of the issues involved.[37] Howe later denied that the Bill's brevity owed anything to sleight of hand, insisting that the legislation was devised at the time of Lord Gardiner, Lord Chancellor in the previous Labour government.[38] Harold Wilson saw the matter differently. At Second Reading, describing the Bill as 'a slick little measure to frustrate Parliament', he recalled of his own administration:

As a Government, had we got the terms we sought from our application, we never contemplated a Bill of either this form or size. We made clear that consequential legislation would take up a whole Parliamentary session. We knew that that would have to be so. I was warned to expect a 1,000-Clause Bill—a phrase that was in common use as indicating the scope and form of parliamentary action consequent on signing the Treaty. The Leader of the House . . . would confirm that I raised our understanding of the form of legislation required with him several times in the debate on the Address last November . . . What we had in mind . . . was a full legislative process to implement whatever obligations we would have shouldered in acceding to the Treaty.[39]

The government's legislative choice was presumably tactical. Foster's suggestion of a single-clause Bill might have affronted wavering Conservatives as too naked a usurpation of parliamentary sovereignty. Conversely a 'Bill of a Thousand Clauses' would have needlessly prolonged the parliamentary battle and exposed MPs to the entirety of Community legislation, within which even government supporters might find something objectionable.[40] Forman suggests an additional reason, that 'an "Act of a thousand clauses" would have implied that the situation was not as in fact it was, namely, that the Community legal order constitutes an *independent* legal order, therefore

---

[34] The remaining clauses were a curious ragbag of consequential substantive changes, dealing with *inter alia* cinematographic films, the sugar market, and perjury before the ECJ.

[35] *The Times*, 27 January 1972.

[36] HC, 829, col 1621, 27 January 1972 (Harold Wilson).

[37] Ibid, col 1629, 27 January 1972 (Peter Shore).

[38] Hillman and Clarke (1988) 108.　　　　　[39] HC, 831, col 640, 17 February 1972.

[40] Kitzinger (1973) 376.

excluding the possibility of *transformation* by national legislatures'.[41] It was suggested at Second Reading that the form of the Bill hampered Members' understanding of the nature of Community law.[42] It is necessarily a matter of speculation whether MPs would have attained a greater grasp of Parliament's prospective status relative to the courts had they been subjected to a far longer legislative process.[43]

The progress of the Bill: adequate opportunity for debate?

Before examining the substantive constitutional issues that arose in debate, it is necessary to consider whether the government's legislative arrangements allowed MPs sufficient opportunity to reflect on the Bill's implications. Controversy centred on both the permissible *scope* of the debate and the adequacy of *time* permitted.

Second Reading commenced on 15 February 1972, less than a month after the Bill's publication. This dashed Labour hopes of a full month to examine the documentation—the authentic English versions of the Treaties and secondary legislation—released in January.[44] However, Rippon presented the three-week time gap as exceptional and done at the Opposition's request.[45] The Second Reading debate lasted three days. Rippon was able to point to only two other Bills in the previous thirty years which had enjoyed such a long Second Reading.[46]

---

[41] Forman (1973) 41. Original emphases. This was confirmed by Howe at Third Reading where he stated that a 'Bill of a Thousand Clauses' would have been constitutionally misleading and would have implied that the situation was not as it was (HC, 840, col 1869, 13 July 1972).

[42] See eg William Baxter (Labour, West Stirlingshire) HC, 831, col 663, 17 February 1972, Denzil Davies (Labour, Lanelli) ibid, col 506, 16 February 1972.

[43] The House in Committee discussed the most relevant Treaty provision, Article 189 EEC, at some length. It is arguable that, had MPs been obliged to undertake a painstaking examination of the Community legislation to which some objections were bound to be raised, this might have concentrated parliamentary minds on whether Parliament could override the ECJ's supremacy doctrine. Equally, however, such a scrutiny could have degenerated into detailed nit-picking on substantive policy with little discussion of fundamental constitutional issues.

[44] See eg Harold Wilson HC, 829, col 1620, 27 December 1972; Michael Foot ibid, col 1621, 27 December 1972.

[45] HC, 836, col 334, 2 May 1972. Originally Second Reading had been scheduled for the week commencing 7 February (*The Times*, 27 January 1972).

[46] HC, 836, col 334, 2 May 1972.

Questions of scope: the ruling out of amendments

It was the Committee stage, however, which proved most contentious in relation to the controversy surrounding the adequacy of debate. The government committed the Bill to a Committee of the Whole House. On the first day in Committee, the Chairman of Ways and Means, Sir Robert Grant-Ferris, ruled out a large number of amendments. He offered the following explanation:

The reason for this is the nature of the Bill itself—[HON. MEMBERS: 'Oh.'] The Bill, as the Explanatory Memorandum says, is one which makes the legislative changes which will enable the United Kingdom to comply with the obligations entailed by membership of [the three Communities] and to exercise the rights of membership. In a word, the Bill provides the legal nuts and bolts which are necessary if the United Kingdom is to be a member of the Communities. It is not a Bill to approve the Treaty of Accession or any of the other treaties which are basic to membership of the Communities . . . If it were such a Bill, then, of course, every article of these treaties would be open to discussion and the majority of amendments would be in order. Since this is not a Bill to approve the basic treaties, Amendments designed to vary the terms of those treaties are not in order, and I have no option to rule otherwise.[47]

This ruling was followed by two hours of points of order from dissatisfied MPs.[48] The next day the Opposition moved a motion criticizing the ruling of the Chairman of Ways and Means as a grave infringement of the House's rights.[49] This was defeated by 309 to 274. A few days later on 6 March the Opposition moved a censure vote on the government for 'framing its European Communities Bill with the intention of removing the possibility of substantial amendment', considering this 'a gross breach of faith in the light of undertakings previously given that the Bill and the Treaties could be fully discussed'.[50] This was defeated by 317 to 270.

The Chairman's ruling sought to distinguish *'nuts-and-bolts'* amendments, relating to the various ways in which Parliament could incorporate past and future Community law into domestic law (involving a greater or lesser degree of parliamentary control), from those concerning *substantive* aspects of the accession 'package', for example fisheries, the protocols on New Zealand and

---

[47] HC, 832, col 269, 29 February 1972.
[48] Ibid, cols 269–308, 29 February 1972. Unusually for Committee proceedings, this became headline news, *The Times* (1 March 1972) leading with 'Labour Stops Commons Debate on Market Bill after Amendments Clash'.
[49] Ibid, cols 432–554, 1 March 1972.   [50] Ibid, cols 1041–1170, 6 March 1972.

Caribbean produce, and free movement of capital. Opponents of the Chairman's ruling raised the following objections:

1. The Chairman's selection was so restrictive and severe as seriously to curtail debate in Committee. Parliament was being gagged and its proceedings on the most important constitutional Bill of our time reduced to a farce.[51] In Peter Shore's words, '[o]n this, the Bill of Bills, by common consent the most important that has ever come before Parliament in time of peace, we have less freedom to amend than we should have with the most insignificant piece of domestic legislation'.[52]
2. The government had repeatedly promised that the Bill would be amendable in a very wide sense, for instance on 20 January when it had employed this argument to answer Opposition complaints as to the lack of a debate on the Treaty of Accession.
3. There was no *constitutional* reason why Parliament should not 'unpick the package' in the sense of permitting some parts of Community law but not others to enter the national legal order. Parliament was sovereign and if it so wished it could legislate contrary to international obligations entered into by the Crown. Admittedly this might put the executive to the trouble of renegotiating the Treaty of Accession, but so what?[53]
4. The House had been denied any opportunity to debate the Treaty of Accession. The October 1971 debate had taken place before important terms (eg on fisheries) had been agreed and before the Treaty's publication. The January 1972 debate had been on a procedural matter, and again the *draft* Treaty (as it still then was) had not at that stage been available outside government circles. Now MPs were being told that questions of approval or disapproval of the Treaty terms were to be excluded from the ambit of debate on the Bill. Yet the first three clauses of the Bill clearly implied approval of the Treaty.[54]

---

[51] Michael Foot HC, 832, col 262, 29 February 1972; Stan Orme ibid, col 284, 29 February 1972; John Morris ibid, col 287, 29 February 1972; Sir Elwyn Jones ibid, col 435, 1 March 1972.

[52] Ibid, col 1044, 6 March 1972.

[53] Sir Elwyn Jones HC, 832, col 438, 1 March 1972; Enoch Powell ibid, col 467, 1 March 1972; Reg Prentice ibid, col 486, 1 March 1972; John Morris ibid, col 509, 1 March 1972.

[54] Ronald King Murray ibid, cols 519–522, 1 March 1972; Sir Elwyn Jones ibid, col 436, 1 March 1972. The following additional points were also made in opposition to the Chairman's ruling: (*a*) Erskine May contained no authority which suggested that Parliament lacked the power to reject any part of treaty packages. (*b*) There was a clear inconsistency between the ruling-out of the amendments and government protestations that the House was perfectly entitled to vote down the motions that each 'Clause stand part of the Bill'. Both would necessitate renegotiation of the

The government, whilst denying having anticipated the Chairman's ruling, predictably supported it.[55] There were several pervasive themes in the arguments of government supporters.

1. The Opposition were not interested in improving the Bill but in obstructing it and thereby blocking implementation of the decision to join the Community approved by a majority of 112 in October 1971.[56]
2. The Bill was intended to be very narrowly defined so that substantive amendments would be wrecking amendments.[57]
3. As a matter of political reality it was simply not possible to send the Crown back to renegotiate; the Treaty of Accession was a carefully negotiated package, the result of long, hard bargaining.[58] 'To exclude from the Bill the implementation of any one portion of the treaties, any single aspect of Community law, could have only one result—that the treaties would not be implemented at all.'[59]
4. 'Not a word was uttered [by the government] to suggest that Parliament was free to pick and choose between this piece and that piece of the treaties finally negotiated.'[60] 'We have said from the outset that the treaties and Community obligations must be taken as a whole.'[61]

The criticism could be levied that some of these arguments may have constituted good reasons for *voting down* the amendments, but not for *ruling them out*. It is hard to see how Grant-Ferris's ruling was compatible with parliamentary sovereignty. A Parliament which can 'make or unmake any law' would surely be perfectly free to incorporate certain aspects of Community law and reject others. On this reading the objection to the amendments would have to be political rather than constitutional.

Treaty. (*c*) The Chair had based his decision on the Explanatory Memorandum, which did not constitute part of the Bill, rather than on the more widely worded Long Title, which did. (*d*) The grounds given for ruling out the amendments did not fit into any of the categories listed in Erskine May on which amendments can properly be disqualified.

[55] Geoffrey Rippon ibid, col 1053, 6 March 1972.

[56] William Whitelaw ibid, col 440, 29 February 1972; John Selwyn Gummer ibid, col 457, 29 February 1972; Geoffrey Rippon ibid, col 1064, 6 March 1972.

[57] Sir John Foster ibid, cols 279–280, 29 February 1972; John Selwyn Gummer ibid, col 457, 29 February 1972. It is noteworthy, however, that at no point did the Chairman of Ways and Means refer to the amendments as wrecking amendments.

[58] David Steel ibid, col 475, 29 February 1972; Sir Geoffrey Howe SG ibid, cols 1155–1156, 6 March 1972.

[59] Sir Geoffrey Howe SG ibid, col 1155, 6 March 1972.

[60] Ibid.   [61] Geoffrey Rippon ibid, col 1056, 6 March 1972.

It could be argued that the restriction of amendments merely reflected the legislative ethos of the 1970–4 Parliament. Norton, in his study of behavioural changes of backbenchers, attributes the increased willingness of MPs to vote against their own side during this and subsequent Parliaments largely to the prime ministerial leadership of Edward Heath. Norton notes that Heath insisted not only that measures introduced by his government should be passed, but that they should be passed in the form in which they were introduced. Such intransigence, he argues, drove Conservative MPs to resort to opposing the government in the division lobbies as the only means of expressing dissent, and this in turn brought about a longer-term shift in parliamentary attitudes in favour of cross-voting.[62] It is surely arguable that the attitudes of government ministers on the one hand and of loyal-minded parliamentary chairmen on the other cannot exist in hermetically sealed boxes. Conceivably the Grant-Ferris ruling represented a 'spillover' effect, however unconscious, of the general hostility to parliamentary 'interference' with government bills.

An alternative explanation would be that the problem lay with the incompatibility between two different constitutional models. According to established British constitutional thinking Parliament was supreme and therefore could pick and choose. UK adherence to international agreements was no bar to Parliament's freedom of action.[63] However, according to emerging Community constitutional thinking the requirement of a uniform body of law throughout the Community meant that the application of EEC law could not vary from state to state.[64] It was therefore incumbent on each new Member State to accept the full *acquis communautaire*, subject only to transitional arrangements.[65] The requirement of uniformity was as much a constitutional fundamental in the Community context as was the doctrine of parliamentary sovereignty in the British context. Uniformity, after all, was the rationale for the supremacy of Community law and underpinned the ECJ's expansive interpretation of the preliminary reference procedure. With Britain poised to join the Community, it might be regarded as legitimate for Community constitutional values to compete against traditional British ones in the event of tensions between the two.

---

[62] Norton (1995) 37.

[63] *Mortensen v Peters* (1906) 14 SLT 227, *Cheney v Conn* [1968] 1 All ER 779.

[64] This was reflected in the ECJ's reasoning in Case 6/64 *Costa v ENEL* [1964] ECR 585.

[65] See eg John Pardoe HC, 832, col 1070, 6 March 1972, and David Steel ibid, col 475, 1 March 1972, both emphasizing that acceptance of the *acquis communautaire* was the price to be paid for the UK's latecomer status.

Questions of time: imposition of the guillotine

On 2 May 1971, after twenty-two days in Committee, the government presented a timetable motion restricting the remaining Committee stage to twelve allotted days.[66] Leader of the House Robert Carr said that the government had to balance two duties: to ensure adequate discussion and to get its business through with reasonable dispatch. While accepting that there had been no filibustering, he considered that most of the Bill's opponents wanted to defeat it, not amend it, and that this invited inevitable consequences. The following arguments were marshalled in favour of the guillotine:

1. There had been unparalleled opportunity for debate on an issue which had been exhaustively discussed for over a decade.[67]
2. The timetable would still give every clause and schedule a reasonable time for debate.[68]
3. It was the clear will of the majority that the matter be brought to a conclusion.[69]

Against these, the Bill's opponents argued:

1. It violated parliamentary tradition to impose a guillotine in the absence of filibustering,[70] and was unprecedented to do so on an important constitutional Bill.[71]
2. They *did* want to improve the Bill—by maximizing parliamentary control over Community matters.[72]
3. Clause 2 was the crux of the Bill, and debate on it (as in the case of Clause 1) should be allowed to run its course.[73] For example there were

---

[66] HC, 836, cols 206–348, 2 May 1972.
[67] Robert Carr ibid, cols 211–213, 2 May 1972; Geoffrey Rippon ibid, col 328, 2 May 1972.
[68] Robert Carr ibid, col 213, 2 May 1972, Geoffrey Rippon ibid, col 330, 2 May 1972.
[69] John Selwyn Gummer ibid, col 308, 2 May 1972.
[70] Sir Robin Turton ibid, col 236, 2 May 1972, Sir Derek Walker-Smith ibid, col 257, 2 May 1972, Ronald King Murray ibid, col 272, 2 May 1972.
[71] Sir Derek Walker-Smith ibid, col 255, 2 May 1972. Government supporters Nicholas Ridley (ibid, col 246) and Alan Haselhurst (ibid, col 270) argued that the Bill's constitutional importance was being exaggerated since it could always be repealed.
[72] Michael Foot ibid, col 228, 2 May 1972; Sir Robin Turton ibid, col 240, 2 May 1972; Neil Marten ibid, col 314, 2 May 1972; Peter Shore ibid, col 325, 2 May 1972.
[73] William Hamilton ibid, cols 303–306, 2 May 1972; Ronald King Murray ibid, col 272, 2 May 1972; Michael Foot ibid, col 226, 2 May 1972. Hamilton was a Labour pro-Marketeer. Another pro-Marketeer, Conservative Capt William Elliot, suggested that the House sit at Whitsun, through the summer, and on Saturdays, to make sure the Bill was properly discussed (ibid, col 319).

eighteen amendments to Clause 2(2) but only one day provided for
their consideration.

4. The Committee stage thus far had been a voyage of discovery.
Superficially Clause 1 appeared to be a definitions clause, but detailed
scrutiny had revealed that it imposed multiple obligations.[74] The inde-
fensibility of these obligations was the real reason for the guillotine.[75]

The timetable motion was, however, carried by 304 to 293.

Before leaving the procedural controversies surrounding the Bill's passage,
it should be noted that the government refused to *accept* any amendments.
Just as it wanted the substantive Treaty 'package' accepted as a whole, so too
it refused to countenance any additional impediments to the transposition of
future Community treaties and legislation. Again, this was in conformity
with the Heath administration's general insistence that legislation should be
enacted in the form in which it was originally presented.

Committee debates were ill attended. During the first debate Powell
remarked that 100–200 Members were compulsorily on duty elsewhere in
the House,[76] and debates throughout tended to feature the same speakers,
mainly anti-Marketeers who seemingly took far more interest in the Bill's
constitutional mechanics than the pro-Marketeers. Divisions, however, were
well attended.

Essential sovereignty

Only Geoffrey Rippon mounted a token defence of the White Paper's claim
that membership would involve no 'erosion of essential national sovereignty'.[77] Other pro-Marketeers cheerfully accepted a loss of sovereignty in
the legal sense, arguing that Britain gained more by membership in terms of
influence.[78]

Anti-Marketeers continued their relentless attack on the 'essential sovereignty' argument. How could the government maintain that there was no loss
of essential sovereignty, in view of the 1,500 regulations poised to become law

[74] Brynmor John ibid, col 296, 2 May 1972; Raymond Fletcher ibid, col 283, 2 May 1972.
[75] Sir Derek Walker-Smith ibid, col 258, 2 May 1972, Eric Deakins ibid, col 317, 2 May 1972.
[76] HC, 831, col 1291, 7 March 1972.   [77] Ibid, col 353, 15 March 1972.
[78] eg David Knox (Conservative, Leek) ibid, cols 478–480, 16 February 1972; James Scott
Hopkins (Conservative, Derbyshire West) ibid, col 513, 16 February 1972.

automatically, with Parliament a mere spectator?[79] How could the government claim that the Treaty would not touch people's lives intimately, yet in the next breath argue that the decision on membership would determine the whole future of the country including its economic well-being and development?[80] Enoch Powell, accepting that, as things stood, the Community's present ambit might seem relatively narrow compared to the broad sweep of politics, warned that

this is intended to be only a start. Of course, the receptacle which is formed by Clause 2 will not initially have much put inside it. It starts life by no means full; but it . . . is a receptacle created to be progressively filled . . . So, although the surrender begins as minimal, it is intended to become maximal; and that intention is implicit in the policy and declarations of the Government.[81]

Heath presented the Luxembourg Compromise as proof that the UK was not joining a federal Europe. He made it clear that he did not foresee an end to the veto, since other countries too had special interests which they wished to protect.[82] Some backbenchers' support for the Bill seemed to rely on this assurance.[83] Nonetheless, eminent lawyers from both parties expressed the conviction that the ECJ would declare the unanimity practice incompatible with the Treaty.[84]

Moreover, there were differences among pro-Marketeers as to whether the EEC would or should develop into fully-fledged political union. Many shared Edmund Dell's view that the real questions of national sovereignty were for the future and that it remained an open question whether the EEC would stay an association of sovereign states or become a federation.[85] However, pro-Marketeers differed in their long-term goals. Some were critical of any rush towards economic and monetary union, arguing that the cause of European unity was best served by free movement of goods, persons, and capital.[86] Others were enthusiastic to see a strengthening of the

[79] Peter Shore ibid, col 295, 15 March 1972.

[80] Michael Foot ibid, col 738, 17 February 1972.

[81] Ibid, col 701, 17 February 1972.

[82] Ibid, col 746, 17 February 1972. See also Geoffrey Rippon (HC, 840, col 1977, 13 July 1972). A veto and federalism are not necessarily incompatible. For example under the US Constitution all states have a veto over any proposal to reduce their Senate representation.

[83] See eg Peter Hordern (Conservative, Horsham) HC, 831, col 327, 15 February 1972.

[84] Sir Elwyn Jones ibid, col 467, 16 February 1972; Sir Derek Walker-Smith ibid, col 319, 15 February 1972.

[85] HC, 833, col 465, 14 March 1972.

[86] See eg Peter Hordern (Conservative, Horsham) HC, 831, cols 328–330, 15 February 1972.

Community's central policy-making institutions and an enlargement of its competences.[87]

The gulf in the pro-Market camp—obscured by the fact that federalists and anti-federalists united in support of the Bill—is reflected in biographical and autobiographical writings. Thus at the time Margaret Thatcher 'saw the EEC as essentially a trading framework—a Common Market—and neither shared nor took very seriously the idealistic rhetoric with which "Europe" was already being dressed in some quarters'.[88] Nicholas Ridley wanted 'a Europe that practises genuine free trade, both within its boundaries and in relation to the rest of the world. We do not want to submerge our identity, nor our freedom to manage our own affairs in some European federal structure which has ultimate control over our destiny.'[89]

In contrast Edward Heath insisted that the Treaty of Rome was never intended to be merely a charter of economic liberty; the aim was ever closer *political* union, albeit achieved by economic means.[90] The situation was well summarized by David Owen's comment highlighted in Chapter 3, that an uneasy truce between federalist and non-federalist pro-Marketeers meant that serious discussion on the Community's destiny was postponed until Britain was firmly embedded within it.[91]

Ultimate sovereignty

Opening the Second Reading debate, Geoffrey Rippon stated that nothing in the Bill abridged the 'ultimate' sovereignty of Parliament. Rippon never spelt out precisely what he meant by 'ultimate' sovereignty. *One possibility* is that it meant that the national courts would enforce subsequent statutes which contravened EEC law, irrespective of whether the statute purported to do this simply by containing provisions which were incompatible with EEC law, or by expressly and intentionally repudiating Community norms. *A second possibility* is that it meant the UK courts would uphold *only* those statutes which evinced an express intention on Parliament's part to legislate contrary to EEC law. *A third possibility* is that it meant domestic courts would enforce *only*

---

[87] See eg Austen Albu (Labour, Edmonton) ibid, cols 331–335, 15 February 1972.
[88] Thatcher (1995) 127.   [89] Ridley (1991) 136.   [90] Campbell (1993) 767.
[91] Owen (1991) 177. He continues: '[i]t is revealing that the federalist debate in Britain only surfaced from 1988 onwards, the moment when it was clear that Labour's internal battle against membership was finally over.'

a statute seeking to repeal the 1972 Act and renounce Community membership in its entirety, but would decline in the meantime to enforce any statute
seeking to 'pick and choose' between Community provisions.

Whatever he meant, Rippon himself muddied the waters by asserting in
the very same speech that Community law was designed to prevail over
conflicting domestic law, that Clauses 2(1) and 3(1) provided 'the necessary
precedence', and that Clause 2(4) provided that future enactments would be
subject to Clause 2(1).[92] Did it follow from this that *every* future enactment,
even one expressly and intentionally repudiating a Community policy, or
even one seeking British withdrawal from the EEC, would be subject to
Clause 2(1)?

When the Committee debated Clause 2(4), Sir Geoffrey Howe more
guardedly argued that the aim of the subsection was that, *as far as could constitutionally be achieved*, Community law should prevail over subsequent
conflicting statutory provisions. He seemed concerned that, despite Clause
2(4), Parliament might retain the ability inadvertently to breach EEC law,
since parliamentary sovereignty was 'inescapable and enduring'; Clause 2(4)
at least tried to push the courts as far as possible in the direction of giving
precedence to Community law. As for express repeal, his statement was mas-
terly in its ambiguity.

Most people have agreed that a subsequent United Kingdom statute—even if not
designed to pull us out of the Communities—which began with the phrase 'notwithstanding the provisions of Clause 2 and Clause X of the European Communities Bill,
black shall be white', would mean that the courts of this country would give effect to
that limited proposition, *certainly as the matter now stands*.[93]

This statement suggests that there could be no implied repeal of EC law. It
also insinuates that Parliament's ability to renounce individual Community
rules by express enactment might not rest on a very firm foundation. As for
withdrawal, however, Howe was more certain. '[A]t the end of the day, if
repeal lock, stock and barrel, was proposed, the ultimate sovereignty of
Parliament would remain intact.'[94] Anti-Market nerves remained
unsoothed. Some Members thought the Bill meant that in *all* instances of
conflict—even in the face of deliberate defiance by Parliament—Community

---

[92] Ibid, col 274, 15 February 1972. This self-contradiction did not escape the attention of the
Opposition. See Sir Elwyn Jones HC, 839, col 251, 20 June 1972.

[93] HC, 838, col 1320, 13 June 1972 (emphases added).

[94] Ibid, col 1319, 13 June 1972.

law prevailed.[95] Others pointed out that the ECJ case law—cases such as *Costa v ENEL*,[96] *San Michele*,[97] *Walt Wilhelm*,[98] and *Internationale Handels-gesellschaft*[99]—meant that Parliament's legislative power would be constrained by the superior law of the Community.[100] However, even within the anti-EEC camp, MPs were not of one accord. Enoch Powell thought that Parliament *would* be able to legislate contrary to Community law, by providing that 'Clause 2(4) shall not have effect for the purposes of this Act' or some such formulation. He considered the issue of whether the UK could leave the Community to be an arid debate, since politically there was always a right to revolution.[101] The differences of opinions as to the effects of Clause 2(4) highlight the confusion as to what exactly Parliament would retain by way of 'ultimate sovereignty'. Nonetheless an amendment to remove Clause 2(4) was defeated by 283 to 268, and an amendment deleting Clause 3(1) was rejected by 281 to 266.

The Opposition sought to remove this confusion by proposing, on the final day of the Committee stage, that a 'Declaration of the Ultimate Sovereignty of Parliament' be incorporated into the Bill.[102] This would read:

It is hereby declared that nothing in the Treaties or in this Act shall detract from the ultimate sovereignty or supremacy of Parliament or shall prejudice the power and right of Parliament to repeal this Act or to alter any of its provisions or effects; and any determination of the European Court or of any of the Communities or their institutions which is inconsistent herewith shall be null and void.

This was moved by Sir Elwyn Jones, who argued that ECJ decisions, together with contradictory ministerial statements, meant there was a risk of uncertainty. The House had to be sure that the Bill was repealable, *and* that future conflicting Acts of Parliament would be enforced.

---

[95]   Sir Arthur Irvine HC, 831, col 343, 15 February 1972; Brynmor John HC, 838, col 1301, 13 June 1972. This would accord with the ECJ's view in *Costa v ENEL* that Community law could not be overridden by domestic legal provisions *however framed*. Harold Wilson was concerned at the ability of *governments*, using Community decision-making, to bind future Parliaments, pointing out that doctrinaire decisions, connived at or initiated by British governments of either Party in the Council, could tie future Parliaments in an indefensible manner, restricting the manifesto commitments that parties could make and the issues on which elections could be fought (HC, 831, cols 645–646, 17 February 1972). Wilson made it clear that he intended to exploit the doctrine that no Parliament could bind its successors as a bargaining chip in his proposed renegotiation of the terms of entry (HC, 823, col 2104, 28 October 1971).

[96]   Case 6/64 [1964] ECR 585, [1964] CMLR 425.   [97]   [1967] 6 CMLR 160.

[98]   Case 14/68 [1969] 8 CMLR 100.   [99]   Case 11/70 [1970] ECR 1125.

[100]   Sir Derek Walker-Smith HC, 835, col 1300, 25 April 1972.

[101]   Ibid, col 1296, 13 June 1972.

[102]   HC, 840, cols 556–648, 5 July 1972.

The government opposed the Declaration. Sir Geoffrey Howe argued that the heart of the matter was how to reconcile the irreconcilable—the supremacy of Community law with the sovereignty of Parliament. The ultimate sovereignty of Parliament was not affected; indeed it could not be affected. He quoted Wade's celebrated 1955 article 'The Legal Basis of Sovereignty' to the effect that parliamentary sovereignty lay beyond the reach of statute and was unalterable by Parliament.[103] Lord Diplock, he noted, had confirmed that the courts would enforce future Acts of Parliament rather than inconsistent provisions of the Treaty of Rome.[104] But Howe then concluded that by joining the Community we had to accept the supremacy of Community law. Thus the second part of the Declaration would be a breach of our Treaty obligations, and should be opposed. The Declaration was rejected by 278 votes to 265.

It is difficult to reconcile the two strands of Howe's argument. Michael Foot joked that whereas Rippon had sought throughout to make the provisions of the Bill plain and had failed, Howe had sought to keep them obscure and had succeeded. Perhaps Howe meant that *from a legal point of view* parliamentary sovereignty was unalterable, but *from a political point of view* British politicians ought not to seek to use parliamentary sovereignty in such a way as to defy Community law, *nor should they threaten to do so.*

It is noteworthy that Howe's parliamentary opponents accorded great importance to his views as a minister and did not appreciate that such questions would ultimately be settled not by the politicians but by the courts. After all, as Wade wrote at the time, '[i]n a country which has no overriding constitutional legislation, a change in [the] grundnorm [ie that the latest expression of Parliament's will is supreme] can be achieved only by a legal revolution and only if the judges elect to abandon their deeply rooted allegiance to the ruling Parliament of the day. No legislative attempt to dictate to them in advance can relieve their dilemma when the clash occurs.'[105]

If the government overestimated the resilience of parliamentary sovereignty, this was hardly unreasonable. Steeped in the writings of Dicey and three centuries of ostensibly unchallengeable statutes, Rippon, Howe, and their advisers were in no position to foresee that judges might eventually come to accord precedence to Community law over Acts of Parliament. Nonetheless, Howe underplayed the role of the political actors when he argued, 'if we were to say, "this Act can be repealed", it would be a pointless exercise because what the House of Commons says about the nature of its [*sic*]

---

[103] Wade (1955) 189.   [104] Diplock (1972) 3.   [105] Wade (1972) 3.

sovereignty can scarcely affect what is one of the ground rules of our constitutional system'.[106] If, as Wade contends, the existence of parliamentary sovereignty rests ultimately on judicial acceptance of a *political* settlement, then surely whilst only the judges can modify the constitutional ground rules, Parliament can *influence* the judges to modify them—as happened for example in 1688 and 1911. The 'political fact' of Parliament's victory over the Crown in the Glorious Revolution and its passage of the Bill of Rights 1689 spurred the courts to accept statute as the highest form of law. The political triumph of the Commons over the Lords which culminated in the passage of the Parliament Act 1911 induced the judiciary to extend the sovereignty doctrine to those Acts passed without Lords consent but in conformity with the Parliament Act procedure. Similarly parliamentary approval of the Declaration of Ultimate Sovereignty, if it had any effect, would surely have served to encourage the judiciary to preserve the constitutional status quo. If at accession Parliament had unequivocally expressed the wish that the existing rules of parliamentary sovereignty be retained, this might have had a decisive influence in subsequent judicial decision-making.

Indeed Howe could be accused of being highly selective in his citation of Wade's famous article. Wade emphasizes that 'the relationship between the courts of law and Parliament is first and foremost a political reality'.[107] He examines the outcomes of the English Civil War, Restoration, and Glorious Revolution to show that the courts accord ultimate legal authority to the victors of *political* revolutions. Might not British accession to the Treaty of Rome be perceived as constituting the change in the 'ultimate political fact', with Parliament's enactment of the European Communities Bill serving as merely an additional parliamentary prompt to push the courts more firmly in favour of according supremacy to Community law? Thus Howe conveniently disregarded Wade's overarching thesis that political events can have a decisive effect on the judicial choice of constitutional ground rules.

There appeared greater consensus on the issue of withdrawal than on the question of Parliament's ability to legislate contrary to Community law while the UK remained a Member State. Not only did Howe consider withdrawal legally possible, but Peter Shore and Douglas Jay threatened that the Bill, if passed, would be interim only, since anything done by one Parliament could

---

[106]   HC, 840, col 628, 5 July 1972. The sovereignty, of course, is that of Parliament, not of the House.

[107]   Wade (1955) at 188.

be undone by the next.[108] The drawing of a distinction between an undoubted right to withdraw and a more questionable right to legislate contrary to Community law on individual matters would appear to have a basis neither in British constitutional theory (according to which domestic courts would enforce Acts of Parliament purporting to do either of these things) or in Community constitutional law (according to which both actions would constitute a breach of Article 5 EEC, which mandated Member States to abstain from action which would jeopardize Community objectives). Presumably the distinction rests on the more pragmatic political consideration that for as long as one chooses to be a member of a 'club', one must abide by the 'club rules'.

Scope of the Bill

Clause 1 listed the three founding Treaties to which the Act would apply. However, it also provided that the Act would apply to 'any other treaty entered into by any of the Communities, with or without any of the Member States, or entered into, as a treaty ancillary to any of the Treaties, by the United Kingdom'.[109] Clause 1(3) established the way in which Community treaties would be incorporated into national law:

(3) If Her Majesty by Order in Council declares that a treaty specified in the Order is to be regarded as one of the Community Treaties as herein defined, the Order shall be conclusive that it be so regarded; but a treaty entered into by the United Kingdom after the 22nd January 1972, other than a pre-accession treaty to which the United Kingdom accedes on terms settled on or before that date, shall not be so regarded unless it is so specified, nor be so specified unless a draft of the Order in Council has been approved by resolution of each House of Parliament.

Thus the means of incorporating additional treaties were twofold:

1. '*The first part of Clause 1(3).*' In the case of any treaty other than those covered by the second part of Clause 1(3), an Order in Council affirming that it constituted a 'Community treaty' would be conclusive for the purposes of the Act.

---

[108] Peter Shore HC, 831, col 301, 15 February 1972; Douglas Jay ibid, col 500, 16 February 1972. Leader of the House William Whitelaw had conceded the point a week before Second Reading.

[109] Clause 1(2).

2. '*The second part of Clause 1(3).*' In the case of treaties entered into by the United Kingdom after 22 January 1972, a draft Order in Council had to be approved by resolution of each House.

Committee debate focused on the issue of parliamentary control. As regards the first part of Clause 1(3), opponents noted that it was drawn very widely. All future treaties *made by the Community* would fall within it, and would therefore not be subjected to parliamentary debate at all. As Ronald King Murray remarked, 'why should the United Kingdom be brought in [as a party to a treaty] when treaties can be entered into with *or without* the Member States?'[110]

As for the second part, there were two main objections. First, although presented as a democratic safeguard, it took away Parliament's existing power to give internal effect to treaties through primary legislation.[111] In particular, revision of the EEC Treaty was itself effected by treaty. According to Article 236 EEC, Treaty amendments had to be approved by all Member States, each according to their respective constitutional requirements. The effect of Clause 1(3) would be that the United Kingdom's 'constitutional require-ment' would be satisfied by each House approving a draft Order in Council by resolution. Thus governments would not have to subject revision of the Treaty to the full legislative process, including a Committee stage. Instead a brief debate on the Order in Council would suffice. Anti-Marketeers argued that a one-and-a-half-hour debate on an affirmative resolution—with no power to amend—was inadequate treatment for, say, a 'second Rome Treaty' aimed at establishing economic and monetary union.[112] Secondly, it was not even clear whether MPs could discuss the merits of a new treaty or merely whether it constituted a Community treaty.[113]

The government argued that treaties extending the scope of the Community's legislative and treaty-making power would require the consent of all Member States and would therefore always be covered by the second part of Clause 1(3). Thus Parliament had a veto over the Community's future development.[114]

An amendment to delete Clause 1(3) was defeated by 249 to 219. Amendments were also tabled seeking to exclude treaties on defence and on

---

[110] Clause 1(2), col 1278, 7 March 1972 (emphasis added).

[111] Ronald King Murray ibid, col 1280, 7 March 1972.

[112] Peter Shore ibid, cols 1373–1375, 7 March 1972.

[113] Enoch Powell ibid, col 1299, 7 March 1972; Michael Foot ibid, col 1309, 7 March 1972.

[114] Sir Geoffrey Howe SG ibid, col 1343, 7 March 1972.

economic and monetary union from the scope of the Clause 1 procedures. Shadow Defence Secretary Denis Healey argued that, as drafted, Clause 1 laid down a mandatory, not permissive, procedure, so that a European defence union, including nuclear cooperation, could only be introduced by affirmative resolution.[115] Geoffrey Rippon assured the Committee that if such an agreement came about, Parliament would have a proper opportunity to examine it: '[i]t would not be a question of the affirmative resolution procedure applying in cases of this kind. We should have the normal parliamentary processes for dealing with a defence treaty.'[116] Michael Foot pointed out that this guarantee was not given in the Bill. Nonetheless, Labour's amendment was defeated by 170 votes to 149. An amendment from Labour pro-Marketeer Edmund Dell, that no new Community treaties be entered into without prior parliamentary approval, also failed.[117]

The picture that emerges, therefore, is that the Committee realized that Parliament would have the right to veto amendments to the Treaty of Rome, and could therefore block major moves towards further integration, but that debate on such future treaties could, in theory, be minimal. It seems unnecessarily draconian that the Heath government sought to sideline the role of Parliament in this way, particularly in view of the fact that substantial Treaty revision was not an immediate likelihood; however, it appears to be on all fours with Norton's account of Heath's disdain for Parliament's legislative participation.

Direct applicability

As we have seen, the controversy surrounding Clause 2(1) and direct applicability was closely related to the Bill's form. Harold Wilson insisted that Labour would have met the Treaty obligations through the normal legislative process, in respect of both past *and future* Community measures. To Wilson this would have two advantages: it would enable the best form of words to be found to ensure the best form of legislation without breaking Treaty commitments,[118] and it would make ministers more cautious before agreeing to new Community legislation.[119]

---

[115] Healey's interpretation is questionable. Clause 1 does not oblige the sovereign to declare a treaty to be a Community treaty.

[116] HC, 833, col 687, 15 March 1972.

[117] Ibid, col 465, 14 March 1972.

[118] HC, 831, col 643, 17 February 1972.

[119] Ibid, cols 644–645, 17 February 1972.

Of course, Article 189 EEC made clear that regulations, unlike directives, do not give Member States a choice of form and methods but enter the legal systems of the Member States automatically. However, the notion that this *precluded* national replication of regulations may not have been clear in 1972. Cases such as *Variola*[120] and *Amsterdam Bulb*[121] which confirmed that Member States were obliged not to obstruct the direct applicability inherent in regulations nor to conceal their Community law nature, and that national legislative measures could not affect their direct applicability, had not yet been decided.

Thus much of the controversy surrounding Clause 2(1) focused on whether Community membership necessitated direct applicability. Oddly the government did not speak with one voice. This may well have been due to Edward Heath's closing speech at Second Reading where he had considered alternative ways of implementing Community law:

One suggestion is that the whole of the legislation which might be affected by any of the instruments should be re-enacted by Parliament . . . But we would not be able to change that part which arose from Community law. I do not think that to ask Parliament to take on that sort of burden is a sensible solution to the problem with which we are faced.[122]

Heath appeared to suggest that, in view of Parliament's inability to amend or reject Community regulations, re-enactment would be absurdly onerous rather than impermissible.

In Committee Sir Geoffrey Howe seemed anxious to accord a restrictive interpretation to the Premier's words: 'I dare say it would be possible to find some other formulation of the proposal. I find it difficult to see what that could be . . . I can think of no other way of achieving it. It may be the best way, and it is certainly the one which commends itself to me and which I commend to the Committee.'[123] Geoffrey Rippon seemed more concerned to justify direct applicability than to defend Heath's comments: 'One cannot escape the obligation as far as directly applicable law is concerned . . . One will not give effect to it by saying "We will not accept that it is directly applicable". In the case of regulations one cannot do that . . . The purpose of having the directly applicable law is that the regulations will be applied uniformly

---

[120] Case 34/73 *Variola SpA v Amministrazione Italiana delle Fiananze*, judgment of 10 October 1973 [1973] ECR 981.

[121] Case 50/76 *Amsterdam Bulb BV v Produktschap Voor Siergewassen*, judgment of 2 February 1976 [1977] ECR 137, [1977] 2 CMLR 218.

[122] HC, 831, cols 747–748, 17 February 1972.   [123] HC, 835, col 1296, 25 April 1972.

throughout the Member States. That is the principle.'[124] Parliament, he maintained, would play its part *before* draft regulations reached the Council.

The *unanimous* anti-Marketeer view was that Clause 2(1) went beyond what the Treaty required. In particular Enoch Powell argued that 'directly applicable' in Article 189 did not mean the same as 'without further enactment' in Clause 2(1). What happened inside a Member State was of no concern to the Community provided that the regulation, once made, was part of the law of all Member States. The Treaty, he maintained, did not prescribe the procedures whereby the regulation becomes national law.[125] Powell's interpretation was supported by Sir Elwyn Jones[126] and Arthur Irvine[127] who both regarded Clause 2(1) as needlessly draconian, and by Ronald King Murray[128] and Sir Robin Turton[129] who viewed it as an unnecessary restriction on parliamentary control. For Sir Derek Walker-Smith, 'the words "directly applicable" do not forbid the use of statutory enactment as a vehicle. What they forbid is any deviation from the *ipsissima verba* of the regulations.'[130] The government response was that direct applicability excluded the possibility of national re-enactment since 'the right to re-enact must carry with it a right not to re-enact', but Rippon seemingly accepted that Parliament retained the power to prevent regulations being enforced:

If, contrary to the wishes of the House, the Government were to allow a regulation to be made [in the Council of Ministers], they would run the risk that the House would, in effect, order our domestic courts not to give effect to it. That would be a breach of the treaty obligations. I cannot conceive of any circumstances in which that would arise. But that is the position.[131]

This statement certainly appears to reinforce Howe's assertion that Parliament retained the power to legislate expressly and intentionally contrary to Community law. It seems to show that Rippon's conception of 'ultimate sovereignty' extended to Parliament's right to pick and choose which items of Community legislation would be enforced in the UK. An amendment to delete the words 'from time to time' from Clause 2(1), thereby precluding its application to future Community legislation, was defeated by 249 votes to 219. An amendment deleting Clause 2(1) was defeated by 244 to 213.

---

[124] Ibid, col 1342, 25 April 1972.   [125] Ibid, col 1359, 25 April 1972.

[126] HC, 835, col 1500, 25 April 1972. Jones was Attorney General 1964–70; later Lord Chancellor 1974–9.

[127] HC, 831, col 344, 15 February 1972.   [128] Ibid, col 361, 15 February 1972.

[129] HC, 835, cols 1560–1563, 26 April 1972.   [130] Ibid, col 1552, 26 April 1972.

[131] Ibid, col 1584, 26 April 1972. Rippon talks of 'the House' when he surely means Parliament.

What had the anti-Marketeers hoped to achieve by advancing an interpretation of 'direct applicability' which would permit parliamentary re-enactment of each and every regulation? On the positive side, it would have provided for greater parliamentary participation in the Community legislative process, since such debates might furnish valuable feedback on the reaction of a national parliament to such legislation. On the less positive side, it might have militated in favour of minimalist Community lawmaking. The 'receptacle' of Clause 2, as Powell had envisaged it, would be less likely to be 'progressively filled', if the Council was mindful that each regulation would be subjected to debate in the British Parliament, with perhaps other national parliaments following Britain's example in the fullness of time. Finally, debates on regulations would have proven a rallying point for those who sought British withdrawal from the EEC. Anti-Marketeers could have exploited such debates to draw attention to the growing scope of Community law, and Parliament's impotence in the face of its obligation to accept (and inability to amend) such legislation.

The debate is also instructive because it again highlights parliamentary underestimation of the ECJ. According to Article 177 EEC, it was for the ECJ to decide how the Treaty was to be interpreted. Furthermore in *Van Gend* the ECJ had made it clear that it would treat questions relating to the effect of Community law within the Member States as questions of Treaty interpretation. Yet anti-Marketeers seemingly assumed that politicians had a monopoly in determining what was meant by direct applicability. For them, it was a matter to be resolved by politics, not by law.

Parliamentary accountability for Community lawmaking

Hostility to direct applicability stemmed largely from the loss of accountability of ministers to Parliament inherent in the concept. The government's solution was that there should be parliamentary involvement at the formative stage of the Community legislative process. It proposed the setting-up of an ad hoc committee of both Houses to examine the best way to ensure adequate parliamentary scrutiny of *draft* regulations and directives.[132] This was welcomed by pro-Marketeers, whereas anti-Marketeers argued that, to be effective, scrutiny had to include the right to reject and that under such

---

[132] Geoffrey Rippon HC, 831, col 275, 15 February 1972.

arrangements Parliament's role would become purely advisory.[133] Some MPs anticipated that the Council's method of legislating through compromise would preclude effective scrutiny.[134]

Objections to direct applicability were accompanied by disapproval of the way in which directives were to be transposed. Clause 2(2) provided that the Queen in Council, ministers, and government departments could make delegated legislation to implement Community obligations and deal with related matters. Clause 2(4) expanded this power to cover 'any such provision . . . as might be made by Act of Parliament', enabling the *executive* to repeal provisions of primary legislation.[135] Yet since Article 189 EEC allowed a free choice of form and methods, some MPs argued that implementation of directives should be by statute.[136] Moreover the Bill laid down no procedure for the form of delegated legislation; it would be a matter for the government of the day. MPs speculated that at best EEC directives would be introduced by affirmative resolution, allowing a mere one-and-a-half-hour debate.[137] More likely, the negative procedure would be used, resulting in only a tiny proportion of implementing measures being debated.[138]

The government's defence was that it had to be left to the good sense of the government of the day to determine whether a directive introduced a major change, necessitating primary legislation. Rippon could not conceive of a future House allowing a government to put into subordinate legislation directives which should be implemented by statute. Rippon also played down the quantity of delegated legislation which would be required.[139] Labour's amendment to remove Clause 2(2) was defeated by 265 votes to 260.

---

[133] Douglas Jay ibid, col 498, 16 February 1972; George Darling (Labour, Sheffield Hillsborough) ibid, col 322, 15 February 1972. This was also the view of Professor J A G Griffith who wrote that 'Parliament has not and cannot have any power to reject the regulations, or amend them, or in any way influence their content' (*The Times*, 7 February 1972).

[134] Ibid, col 316, 15 February 1972 (Sir Derek Walker-Smith). See also Neil Marten ibid, cols 520–521, 16 February 1972.

[135] Douglas Jay pointed out that Clause 2(2) was a 'Henry VIII clause'; Parliament was being asked to make all its laws 'subject to correction and alteration, by whom we are not quite clear' (HC, 837, col 1468, 24 May 1972). On Henry VIII clauses generally, see Loveland (2000) 126–127.

[136] Sir Derek Walker-Smith HC, 837, col 1463, 24 May 1972; Enoch Powell ibid, col 1480, 24 May 1972.

[137] Peter Shore HC, 831, col 299, 15 February 1972.

[138] Denzil Davies ibid, col 508, 16 February 1972.

[139] HC, 837, cols 1506–1508, 24 May 1972. He claimed that had the UK been in the Community in 1971, only some 2% of Community measures would have been dealt with under Clause 2(2).

Power of the ECJ

MPs hostile to Community membership showed little inkling of Parliament's demotion *vis-à-vis* the European and domestic judiciary. If we take the Second Reading debate as a snapshot of anti-EEC opinion at the time, it is noteworthy that none of the anti-Marketeers highlighted enhanced judicial power. Of twenty-six who spoke, only six mentioned the courts, domestic or ECJ, and none of these mentions can be described as critical. Indeed one of the anti-Marketeers' leading spokesmen, Sir Derek Walker-Smith, viewed the ECJ as 'one of the bright spots if we entered the Community', predicting that it would prevent encroachments by the Community executive.[140]

In contrast, fifteen contributors to the Second Reading debate attacked the Commission and twelve criticized the Council. There was considerable concern, not confined to the Bill's opponents,[141] as to how Community membership would increase the power of the *executive*, British and Community, against the legislature. The Commission, not the Court, and certainly not the UK courts, was the anti-Marketeers' *bête noire*, and there was considerable argument about whether its legislative powers were restricted to detailed implementation of Council decisions, as the government contended, or whether it enjoyed wider legislative competence. In his opening speech, Geoffrey Rippon dealt with the ECJ almost as an afterthought:

Before I leave the directly applicable Community provisions, I should like to mention one further feature of this concept. In order to ensure impartial administration and interpretation, it is inherent in the concept that in the last resort a single authority should determine questions about the interpretation and validity of the provisions. This is a function of the European Court, in respect of Community provisions, whether directly applicable or not.[142]

This makes no mention of the fundamental role of preliminary references in monitoring the compatibility of *Member State measures* with Community law. Without this, one is left with a pre-*Van Gend* picture of the ECJ, focusing only on its role in preventing the Community institutions from acting *ultra vires* the Treaty.[143]

---

[140] HC, 838, col 1625, 14 June 1972.

[141] See eg the contributions of Edmund Dell (HC, 835, col 1379, 25 April 1972), Kenneth Baker (HC, 831, col 688, 17 February 1972), and Charles Fletcher-Cooke (HC, 837, cols 1487–1488, 24 May 1972).

[142] HC, 831, col 278, 15 February 1972.   [143] See Weiler (1986).

A rare exception to the general lack of interest (and insight) regarding the ECJ's role was the comment of Brynmor John (Labour, Pontypridd) during the Committee debate on Clause 2(4) that 'for the first time ... we have a constitutional court which is set above Parliament'.[144] This view could, however, be contested. It could be argued, as Hamilton argued in *The Federalist Papers No. 78*, that far from the judiciary being superior to the legislature, the power of 'the people' is superior to both and that, by according supremacy to a constitution (here, the Treaty) rather than to statutes, the judges are merely regulating their decisions by the fundamental law rather than the nonfundamental law.[145] This argument in turn raises difficulties about whether the Treaty can convincingly be equated to the will of the people.

Direct effect and the empowering of the domestic courts

MPs also failed to appreciate the impact of direct effect. Many saw the challenge to sovereignty chiefly in terms of the Commission bringing the UK before the ECJ via enforcement proceedings under Article 169.[146] The far greater 'risk' of British courts preferring Community law over domestic law[147] was not anticipated. Sir Derek Walker-Smith posed the following scenario:

Suppose Parliament had the temerity to reject, or even to amend, a regulation. Suppose Parliament sought to pit its sovereignty against the overriding authority of the Community. Parliament would clearly be embarking on a lost cause. The Treaty would decide decisively against us. The Treaty tells us that Community law must prevail and that the regulations are 'directly applicable'. Clearly, we should be in breach of our self-assumed obligation. The Treaty provides remedies for such breaches. It can be seen from Articles 169 and 171 that this is a matter, first for the Commission and then for the Court of Justice. The Community Court would decide, and Westminster would yield to the wisdom of Luxembourg.[148]

It is not, however, the Treaty which is the source of Community law supremacy but rather the case law of the ECJ, issuing instructions to the

---

[144] HC, 838, col 1299, 13 June 1972.   [145] Rossiter (1961) 467–468.

[146] This misconception had been shared by the Belgian, Dutch, and German governments who had argued in *Van Gend* that enforcement actions constituted the sole means of remedying a Member State's failure to observe its Community obligations.

[147] The advantages of direct effect over Article 169 proceedings as a means of enforcing Community law are well set out in Craig (1992).

[148] HC, 831, col 317, 15 February 1972.

national courts to allow Community rules to prevail over conflicting national ones. Indeed the textual foundation for the supremacy doctrine is not as strong as its teleological rationale.

Generally, MPs still failed to perceive parliamentary sovereignty in terms of judicial power. Enoch Powell at Second Reading analysed most skilfully the Bill's effects on all the elements of parliamentary sovereignty (Parliament's ability to legislate on any subject matter, its inability to bind its successors, its status as supreme lawmaker), but omitted any reference to the relationship between Acts of Parliament and the courts.[149] This constitutes a vivid example of the chasm between the politician and the lawyer. To the lawyer, parliamentary sovereignty is not about what Parliament can do but how the courts react to what Parliament does. To the lawyer, parliamentary sovereignty means that *the courts* recognize Parliament's right to make or unmake any law, that *the courts* will not allow Parliament to be bound by its predecessors, and that *the courts* accord Parliament the status of supreme lawmaker. Powell's neglect of direct effect was reflected in his extra-parliamentary writings. In his two books of speeches on the Community[150] the only reference to the ECJ was that if Parliament rejected Community legislation 'the Commission will trot along to the Court of Justice'.[151] Direct effect—in practice far more devastating to parliamentary sovereignty than enforcement proceedings—went unmentioned, as did the role of the national courts. Peter Shore at Third Reading said Parliament had no right to legislate contrary to Community law, 'no right, that is, unless we breach the Treaty'[152]—seemingly assuming that British courts would allow Parliament that option. Sir Elwyn Jones, Wilson's Attorney General, even perceived the Bill in terms of '*restrictions* which will be placed on the rights and powers of our courts of law'.[153] He seemed oblivious to the ECJ's strategy of empowering the national courts.

Only three MPs anticipated the impact of direct effect on the power of the national courts. Denzil Davies noted a clear movement in the six Member States in favour of municipal courts according priority to Community law over conflicting national legislation.

It may be that in the first few years following our entry the English courts, with their long tradition of enforcing Statutes of this Parliament and nothing else, will shrink from that ultimate step. But I have little doubt that, before long, once the idea of what Community law means has been instilled in them, this will be the final step. Whatever

---

[149] HC, 831, cols 698–707, 17 February 1972.   [150] Powell (1971) and (1973).
[151] Powell (1973) 62.   [152] HC, 840, col 1883, 13 July 1972.
[153] HC, 832, col 435, 1 March 1972 (emphasis added).

Parliament says, should it say something contrary to Community law, the courts of this country will overturn all that they have done for centuries in order to enforce the law of an outside body which may be contrary to the law of this Parliament.[154]

The second MP was Eric Deakins (Labour, Walthamstow West). When the Committee debated Clause 3(1) he criticized the subsection as 'surely sowing the seeds of a potentially serious constitutional conflict between the courts of this country—acting on behalf of the European Court of Justice, in asserting the supremacy of the Treaty of Rome—and the Government of this country'.[155] Finally pro-Marketeer Harold Lever (Labour, Manchester Cheetham) noted that Member State governments did not have the final say on whether they were complying with the Treaty:

Whether they are doing what they ought to do under their agreement will be decided not by the Governments themselves, but by the courts of their lands. So it will be by the courts of our own land. That is not a matter of regret. That is a remarkable advance in the mechanism for giving effect to collective agreements.[156]

These three contributions appear to be the sum total of parliamentary consciousness of the way in which membership would modify the UK's internal separation of powers.

Yet despite the failure of most of the Bill's opponents to appreciate the full implications, the government did flag up to MPs, albeit tersely, the role which the judiciary would play in enforcing the supremacy of Community law. At the Committee stage debate on Clause 3(1), Sir Geoffrey Howe reminded MPs of the principle in *Costa v ENEL* and added that '[w]hen I say that Community law takes precedence over each of our three jurisdictions, *it will be applied by the judges of our three systems*'.[157]

Parliamentarians also misunderstood the nature of directives. The ECJ had already resolved in *SpA SACE*[158] that individuals could enforce in their national courts rights laid down in unimplemented directives. Nonetheless MPs got the wrong end of the stick. Michael English (Labour, Northampton North) argued that '[u]nlike a regulation, a directive cannot be enforced'.[159] Government spokesmen did not disabuse MPs of this idea. Geoffrey Rippon speculated as to what would happen if Parliament rejected an Order in Council transposing a directive:

---

154 HC, 832, col 1302, 7 March 1972.
155 HC, 838, col 1634, 14 July 1972.
156 HC, 840, col 1900, 13 July 1972.
157 HC, 839, col 265, 20 June 1972 (emphasis added).
158 Case 33/70, [1970] ECR 213.
159 HC, 837, col 1485, 24 May 1972.

Parliament has the authority to reject, and then the Government of the day must mend their fences accordingly. They may choose to be in breach of their treaty oblig-ations ... If the Government were forced into a breach because this House would not agree to proceeding in the way proposed, either the breach would have to be tolerated by the Community or the Government would have to proceed in a different way.[160]

Despite *SpA SACE* Rippon did not appear to acknowledge the possibility that the courts would enforce directives in the event of Parliament's failure to transpose them. Indeed, when Douglas Jay raised the spectre of Parliament refusing to implement a directive, Rippon likened this to the Labour govern-ment's successful defiance of EFTA rules when it had imposed a 10 per cent surcharge on EFTA products, thereby equating the Community (and the effectiveness of its enforcement machinery) with a conventional inter-national organization, and ignoring the ECJ's clear statements in *Costa* and *Van Gend* that it was no such thing.[161]

The politics of the votes

The government struggled to win the votes. The Jenkinsites were committed to voting with the Opposition, and the government would not accept amend-ments to placate Conservative rebels. Several factors secured victory. First, a few Labour backbenchers abstained throughout the Bill's passage.[162] Secondly, government Whips liaised with the Jenkinsites to ensure that Committee votes were won by selective absenteeism.[163] Thirdly, to minimize

---

[160] Ibid, cols 1508–1509, 24 May 1972. In passing it is interesting to note that Lord Howe has recently conceded that in presenting the effect of directives, he and his advisers overemphasized the 'choice of form and methods' enjoyed by Member States, and underestimated the importance of directives being 'binding on each Member State' to which they are addressed (Howe (1996)).

[161] Ibid, col 1470, 24 May 1972.

[162] *The Times*, 18 February 1972, lists Carol Johnson, Freda Corbet, Austen Albu, George Lawton, Christopher Mayhew, and John Rankin as Labour abstainers and Michael Barnes, Richard Crossman, and Ray Gunter as absentees. Owen comments, '[w]e hid behind their bravery and were demeaned. It was the memory of this shabbiness that sustained my resolve when it came to the agony of leaving the Labour Party and creating the SDP in 1981' (Owen (1991) 189). Jenkins remarks, '[t]hey at once provided us with an essential little shield behind which to shelter ... It is never comfortable to be dependent on men braver than oneself' (Jenkins (1991) 338).

[163] Kenneth Clarke explained: 'We [would] not have got into the Community if we hadn't had an unofficial arrangement in which I was the go-between. I would meet John [Roper] each day and discuss with him how many Jenkinsites should fail to turn up that evening. We'd have to negotiate it, because they all had trouble with their constituency associations. I'd suggest the number we needed to match the number of Conservative rebels we knew we were going to have that night. The

Conservative rebellion, Heath turned the Second Reading into a vote of confidence:

I must tell the House that my colleagues and I are of one mind that the Government cannot abdicate their responsibilities in this matter. Therefore, if this House will not agree to the Second Reading tonight and so refuses to give legislative effect to its own decision of principle, taken by a vast majority less than four months ago, my colleagues and I are unanimous that in these circumstances this Parliament cannot sensibly continue.[164]

This strategy secured a majority of eight on Second Reading, seventeen on Third Reading, and similarly thin majorities throughout the Committee stage.

Consideration of the constitutional issues in the House of Lords

Lords' Second Reading was dominated by general argument as to the merits and demerits of EEC membership. However, Lord Hailsham LC in moving Second Reading analysed the legal implications in a way which was curiously at odds with the approach of his Commons colleagues. He referred to the possibility of conflict between EEC law and 'the doctrine of the sovereignty of Parliament and its corollary (I believe judge-made) the doctrine of the priority of later Acts over previous Acts: that rule of construction whereby when two Acts conflict the later is construed as amending or repealing the earlier one'.[165] Lord Hailsham's sleight of hand is admirable. By characterizing the doctrine of 'the priority of later Acts over previous Acts' as a mere rule of construction, and singling it out as 'judge-made' when in reality parliamentary sovereignty as a whole is a judicial creation, he presented it as a discrete entity, distinct from parliamentary sovereignty. He then argued that Clause 2(4) merely provided a *new* rule of construction, 'to substitute in the appropriate case . . . for the judge-made rule',[166] whereby Community obligations would prevail over subsequent enactments. Echoing Lord Gardiner's 1967 statement, he argued that this would not be inconsistent with parliamentary sovereignty but an application of it.

nearest we got to losing the European Communities Bill was when John and I made a slight error and the majority went down to three or four' (Balen (1994) 81).

[164] HC, 831, col 752, 17 February 1972. [165] HL, 333, col 1230, 25 July 1972.
[166] Ibid.

Rules of construction can vary in the strength of their interpretative obligation. One possibility was that the supremacy of EEC law would have to yield
to the sovereignty of Parliament whenever statutory wording could not be
reconciled with EEC provisions according to traditional (literalist) English
canons of statutory interpretation. A second possibility would be that the
courts would progressively adopt the ECJ's teleological interpretative
approach, but would again accord precedence to Acts of Parliament where
not even the added flexibility of purposivism could reconcile statute with
EEC law. A third possibility, particularly in the wake of the blurring of interpretation and validity in *Anisminic*, was that the rule might be perceived as
requiring nothing short of an express statutory declaration of Parliament's
intention to override EEC law before the courts would enforce a conflicting
statute.

The nature of Lord Hailsham's 'rule of construction' was clarified in a
Committee debate on Lord Stow Hill's probing amendment to delete Clause
2(4). For the government, Viscount Colville explained that '[w]hat we are
telling [the courts] to do, if they possibly can, is to construe that later Act so
that it does not conflict with the directly applicable law. It is only if they cannot do so that the law of the English courts allows them to give precedence to
the later English Act.'[167] So it would be very easy for Parliament to legislate
contrary to EEC law. Parliament would not even need to insert a provision in
a statute stipulating that the Act applied 'notwithstanding any provision of
Community law' (or some such formulation). Viscount Colville seemed to
suggest that whenever Parliament enacts provisions which so clearly
conflicted with EEC law that they could not be interpreted so as to conform
with it, then the courts must enforce the statute. This is a marked contrast
with the position put forward by government ministers in the Commons,
where Sir Geoffrey Howe had suggested that the courts would enforce Acts
contravening EEC law only if Parliament used statutory wording explicitly
expressing an intention to do so. On the other hand, Viscount Colville
confirmed that Clause 3(1) meant that British courts would have to follow the
ECJ's rules and practices of interpretation.[168] It therefore appeared that
the government was adopting the second of the three possible meanings of
'rule of construction' suggested above.

Lord Hailsham himself drew out the consequences of his characterization
of Clause 2(4) as a rule of construction during Committee debate on a probing amendment to delete Clause 2(1). Lord Hailsham confirmed that parlia-

[167] HL, 334, cols 1026–1027, 8 August 1972.   [168] HL, 333, col 1364, 26 July 1972.

mentary sovereignty remained 'the fundamental dogma of our unwritten constitution'. Since the courts were subject, 'as is every institution within this country', to the constitution, there was no doubt that Parliament could breach its obligations under the Treaty. Parliamentary sovereignty prevailed over 'any treaty you choose to name, including this one'.[169] Despite *Van Gend* Lord Hailsham did not appear to envisage the possibility that the Treaty might prove something more than an international agreement, and might provide a surrogate constitution to which British courts could attach a certain allegiance.

Lord Hailsham received support from Lord Diplock, who accepted that Clause 2(4) constituted a rule of construction. This meant that *in cases where there was an ambiguity*, the courts would interpret subsequent Acts in conformity with EEC law. However,

[I]f on the other hand—and here I do not speak of course for the Government but I express solely my own view—it were decided by Parliament to pass an Act of Parliament repealing or amending some directly applicable Community law, that would be a breach of our Treaty obligations. If it were on a serious matter it would no doubt be the end of the European Community so far as we were concerned. But the courts would be bound to give effect to a subsequent Act of Parliament under the law as it is administered in the courts today, *and as it will continue to be administered, because this Bill does not alter that*.[170]

Lord Diplock's views seem to tally with those of the government's Lords spokesmen in three respects. First, he shares their view that ambiguity in a statute would be required to trigger the operation of Clause 2(4). Secondly, he subtly belittles his 'own view' in comparison to the view taken by the government, which is ironic given that the judiciary not the government would have the final say on the fate of parliamentary sovereignty. Thirdly, he takes the position that the law will 'continue to be administered' in conformity with parliamentary sovereignty, and that the Bill would not alter this fundamental position.

Attempts to amend Clause 2(4)

Lord Shackleton appeared to be reinforcing Lord Hailsham's view of Clause 2(4) when he moved an amendment that the words 'unless the contrary

---

[169] HL, 334, cols 812–813, 7 August 1972.
[170] Ibid, col 1029, 8 August 1972 (emphasis added).

appears' be inserted, so that the Clause would read: 'any enactment passed or to be passed . . . shall *unless the contrary appears* be construed and have effect subject to the foregoing provisions of this section.' Pointing to 'the lack of absolute certainty that Parliament retains its supremacy',[171] Lord Shackleton explained that the amendment intended to clarify that any subsequent enactment which clearly sought to override a Community obligation would prevail.[172] The amendment got short shrift from the Lord Chancellor who argued that it would be dishonourable to insert in the Act something that would be inconsistent with Britain's Community obligations, and that in any case Clause 2(4) did not destroy parliamentary sovereignty because no Act of Parliament could do that. The amendment was rejected without division.

The question of supremacy attracted further discussion when Lord Beswick proposed that the following sentence be added to Clause 2: 'Provided that nothing in this Act shall be held to detract from the ultimate sovereignty or supremacy of Parliament or to prejudice the right of Parliament to repeal it or alter its provisions.'[173] This echoed Elwyn-Jones's 'Declaration of Ultimate Sovereignty' in the Commons. Lord Beswick pointed to the difference between the Lord Chancellor's explanation of Clause 2(4) and that of the Solicitor General in the Commons. Suggesting that the question of precedence would be for the national courts, he argued that it would be advisable to put the matter of 'ultimate sovereignty' beyond doubt by writing it into the Bill.[174] Once again the government riposte was two-pronged. First, legally, parliamentary sovereignty lay beyond the reach of statute so Lord Beswick's formulation would add nothing. Secondly, politically, it would be wrong at the very moment of accession to suggest that the United Kingdom was considering violating EEC law. The amendment was defeated by 103 votes to 22. On Report Lord Beswick pressed his amendment again, arguing that 'we should make it clear in the ultimate that Parliament is sovereign, and that what this Parliament of this country decides shall be done will in fact be done'.[175] The Lord Chancellor in reply took his argument one step further: the amendment was '*not merely unnecessary but constitutionally vicious*, because it suggests that it is possible for one Parliament to do that which no Parliament in this country is permitted to do, and which might be destructive of our liberties if it sought to do so'.[176] Arguably Lord Hailsham was here advancing an absurd thesis. The passage of such an amendment

---

[171] HL, 334, col 1049, 8 August 1972.   [172] Ibid, col 1047, 8 August 1972.
[173] HL, 334, col 893, 7 August 1972.   [174] Ibid, col 897, 7 August 1972.
[175] HL, 335, col 290, 12 September 1972.
[176] Ibid, col 292, 12 September 1972 (emphasis added).

would have expressed the determination of the polity to preserve the legislature's omnipotence. Since parliamentary sovereignty constitutes a *judicial* response to a *political* settlement, then enactment by Parliament of statutory wording *reinforcing* that political settlement can hardly serve to undermine the doctrine. More likely it would have fortified judicial deference to Acts of Parliament. Lord Wynne-Jones and Lord Greenwood found it impossible to accept Lord Hailsham's reasoning, and Lord Beswick in closing the debate suggested that the Lord Chancellor's line of argument

would be quite beyond controversy if it were applying to a situation such as we have known in this country up to the present time. But as from the time we go into the European Community, the situation will be quite changed: the sovereignty of Parliament will be subjected to a constant process of erosion. . . . This is the dynamism theory . . . slowly but certainly the sovereignty of the individual states disappears.[177]

Lord Beswick, like Denzil Davies in the Commons, was commendably far-sighted in anticipating that the courts might adopt an evolutive approach to the limitation of parliamentary sovereignty in the wake of the Act rather than placing excessive emphasis on the original intention of 1972 parliamentarians. The amendment was defeated by 111 votes to 22.

There was marginally more awareness than in the Commons that the enforcement of directly effective EEC law would rest with the national courts. This is implicit in the arguments of Lord Beswick, Viscount Colville, and Lord Hailsham.[178] Despite this, though, at Third Reading the Lord Privy Seal Earl Jellicoe accorded an exaggerated importance to Hailsham's and Colville's statements on sovereignty, extolling them as 'an invaluable quarry for those who wish in future to dig into the legal and constitutional implications of this Bill'.[179] In reality the final decision on sovereignty would lie with the courts—which would in any case be prevented by the exclusionary rule from examining the pronouncements of Hailsham and Colville.

The Lords: conclusion

By the time the Bill reached the Lords the government had clearly settled upon a more consistent position as to the effects of EC membership on

---

[177] Ibid, col 298, 12 September 1972.
[178] See eg Viscount Colville HL, 333, col 1359, 26 July 1972; Lord Hailsham LC HL, 334, col 772, 7 August 1972.
[179] HL, 335, col 1137, 20 September 1972.

parliamentary sovereignty. Unfortunately this position was consistently wrong. By insisting that the British courts would never treat Clause 2(4) as anything other than a rule of construction, ministers in the Upper House were purporting to know the unknowable. In so doing they displayed an unjustified confidence that the courts would stand by parliamentary sovereignty rather than embrace the supremacy of Community law.

Post-Bill academic critiques

With the Bill enacted, academic attention fastened on whether the courts would indeed be prepared to disapply statutes or whether the Act would be vulnerable, like any other, to parliamentary sovereignty. Opinion was divided, though (unlike ministers) all commentators acknowledged that no *firm* prediction of judicial conduct could be made. Forman thought there was a danger that UK courts would interpret the Act like any other UK legislation rather than regarding it as a 'stepping-stone' to the new legal order.[180] Trindade too doubted that the judicial 'revolution in legal thought' would be swiftly achieved; in the meantime, he suggested, judges faced with conflicting UK statutes could stay proceedings for a year so that the offending legislation could be repealed.[181] In contrast Mitchell, Kuipers, and Gall were more optimistic, noting that the Act did not seek to give instructions to future Parliaments but rather to the domestic courts, and proposing that this be taken as an invitation to the courts, by legal revolution, to accept the ECJ's legal order in place of their traditional allegiance to the Parliament of the day. To refuse to do so would be on a par with rejecting the legal order of 1707.[182] The fact that academics could reasonably hold different views on the prospects of the Act achieving its aims perhaps goes some way in excusing the tergiversation of government ministers.

Conclusion

The form of the European Communities Bill (which possessed a certain logic) and the use of the guillotine (which was less excusable given the constitutional enormity of the issue) did not prevent considerable debate as to the

---

[180] Forman (1973).   [181] Trindade (1972).   [182] Mitchell, Kuipers, and Gall (1972).

constitutional implications of membership. The substance of this debate, however, left much to be desired.

Pro-Market MPs largely opted out of the detailed consideration of the Bill. No doubt some (for example, Harold Lever) understood the constitutional law ramifications perfectly well, but did not object to the probable modification of the relationship between Parliament and the courts. Others (such as Margaret Thatcher) may have been quite unaware of the likely change. Others must have been wilfully blind to the effect of membership on parliamentary sovereignty. Their overwhelming preoccupation was that Britain should join the Community, so they simply 'turned a deaf ear' to the constitutional implications.

Most anti-Marketeers, with the Commission as their hate object, perceived the main threat as coming from an over-mighty executive, and this distorted their view of enforcement. The vast majority assumed that the chief agent of compliance would be the Commission. They disregarded entirely the role of the national courts.

Neither does the executive come out of this story well. The failure of government spokesmen to adopt the same position in each House of Parliament is quite extraordinary. In the Lords, peers were told in no uncertain terms that future statute would prevail over Community law whenever the two could not be interpreted in conformity with each other. In the Commons, MPs were told that the Bill pushed our courts 'as far as can constitutionally be achieved' in favour of according supremacy to Community law. In the Commons, the long-term future of parliamentary sovereignty was presented as somewhat precarious: expressly conflicting statute would prevail over EEC law 'certainly as the matter now stands'; whereas in the Lords, peers were assured that the Bill in no way modified the rules of parliamentary sovereignty.

Even within the Commons, however, ministers proved unable to stick to a consistent collective 'line'. Sir Geoffrey Howe declared that the courts of the UK's three jurisdictions would enforce the supremacy of Community law, whereas Geoffrey Rippon insisted that Parliament retained the right both to reject regulations and to refuse to implement directives, in which case the Community provision in question would have no legal effect within the UK. All that the government would be able to do would be to mend its international fences accordingly. Rippon conceded not the slightest possibility that the courts might in such circumstances bypass the legislature by enforcing Community legislation in preference to the will of Parliament.

In assessing the equivocations and contradictions of government ministers over 'ultimate sovereignty' one must bear in mind that they were on virgin territory. Never before had the enactment of a statute presented such a direct potential threat to the legislative supremacy of Parliament. However, such uncertainty merely strengthens the case for the government stressing that questions of the permissibility of implied repeal, express repeal, and withdrawal would depend on future court judgments, not on their own ministerial pronouncements. This was not emphasized enough. Perhaps the unwarranted confidence of ministers in their own powers of statutory interpretation stemmed from their anxiety to reassure wavering Conservatives.

All in all, there was little interest in the ECJ and very little realization by parliamentarians that they were voting for a fundamental change in the constitutional relationship between Parliament and the national courts. In part, this can again be attributed to unfamiliarity with the intrusion of law into politics, in a constitution based on so much convention and so little law. MPs seem to have tacitly assumed that government and Parliament would in future comply with Community law as a matter of political not legal obligation.

5

The Irish Comparison

This chapter examines whether the constitutional naïveté of British parliamentarians at accession was shared by their Irish counterparts. It also seeks to establish whether the Irish government provided its legislature and electorate (since the necessary constitutional amendment was effected by referendum) with a more accurate picture of the constitutional consequences of membership. Ireland provides a suitable comparison because it joined contemporaneously with the UK, when *Van Gend*, *Costa*, and *Internationale Handelsgesellschaft* had already been decided. At the same time it furnishes a useful contrast since Eire's 1937 constitution firmly rejects parliamentary sovereignty in favour of limits on parliamentary power. This has been accompanied since the 1960s by active judicial review of Acts of the Oireachtas, the Irish Parliament, by the Irish Supreme Court.[1] We will need to consider throughout whether a *law-based* constitution, rather than one based largely on convention and politics, served to clarify the prospective impact of membership.

Irish constitutional culture 1: national sovereignty

Although Ireland was formally independent from 1922, Irish public life had long been imbued with a strong sense that national sovereignty was severely limited. This largely derived from Ireland's economic dependence on the UK.[2] Eighty per cent of Irish trade was with Britain; the value of the punt was linked to that of sterling. Irish politicians were preoccupied with the

---

[1] See eg Casey (1987) 29, Reid (1990) 3.   [2] Coakley (1983) 48.

Community as an *economic* entity partly due to Ireland's perception of her own economic vulnerability.[3]

Lack of Irish concern about sovereignty may also have stemmed from Ireland's lowly status in international relations, vividly illustrated by the way in which her prospects of Community membership rested on the fate of the British application. This militated towards a perception of the Community as a chance to enter an exciting new alliance rather than as a threat to sovereignty. Moreover nationalism was diminishing as a factor in elections with a greater preoccupation on economic issues.[4] This was mirrored by a shift in outlook among the country's political elite from concern to preserve cultural nationalism to overriding economic pragmatism.[5]

Thus, both economically and in foreign policy, Ireland felt herself buffeted by external forces. Economic dependence and diplomatic impotence inevitably strengthened the perception of sovereignty in terms of real influence over her future (which she lacked) rather than in terms of legislative freedom (which she enjoyed).

Irish constitutional culture 2: parliamentary sovereignty

The 1922 constitution purported to contain guarantees of 'fundamental' rights but was at all times capable of amendment by Act of the Oireachtas.[6] The result was *de facto* parliamentary sovereignty. By contrast the 1937 constitution is rigid,[7] though it has been doubted whether its framers really envisaged the part which judicial review would ultimately play.[8] Nonetheless Article 15.4.1° forbids the Oireachtas to enact law repugnant to the constitution and Articles 34.3.2° and 34.4.3° give the High Court and Supreme Court

---

[3] Laffan (1991) 187.   [4] Ibid 49.   [5] Cohan (1972) 2.

[6] Kelly (1967) 63. Although the 1922 constitution adopted referendums as the method of constitutional amendment, this did not apply for the first eight years. During that period the Oireachtas was authorized to enact constitutional amendments by ordinary legislation. Since the Oireachtas was entitled to amend *any* article, it was able subsequently to extend the term of amendment by ordinary legislation by a further eight-year period (Kohn (1932) 251–252).

[7] Article 46 provides that a constitutional amendment must originate in the Dáil, must describe itself as an 'Act to Amend the Constitution', must be passed or deemed to have been passed by both Houses of the Oireachtas, *and must be approved by a referendum majority*. The President can then sign the Bill and, when duly promulgated as a law, it amends the constitution (Forde (1987) 18).

[8] Kelly (1994) p lxxxix. De Valera, the 1937 constitution's principal drafter, remarked extensively on the modest role of judges under the constitution during the Dáil debate on its adoption (Chubb (1991) 64).

jurisdiction to consider the constitutionality of any law. Until the 1960s there were few such cases, and in those which did arise judges, unfamiliar with judicial review, adopted an inhibited role. Yet even at this stage there were exceptional cases which showed that the constitution really did have bite. In *Buckley and others (Sinn Féin) v Attorney General and another*[9] in 1950 the Supreme Court held that a statute purporting to preclude the courts from hearing further proceedings relating to an ongoing dispute as to who was entitled to the funds of Sinn Fein was *ultra vires* the Oireachtas since it constituted an unwarrantable interference in the judicial domain.[10] In the mid-1960s, however, there was a dramatic increase in judicial review of Acts of the Oireachtas, relating in particular to the constitution's fundamental rights articles.[11] Eschewing its earlier approach—that the balancing of rights protection between individuals and citizens as a whole lay solely within the province of the Oireachtas[12]—the Supreme Court held in *Ryan v The Attorney General*[13] that there existed an undefined residue of personal rights guaranteed by the constitution, not specifically enumerated therein, which it would protect from legislative intrusion. This case marked a sea-change so that, in contrast to Britain, the Irish were growing accustomed to judicial review of primary legislation by the time of accession.

Background to the Irish application

Ireland's first attempt to join the Community had been in 1961–3. At that time, one of the government's main motives in seeking membership was to facilitate economic reform.[14] Fianna Fáil governments in the 1930s–1950s maintained a policy of protectionism, an overvalued exchange rate, and little encouragement of manufactured exports. The result was a deep recession in the 1950s, characterized by high unemployment, low growth, and emigration.[15] In 1958 the Department of Finance published *Economic Development*,

---

[9] [1950] IR 67.

[10] It is interesting that on this very issue of parliamentary attempts to preclude access to the courts, what the Irish Supreme Court achieved by invalidation in *Buckley* the House of Lords achieved through statutory interpretation in *Anisminic v Foreign Compensation Commission* [1968] 2 QB 862, discussed in Ch 2 above.

[11] Kelly (1967) 37–41 and 63–64, Casey (1987) 29.

[12] eg in *Re Article 26 and the Offences against the State Act 1940* [1943] IR 470.

[13] [1965] IR 294.   [14] Keogh (1997) 83–84.   [15] Coughlan (1979) 11.

an influential programme advocating export-orientated expansion.[16] This was adopted by Sean Lemass, in 1958 as Tánaiste[17] and Minister for Industry and Commerce and from 1959 as Taioseach. Convinced that free trade was inevitable, Lemass was anxious to attract foreign industrial capital and to find higher-priced continental food markets on which to sell Ireland's agricultural output. Moreover when it was rumoured in early 1961 that the UK was seeking membership, Ireland had no choice but to follow suit. The Republic was wholly dependent on its British market and its economy would be ruined by the application of the common customs tariff. Accordingly in July 1961 Lemass announced that Ireland would apply for full membership if the UK also applied, and Ireland swiftly submitted her formal application.

The government's 1961 White Paper *European Economic Community* emphasized that 'all authoritative comment as well as the actual [Treaty] text suggest that the possible adaptations to the Treaty on accession of a new member would not be such as to modify in any important respect the basic provisions of the Treaty'.[18] This is a sharp contrast with the initial attitude of the Macmillan government (and the consistent attitude of the Gaitskell/Wilson opposition) that substantial Treaty change would be necessary to secure British membership. At this pre-*Van Gend* stage the Irish government seemed—not unreasonably—to view the Community simply as an international organization, the White Paper merely stating that 'membership would entail acceptance of the principles and obligations of the Treaty'.[19]

Negotiations became bogged down by fears of some Member States that Ireland would not play her part in a future defence or political community, something firmly denied by the government which protested that Ireland would fully participate in the integration of a United States of Europe and was not neutral 'in the present world division between communism and freedom'.[20] The application failed because the Six, under French pressure, insisted that formal talks with Ireland could not begin until negotiations with Britain were completed. They rejected Lemass's promptings that the Irish application should be pursued independently if the British application failed.[21]

By way of a substitute, Lemass signed the British-Irish Free Trade Area Agreement in December 1965. Ireland's application was formally 'reactivated' in 1967 though no serious diplomatic effort was made, since by then it

---

[16] Whitaker (1973) 416, Hederman (1983) 60.   [17] Deputy to the Taioseach.
[18] Pr 6106 (June 1961) Dublin, para 94.   [19] Ibid, para 97.
[20] Speech of Mícheál O'Moráin, Minister of Lands, 5 February 1962 in Co Mayo.
[21] *Irish Press*, 6 September 1962, *Irish Times*, 6 September 1962.

was plain that Irish membership depended on British membership. However, the Lynch government issued a White Paper which revealed that the Ministries of Finance and External Affairs were having periodic discussions with the Commission to discuss 'issues likely to arise in connection with Ireland's application'.[22] The same White Paper stated that Community law created 'obligations and rights for [Member States'] citizens . . . *which the national courts are obliged to enforce and uphold*'.[23] It also included an account of *Costa v ENEL*, which pointed out that Member States had 'given up their power to override the Treaty by subsequent legislation'.[24] This represents a far more forthright approach than that adopted in the British 1967 White Paper, which played down the effect of *Costa*.[25]

The 1970 application: positions of the parties

The Heath/Pompidou rapprochement re-energized Irish efforts to join, and formal negotiations commenced on 30 June 1970. Crucially, both Fianna Fáil and Fine Gael supported Community membership with negligible backbench dissent. Fine Gael, in the words of frontbencher Richie Ryan, 'will not be a British Labour Party, prepared to play politics in the best interests of its own members in order to get into power'.[26] The Irish Labour Party's position was that Ireland should not join the Common Market and that the option of association had not been properly considered.[27] Furthermore Labour saw no reason why negotiations had to be premised on the conditions laid down in the Rome Treaty.[28] Like its British sister party, Labour's animosity owed much to the Treaty being 'anti-planning and based on the principles of laissez-faire and free competition'[29] and indeed 'Adam Smith textbook free trade'.[30]

The government's White Paper *Membership of the European Communities: Implications for Ireland*[31] made it clear that '[p]articipation in the European Communities involves the exercise by Community institutions of certain

---

[22] *European Communities* (April 1967) Pr 9283, para 14.

[23] Ibid, para 52 (emphasis added).   [24] Ibid, para 53.   [25] See pp. 48–9 above.

[26] Dáil, 252, col 815, 10 March 1971.

[27] Dáil, 247, col 2092, 25 June 1970 (James Tully).   [28] Ibid.

[29] Ibid, col 1672, 23 June 1970 (Brendan Corish, Labour Leader), ibid, col 1701, 23 June 1970 (Dr Noel Browne, Labour, Dublin South East).

[30] Dáil, 259, col 1940, 21 March 1972 (Justin Keating, Labour, North County Dublin).

[31] Prl 1110 (April 1970) Dublin.

powers previously reserved to the Governments, legislatures and judiciaries of the member States'.[32] The White Paper listed constitutional provisions which might require amendment:[33]

Article 5	Ireland is a sovereign, independent, democratic state.
Article 6	2. [P]owers of government are exercisable only by or on the authority of the organs of State established by this Constitution.
Article 15(2)	The sole and exclusive power of making laws for the State is hereby vested in the Oireachtas; no other legislative authority has power to make laws for the State.
Article 29	5.2° The State shall not be bound by any international agreement involving a charge upon public funds unless the terms of the agreement shall have been approved by Dáil Éireann.
	6. No international agreement shall be part of the domestic law of the State save as may be determined by the Oireachtas.
Article 34	1. Justice shall be administered in courts established by law and by judges appointed in the manner provided by this Constitution . . .
	4.6° The decision of the Supreme Court shall in all cases be final and conclusive.

A committee chaired by the Attorney General would consider the form of the constitutional amendment.[34]

The section of the White Paper on 'Political Implications' was also candid. It stated that the first aim of the Treaty was to establish ever closer union among the European peoples. Applicant countries had to be fully aware of the Community's essentially *political* goal.[35] Ireland would help achieve this goal, and would also be prepared to assist, if necessary, in the defence of the new Europe.[36]

The Community and its destiny: a more consistent story?

On 23 June 1970, the Taoiseach, Jack Lynch, moved a motion in the Dáil to take note of the White Paper. In spite of its contents, he played down the limitation of sovereignty, claiming that Community obligations were 'not dissimilar' to those under GATT and the British-Irish Free Trade Area Agreement.[37] Whatever the merits of this argument in the context of Irish

---

[32] Para 1.1.   [33] Paras 1.5–1.8.   [34] Para 1.9.   [35] Para 2.2.
[36] Para 2.6.   [37] Dáil, 247, col 1648, 23 June 1970.

political practice, as a matter of Irish constitutional law it was debatable. The question of whether the Oireachtas could legislate contrary to Irish international obligations was unsettled. In *State (Somers Jennings) v Furlong*[38] in 1966, Henchy J had held in the High Court that where there was an irreconcilable conflict between a domestic statute and the provisions of an international convention, the domestic courts must give effect to the statute. However, Lynch conceded that the existing sphere of Community activity—economic, fiscal, and monetary harmonization—though limited, was a wide one.[39] There was thus no talk of Ireland retaining 'essential sovereignty'.

The Minister for External Affairs, Dr Patrick Hillery, was even more frank. Throughout the negotiations and Oireachtas debates Hillery served much the same role as Howe and Rippon in the UK. In this first debate, Hillery reiterated that political unification remained the ultimate goal of the Treaty,[40] and stated that a united Europe was an ideal to which the government fully subscribed.[41] Ireland would also participate in the defence of the Community in the event of a common defence policy. Hillery noted that there were two schools of thought about how the Community should develop: some Member States sought speedy development of supranational institutions like the European Parliament, others wanted national governments to retain control. He continued: '[a]s far as I am concerned, I want to be where decisions are made. This should be our attitude also as a nation.'[42] This cryptic comment perhaps suggests that the Irish government would be happy to go along with whichever future course for the Community became the prevailing consensus among Member States. That interpretation was consistent with a more general remark made by Hillery in the Dáil two years later that '[w]e do give some overall policy direction to our foreign relations. But for a small country like ours, the role of Government is not to try to impose a grand "foreign policy design".'[43] Hillery clearly assumed that Ireland's role would be cooperative rather than obstructionist, unlike UK politicians who emphasized the Luxembourg Compromise and the veto on Treaty change. Although Hillery repeated Lynch's mistake of likening Community membership to that of UNO or GATT, he acknowledged that constitutional amendments would be required to provide for the application in Ireland of directly effective and directly applicable Treaty provisions and regulations, and ECJ jurisdiction. He noted that '[o]ne of the functions of the European Court . . . is to decide, when called upon, whether acts of the

---

[38] [1966] IR 183.
[40] Ibid, col 2067, 23 June 1970.
[42] Dáil, 254, col 754, 1 June 1971.

[39] Dáil, 247, col 1648, 23 June 1970.
[41] Ibid, col 2011, 23 June 1970.
[43] 18 April 1972. Quoted in Keatinge (1978) 193.

Council . . . or acts of the Commission, *or individual member Governments in relation to matters covered by the Treaties*, are, in fact, compatible with the Treaties'.[44] Unlike British politicians, Hillery made no distinction in this context between enforcement actions and preliminary rulings. This suggests that he was attuned to the use of the Article 177 procedure for monitoring Member State compliance with Community law.

The Taoiseach adopted a similar position with regard to the Community's future. Although the status quo was that the interests of all Member States were fully taken into account, the government was wholeheartedly ready to join in working towards the achievement of the ever closer union among European peoples of which the Treaty spoke.[45] The Tánaiste Erskine Childers predicted that economic and monetary union would benefit Ireland by boosting EEC regional policy.[46] Finance Minister George Colley noted approvingly that the Werner Report envisaged that by 1980 the main economic policy decisions would be taken by the Community, but that such a fundamental change would require Treaty amendment.[47] This contrasts with the British government's position, whereby commitment to EMU sat uneasily with insistence that the veto was there to stay. The Fine Gael front bench shared the government's enthusiasm for 'ever closer union'. Dr Garret FitzGerald, for example, noted approvingly that economic and monetary union would mean in effect a single state.[48]

Most backbenchers approved the government's long-term aims. Thomas O'Higgins (Fine Gael, Dublin County South) welcomed the fact that the Community was not merely concerned with trade but meant 'embarking towards the greatest adventure in our history, towards a united states of Europe'.[49] Patrick Belton (Fine Gael, Dublin North East) sought 'the formation of some sort of European Community like the United States of America, where different countries will be bound together'.[50] Major Vivion de Valera (Fianna Fáil, Dublin Central) noted that the trend towards enlargement of the Community reflected the evolution of the United States.[51]

As for the Seanad, not a single member spoke against membership during debate. Senator Alexis FitzGerald, a distinguished lawyer, linked the Community's federal nature to the status of the ECJ within it:

---

[44] Dáil, 247, col 2069, 25 June 1970 (emphasis added).
[45] Dáil, 254, col 652, 1 June 1971.   [46] Dáil, 252, cols 848–849, 10 March 1971.
[47] Dáil, 247, col 1825, 24 June 1970.   [48] Dáil, 254, col 748, 1 June 1971.
[49] Dáil, 247, col 1855, 24 June 1970.   [50] Ibid, col 708, 8 July 1970.
[51] Dáil, 254, col 717, 1 June 1971.

We are entering a unique federation. It is a functional, if not a political federation. . . . The *supreme* institution which gives evidence of the federative nature of this Community is the European Court, which has been developing, in its interpretation of the Treaty and the regulations, directives and decisions made under the Treaty, into a system of law that is self-enforcing.[52]

FitzGerald's characterization of the Community legal system as self-enforcing connotes an appreciation of the role of the national courts under the doctrine of direct effect in ensuring observance of Community rules.

Some Deputies did not believe that Ireland would be in any position to veto future integration, even on the sensitive defence issue, despite the formal unanimity requirement relating to Treaty amendment.[53] Certainly (in contrast to Britain) leading politicians did not seek to emphasize Ireland's right under the Treaty to block 'ever closer union', doubtless because it was 'an ideal to which [they] fully subscribed'.[54]

The consistency of the Irish polity is readily distinguished from the Heath government's zigzagging between its claims that 'essential' and 'ultimate' sovereignty were not at stake, and its ambitions that the Community prove a strong influence in world affairs with a single foreign policy.

Legislative freedom versus real influence

The dominant theme of British pro-Marketeers, that a sacrifice of legislative freedom would be more than compensated by greater political influence, also pervaded the arguments of Irish Europhiles. Indeed, their case was all the more compelling since Ireland had never achieved economic independence from the UK. Fine Gael's foreign affairs spokesman Richie Ryan stated that Ireland would be 'shedding some of our purely legal sovereignty in order to gain real power and real control'.[55] Party leader Liam Cosgrave suggested that Community membership opened up the prospect of escaping British economic dominance. The Taoiseach agreed that it was 'misleading to refer to the limitations on this country's freedom of action which will result from membership and to ignore the very real limitations on our freedom that now exist, especially at the present time when we are not a party to any

[52] Seanad, 73, col 929, 23 November 1972 (emphasis added).
[53] eg James Tully (Labour, Meath) (Dáil, 259, cols 2015–2016, 21 March 1972).
[54] The Taoiseach, Dáil, 247, col 2068, 25 June 1970.
[55] Dáil, 252, col 818, 10 March 1971.

international agreement or any international grouping such as the European Communities'.[56] Garret FitzGerald noted that Ireland needed to secure a diminution of *British* sovereignty that would prevent Britain exploiting her. He argued that membership offered a massive extension of Irish sovereignty, preventing 'further exploitation of our people by a former colonial power'.[57]

Ireland's smallness was also seen as militating in favour of membership, reflecting the way in which the interests of small states are best served by rule-bound, multilateral agreements. Lynch noted that any small country's economic policy was substantially influenced by the actions of larger nations. Membership would increase Irish influence since 'as a member we would participate in the formulation of common codes of action by Member States'.[58]

Politicians were also mindful that Ireland would benefit from the formal equality between Member States underpinning the Treaty. Cosgrave pointed out that the Treaty ensured that the rights of small countries as well as stronger ones were protected, for example by the Luxembourg Compromise.[59] Finance Minister George Colley emphasized that, as a small, economically weak country, the scope for Ireland to control her economic destiny was very limited. Ireland would therefore benefit from the EEC's inbuilt structures controlling the power of all Member States irrespective of size and economic power.

One element in the debate not seen in Britain was the argument that national sovereignty was in any case ignoble and undesirable. Fine Gael's Richie Ryan suggested that '[a]bsolute sovereignty belongs to the time of the kings . . . The truth is that qualified sovereignty is a better guarantee of individual rights and personal rights.'[60] Similarly Fianna Fáil's Vivion de Valera dismissed national sovereignty as a concept belonging to the earlier part of the century which was no longer valid.[61] Garret FitzGerald wanted attachment to national sovereignty to be superseded by a concept of multi-layered sovereignty.[62] These statements reflect the extent to which Irish politicians had eschewed traditional nationalism.

---

[56] Dáil, 257, col 1721, 9 December 1971.   [57] Dáil, 247, col 1935, 25 June 1970.

[58] Ibid, col 1648, 23 June 1970.   [59] Ibid, col 1660, 23 June 1970.

[60] Dáil, 252, col 816, 10 March 1971.   [61] Dáil, 254, col 722, 1 June 1971.

[62] Dáil, 247, col 1928, 25 June 1970.

Irish unity

One aspect of traditional nationalism, however, had not diminished. Article 2 of the constitution defined the national territory as the whole island of Ireland and Article 3 both envisaged reintegration of that territory and stated that the Irish government and Parliament enjoyed jurisdiction over it. With the violence in Northern Ireland only just begun, most Deputies passionately believed in a united Ireland. For anti-Marketeers, acceding to the Treaty implicitly involved accepting the existing frontier with the UK.[63] For pro-Marketeers, the very fact that so many decisions would be taken at a European level would erode the significance of 'the Border',[64] whereas an Irish 'No' would place the Community's external frontier between Northern Ireland and the Republic. This argument was powerfully exploited in a Fianna Fáil full-page press advertisement, which featured a silhouette of Ireland with Northern Ireland removed, together with the emotive caption:

Is this the kind of Ireland you want? Part of an island cut adrift from the great family of nations in the European Community?[65]

Cultural sovereignty

The question of whether national identity would suffer or be enhanced by membership had more resonance in Ireland than in Britain.[66] The Taoiseach argued that Irish culture would flourish in the enriched climate of a wider Community in the face of active two-way interchange.[67] The Tánaiste suggested that contact with different cultures would stimulate the Irish personality, replacing Irish passivity in preserving national identity in the face of one dominating foreign culture—that of Britain.[68] In contrast some

[63] Dáil, 248, col 71, 30 June 1970 (James Tully, Labour, Meath); ibid, col 383, 2 July 1970 (Dr John O'Donovan, Labour, Dublin South Central); Dáil, 254, col 667, 1 June 1971 (Justin Keating, Labour, North County Dublin).

[64] eg Dáil, 247, col 1693, 23 June 1970 (the Tánaiste, Erskine Childers), FitzGerald (1972) 108.

[65] *Irish Times*, 4 May 1972.

[66] The comment repeatedly made by Edward Heath, that under the Treaty 'the French are no less French, the Germans no less German', attracted little comment from British anti-Marketeers perhaps because they were primarily interested in retaining the freedom of action of UK governments and Parliament, rather than in preserving British cultural identity.

[67] Dáil, 247, col 1651, 23 June 1970.   [68] Ibid, col 1689, 23 June 1970.

anti-Marketeers perceived a threat to the Irish language, traditional family life,[69] and Christian values.[70]

Ultimate sovereignty

There was less belief in Ireland than in Britain that the national legislature could defy Community law or indeed leave the Community. Significantly— and in sharp contrast to their British sister party[71]—it was Labour which took the strongest line on this. For instance, Dr John O'Connell (Labour, Dublin South West) considered that once Ireland entered she could not withdraw.[72] James Tully (Labour, Meath)[73] and Justin Keating (Labour, Dublin County North)[74] did not believe that withdrawal was possible 'by any legal process'. Barry Desmond (Labour, Dun Laoghaire & Rathdown) spoke of the 'political finality' of accepting the Treaty of Rome.[75]

Pro-Marketeers adopted the same view. Garret FitzGerald conceded that the Treaty involved *alienating* Irish sovereignty.[76] Seemingly he recognized that Community membership was a permanent commitment—an approach which contrasts with that of Rippon and Howe in Britain. Another pro-Marketeer, Senator Alexis FitzGerald, spoke of an *irretrievable* limitation on the sovereignty referred to in Article 5 of the constitution,[77] and that in enacting the European Communities Bill 1972 the Oireachtas was adopting a law it could never constitutionally or legally repeal.[78]

Anti-Marketeers also recognized that the Oireachtas would not be able to legislate contrary to Community law *on any particular issue*. As Labour's James Tully observed, 'we cannot pick out the little bits we like and discard what we

[69] eg Sean Treacy (Labour, Tipperary South) suggested that family life would be subjected to the influences of Paris, with 'the likelihood of immoral literature and pornography invading our homes' (Dáil, 252, col 790, 10 March 1971).

[70] eg Oliver J Flanagan (Fine Gael, Laoighis-Offaly) suggested that if Ireland was obliged by European legislation to introduce divorce, this would sound the death knell of Christian life in Ireland (Dáil, 252, col 657, 10 March 1971).

[71] Unlike British Labour, Irish Labour were in no position to form the next government, which perhaps affected their thinking.

[72] Dáil, 247, col 1913, 24 June 1970.

[73] Dáil, 258, col 554, 26 January 1972. Tully also thought there were practical reasons precluding withdrawal: 'If we accept membership of the EEC and gear all our economy to membership, the Minister knows that after a number of years there is no way in which we can pull out.'

[74] Dáil, 258, col 462, 25 June 1970.   [75] Dáil, 254, col 690, 1 June 1971.

[76] Dáil, 257, col 1345, 2 December 1971.   [77] Seanad, 73, col 928, 23 November 1972.

[78] Ibid, col 925, 23 November 1972.

dislike'.[79] Only Senator Neville Keery (a pro-Marketeer) raised the possibility that Ireland might quietly ignore directives,[80] and he was condemned for saying so.[81]

The institutional balance between the Oireachtas and the courts

Deputies appeared far more aware than British MPs of the ECJ's importance in the Community constitution. Barry Desmond (Labour, Dun Laoghaire & Rathdown) demanded a clear statement from the government about the ECJ's role in the Irish legal system: '[w]e might even ask at what point in various types of situation is the focus directly on Luxembourg. What are the powers of that court in Luxembourg? What sanctions does it possess? Most important, what has been done, what has been its record in practice to date?'[82] Sean Treacy (Labour, Tipperary South) recognized that the ECJ would have the final say as to which Irish laws remained on the statute book: '[t]he court in Brussels [*sic*] can determine who shall buy land in any particular country and can give non-nationals the power and the right to buy land. The decision of the court in Brussels supersedes the decision of the High Court and the Supreme Court in that regard. I do not see what degree of manœuvrability or independence we shall have to determine our own future.'[83]

Nor was recognition of the seminal role to be played by the ECJ limited to anti-Marketeers. Patrick Donogan (Fine Gael, Louth) derided the Taoiseach's claim that the Community worked in the interests of all Member States by suggesting that the ECJ would oblige Ireland to observe decisions not to its liking.[84] John Bruton noted that Irish courts might have to enforce directives even where these had not been implemented by domestic legislation. He was questioned by a Fianna Fáil Deputy:

Major de Valera: What court would ultimately decide the question the Deputy is raising?

---

[79] Dáil, 258, col 456, 25 January 1972.   [80] Seanad, 73, col 845, 22 November 1972.
[81] eg by Senator Pierce Butler: 'If directives are passed it is binding on us to accept them and put them into effect', ibid, col 936, 23 November 1972.
[82] Dáil, 257, col 1131, 2 December 1971.   [83] Dáil, 252, col 791, 10 March 1971.
[84] Dáil, 255, col 575, 6 July 1971.

Mr Bruton: The European court.

Major de Valera: The European court would be the final court.[85]

Oddly, Bruton's colleagues Garret FitzGerald and Richie Ryan, in spite of *SpA SACE*, assumed that unimplemented directives could not be enforced.[86]

Kompetenz-Kompetenz

The Dáil's greater awareness of the ECJ's importance evidently derived from the centrality of the courts to the Irish constitution and the veneration of their role in Irish public life. This respect is readily apparent from the Oireachtas debates. The fact that areas falling within the scope of Community law would be removed from the purview of the Supreme Court proved a significant grievance when the European Communities Bill was debated. Although Deputies, unlike their British counterparts, appreciated the power which the ECJ would wield, many disapproved of it, not so much out of concern for the legislative freedom of the Oireachtas as out of anxiety to preserve the Supreme Court's constitutional standing.

This anxiety manifested itself in the widespread delusion that after accession the Supreme Court would *exclusively and routinely* determine the respective scope of national and Community law. Thus the Taoiseach asserted that the *final* decision on whether domestic implementing legislation was 'consequent on membership' would rest with the Supreme Court.[87] Some eleven months later, he was still pushing the same point, that (in the context of power under the European Communities Act 1972 to make ministerial regulations to implement Community directives) 'our courts will be the *ultimate* safeguard against any attempted use of the section in excess of the powers conferred'.[88] Similarly Finance Minister George Colley argued that '[i]f anyone wants to contest [an Irish law], he can contest it before our courts unless it is an act which arises directly from the terms of the Treaties . . . *This would be a matter for interpretation by our courts.*'[89]

---

[85] Dáil, 263, col 959, 7 November 1972.

[86] Ibid, col 968, 7 November 1972 (FitzGerald); ibid, col 1688, 15 November 1972 (Ryan). FitzGerald and Bruton are both barristers; Ryan was a solicitor.

[87] Dáil, 257, col 1725, 9 December 1971.

[88] Dáil, 263, col 97, 25 October 1972 (emphasis added).

[89] Dáil, 258, col 420, 25 January 1972 (emphasis added).

Garret FitzGerald asserted that Irish courts, not just the ECJ, would be able to declare Community acts *ultra vires* the Treaty, thereby for instance preventing abuse of Article 235 EEC.[90] In the Seanad Professor Patrick Quinlan argued that '[a]ny groups within the country that feel there is a challenge involved either in our neutrality, foreign policy *or any other matter in the political field*, have a remedy, because if any directive comes within those particular areas then it is automatically outside the scope of the three Treaties mentioned and consequently they can refer such a directive to the Supreme Court'.[91]

It is important to clarify what was at issue here. What was being argued was that the Irish courts, *as a matter of routine practice*, would determine the scope of Community law. The issue was not what the Irish courts *could* do,[92] but what they *would* do. Irish politicians seemingly assumed that keeping the EEC institutions within their powers would become the staple fare of Irish public law.

It is notable that Dr Hillery eventually conceded that the extent of conflicts between Irish and Community law would be a matter for the European Court.[93] Trinity law lecturer Kadar Asmal commented that the Taoiseach had erred in assuming that the Supreme Court would interpret the Treaty: it was for the *ECJ* to decide what was and what was not a Community matter. He argued that, 'as regards what is known as sovereignty, the ultimate decision-making bodies will no longer be the ones identified by the Constitution. Ultimate decision-making in a large area will be transferred to . . . the European institutions.'[94]

To what extent should the Irish government have realized that the ECJ would draw the boundary line between national and Community law? Most subsequent writers have acknowledged that 'the final word . . . might have to lie with the European Court of Justice'.[95] Without hindsight, it might have

---

[90]   Dáil, 257, cols 1356–1357, 2 December 1971. Article 235 EEC provided that 'if action by the Community should prove necessary to attain, in the course of the operation of the common market, one of the objectives of the Community and this Treaty has not provided the necessary powers, the Council shall, acting unanimously on a proposal from the Commission and after consulting the European Parliament, take the appropriate measures'. For an analysis of the usage of this article see Weiler (1999) 52–63.

[91]   Seanad, 72, col 528, 24 November 1972 (emphasis added).

[92]   Here one must agree with Weiler that 'there has not yet been a full ventilation of the "Kompetenz-Kompetenz" issue and it is not yet clear whether at least the courts such as the German, Italian or Irish highest courts would cede that power so easily'. Weiler (1999) 212.

[93]   Seanad, 73, col 1007, 29 November 1972.   [94]   *Irish Times*, 9 May 1972.

[95]   Casey (1987) 179. See also Murphy (1983) 32, McCutcheon (1991) 212, Whelan (1992) 61, Hogan (1987) 60.

been possible that the Supreme Court would have adopted a more bullish position, especially in view of the natural law ethos of the constitution (which speaks, for example, of inalienable rights, antecedent and superior to *all* positive law).[96] Yet it was surely predictable that such cases would be the exception rather than the rule, and that the domestic courts would *generally* defer to the ECJ's opinion of the legal requirements of membership. This, after all, had been the experience of the Six until the early 1970s. This issue is intimately linked to the question of the status of the constitutional amendment *vis-à-vis* the rest of the constitution, and will be discussed further below.

The form of the constitutional amendment

Temple Lang had already identified in 1963 the need for a constitutional amendment if Ireland were to join the Community, since the constitution did not permit the surrender of any legislative, executive, or judicial powers of government to international institutions.[97] In June 1970 the government readily accepted the conclusion of its Attorney General's Committee that a constitutional amendment was required,[98] but the amendment did not materialize until November 1971. In the meantime there was considerable speculation as to the scale of amendment that would be necessary. For example Opposition justice spokesman Tom Fitzpatrick (Fine Gael, Cavan) considered it important to spell out the changes involved in Community membership, and suggested that therefore *all* the constitutional provisions mentioned in the 1970 White Paper[99] should be amended.[100] Indeed such substantial changes might be better handled by introducing an entirely new constitution.[101]

---

[96] Article 41 ('The Family'). Emphasis added.   [97] Temple Lang (1963) 552.

[98] Dáil, 247, col 1646, 23 June 1970 (the Taoiseach).

[99] Articles 5, 6.2, 15.2, 34.1, 34.4.6°, 29.5.2°, and 29.6.

[100] Dáil, 252, cols 758–762, 10 March 1971. Fine Gael leader Liam Cosgrave appeared to back this position when he argued for 'specifically and clearly-defined amendments in the Constitution' (Dáil, 254, col 661, 1 June 1971).

[101] Fine Gael generally considered the 1937 constitution 'miserable and mischievous' (Richie Ryan, Dáil, 257, col 1139, 2 December 1971). A parliamentary committee had sat in 1967–8 to consider a more comprehensive programme of constitutional change on matters such as divorce, private property, and the language of the 1937 constitution. Its activities were sidelined by the outbreak of violence in Northern Ireland in 1969.

This was not, however, the government's solution. On 2 December 1971 Lynch introduced in the Dáil the Third Amendment of the Constitution Bill 1971, providing for a single omnibus constitutional amendment:

29.4.3° The State may become a member of the European Coal and Steel Community (established by Treaty signed at Paris on the 18th day of April, 1951), the European Economic Community (established by Treaty signed at Rome on the 25th day of March, 1957), and the European Atomic Energy Community (established by Treaty signed at Rome on the 25th day of March, 1957). No provision of this Constitution invalidates laws enacted, acts done or measures adopted by the State consequent on membership of the Communities or prevents laws enacted, acts done or measures adopted by the Communities, or institutions thereof, from having the force of law in the State.

The Taoiseach explained that the government had eschewed the article-by-article approach on the grounds that the extent to which the constitution would need to be amended would in the final analysis be a matter for the courts. It was therefore most appropriate to achieve the desired result through an amendment which would remove incompatibilities in a general way.[102] Thus the government were giving considerable leeway to the courts. Labour tabled an amendment that 'Dáil Éireann declines to give a Second Reading to the Bill on the grounds that it seeks to amend the Constitution without enumerating the Articles so affected and in a manner contrary to that intended in Article 46.1 of the Constitution.'[103] Justin Keating (Labour, North Co Dublin) suggested that the government's motive in wrapping up the most profound changes since the State's formation in 'four vague lines' was to make the amendment seem innocuous, when in reality Ireland was being asked to scrap her constitution.[104]

In the event, Labour's amendment was defeated by 106 to 17 and the Bill's Second Reading was carried without a division. This easy passage was facilitated by the pledge of Fine Gael Leader Liam Cosgrave, departing from his Party's previous position, that Fine Gael would not oppose the Bill's second stage, but would promote three amendments in Committee along the following lines:[105]

1. The phrase 'consequent on membership' was too wide, and should be replaced by 'necessitated by the obligations of membership'.

---

[102] Dáil, 257, col 1073, 2 December 1971.

[103] Ibid, col 1074, 2 December 1971.

[104] Ibid, col 1075, 2 December 1971.

[105] Ibid, cols 1112–1119, 2 December 1971.

2. It should be made clear that the Oireachtas retained exclusive control over measures relating to national emergencies and the raising and maintenance of armed forces.
3. There should be no abridgement of or doubt about the position of the constitutional guarantees of fundamental rights and personal freedom in Articles 40–44 of the Constitution.[106]

The substance of the constitutional amendment

The first sentence of the Third Amendment attracted scant attention. Murphy and McMahon suggest that as a purely enabling provision, permitting the State to join the (named) Communities if the Oireachtas so decided, its legal interest is limited.[107] However, an alternative view is possible. By allowing the State to join the Communities, it could be contended that the first sentence by implication provides *constitutional* sanction for the importation into the Irish legal order of the doctrines of direct effect and supremacy inherent in membership, something which the second sentence clearly does not purport to do. Otherwise the incorporation of these doctrines into Irish law would depend on the European Communities Act 1972, which would have the curious consequence that a lower form of law (statute) would regulate the relationship between two higher forms of law (the constitution and Community law).

Although the government emphasized that any new political or defence Community would probably be based on a *new* treaty, necessitating a fresh referendum, recourse to the people before the government agreed to amend the *existing* treaties was not required by the constitutional amendment. As Murphy and McMahon have commented, in joining the EEC the Irish were joining a dynamic, not static, Community. 'It was a commitment to a moving train. The Irish people might not have known where exactly the journey would terminate, but they committed themselves to a forward movement.'[108] Conversely, had the Treaty been so drastically altered as to remove its predominantly economic nature, this might require a referendum.[109]

---

[106] These articles are titled, respectively, 'Personal Rights', 'The Family', 'Education', 'Private Property', 'Religion'.

[107] McMahon and Murphy (1989) 265, McMahon (1976) 87.

[108] McMahon and Murphy (1989) 267.   [109] McMahon (1976) 87.

The second sentence of the constitutional amendment can be divided into two parts. The first protected from constitutional challenge governmental acts 'consequent on' Community membership. The second protected Community acts from such challenge. These provisions proved highly controversial, since they removed from the Supreme Court its right to invalidate measures on constitutional grounds.

Justin Keating considered the first part of the second sentence scandalous, since it meant that simply by showing that a law or act was consequent upon EEC membership, recourse to the constitution would be swept away.[110] As for the second part, Community provisions would have force of law in the State even if they violated the constitution.[111] Keating was also mindful that, despite Labour's criticism of the 1937 constitution, the Supreme Court, which had 'enshrined a good deal of liberties', would find itself subservient to the European Court.[112] Barry Desmond (Labour, Dun Laoghaire & Rathdown) considered it dangerous to remove the constitutional sanction from a broad area of Irish legislation because it would change the 'whole environment of legislative thought'.[113] Irish governments would be able to flout the constitution simply by finding some tenuous link with EEC law.[114]

Although Fine Gael eschewed this generalized attack on the diminution of judicial review, they considered it essential that the Supreme Court retain the right to invalidate Community norms and implementing measures which violated the fundamental rights in Articles 40–44 of the constitution. Fine Gael did not envisage any legal problems with such a qualified acceptance of Community law.[115] It is unclear whether Fine Gael wanted Ireland to make a unilateral qualification to the supremacy doctrine, similar to that made by the German courts in *Internationale Handelsgesellschaft*,[116] or whether they considered that it would be possible to negotiate a protocol with the other Member States.

As it was, Fine Gael again retreated. At the Committee stage on 25 January 1972 Liam Cosgrave announced that on reconsidering and further examining the Bill, Fine Gael had decided not to press its amendments regarding involvement of the State in war and fundamental human rights since the

---

[110] Dáil, 257, col 1077, 2 December 1971.   [111] Ibid, col 1078, 2 December 1971.
[112] Ibid, cols 1081 and 1091, 2 December 1971.   [113] Ibid, col 1131, 2 December 1971.
[114] Ibid, col 1132, 2 December 1971. This quotation provides an interesting contrast with the British Labour Party's pre-1990s hostility to judicial 'sanctions' in the context of British proposals for a Bill of Rights.
[115] Ibid, col 1298, 2 December 1971 (Richie Ryan).
[116] [1972] CMLR 177, [1974] 2 CMLR 540.

specific terms of the Treaty in no way affected the relevant articles of the constitution.[117]

Cosgrave confirmed that Fine Gael would accordingly only move its amendment to delete 'consequent on' and substitute 'necessitated by the obligations of' membership. He continued: '[w]e expressed some concern about other sections but on reflection we decided the best way is to put this as clearly as possible—to put the issue, when the Act is put before the people, not in a complicated way by discussing matters not in it.'[118]

Ostensibly, therefore, within the scope of application of the Treaty, Irish fundamental rights were to be sacrificed purely to make the constitutional amendment more straightforward to the electorate. In view of the veneration of the Irish for their constitution, is it not more convincing to argue that the inclusion of a human rights guarantee would have made the constitutional amendment *more* attractive to voters? Fine Gael's retreat reflected the highly bipartisan approach to Community membership between the two major parties. This was reinforced by the fact that Fine Gael's sole surviving amendment was accepted by the government at Committee stage without controversy.

In fairness, the government made it quite clear that the object of the constitutional amendment was to diminish the Supreme Court's role. As Dr Hillery told the Seanad:

The application of the Treaty of Rome to Ireland would require that some of the institutions of Europe in relation to certain aspects of the Treaty of Rome would take the functions reserved for institutions here like our Supreme Court. Our Constitution could prevent the application of the Treaty of Rome to Ireland. Basically this is why changes in the Constitution are necessary.[119]

As if to compensate for the Supreme Court's loss of authority, the Taoiseach presented a misleadingly rosy picture of the opportunities for judicial review before the ECJ. He asserted that 'anyone may have recourse to the Court in respect of regulations and decisions of the Communities which affect him'[120]—overlooking the restrictive standing rules for non-privileged applicants.[121] He also suggested that Article 177 references were mandatory for courts dealing with questions of the interpretation of Community law.[122]

It is notable that Deputies were concerned with defending the Supreme Court's ability to uphold Irish constitutional rights but paid scant attention to

[117] Dáil, 258, col 395, 25 January 1972.
[118] Ibid, col 396, 25 January 1972.
[119] Seanad, 71, col 1406, 18 November 1971.
[120] Dáil, 257, col 1071, 2 December 1971.
[121] See generally Craig (1994).
[122] Dáil, 257, col 1071, 2 December 1971.

the fact that Community membership would provide an expansive new ground for judicial review of national legislation (and administrative actions) by all domestic courts and tribunals, namely incompatibility with Community law. The Irish attitude provides an instructive contrast with the British situation, where although MPs were similarly unaware of the enhanced judicial power involved in Community membership, unlike their Irish counterparts they were almost entirely uninterested in the position of the national courts.

The status of the constitutional amendment

Ostensibly the constitutional amendment sought to establish the primacy of Community legislation over the Irish constitution. However, the new Article 29.4.3° was also *itself* widely perceived as a 'super-Article', prevailing over any conflicting provision of the constitution, even those relating to fundamental rights, because of the words '[n]o provision of this Constitution invalidates . . .' in the second sentence. The dominant academic view was expressed by John Temple Lang:

> The amendment probably unnecessarily ensures that any Community legislation which in its content . . . is incompatible with eg the fundamental human rights provisions of the Irish Constitution (Arts 40–44) will nevertheless be beyond challenge on constitutional grounds in the Irish courts. On this interpretation, the only limitations under Irish law will be those laid down by the Treaties themselves. . . . The amendment has therefore eliminated any chance of conflict between the Constitution of Ireland and Community law.[123]

An opposing view has been put by Kelly, who suggested that the principle of harmonious interpretation of the constitution (ie that all articles share the same legal status) makes it questionable whether Article 29.4.3° qualifies the rest of the constitution.[124]

Legislators appear to have assumed that Article 29.4.3° *would* prevail over all others. For example David Andrews (Parliamentary Secretary to the Taoiseach) told the Seanad that the amendment was required to remove the incompatibilities between the Treaty of Rome and constitutional provisions. So, for instance, the constitutional amendment would ensure that Article 34 would not prevent the ECJ from exercising its jurisdiction.[125] The point was

---

[123] Temple Lang (1972) 168–169.   [124] Kelly (1994) 284–285.
[125] Seanad, 72, col 512, 24 February 1972.

not lost on the Third Amendment Bill's opponents. Labour Leader Brendan Corish noted that the constitutional amendment overrode all other articles of the constitution;[126] Justin Keating pointed out that, in effectively abrogating many sections of the constitution, it bypassed the people;[127] Dr John O'Donovan (Labour, Dublin South Central) considered that its real effect would be to abolish the constitution.[128]

It is ironic that the government accorded the constitutional amendment such pre-eminent status in view of the Taoiseach's response to Fine Gael's short-lived attempt to make the constitution's fundamental rights provisions prevail over Community law: '[t]he Constitution is the fundamental law of this country and there would be no obvious criterion by reference to which any Articles could be classified as being more fundamental than others.'[129]

Constitutional issues in the referendum campaign

At the start of the campaign, four citizens launched an abortive legal challenge to the constitutionality of the Third Amendment Act.[130] Their statement of claim argued that (*a*) the Community treaties were repugnant to the constitution, and in particular to various articles of it; (*b*) those articles must therefore be amended; (*c*) the Act's provisions were contrary to Article 46(1); and (*d*) the parties were entitled to a referendum vote on each specific article.[131] Without explanation, the action was withdrawn before preliminary hearing.

The referendum campaign generated few new arguments on sovereignty. The main pro-Community pressure group, the Irish Council of the European Movement, published a series of leaflets, one of which was entitled 'Sovereignty'.[132] This placed heavy emphasis on the unanimity requirement and asserted that membership was not an irreversible handing-over but that Ireland could, simply by ceasing to accept the rules, automatically drop out of membership. The Community, it argued, had no army or other force to compel countries to remain in membership. The rival Common Market Study

---

[126] Dáil, 257, col 1371, 2 December 1971.   [127] Ibid, col 1104, 2 December 1971.
[128] Dáil, 258, cols 572–575, 26 January 1972.   [129] Dáil, 257, col 1726, 9 December 1971.
[130] The four were: Dr Vincent Barry, President of the Royal Irish Academy, G H C Crampton, chairman of a firm of building contractors, Michael Mullen, General Secretary of the Irish TGWU, and Maire Comerford, journalist.
[131] *Irish Times*, 28 April 1972.
[132] *Understanding EEC No. 4: Sovereignty* (Irish Council of the European Movement).

Group's pamphlet, *The Common Market: Why Ireland Should Not Join*, suggested that the surrender of sovereignty involved in membership was unique because the extent to which the power of individual decision was being renounced was unknown at the time of signing the Treaty. Accordingly it was more akin to a state joining the USA than to a country entering an international agreement. The role of the ECJ was highlighted, and its superior status to the Supreme Court was emphasized. 'The Court . . . is the supreme court of appeal so far as the Treaty is concerned, and individual governments, firms and organizations within the EEC must conform to its judgments, which overrule national law and national Supreme Courts.'[133] Labour continued to stress that the omnibus amendment hid the true extent of the abandonment of national sovereignty.[134] Brendan Corish argued that the people were being asked to sign away that basic and fundamental right enshrined in the constitution which limited the power of the Dáil by preventing it from enacting legislation in conflict with the fundamental rights of the State. Furthermore, 'in any situation which we consider hostile to Irish interests, in the future, there is nothing we could do by having recourse to our own Constitution in the courts to block or prevent any measure carried out by the European Communities'.[135]

As the campaign wore on, the sovereignty issue became increasingly emotive. Liam Cosgrave argued that by voting 'Yes', the Irish people would be following in the traditions of Wolfe Tone and Arthur Griffith;[136] Corish countered that surrendering Irish sovereignty would be a betrayal of the 1916 Proclamation.[137] Fianna Fáil's final full-page advertisement ludicrously asserted that: '[j]oining a prosperous Europe will mean an immensely better future for all of us; and joining does not mean that we sacrifice control of our affairs. We will retain control of our land and housing, of our education, health, of our industry and agriculture, and of our social, economic, cultural and political affairs.'[138]

On the other side of the divide, the Common Market Defence Campaign sent leaflets to each convent and monastery claiming that membership would be a blow to Christianity.[139] Their eve-of-poll advertisement urged voters not to betray the rights and liberties 'dearly bought by the blood and tears of some of the noblest and bravest men and women any country ever produced'.[140]

---

[133] Ibid 21.
[134] *Irish Times*, 1 May 1972, reporting speech by Sean Treacy TD.
[135] Ibid, 5 May 1972.
[136] Ibid, 9 May 1972.
[137] Ibid, 6 May 1972.
[138] Ibid, 8 May 1972.
[139] Ibid.
[140] Ibid, 10 May 1972.

Political and press consensus helped achieve a 'yes' victory. So too did the fact that, with British entry seemingly certain, Ireland's accession was no longer a choice between entry and the status quo.[141] The possibility of associate status was presented throughout as a non-starter. Indeed Fianna Fáil used press advertisements to ram home their argument that '[i]t's either in or out—association just isn't on. . . . There's no middle course.'[142]

In the event, the result of the poll was 1,041,880 for, 211,888 against, on a 71 per cent turnout. This represented slightly more than 58 per cent *of the total electorate* voting for membership, 29 per cent abstaining, and only 12 per cent voting against.[143] Lynch claimed that the victory had exceeded his expectations.[144] The *Irish Press* pointed out that the result was the most decisive response by the electorate since the Sinn Fein landslide of 1918.[145] Commentators noted a high correlation between the 'yes' vote and support for Fianna Fáil and Fine Gael in the elections which preceded and followed the referendum.[146]

European Communities Bill 1972

Since the constitutional amendment did not of itself incorporate Community law into Irish law, on 25 October 1972 the Dáil was asked to approve the European Communities Bill, section 2 of which provided that

From the 1st day of January 1973, the treaties governing the European Communities and the existing and future acts adopted by the institutions of those Communities shall be binding on the State and shall be part of the domestic law thereof under the conditions laid down in those treaties.

The treaties were defined in section 1, together with a provision to add future treaties to the definition by affirmative vote of both Houses. Section 3 authorized ministers to make regulations 'for enabling section 2 of this Act to have full effect', and, as in Britain, these regulations could repeal or amend any other law, including primary legislation. Controversially, section 4 provided that ministerial regulations would have statutory effect subject to being confirmed by an Act of the Oireachtas passed no later than the end of the year following that in which they were made.

---

[141] McAleese (1977) 144.   [142] *Irish Press*, 1 May 1972.   [143] Keatinge (1973) 144.
[144] *Irish Times*, 12 May 1972.   [145] *Irish Press*, 12 May 1972.
[146] Coakley (1983) 51.

Ostensibly there was no equivalent to section 3(1) of the British Act, making ECJ principles binding on national courts. However, these principles were presumably imported into the Irish legal system by the phrase 'under the conditions laid down in those treaties' in section 2. Those 'conditions' would include Article 164 EEC, that '[t]he Court of Justice shall ensure that in the interpretation and application of this Treaty the law is observed', and this would doubtless furnish the required nexus.

Supremacy of Community law

This was not clear enough for Charles Haughey, who moved in Committee that the following be added to section 2: 'and in cases of conflict shall prevail over any other part of the domestic law now in force or hereafter to be enacted or to come into force'. Haughey's amendment was aimed in particular at leaving *Irish* courts in no doubt as to which law prevailed.[147] It is notable that his amendment would be wide enough to deal with incompatibility between Community law and constitutional provisions—underlining the curious phenomenon of an Act of the Oireachtas purporting to lay down a hierarchy of norms between two forms of law higher than itself.[148]

Two Deputies, James Tully[149] and Oliver J Flanagan,[150] opposed the amendment on the grounds that the Oireachtas should have the right consciously to pass a law contrary to Community law, Flanagan raising the spectre of divorce and abortion becoming 'binding in the Community'. Vivion de Valera suggested that if this occurred, then the solution would be to reject Community membership *in toto*.[151] The government's position, however, was that it was unnecessary to spell out the supremacy of Community law since, in Hillery's words, 'Community law within the areas covered by the Bill prevails and that is that. What we put in this Bill does not change that.'[152]

This statement suggests that—in contrast to the British government—the Irish government assumed that once the Bill was in force it would be legally impossible for the Oireachtas to legislate contrary to Community law, even if

147 Dáil, 263, col 944, 7 November 1972.
148 If one takes the view that this was not achieved by the constitutional amendment.
149 Ibid, col 933, 7 November 1972.   150 Ibid, col 937, 7 November 1972.
151 Ibid, col 938, 7 November 1972.
152 Dáil, 263, col 939, 7 November 1972. Hillery possibly shared the author's view that the constitutional amendment itself provided for the importation of direct effect and supremacy into the Irish legal system.

it attempted to do so intentionally and expressly. Furthermore it also implies that the quality of supremacy did not owe its existence to anything in the 1972 Act. It is paradoxical that Hillery perceived the supremacy of Community law as immutable just as Sir Geoffrey Howe considered that the sovereignty of Parliament was 'inescapable and enduring'. As a result of the government's opposition, Haughey withdrew his amendment.

Judicial review 1: Irish courts preventing governmental abuse in the name of Community law

At second stage Lynch told the Dáil that the Oireachtas would have no function in the implementation of most Community legislation since it was directly applicable. This, he stated, was part and parcel of the limitations of freedom of action at national level which Community membership involved—something which had been fully appreciated by Deputies and the electorate. As for ministerial regulations made under section 3, 'our courts will be the ultimate safeguard against any attempted use of the section in excess of the powers conferred'.[153] Once more, this quotation reflects the centrality accorded to the role of the courts in Irish public life. It is not the sort of comment that was made in the House of Commons, despite judicial review of delegated legislation being well established in the UK. Yet, as discussed above, Lynch's confidence in the Irish courts' role in striking down *ultra vires* abuses of section 3 was at best naïve. Whether ministerial regulations were 'necessitated by' Community obligations would rest on the interpretation of those obligations—generally a function not of the national courts but of the ECJ, which was unlikely to accord such obligations a restrictive construction if *Van Gend* and *Costa* were anything to go by. Some Deputies seemed to sense this; for example Patrick Cooney (Fine Gael, Longford-Westmeath) could not see how the courts could be a safeguard since it would scarcely be possible to exceed such excessive powers.[154] James Tully did 'not buy for one moment the Taoiseach's comment that the courts are there to protect. . . . We will be in the EEC. We have decided to go in and, once we are in, we are stuck there, warts and all.'[155]

---

[153] Dáil, 263, col 97, 25 October 1972.   [154] Ibid, col 230, 25 October 1972.
[155] Ibid, col 128, 25 October 1972.

Judicial review 2: Irish courts ensuring compliance with Community law

Significantly there was little discussion of the new power that national courts would enjoy to set aside Irish laws in favour of conflicting Community law. John Bruton suggested that if a directive were not implemented promptly there might be some difficulty in deciding whether an individual could sue in the Irish courts to have its provisions enforced.[156] His colleague Richie Ryan suggested that if the State failed to fulfil its obligations, an action would lie against it. If a remedy were unavailable in the Irish courts, it would be available in the Community court.[157] However, Hillery retorted that 'it is true that if you had to force a government to do its job it is through the institutions of the Community that you would have to make your approach, not through a section of our own legislation'.[158] This misleadingly suggests that aggrieved individuals could not exploit domestic legal machinery but would presumably have to rely on the Commission to bring enforcement proceedings. Such underemphasis on the role of national courts in enforcing Community law has strong echoes in the British debate.

Hillery (unlike Geoffrey Howe and Geoffrey Rippon) recognized that directives could have direct effect, and that the question of whether specific directives were directly effective was ultimately for the ECJ.[159] Quizzed further on this point by Mary Robinson in the Seanad, he cited *SpA SACE* and *Grad* as cases in which directives and decisions had been held directly effective.[160]

Passage of the Bill

The Fianna Fáil/Fine Gael consensus broke down over the issue of the role of the Oireachtas in the implementation of Community obligations and its participation in the Community legislative process. These issues, though intrinsically important, are peripheral to the main themes of this book, since—unlike the anti-Marketeers in Britain—there was no question that Fine Gael accepted the concept of direct applicability and that their demands fell within the constraints of Community law. They will therefore be dealt

[156] Ibid, cols 1011–1012, 8 November 1972.   [157] Ibid, col 1016, 8 November 1972.
[158] Ibid, col 1017, 8 November 1972.   [159] Ibid, cols 1026–1027, 8 November 1972.
[160] Seanad, 73, col 942, 23 November 1972.

with briefly. Fine Gael and Labour rejected *ex post* confirmation of ministerial regulations, arguing instead that these should be subject to prior approval by Dáil Éireann, which should be able to amend, not just reject, them.[161] In addition there should be limitations on the ministerial right to make regulations similar to those in the British Act.[162] The opposition parties also wanted a Dáil committee which would (*a*) determine whether individual directives should be implemented by delegated legislation or statute and (*b*) advise ministers on proposals coming before the Council. All draft Community regulations and directives should also be laid before both Houses for consultation.[163] Fine Gael emphasized that its motive was simply to prevent Irish ministers from 'going berserk and running amok' by exploiting their new powers.[164]

One amendment was particularly interesting from the point of view of the interplay between legislature and courts. Richie Ryan moved that all repeals and amendments to existing statutes be specified in a schedule to the Act. The government opposed this since '[m]any areas will not be clear, could not be clear. If there is a conflict the extent of it would have to be confirmed by our own courts and some by the European courts.'[165] This was a significant acknowledgement of the potential role of the Irish courts in enforcing Community law over Irish statutes, and denotes a deference to courts not shared by the British, who repealed various provisions of incompatible legislation in sections 4–12 and Schedules 3 and 4 of the British Act. It shows the same underlying philosophy evinced in the government's choice of a constitutional amendment which did not specify how other constitutional provisions were affected but left the matter to judicial determination. Irish politicians were happy to leave such decisions to courts in a way which British

---

[161] Amendment No 7, moved by James Tully (Labour, Meath) (Dáil, 263, col 1035, 8 November 1972). The amendment was defeated by 65 votes to 53.

[162] Amendment No 9, moved by Richie Ryan (Dáil, 263, cols 1152–1153, 8 November 1972). It excluded from the scope of s 3 any regulations which *inter alia* imposed or increased taxation, operated retrospectively, created new criminal offences, conferred any power to limit the personal rights guaranteed by the constitution or the European Convention on Human Rights. The amendment was defeated by 59 votes to 48.

[163] Amendment No 13, moved by Richie Ryan, contained both this demand and the demand for a Dáil Committee (Dáil, 263, col 1194, 8 November 1972). The amendment was defeated by 58 votes to 46.

[164] Dáil, 263, col 1162, 8 November 1972.

[165] Ibid, col 1208, 8 November 1972, and cols 1232–1234, 9 November 1972 (Dr Hillery). Ryan counter-argued that the function of Parliament was to state the law (ibid, col 1242, 9 November 1972).

politicians were not, such was their reverence for the constitutional role of the judiciary. Ryan's amendment was defeated by 59 to 43.

Since all its amendments were voted down, Fine Gael, with Labour, opposed the Final Stage of the European Communities Bill, which was only passed in the Dáil by 58 to 45.

The epilogue was that the *ex post* system of parliamentary control proved unsatisfactory. The government railroaded its first and only confirmation Act through the Oireachtas without even making available the texts of the twenty-two regulations to be confirmed. The new coalition government introduced the European Communities (Amendment) Act 1973. This accorded full statutory effect to ministerial orders subject to a proviso that the Oireachtas could annul them on a recommendation of a new Joint Committee on the Secondary Legislation of the European Communities, also established by the Act.[166] One further aspect of the immediate aftermath deserves mention: Labour formed part of the new coalition, along with Fine Gael. On election night (28 February 1973) Corish, who was to become Tánaiste in the new government, immediately announced that the Labour Party would accept the verdict of the people in the 1972 referendum. Thus within two months of accession all three main parties had embraced Community membership.

Conclusion

Eighteen years after accession Jack Lynch felt able to declare, 'we went in with our eyes open . . . We knew exactly what we were doing, and there was no hidden agenda.'[167] The parliamentary debates largely bear this out. Familiarity with judicial invalidation of statute served to make Ireland's legislature far more acutely aware of the importance of the ECJ within the Community constitutional order and of the way in which membership would affect the role of the national courts. Yet this latter awareness was one-sided. Deputies were intensely preoccupied with the way in which Community provisions and national implementing measures would be immune from judicial review for breach of 'Eire-rights'. They were less perturbed at the prospect of the *national* courts being obliged to exercise a new and expansive jurisdiction to quash Irish legislation for breach of 'Euro-rights'. Perhaps, having chosen

[166] McMahon (1976) 89, Robinson (1973*b*) 352–354 and (1973*a*) 467–470.
[167] O'Mahony (1991) 122.

since the foundation of the Republic to eschew a sovereign Parliament, merely to add additional grounds for judicial review of Acts of the Oireachtas was less constitutionally objectionable than having to sacrifice fundamental rights embodied in the Irish constitution.

Furthermore both executive and legislature largely assumed that the decision as to whether a measure was 'necessitated by the obligations of membership' would lie solely within the domain of the Irish courts. This belief may have provided a reassuring quid pro quo to compensate for the fact that such measures would be exempt from constitutional review. However, Deputies were not made aware of the strong possibility that, in the normal course of events, the Irish courts would accept the ECJ's view of what was legally required of Community members, and that only in the most exceptional circumstances might the Supreme Court consider defiance.

With the benefit of hindsight, it is interesting to note in passing that the issue of whether an Irish court can, constitutionally, favour a fundamental Irish constitutional norm (ie a natural law right) over a competing Community law requirement remains a question which divides Irish academic lawyers to this day.[168] Indeed, only a year after accession, Walsh J (in the majority in the Supreme Court) held in *McGee v Attorney General*[169] that justice was placed above the law, that natural rights were not created by law, and that the State had no control over such rights. Von Prondzynski commented that such a natural law perspective places the guarantees of fundamental freedoms in Articles 40–44 above all other articles of the constitution, and that consequently provisions of those articles could be used to invalidate purported amendments of any part or parts of the constitution.[170] If natural law assumptions loomed so large in judicial minds in the 1960s/1970s, this makes it all the more interesting that there was no discussion whatsoever about the fundamental or supreme character of natural rights in the Oireachtas during the accession debates, and that the possibility of an Irish court according priority to a natural law right over a Community norm never occurred to legislators.[171] In this context the cross-fertilization of ideas between judiciary and legislature is curiously absent.

Nonetheless, Dáil Éireann was more aware than the House of Commons that there could be no evading the supremacy of Community law, and that

---

[168] Hogan and Whelan (1995) 7–16 and 121–142, cf Phelan (1997).
[169] [1974] IR 284.   [170] Von Prondzynski (1977) 35.
[171] It also makes it yet more curious that in contrast, at the same time, the government and most Deputies assumed that the Irish courts would hold a monopoly on determining whether legislation was 'necessitated by the obligations of membership'.

unilateral lawful withdrawal might prove impossible. The Irish legislature was also presented with, and had a better understanding of, the likely future development of the Community. To an extent the government—with a united backbench and cooperative main opposition party—could afford the 'luxury' of giving a more accurate perception of the Community constitutional order. Community membership was a consensus issue not, as in Britain, a politically sensitive one. However, unlike Britain, Ireland did not have to make the quantum leap from a political to a legal constitution. The limits on the legislative powers of the Oireachtas, the corresponding powerful role played by the nation's courts, and the veneration of Irish legislators for the judicial role served to make Irish accession less of a journey into the unknown. As a result the Oireachtas enjoyed a more realistic expectation of the constitutional shape of things to come.

6

From Accession to *Factortame*

We have seen little indication that MPs, in voting for Community membership at the various stages, were aware that accession would open up the possibility of national courts declining to enforce statutory provisions. This
chapter asks whether the initial experience of membership led to greater
awareness of the immense constitutional change to which parliamentarians
had unwittingly acquiesced. It examines parliamentary discourse during the
period between accession on 1 January 1973 and the Second Reading of the
Merchant Shipping Bill on 28 January 1988, the legislative genesis of the
Factortame saga which culminated in House of Lords approval of the ECJ's
supremacy doctrine.

The 1975 referendum

The years immediately following accession were marked by a striking lack of
interest on the part of MPs in the ECJ and Community legal principles. In
the parliamentary Sessions 1972–3, 1973–4, 1974, and 1975–6, there were
no debates and no questions, oral or written, in the House of Commons on
the ECJ or on the doctrines of supremacy and direct effect. The general
picture is of considerable discussion of substantive Community secondary
legislation, but in the absence of any direct conflict between Acts of
Parliament and Community provisions, no discussion of the supremacy
issue. The decision in *Van Duyn v Home Office*[1] that directives were capable of
having direct effect flatly contradicted what MPs had been told during the
passage of the 1972 Act, yet gave rise to just one written question, from Sir

[1] Case 41/74 [1974] ECR 1337, [1975] 1 CMLR 1.

Derek Walker-Smith, asking whether future directives would be so formulated as to preclude direct effect.[2]

The main relevant event of the UK's early years in the Community was the 1975 referendum on continued membership. Wilson had been converted by Tony Benn to the idea of a referendum as a means of uniting the Labour Party.[3] *Labour's Programme 1973* committed the Party to renegotiating the terms of entry, the most important constitutionally being '[t]he retention by Parliament of those powers over the British economy needed to pursue effective regional, industrial and fiscal policies'. Once again Labour's commitment to parliamentary sovereignty was not general, but rather restricted to ensuring that Parliament retained power to operate a progressive economic policy. If renegotiations proved successful, 'the people should have the right to decide the issue through a General Election or a Consultative Referendum'; if unsuccessful, 'we should not regard the Treaty obligations as binding on us. We shall then . . . consult [the British people] on the advisability of negotiating our withdrawal from the Communities.'[4] This formulation suggests that either Labour was prepared for Britain to flout Community law, or, more likely, it did not seriously envisage that the negotiations would be unsuccessful. Labour fought both 1974 general elections on this formula.

The Wilson government claimed that the outcome of the renegotiations preserved parliamentary supremacy on regional, industrial, and fiscal matters, but these claims were not particularly convincing. The government readily accepted that renegotiation did not mean Treaty revision,[5] so Britain would remain bound by the controversial Treaty provisions on state aids, Articles 92–94 EEC. Instead the government appeared satisfied with a restatement of Commission policy.

The Commission has acknowledged that national governments are the best judges of what is required in their own country and that the Commission will be prepared to consider changes in national aid systems compatible with the Common Market, when they are justified by problems of employment, unemployment, migration and by other valid requirements of regional development policy which constitute essential national problems.[6]

---

[2] HC, 893, cols 22–23w, 9 June 1975.
[3] Wilson (1979) 50–51. 'Labour M.P.s . . . were against entry, many of them regardless of the terms. But . . . a good number [of the pro-Market minority] believed more strongly in British membership than in any other tenet of policy, and would, if the choice had to be made, reject the Party in favour of what was to them the wider aim, Europe. . . . In all my thirteen years as Leader of the Party, I had no more difficult task than keeping the Party together on this issue.'
[4] *Labour's Programme 1973*, 134.   [5] Wilson (1979) 95.
[6] *Membership of the European Community* (1975) Cmnd 5999, 4.

The government did not explain why a supposedly permanent commitment, Community membership, should rest on an eminently changeable Commission policy. In any case, the Commission's formulation left it up to the Commission to determine when a national problem was 'essential', a notion perhaps as flexible as that of 'essential sovereignty' in the Heath era. As for industrial policy generally, Labour's programme was 'in no way incompatible with the Treaty, provided that the government's powers are not exercised so as to damage the competitive position of undertakings in other Member States—a principle which we accept, as we have in the case of regional policy'.[7] It is hard to see how substantial industrial investment could avoid as its corollary damage to the competitive positions of other undertakings, including those established in other Member States. Perhaps what this statement really reveals is that the government did not intend to pursue a particularly interventionist industrial programme. As for the issue of fiscal policy, this had 'not proved difficult. There are proposals for certain measures to harmonise the structure of some indirect taxes, but any which were objectionable to us would require our agreement.'[8]

The White Paper *Membership of the European Community: Report on Renegotiation*[9] covered the general issue of sovereignty, both national and parliamentary. It argued that no country nowadays enjoyed unqualified freedom of action, but that countries were increasingly coming together in interdependent groupings, each of which imposed rights and duties. However, the Community had certain distinctive features setting it apart from other such groupings, of which four warranted comment: the direct applicability of Community law (there were 'common rules applying uniformly . . . and not depending on separate national legislation'); the power of member governments through the Council; the role of the Commission; and the open-ended nature of the Community's future development. It is curious that the direct *effect* and supremacy of Community law and the power of the ECJ and the national courts were not considered to merit comment. This suggests that governmental understandings of the way in which Community law would work had in no way developed since accession.

As for the role of the UK Parliament, the White Paper stated that 'membership involves some changes in the position of Parliament and in its relationship with the Executive'. Parliament's relationship with the judiciary went unmentioned. It was recognized that membership involved reconciling

---

[7] *Membership of the European Community* (1975) Cmnd 5999, 5.   [8] Ibid 6.

[9] Cmnd 6003 (1975), paras 114–141.

the 'system of directly applicable law made by the Community with our constitutional principle that Parliament is the sovereign legislator and can make or unmake any law whatsoever'. The real source of the conflict—the ECJ's supremacy doctrine—was not discussed. The White Paper then reverted to Labour's 1967 arguments: that parliamentary sovereignty remains unaltered; that Parliament 'retains its ultimate right to legislate on any matter'; and that Parliament's compliance with Community obligations would depend on it voluntarily refraining from passing inconsistent legislation. Parliament had merely *delegated* legislative powers to the Community, and since it could repeal the 1972 Act, Community membership depended on the continuing assent of Parliament. The suggestion seemed to be that Parliament, as delegator, could retrieve *part of* its powers from the delegate as well as the whole of them. Moreover the White Paper tacitly assumed that government, not judiciary, determines whether the rules of parliamentary sovereignty survive Community membership.

Opposition as well as government played down the loss of sovereignty. In the Commons debate on continued membership Margaret Thatcher, now Opposition Leader, delivered a thirteen-column speech in favour of Community membership without a single mention of sovereignty.[10]

There were two debates prior to the referendum: the first on whether to approve the government's recommendation in favour of continued membership, the second on the Referendum Bill itself. The three-day debate on membership indicated that the arguments on sovereignty presented by each side had not evolved significantly since 1971. As in the pre-accession debates, pro-Market MPs counterposed traditional perceptions of sovereignty to real influence.[11] One subtle change was a greater willingness by some to tackle each other's competing ideas about sovereignty rather than simply pronounce on their own.[12] Enoch Powell for instance attacked the 'real influence/real power' argument as based on 'the largely illusory notion that Britain was once great because she had an Empire and is now small and weak

[10] HC, 889, cols 1021–1033, 8 April 1975. Rather Mrs Thatcher focused on peace, security, and economics.

[11] See eg Sir Geoffrey Howe (HC, 889, col 1139, 8 April 1975), Maurice Macmillan (Conservative, Farnham) (ibid, cols 1169–1170, 8 April 1975), and Michael Stewart (Labour, Fulham) (ibid, col 1290, 9 April 1975).

[12] By contrast Butler and Kitzinger (1996) noted a general lack of dialogue during the referendum campaign as a whole. They make the point that by and large 'each utterance [by a politician] tends to be an isolated event and is seldom directed to answering the arguments of the other side. Sometimes the observer has a sense of two entirely separate campaigns, each aimed against straw armies of their own devising' (160).

and must seek salvation in being submerged or merged in what is large and, by hypothesis, therefore powerful'.[13] He further argued that the 'we' who would benefit from any increase in power or influence would not be Britain but the Community; but that in any case the EEC would attain superpower influence only if it adopted a similar political structure to the USA or USSR, something which was not going to happen. On the opposing side, Brian Walden (Labour, Ladywood) thoroughly analysed the perceptions of sovereignty of his anti-Market comrades, concluding that they must be concerned with the preservation of parliamentary, rather than national, sovereignty, but that the referendum idea represented the most brazen affront to parliamentary sovereignty and that in any case 'what a member country [of the Community] finds insupportable it is not required to support'.[14] This was not the case. Although the UK could invoke the Luxembourg Compromise to veto new legislation, it could not prevent the application of unexpected ECJ decisions.

The Commission, not the ECJ, remained the only institution that inspired animosity. Even Wilson described it as 'over-large, over-bureaucratic, over-staffed and over-expensive'.[15] There was marginally more consciousness of the impact of direct effect. Three Members in the course of the three-day debate emphasized the role of the national courts in enforcing Community law. This may seem unimpressive, but it contrasts with the three mentions during the *entire passage* of the 1972 Act. Possibly this was in part attributable to the *Van Duyn* judgment of December 1974. The first was Richard Body (Conservative, Holland with Boston), who perceived the ECJ as

now the supreme court of this country. As long as we are members of the European Community, that court has the power to change our laws, because it acts quite differently from our own courts of law. Our own courts will interpret strictly the law as the European Court of Justice interprets the spirit of the law and in that way develops and changes the law of the Community.[16]

Admittedly it is not clear in this last sentence whether Body is simply drawing a distinction between the interpretative technique of the national courts and the ECJ, or whether he is referring to the national courts' obligation under section 3(1) of the 1972 Act to follow ECJ interpretations. However, it is significant that Body linked two objections: the ECJ's new constitutional status and its teleological interpretative approach. The second MP was Doug Hoyle (Labour, Nelson & Colne), who noted that '[i]f necessary, [the

---

[13] HC, 889, cols 1300–1302, 9 April 1975.   [14] Ibid, cols 1037–1039, 8 April 1975.

[15] Ibid, col 832, 7 April 1975.   [16] Ibid, cols 1182–1183, 8 April 1975.

Commission] can overrule our laws, passed in Parliament, by going to our courts. We could have the ludicrous situation when an appeal could go to the House of Lords and could overrule the Commons.'[17] The fact that Hoyle equated 'Parliament' with 'the Commons' again shows the gulf between political and legal thinking. Additionally it is not the Commission which applies to the national courts but individual litigants. It was precisely the ECJ's harnessing of the 'people-power' of individual litigants concerned to protect their rights at national level which made the enforcement of Community law so effective. Finally, Reginald Maudling, winding up for the Opposition, gave perhaps the first establishmentarian defence of direct effect:

> Of course, it is true that the Treaty involves the acceptance and enforcement by the British courts of Community law. But there are many examples of treaties which oblige us to enact legislation which is effective in the British courts. I cannot see very great differences in practice between being obliged ourselves to enact the legislation or telling the courts to follow legislation which has been enacted by a body of which we are a member.[18]

Maudling omits to discuss his opponents' most strongly held objection, that the national courts are obliged to accord precedence to such Community legislation over subsequent Acts of Parliament.

One pervasive issue was new; that the House was considering *withdrawal.* Curiously MPs at no point considered whether withdrawal would be unilateral or effected by Treaty amendment. If the former were the case, this would involve breaching a Treaty obligation since the Community was of unlimited duration. If the latter were the case, no Treaty breach would be involved. Parliamentarians simply proceeded on the basis that withdrawal would be unilateral. As Margaret Thatcher put it, '[f]or Britain to abrogate a treaty is bad for Britain, bad for our relations with the rest of the world and bad for our future trading relationships'.[19] The same theme was echoed by Opposition spokesmen Reginald Maudling[20] and Sir Geoffrey Howe,[21] indicative of a coordinated effort. Veteran anti-Marketeer Sir Derek Walker-Smith was so wary of the breach of international law involved, combined with Britain's potential loss of reputation, that he voted for continued membership.[22]

The House approved the government's pro-membership position by 396 votes to 170, Labour MPs voting 137 for and 145 against.[23]

---

[17] Ibid, cols 1160–1161, 8 April 1975.
[18] Ibid, cols 1351–1352, 9 April 1975.
[19] Ibid, col 1033, 8 April 1975.
[20] Ibid, cols 1343–1344, 9 April 1975.
[21] Ibid, cols 1134–1135, 8 April 1975.
[22] Ibid, cols 1309–1314, 9 April 1975.
[23] Wilson (1979) 105. Wilson records that 'seven Cabinet ministers, and thirty-one ministerial other ranks, exactly half the juniors, voted against the Government' (ibid 104).

The debate on the Referendum Bill focused mainly on the compatibility of referendums with parliamentary democracy, an issue which falls outside the scope of this book. However, in moving Second Reading, Leader of the House Edward Short presented the effects of Community membership on parliamentary sovereignty as the main justification for holding the referendum. In so doing Short equated 'ultimate sovereignty' solely with the right to withdraw.

Sovereignty was an important issue in the campaign itself, but again the ECJ was hardly mentioned. Seemingly the only attack on it from a politician came from Eric Heffer who described it as the most important organ of the Community and thought that it harmed democracy since it could override not only Community decisions but the government, Parliament, and constitution of every Member State. He further noted that the courts had 'disallowed' laws passed by the Italian, Dutch, and Belgian Parliaments.[24] In contrast Michael Foot and Enoch Powell both wrote major *Times* articles on sovereignty without mentioning the ECJ or national courts, Foot lambasting instead 'the bureaucratic meshes of the Brussels Commission' and 'the secret or semi-secret lawmaking processes of the Council . . . a dumb legislature',[25] Powell focusing entirely on the loss of parliamentary self-government.[26]

Academic lawyers and government law officers also entered the fray. Disagreement focused on at least three issues. The first issue involved the scope of Community law. Lord Elwyn-Jones LC rehashed the argument of his predecessors, that the legal changes involved in membership would not affect the ordinary citizen,[27] and William Whitelaw said that Community law only existed for a few commercial and industrial purposes.[28] These claims were rebutted by former Solicitor General Sir Arthur Irvine QC and also by Professor Wedderburn who pointed out that Community law applied to the fields of industry, jobs, prices, food, and energy—fields which affected the citizen far more than criminal law.[29] The second issue was the ECJ's teleological interpretative technique. There was an exchange between Irvine, who feared that English common law, with its 'careful rules of interpretation', would be influenced by the ECJ's purposive technique whereby judges had regard to 'such novel objectives as the advancement of European unity',[30] and Solicitor General Peter Archer QC, who did not deny the likely

---

[24] *The Times*, 29 May 1975.   [25] Ibid, 23 May 1975.   [26] Ibid, 4 June 1975.

[27] Ibid, 28 May 1975.

[28] Ibid, 5 May 1975. This claim was repeated in Britain in Europe's 'Why You Should Vote Yes' pamphlet.

[29] *The Times*, 28 May 1975.   [30] Ibid, 5 May 1975.

influence of Community law but thought this would benefit English law.[31] The third issue related to the ability of Community law to bind successor Parliaments. Patrick Neill QC of All Souls said that the European Communities Act overthrew centuries of established constitutional law and tradition by making an Act purporting to repeal Community law impossible.[32] Wedderburn agreed that the electorate was now unable to eliminate a Community provision by voting out a government; new Parliaments were irrevocably bound by Community regulations agreed by ministers in earlier Parliaments.[33] Lord Advocate Ronald King Murray QC rejected the White Paper's proposition that Community law involved delegation: delegation meant giving power to a subordinate body for subsidiary ends whereas 'the powers conferred on Brussels are transferred to a superior authority which can overrule British law for economic ends which are far-reaching'.[34]

Both the 'Yes' and 'No' campaigns were permitted government-financed pamphlets which were delivered to every household together with a pamphlet outlining the government's position. Almost a quarter of the government's pamphlet was devoted to parliamentary sovereignty.[35] It argued that Parliament would not lose its power because:

1. No country, not even superpowers, enjoyed complete freedom of action, but this did not mean they lost their national identity.
2. No important new Community policy could be decided without the consent of a British minister answerable to a British government and Parliament. The Council, not the Commission, took the major decisions and Britain *always* had a veto. (It did not of course have a veto over ECJ decisions, but this was not mentioned.)
3. Parliament retained the final right to repeal the 1972 Act and withdraw Britain from the Community.
4. The new terms protected our national interests—the essence of sovereignty.
5. The Commons had voted by 396 to 170 in favour of staying in.

With regard to the third point above, it is interesting that the government did not repeat its White Paper mantra that Parliament would retain 'its ultimate right to legislate on any matter'.

The 'Yes' pamphlet reprised the 'real influence' argument, contending that much of the argument about sovereignty was false because 'it's not a

---

[31] Ibid, 10 May 1975.   [32] Ibid, 28 May 1975.   [33] Ibid.
[34] Ibid, 30 May 1975.   [35] *Britain's New Deal in Europe.*

matter of dry legal theory'.[36] The 'No' pamphlet emphasized that, since Community law prevailed over British law, the right of the British electorate, by their votes, to change laws and policies in Britain would steadily dwindle.[37]

The press (except the *Morning Star*) lined up solidly in favour of continued membership throughout the campaign. There was some comment by the broadsheets on the subject of sovereignty. The *Guardian* noted that '[w]hen the pro-Marketeers say we would have more of it, and the anti-Marketeers flatly contradict this and say we would have less of it, it is clear that they are not talking about the same thing'.[38] Pro-Marketeers equated sovereignty with the power to control the political environment in which the nation lived, whilst anti-Marketeers saw it as a juridical matter, that the state—large or small, powerful or weak—should be the source of all law and legitimate public authority. It would assist the debate, the editorial concluded, if these two distinct conceptions of sovereignty could be disentangled and kept separate.

More generally, the press concentrated on the Labour Left's motives for opposing membership. As William Whitelaw put it, 'sovereignty is being used as a catchword to service the interest of many people who believe in an extreme form of socialism'.[39] The *Daily Telegraph* predicted that Labour might break up since '[u]nderlying whatever unity may appear on the surface there were always profound cleavages about the uses to which power, once achieved, should be put. To isolate Britain into a fully socialist siege economy, or to cooperate in a mixed economy with others; that is the cleavage about Europe.'[40] Similarly the *Guardian* noted that '[s]ome of the anti-Market heat stems from the belief that the European Community is a capitalist affair. From this comes the fear of interference with British industry and of a brake on socialist policies. Yet, as the Foreign Secretary said, neither the Commission nor anyone else can or will challenge the effective management of a mixed economy which is the government's stated aim.'[41] It should perhaps be noted that the 1974–9 Labour *government's* 'stated aims' on economic policy were quite different from the Labour *Party's*. Its 1973 programme had included, in Harold Wilson's words, the 'outlandish proposal to commit the party to nationalise 25 of the 100 biggest companies'.[42] *The Times* too focused

[36] *Why You Should Vote Yes: A Statement by Britain in Europe.*
[37] *Why You Should Vote No: A Statement by the National Referendum Campaign.*
[38] *Guardian*, 19 April 1975.   [39] *The Times*, 19 April 1975.
[40] *Daily Telegraph*, 11 April 1975.   [41] *Guardian*, 11 April 1975.
[42] Wilson (1979) 30.

on the gulf between social democrats and socialists in the Party and linked Community membership to the survival of the mixed economy.[43]

In the event 17,378,581 (67.2 per cent) electors voted 'Yes' whereas 8,470,073 (32.8 per cent) voted 'No', a majority of 8,908,508.

From referendum to Single European Act

There was no discussion of the ECJ in the Commons in 1976–7 and 1978–9 and just two written questions in 1977–8. There were five written questions in 1979–80, one in 1980–1, none in 1981–2, four in 1982–3, and two in 1983–4. The same general picture reasserted itself of a vast amount of discussion on Community matters but no discussion of the sovereignty issue.

Two themes emerge from the very few questions asked. The first was that far from being concerned about the UK's own national/parliamentary sovereignty, MPs seemed more anxious that ECJ judgments should prevail in *all* Member States. Commission research had shown that more than 50 per cent of enforcement judgments were not being implemented within a year.[44] Thus in November 1979 Shadow Attorney General John Morris asked Sir Michael Havers AG what state assistance was available to British nationals to sue other Member States in their own national courts for disregarding an ECJ judgment. The Attorney General replied that legal aid was only available for UK proceedings. Morris also asked if he would make a statement as to what legal action if any could be taken to enforce ECJ judgments in the Member States, for example damages actions. Oddly the Attorney General simply replied 'No'.[45] Perhaps his refusal to be drawn reflects the fact that Member States prefer to leave enforcement actions to the Commission rather than face the diplomatic opprobrium of suing their 'European partners' themselves or actively inciting others to do so. The notion of exclusive reliance on the Commission to enforce Community law also fitted snugly into a somewhat less supranational perception of EEC constitutional arrangements. In March 1982 Tim Eggar (Conservative, Enfield North) moved a Private Member's Bill (later withdrawn) 'To provide for the temporary prohibition or restriction on imports of goods in transit from Member States which remain in breach of judgments of the Court of Justice of the European Communities.'[46] He instanced the ECJ's 1980 judgment in

---

[43] *The Times*, 10 April 1975.
[45] HC, 972, cols 642–643w, 1 November 1979.

[44] Audretsch (1986) 400.
[46] HC, 21, cols 320–322, 31 March 1982.

Commission v France[47] condemning discriminatory taxation against Scotch whisky, a decision ignored by the French government. A final example was a written question from Anthony Steen (Conservative, Liverpool Wavertree) in July 1984, asking the Foreign Secretary what steps were being taken to reduce infractions of Community law. The response of Foreign Office Minister of State Richard Luce was revealing: '[t]he United Kingdom has a clear interest in Community law being upheld. But under the Community Treaties it is the Commission which is responsible for ensuring that Community obligations are observed.'[48] Again the government disregarded direct effect, ignoring the ECJ's long-standing statement that 'the vigilance of individuals concerned to protect their rights amounts to an effective supervision in addition to . . . the diligence of the Commission and the Member States'.[49]

The second theme was concern at the ECJ's caseload. In July 1979 the Attorney General expressed the government's willingness to agree procedural amendments to remedy the ECJ's backlog.[50] Four years later he revealed that the UK was promoting the establishment of a staff tribunal to reduce substantially the number of staff cases coming before the ECJ.[51]

One might expect parliamentary comment on the leading Community law cases of the period, as well as the domestic cases on the application of Community law to the national legal system. Such comment was sparse.

It is significant, for instance, that *Macarthys v Smith*[52] provoked no political discussion. In it, Lord Denning MR suggested *obiter* that there could be no implied repeal of Community law. English courts, he maintained, would accord priority to statute over conflicting Community law only where Parliament 'deliberately passes an Act with the intention of repudiating the Treaty or any provision in it or intentionally of acting inconsistently with it and says so in express terms'.[53] Cumming-Bruce LJ agreed that if the ECJ held the Treaty to be incompatible with a UK statute, EC law would prevail. Conversely Lawton LJ emphasized that Parliament's recognition of EC law and ECJ jurisdiction by one enactment could be withdrawn by another: he would not presume to take any judicial step which it would be more appropriate for the House of Lords, as part of Parliament, to take.[54] Hood Phillips

---

[47]   Case 168/78 [1980] ECR 347, [1981] 2 CMLR 631.
[48]   HC, 64, cols 510–511w, 23 August 1984.
[49]   Case 26/62 *Van Gend en Loos* [1963] ECR 1, 13.
[50]   HC, 971, cols 352–353w, 26 July 1980.   [51]   HC, 46, cols 355–356w, 26 July 1983.
[52]   [1979] 3 All ER 325. Judgment of 19 July 1979.   [53]   Ibid 329 c–e.
[54]   Ibid 334 d–h.

thought that the differences between the judgments highlighted the need for clear House of Lords guidance on the constitutional effect of the 1972 Act.[55] If parliamentarians had any interest in court decisions, this divergence of judicial opinion would have underlined to them that the fate of parliamentary sovereignty now lay in judicial hands. When *Macarthys* returned from the ECJ, Lord Denning repeated three times that Community law prevailed over *any* inconsistent part of English law.[56] Whether this represented a change from his previous position was uncertain, but again his judgment inspired no parliamentary comment.[57]

Nor did *Garland v British Rail Engineering Ltd* elicit any criticism.[58] In it, Lord Diplock held that there was a strong presumption in favour of interpreting national legislation in conformity with Community obligations. His Lordship somewhat teasingly commented that the case before him was not an appropriate occasion to consider whether anything short of an express positive statement in an Act that a particular provision is intended to breach EC law would justify an English court in construing a statutory provision inconsistently with an EC obligation.[59] Again this could have brought home to MPs that the extent to which EC membership would modify parliamentary sovereignty was a matter for the courts. Indeed, Allan suggested that it 'seems only one step further to change the [statutory] language completely, (or ignore it) when there is no sign that Parliament foresaw or intended any conflict with Community law', thereby resolving the conflict between parliamentary sovereignty and EC law supremacy by stretching the concept of interpretation.[60] Clarke and Sufrin reached basically the same conclusion.[61]

As for ECJ case law, *Commission v United Kingdom (Beer and Wine)*[62] had profound fiscal policy implications, yet inspired neither a ministerial statement nor questions. Even where a judgment did attract comment, it is surprising how little controversy ensued. When *Simmenthal*[63] was decided Neil Marten asked the Attorney General for a statement on its implications, only to be told that the judgment accorded with previous ECJ decisions.[64] This was surely an inadequate dismissal of a decision which established that *every*

---

[55] Hood Phillips (1980).

[56] [1981] 1 QB 180, 200 D–G. Judgment of 17 April 1980.

[57] He attributed the supremacy of EC law to the 1972 Act rather than to entry into a new legal order. This suggests that the courts would recognize Parliament as being able to amend the Act.

[58] [1983] 2 AC 751. Judgment of 22 April 1982.   [59] Ibid 771 C–F.

[60] Allan (1982).   [61] Clarke and Sufrin (1983); cf Ellis (1980).

[62] Case 170/78 [1983] ECR 2265, [1983] CMLR 512.

[63] Case 106/77 [1978] ECR 629, [1978] 3 CMLR 263.

[64] HC, 946, col 560w, 22 March 1978.

UK court and tribunal was duty-bound to disapply Acts of Parliament which conflicted with Community law. (It is worth noting in passing that Hood Phillips wrote of *Simmenthal* at the time that 'we should expect United Kingdom courts not to ask the European Court for a preliminary ruling or to apply *Simmenthal (No 2)*, but to allow appeals all the way up to the House of Lords on a matter of national law; and we find it difficult to believe that the House of Lords in its judicial capacity would reject the legislative supremacy within the United Kingdom of the Parliament of which it is part'.[65])

In the entire period there was only one debate—brief and late at night—on the ECJ. In January 1980 the Attorney General moved 'That this House takes note of Council Documents Nos. R/2075/78 and 4679/79 on reorganisation of the Court of Justice and considers that any enlargement of the Court should take place only if a genuine need for it is clearly established.'[66] These documents suggested an increase in the numbers of ECJ judges and Advocates General to ease the ECJ's burden. Outlining the ECJ's work, Havers once again made it clear that the government considered preliminary rulings less significant than enforcement actions: '[o]f the first importance are cases brought by the Commission against a Member State . . . A second category of case [preliminary references] vary greatly in importance, depending on the principle of Community law that is being interpreted.'[67]

The debate gave a couple of anti-Marketeers the opportunity to air misgivings about the ECJ's constitutional role. Gwynneth Dunwoody, commenting that the House had not adequately discussed the ramifications of the Community institutions prior to accession, remarked that the ECJ 'is a very different institution from those we are used to. It has the right not just to look at legislation but to tell Member States and their legislatures not just that their existing legislation is not acceptable, but that they should change it. The average Briton is not used to that concept.'[68] Here Dunwoody makes the same mistake of placing emphasis on enforcement proceedings and thereby underestimating the ECJ's authority. A preliminary ruling interpreting Community law as incompatible with Member State measures issues an instruction not only to the national legislature to change the law but to the domestic courts to disapply the offending provision in the meantime. As Peter Archer remarked, there was nothing surprising in the concept of an international tribunal which could tell 'the almighty nation state' when it had infringed its obligations.[69]

---

[65] Hood Phillips (1979).
[66] HC, 977, cols 361–393, 22 January 1980.
[67] Ibid, col 362, 22 January 1980.
[68] Ibid, col 374, 22 January 1980.
[69] Ibid, col 386, 22 January 1980.

For Enoch Powell, the ECJ's assumption of a lawmaking role was not accidental. Where there is a written constitution, the interpretation of that constitution will lie with a court and not with any representative body. Like the United States Supreme Court, the ECJ would evolve its own principles of law, which again could not be corrected by any legislative body.[70] Interestingly, Powell also saw the ECJ's power as incompatible with the rule of law, although he appeared to be saying that the rule of law was the same thing as parliamentary sovereignty.[71]

A revealing remark was made by Peter Archer when he commented that there was nothing shocking in having international obligations relating to ordinary domestic life in a nation state.[72] Earlier statements that Community law would have little impact on 'ordinary domestic life' plainly lacked credibility by now.

Origin of the Single European Act

The impetus for the Single European Act (SEA), the first major amendment of the Treaty of Rome, stemmed from two aspirations. The first, about which the British government was enthusiastic, was to carry through the original Treaty aim of creating a common market.[73] The second, not shared by the British government, was to make further progress towards European integration.[74]

At the Milan summit of the European Council (28–9 June 1985), the Italian Presidency and Commission persuaded the Council to schedule an intergovernmental conference. Although Treaty amendments required common accord, the calling of an IGC merely demanded a majority vote.[75] Margaret Thatcher did not consider constitutional change necessary in order to carry through the single market legislative programme. As she told the House on her return: 'the United Kingdom's view was that some positive improvements in the Community's decision-making could have been decided in Milan and did not require any Treaty amendment.'[76] Nor did she

---

[70] Ibid, col 384, 22 January 1980.   [71] Ibid.   [72] Ibid, col 386, 22 January 1980.

[73] See eg *Completing the Internal Market*, White Paper from the Commission to the European Council (June 1985).

[74] See eg the European Union Draft Treaty, approved by the European Parliament on 14 February 1984, and the Dooge Report of March 1985 (Pinder (1995) ch 4). See also Thatcher (1993) 549–550.

[75] De Zwaan (1986), Grant (1994) 72.   [76] HC, 82, col 185, 2 July 1985.

favour the reform deemed necessary for market integration, namely the application of qualified majority voting to Article 100A:

One of those proposed Treaty amendments at the intergovernmental conference would change the unanimity rule, and I think most of us—I certainly—would wish to keep the unanimity rule on directives which could be quite vital to many of our industries. That is a matter that will be dealt with at the IGC and I thought that our proposals, which would not have required Treaty amendment, would be better. It is important that the internal market be completed, but I think it can be completed keeping the unanimity rule.[77]

She favoured a modest change to the Luxembourg Compromise (namely that the reasons for which it were used should be clearly expressed) as the only institutional reform required. She echoed Heath's emphasis on the importance of the veto to preserving the Community's *sui generis* status: '[w]e have fought for the British right to a veto. Where we have unanimity in the Treaty, it is inbuilt . . . Otherwise we still fight for the Luxembourg compromise. . . . I agree wholly . . . that there is no question of a federal Europe.'[78]

She asserted—citing statistics of Commission enforcement actions—that Britain's record in obeying Community law was one of the best. The persisting preoccupation with enforcement proceedings as the benchmark of compliance with Community norms is remarkable, when the fusion of direct effect, supremacy, and the preliminary reference procedure had long since proven more effective.

Government response

It is a matter of speculation why at the Luxembourg European Council (2–3 December 1995) Mrs Thatcher agreed to the SEA. In her memoirs she argues that it was right to sign it in order to achieve a single European market.[79] However, Grant suggests that the Foreign Office had to persuade her, just before midnight on the final day, that vetoing the Treaty changes would not be in the national interest, such was her fury with the Economic and Monetary Union chapter and much else.[80] Foreign Secretary Geoffrey Howe's memoirs fail to mention any prime ministerial reluctance to approve

---

[77] Ibid, col 189, 2 July 1985.
[78] Ibid, col 192, 2 July 1985 (answer to an oral question from Tony Marlow MP).
[79] Thatcher (1993) 557.
[80] Grant (1994) 73.

the Treaty changes; rather, he presents the SEA as a closely fought package ultimately satisfactory to the UK.[81] Nigel Lawson records that the Premier grudgingly allowed herself to be persuaded that majority voting was essential if the single market was ever to be achieved, consoling herself that the Luxembourg Compromise remained unaffected.[82]

On the day, *The Times* reported Thatcher as saying that she had not wanted to make the Treaty changes, 'but if they [the other Member States] wanted to do it this way, so be it'.[83] In reporting on the IGC, she was asked by Jonathan Aitken why she had reversed her previous position that no changes were necessary. She replied that Britain 'wanted something from our European partners and they wanted something from us. It seemed a reasonable compromise.'[84] It is difficult to identify this quid pro quo, in view of Thatcher's earlier insistence that the British goal, completion of the internal market, required no Treaty amendments whatever.

Select Committee response

The House of Lords Select Committee on the European Communities considered that the SEA would in the long term weaken the position of the UK Parliament.[85] Qualified majority voting, by reducing the power of UK ministers in the Council, would undermine accountability to Parliament.[86] As for the survival of the Luxembourg Compromise, despite government assurances it was questionable whether it could be invoked where the Commission, the majority of the European Parliament, and a qualified majority of Member States were united against Britain.[87] In particular, under the cooperation procedure the Council would only be able to reject amendments proposed by the European Parliament and adopted by the Commission if it voted them down unanimously. It was difficult to see how the Luxembourg Compromise could fit into this legislative arrangement. The Select Committee could perhaps usefully have added that in any case the powerful *political* momentum in favour of completing the single market in the wake of the SEA was likely to make the Luxembourg Compromise a less powerful tool.

---

[81] Howe (1994) 455–457.   [82] Lawson (1993) 889.

[83] *The Times*, 4 December 1985.   [84] HC, 88, col 436, 5 December 1985.

[85] *Single European Act and Parliamentary Scrutiny*, 12th Report of the House of Lords Select Committee on the European Communities (Session 1985–6) HL, 149, para 12.

[86] Ibid, para 13.   [87] Ibid, para 15.

In contrast the First Special Report from the House of Commons Select Committee on European Legislation was mealy-mouthed, doubtless reflecting its government majority but also its limited terms of reference compared to its Lords counterpart: it was restricted to scrutinizing Community legislation, so tended to neglect wider institutional questions.[88] It argued that the increase in majority voting 'would not affect the accountability of ministers to the House of Commons for their actions in Council',[89] but conceded that the extent to which the Luxembourg Compromise would survive was 'one uncertain element'.[90]

Media and academic response

The Times considered the SEA a 'modest but useful step forward in the development of the Community'. Interestingly, *The Times* still appeared to believe that Parliament could decline to give effect to directives.[91] The *Guardian* approved the Treaty changes as 'modestly historic'.[92] The *Daily Telegraph* also emphasized the 'extremely modest' nature of the reform package.[93] *The Economist* too was contemptuous of the SEA's 'tiny reform to the Rome Treaty'.[94]

However, after the initial reaction to the SEA changes, media interest waned. As Paul Johnson remarked, the SEA 'aroused no passion in the Cabinet, in the Commons or in the media'.[95] The Left appeared particularly uninterested; *New Statesman* contained nothing on the SEA, either in the wake of the Luxembourg statement or during the Bill's passage. The Right were seemingly more interested, the *Spectator* commenting that '[o]n 1 July Britain takes over the presidency of the EEC. During our six months of office, we could safeguard the sovereignty of the British Parliament, and also spare Europe a yet more unworkable bureaucracy, by taking any opportunity we can to scupper the Single European Act.'[96]

---

[88] Coombes (1981) 250.

[89] *The Single European Act and Parliamentary Scrutiny*, First Special Report from the Select Committee on European Legislation (Session 1985–6) HC, 265, para 21.

[90] Ibid, para 23.   [91] *The Times*, 6 December 1985 (emphasis added).

[92] *Guardian*, 5 December 1985.   [93] *Daily Telegraph*, 5 December 1985.

[94] *The Economist*, 22 February 1986.

[95] *The Times*, 23 January 1986. Johnson blamed 'the sheer soporific effect of the leaden jargon with which the EEC conceals its doings . . . combined with the trance-enducing character of Sir Geoffrey Howe'.

[96] *Spectator*, 27 June 1986.

As for academic comment, British constitutional journals showed little interest. *Public Law* in 1985, 1986, and 1987 contained only the skimpiest references to the SEA, and no analysis whatever. There was nothing on the SEA or Community in 1985, 1986, and 1987 *Political Quarterly*, nor did *Parliamentary Affairs* run a separate article on the SEA until 1988,[97] though Shell's 1987 annual summary of constitutional developments contained a short section on 'European Community' outlining the changes.[98] All in all, the UK and EEC constitutions were still seen as highly discrete subjects for academic study.

In contrast Community law and Community politics journals contained a wealth of comment. The *European Law Review* welcomed the SEA as the most significant step in *political* as well as economic integration since 1957.[99] The *Common Market Law Review* defended the SEA against critics who considered it meagre, observing that at one stage it hardly seemed likely that any Treaty amendments would be agreed on, and that the compromise nature of the SEA had spared the Community the most serious crisis of its existence.[100] The 1986 *Journal of Common Market Studies* contained a major article by Juliet Lodge characterizing the SEA as a pragmatic compromise aimed at safeguarding national interests in the face of pressures for greater Community action.[101]

ECJ case law

Two things should be noted about the ECJ's activities in the run-up to SEA incorporation. First, the number of enforcement actions against the UK had risen. In the first four years of Community membership there had been no ECJ judgments against the UK. However, in 1977 the Commission changed its enforcement strategy, eschewing a selective, cautious approach in favour of taking action against recalcitrant Member States as a matter of course.[102] As a result there were twelve judgments against the UK by 1983. As we have

---

[97] Judge (1988) 441–453.

[98] Shell (1987) 293–295. In its April 1989 issue Norton asserted that in the event of express repeal of Community law by an Act of Parliament, British courts would enforce the provisions of that Act, commenting that this gave the UK an option not enjoyed by many countries (Norton (1989) 142).

[99] (1986) 11 EL Rev 117.

[100] (1986) 23 CML Rev 251.

[101] Lodge (1985–6).

[102] Audretsch (1986) 279–289.

seen, politicians tended to place an unwarranted emphasis on the importance of Commission enforcement actions.

Secondly, during the Bill's passage, the ECJ made two controversial pre-liminary rulings on UK cases which provided ammunition for the SEA's opponents. The first was *Conegate Ltd v HM Customs & Excise*.[103] Here the ECJ decided that a Member State could not use its obscenity laws to prohibit importation of goods (here, blow-up sex dolls) which could be made and traded lawfully within it.[104] The reaction of Lord Denning was that the ECJ had misinterpreted Article 36 EEC and accordingly '[a]re we not entitled to go by the Treaty of Rome and to ignore these wrong decisions of the European Court? Or cannot we tell our courts to cock a snook at them?'[105]

The second case was *Drake v Chief Adjudication Officer*, in which the ECJ held that refusal to pay disability benefit to a married woman merely because she was married (where there was no such refusal to pay it to a married man) contravened Directive 79/7 on non-discrimination in social security.[106] The decision was all the more humiliating because the government 'caved in' the day before the judgment, permitting some 11,000 women to apply for the benefit.[107]

European Communities (Amendment) Bill 1986: content and progress

Incorporation of the SEA necessitated primary legislation since section 6 of the European Assembly (Elections) Act 1978 provided that where a treaty increased the powers of the European Parliament, it had to be approved by statute.[108] Clause 1 of the Bill included the SEA within the definition of 'Community treaties' for the purposes of the 1972 Act. Clause 2 expanded section 3(1) of the 1972 Act by obliging domestic courts to determine ques-tions of Community law in accordance with principles laid down by the ECJ *or any court attached thereto*—paving the way for the establishment of the Court of First Instance.

---

[103] Case 121/85 [1986] ECR 1679, [1986] 1 CMLR 739.   [104] *Guardian*, 12 March 1986.

[105] Ibid, 4 June 1985. Lord Young responded that the government was bound by the ECJ judg-ment under the Treaty of Rome.

[106] Case 150/85 [1986] ECR 1995, [1986] 3 CMLR 43.   [107] *Guardian*, 25 June 1986.

[108] The then Foreign Secretary Dr David Owen had introduced this clause during the Committee stage to reassure the House that direct elections to the Assembly would not lead to a federal Europe. See HC, 943, col 794, 2 February 1978.

First Reading took place on 27 March 1986.[109] A mere five and a half hours were devoted to Second Reading on 23 April 1986.[110] The debate was ill attended; William Cash observed that only six Labour Members, one Scottish Nationalist, one Unionist, one Liberal, and not a single SDP Member were present.[111]

Second Reading was carried by 319 to 160, the Liberals and SDP largely absenting themselves from the vote, and a handful of Conservatives voting with Labour. The Bill was then committed to a Committee of the Whole House. However, after eighteen hours of debate on just three groups of amendments, the government presented a guillotine motion proposing that the remaining Committee proceedings be telescoped into two hours with a Third Reading of just one hour.[112] The government presumably realized that such a time allocation was somewhat outrageous, for it accepted an amendment from Teddy Taylor to extend the Committee stage to five hours—one hour for each of the remaining sets of amendments.

Opponents of the guillotine focused on the seminal importance of the SEA which necessitated thorough debate. For the Opposition, Peter Shore (in notable contrast to his remarks thirteen years earlier about the eminent repealability of the 1972 Act) pointed out that, once passed, the Bill could not be repealed by a subsequent Parliament, unless that Parliament were prepared to tear up the underlying EC Treaty.[113] He accused the government of responding to the SEA's importance first with deception—the pretence that the Bill was a piffling measure—and secondly with an arrogant attempt to bulldoze it through the House on a derisory timetable. Teddy Taylor moved his amendment somewhat shamefacedly, accepting that the time proposed therein was pathetically inadequate, but believing that the alternative would set an appalling precedent whereby future extreme governments could change the constitution.[114] Opponents of the guillotine also argued that its use was inappropriate for a major constitutional issue and that the aim laid down in the SEA preamble of transforming relations into a European Union should not be brought about by stealth.

Strikingly—given the procedural nature of this debate—four Members justified their demand for more time by attacking the ECJ. First, Teddy Taylor pointed out that, for all the debate on QMV, many of the new Treaty articles would give power not to the Council but to the ECJ.[115] Secondly,

---

[109] HC, 94, col 1083, 27 March 1986.   [110] HC, 96, cols 316–397, 23 April 1986.
[111] Ibid, col 325, 23 April 1986.   [112] HC, 100, cols 927–978, 1 July 1986.
[113] Ibid, col 933, 1 July 1986.   [114] Ibid, col 937, 1 July 1986.
[115] Ibid, col 938, 1 July 1986.

plainly referring to *Drake v Chief Adjudication Officer*, Sir Edward du Cann complained that 'European law is increasingly taking primacy over United Kingdom law. Look at the way in which the government scuttled, a fortnight ago, just one day before a decision on social matters was promulgated by the European Court.'[116] Thirdly, Tony Marlow condemned the Bill as an anti-democratic vice with which the ECJ would squeeze European nation states into a union against their wills, by exploiting to the full the SEA preamble's reference to transforming relations between the States into a European Union.[117] Fourthly, Eric Deakins (Labour, Walthamstow) instanced the fundamental importance of a Committee stage debate on the ECJ that had already taken place as a reason for not truncating further debate. Just as the future of the ECJ was worth half a day's debate, so too were other aspects of the SEA.[118] Despite these arguments the Taylor amendment was carried by 286 to 150 and the amended motion was carried by 270 to 153.

SEA: Sovereignty and federalism

The government strategy was to allay fears that the SEA involved any marked loss of sovereignty. Thus Foreign Secretary Sir Geoffrey Howe argued that British national interests would be protected because, first, key safeguards had been secured, namely the retention of unanimity for legislation relating to taxation, free movement of persons, and employees' rights; secondly, it would be open to Britain to combine with other Member States to form a blocking minority; and thirdly, as a last resort, the Luxembourg Compromise remained untouched and unaffected.[119] Howe also argued that the reference to 'European Union' in the SEA preamble should not be seen as something ominous.[120] He mocked the Eurosceptics' 'fearful constitutional fantasies' as 'terrors for children: not for me'. In reality cooperation with Community partners was the way to realize *national* goals.[121]

---

[116] HC, 100, cols 943–944, 1 July 1986.   [117] Ibid, col 953, 1 July 1986.

[118] Ibid, col 958, 1 July 1986.   [119] HC, 96, col 320, 23 April 1986.

[120] This stated that the High Contracting Parties were 'moved . . . to transform relations as a whole among their States into a European Union' and were 'resolved to implement this European Union on the basis, firstly, of the Communities operating in accordance with their own rules and secondly of European Cooperation among the Signatory States in the sphere of foreign policy and to invest this union with the necessary means of action'.

[121] HC, 96, cols 325–326, 23 April 1986.

Labour's opposition to the Bill was only to a limited extent based on general concerns over sovereignty. Whilst characterizing the SEA as the first major transfer of sovereignty from Westminster to Strasbourg and Brussels,[122] Opposition spokespersons placed far more emphasis on the argument that the SEA was at best irrelevant to the Community's deep-seated problems—the CAP, unemployment, trade, and relations with the USA. Moreover its ethos was Thatcherite. Labour objected to the worship of the single market, arguing that even right-wing governments on the Continent recognized the need for a social dimension. No doubt underlying Labour's downgrading of the sovereignty issue was a shift in Party policy. Although *Labour's Programme 1982* had advocated withdrawal, this had by now been toned down by the Party's parliamentary leadership, so that the major objection to the SEA was that it was perceived as the triumph of 'Euro-Thatcherism'.[123]

Arguably the SEA provision with the greatest long-term federalizing potential was on economic and monetary union. During the negotiations Thatcher had held out for no mention of EMU whatever, but confronted by a German volte-face she had been obliged to accept an extremely short Treaty chapter entitled 'Cooperation in Economic and Monetary Policy (Economic and Monetary Union)'.[124] She hoped that this title would set limits on the meaning of EMU; nonetheless the new chapter meant that there was finally a mention, however fleeting, of this aim in the Treaty. Clearly this raised afresh the question of whether 'essential national sovereignty' was under threat.

During the Committee stage Teddy Taylor moved an amendment to deny the new chapter parliamentary approval. George Foulkes for the Opposition used the occasion to underline Labour's hostility to the perceived federalism of the SEA: Labour supported European cooperation, not a united states of Europe or European superstate.[125] Here too, anti-Marketeers emphasized the way in which ECJ interpretations could bring about this transformation. The EMU provisions could not be simply taken at face value but would be interpreted by the ECJ, with its completely different interpretative technique.[126] In so doing the ECJ would make optimum use of the SEA preamble if the British government and Parliament were arraigned before it for failing to move towards EMU.[127] By contrast Lynda Chalker for the government

---

[122] HC, 101, col 567, 10 July 1986 (George Foulkes).

[123] Judge (1988) 453.

[124] Thatcher (1993) 555, Grant (1994) 73.

[125] HC, 101, col 525, 10 July 1986.

[126] Ibid, col 527, 10 July 1986 (William Cash).

[127] Ibid, col 528, 10 July 1986 (Nigel Spearing).

played down the importance of the EMU chapter, arguing that it imposed no new commitments and did not represent a step towards a united states of Europe.[128]

Pro-Marketeer backbenchers tended to be more candid than the government about the likely loss of sovereignty. Sir Russell Johnston cheerfully accepted that the Prime Minister's oft-quoted statement against federalism was unrealistic; it was atavistic not to accept that the integration process involved something like federalism.[129] Similarly Ann Clwyd happily predicted that within twenty years the European Parliament would be more important than the UK Parliament.[130]

More generally, as in 1971–2 and 1975, pro-Market backbenchers emphasized the reality of *political* power rather than *legal* precedence. Some argued, for instance, that since parliamentary sovereignty was not a *political* reality in the United Kingdom (ie political power rested with government not Parliament), European integration should hold no fears. For instance Michael Knowles (Conservative, Nottingham East) argued that an increase in the European Parliament's powers did not necessarily affect Westminster adversely, since power really resided with the executive, domestic and European.[131] Hugh Dykes was critical of his colleagues' bouts of 'constitutional madness' in view of the deficiencies of the British constitution, whereby Parliament annually churned out a monumental amount of ill-digested, unexamined, legislation.[132] The pervasive theme was that talk of 'parliamentary sovereignty' obscured the reality of backbench feebleness in the face of an over-mighty executive. This reality militated in favour of a stronger role for the European Parliament as a more effective check on the Community executive. In presenting this argument, pro-Marketeers such as Dykes made the common mistake among politicians of confusing the legal character of the parliamentary sovereignty doctrine with its political consequence, which is to strengthen the executive.[133]

Other pro-Marketeers asserted more generally that the notion of a sovereign, independent Britain was a myth. Anti-Marketeers, they argued, were defending the shadow rather than the substance of sovereignty.[134] How

---

[128] Ibid, col 529, 10 July 1986.   [129] HC, 100, col 641, 27 June 1986.
[130] HC, 96, col 355, 23 April 1986.   [131] Ibid, col 344, 23 April 1986.
[132] HC, 100, col 559, 26 June 1986.

[133] This impact is cheerfully accepted by some academic supporters of parliamentary sovereignty, eg Norton (1989) who argues that an elected dictatorship is preferable to the non-elected dictatorship of a court permitted to invalidate Acts of Parliament.

[134] HC, 100, col 499, 26 June 1986 (Sir Anthony Meyer).

could Britain be said to suffer a loss of sovereignty if, in exchange, she gained part of the sovereignty of eleven other nations?[135] Indeed, unless they united, Britain and the other European countries risked becoming economic colonies of the United States and Japan.[136]

SEA and the Luxembourg Compromise

The issue of the Luxembourg Compromise pervaded the Bill's passage. As we have seen, both Thatcher and Howe had emphasized its post-SEA survival. It was, however, questionable whether there was a Luxembourg Compromise worth saving. In 1982 UK Agriculture Minister Peter Walker had sought to invoke the compromise over farm prices only to be overruled in Council. In the particular circumstances, this was fair enough: Walker had made it quite clear that there was no vital national interest involved but that the UK sought a satisfactory settlement in another policy area. However, as Lawson explained, the Foreign Office, believing that the Walker episode had severely wounded the Luxembourg Compromise, had developed a two-pronged policy designed to ensure its survival. First, if any other member country sought to invoke the compromise, the UK should always support it; secondly, the UK should never itself invoke the compromise, since it could not risk having it overridden a second time.[137] Lawson credits himself with getting 'this perverse policy' overturned.

Unsurprisingly, doubts about the value of the compromise (even without the SEA changes) surfaced during the parliamentary debate. Several MPs drew attention to the 1982 incident.[138] Eric Deakins referred also to the Commission's conduct in 1985 when Germany invoked the compromise to veto a cereal price reduction. He claimed that whereas under Community rules the previous year's cereal prices should have been retained, the Commission simply imposed its own prices, thereby negating the German veto.[139] Eric Forth (Conservative, Mid-Worcestershire) went further, arguing that even unanimity rules laid down in the Treaty were no protection, since any harmonization would be done as part of a package, with quid pro quos or trade-offs, with other Member States.[140]

---

[135] Ibid, col 644, 27 June 1986 (Jeremy Hanley).

[136] HC, 96, col 342, 23 April 1986 (Michael Knowles).   [137] Lawson (1993) 890.

[138] Sir Edward du Cann HC, 96, col 334, 23 April 1986; Eric Deakins ibid, col 346, 23 April 1986; Teddy Taylor HC, 100, col 938, 1 July 1986.

[139] HC, 101, col 543, 10 July 1986.   [140] Ibid, col 511, 10 July 1986.

As to the effect of the SEA, there was scepticism as to whether the compromise could survive unscathed. Peter Shore noted the conclusion of the House of Lords Select Committee on the European Communities that it was doubtful that the Luxembourg Compromise would survive the SEA,[141] and both he and George Foulkes[142] contended that the compromise would be fatally weakened by the cooperation procedure. Here, a plea by a single Member State that a European Parliament amendment violated its vital national interests would be of no avail.[143] This was because the Council would need nothing short of a qualified majority to reject a European Parliament amendment adopted by the Commission. Geoffrey Rippon, now a backbencher, thought that the SEA put down a marker that Member States should not invoke the compromise unless *very* important national interests were at stake.[144] One might have expected the government to speak with one voice, but in the dying seconds of the Third Reading debate Lynda Chalker revealingly blurred the issue:

[Mr Shore] asked about the veto. Where important interests are at stake, discussion must be continued until unanimous agreement is reached. That is exactly what we mean by the Luxembourg compromise. . . . The unanimity rule has been replaced by qualified majority voting, but . . . [this] has been agreed for those issues where we wish to make progress and where it is in Britain's interest to make progress. It is right to make progress, but we still have the right *on other issues* to exercise the veto where it is in the interests of Britain to do so.[145]

The whole point of the Luxembourg Compromise is that it constitutes a *de facto* veto (or unanimity rule) in precisely those fields where the Treaty stipulates majority voting. Under it, invocation by a Member State of an essential national interest should suffice to frustrate *any* Treaty provision calling for decision-making by QMV. It is notable that Lord Young, with the benefit of hindsight, stated in his memoirs that 'the result of the Single European Act was that the veto could no longer save us from the consequences of changes in Europe'.[146] Similarly with hindsight, Lord Tebbit was furious at the SEA's erosion of the veto, and outraged that such a huge decision came to be taken by government and Parliament with so little debate.[147]

---

[141] HC, 100, col 934, 1 July 1986.

[143] See Edwards (1987) 26.

[145] HC, 101, col 570, 10 July 1986 (emphasis added).

[147] Tebbit (1991) 44.

[142] Ibid, col 490, 26 June 1986.

[144] HC, 96, col 352, 23 April 1986.

[146] Young (1990) 241.

SEA and the power of the ECJ

Attention focused on the ECJ partly because Clause 2 incorporated the IGC's decision to permit an additional court to be attached to it. The first amendment to be debated in Committee sought to exclude incorporation of this commitment. Anti-Market MPs were angered at ECJ case law which attributed an expansive scope to Community law. Teddy Taylor for example singled out *Conegate* as an incursion into what should properly be the preserve of the Member States.[148] Thus for Taylor it was impossible to determine the SEA's scope: '[t]he fact is that none of us knows. The European Court will decide what the SEA does. It will not be the Government, me or other MPs.'[149]

The objection to the ECJ's broad interpretation of the ambit of Community law was inextricably linked to criticisms of its teleological mode of interpretation, regarded by anti-Marketeers as illegitimate. Since the ECJ was driven by what the Community's policy should be, it took a far wider view of its powers than that taken by British courts, and took political rather than legal decisions.[150] The government claim that the SEA preamble did not confer rights or impose duties ignored the fact that the preamble provided the context for interpretation of the operative text.[151]

Institutional fears were also voiced. Anti-Marketeers argued that it was not clear from the SEA text whether the House was assenting to the setting-up of one court or several.[152] It was easy to envisage the ECJ sitting at the apex of a network of Community courts based in the individual Member States.[153] Certainly nothing in the SEA prevented the establishment of circuits of Community courts in all EEC countries.[154] MPs raising these arguments plainly did not appreciate the impact of direct effect and supremacy, under which every national court becomes a Community court. Tony Marlow made a more general, perceptive, comment that the European debate was becoming increasingly intricate and increasingly based on the *legal* aspects—the ECJ, its powers, and the balance of powers between courts.[155] Strangely

---

[148] HC, 99, cols 813–815, 16 June 1986.   [149] Ibid, col 815, 16 June 1986.

[150] Ibid, cols 813 and 818, 16 June 1986 (Nicholas Budgen).

[151] Ibid, col 818, 16 June 1986 (Teddy Taylor).

[152] Ibid, col 829, 16 June 1986 (Enoch Powell).

[153] Ibid, col 841, 16 June 1986 (Eric Deakins).

[154] Ibid, col 857, 16 June 1986 (Nigel Spearing).   [155] Ibid, col 843, 16 June 1986.

Marlow was the only MP to highlight expressly the lack of accountability of the ECJ in comparison to Parliament.[156]

The anti-Market case was therefore that the ECJ's decisions were so objectionable that creating more courts would only encourage it. Teddy Taylor argued, '[l]et us try to find out whether, by restricting the number of courts, we may put some restriction on the ever-increasing role of the Court in deciding British issues, which should be decided by British courts'.[157] (It is curious that he did not think that British issues should be decided by Britain's Parliament rather than her courts.) Or, as Eric Deakins put it: 'I want to reduce the number of cases and the scope of the European Court and limit it until we have changed the relationship between this country and the rest of the Community.'[158]

The ECJ had supporters as well as detractors. Some emphasized its positive merits. For instance the ECJ usually worked to the benefit of the UK in the sense that it prevented infractions of Community law by other Member States.[159] There was 'plain, common sense' in the way in which the ECJ had obliged Britain to improve her laws on sex discrimination.[160] More generally the European courts were less bogged down by establishmentarian commitments than their British counterparts.[161] Other pro-Marketeers emphasized the modest nature of the constitutional change. The CFI would simply provide for the more efficient disposal of the ECJ's growing caseload.[162] The SEA merely created a *subsidiary* court, which, far from having sweeping new powers, would only have some of those possessed by the ECJ.[163] Thus there would be no net increase in ECJ power; the CFI would merely deal with detailed probing.[164]

Some MPs still assumed that in the event of a clash between Parliament and the ECJ, British statute would prevail. For example Eric Deakins asserted that Labour would put before the electorate a policy of exchange controls. When Teddy Taylor intervened to say, 'You cannot do that', he responded, '[t]he hon. Gentleman says that we cannot do that. Within rea-

---

[156] HC, 101, col 562, 10 July 1986.   [157] HC, 99, col 815, 16 June 1986.
[158] Ibid, col 841, 16 June 1986.
[159] Ibid, cols 816–817, 16 June 1986 (Sir Anthony Meyer).
[160] HC, 96, col 357, 23 April 1986 (Ann Clwyd, referring in particular to Case 152/84 *Marshall v Southampton and South West Hampshire Area Health Authority (Teaching)* [1986] ECR 723).
[161] HC, 96, cols 369–370, 23 April 1986 (Tom Clarke, Labour, Monklands West. Presumably he was referring to the European Court of Human Rights in addition to the ECJ).
[162] Ibid, col 317, 23 April 1986 (Sir Geoffrey Howe).
[163] HC, 99, col 832, 16 June 1986 (John Butterfill, Conservative, Bournemouth West).
[164] Ibid, cols 861–866, 16 June 1986 (Lynda Chalker).

son, the British Government can do whatever they like. Whether they are breaking international obligations is another matter.'[165] This connotes a significant lack of insight from one of the three MPs who anticipated during the passage of the 1972 Act that the British courts might side with the ECJ against national authorities. In the same vein Tony Marlow asserted: 'Parliament can be obliged to do nothing. Parliament is sovereign and can make its own decisions on these issues.'[166] But again anti-EEC opinion was divided, Sir Edward du Cann interjecting that the House of Commons would become impotent if the legislation were passed, and Nigel Spearing remarking that Marlow did not understand the notion of 'enforceable Community rights' introduced by the 1972 Act.

House of Lords: Lord Denning's intervention

The otherwise unremarkable Lords Second Reading[167] was enlivened by Lord Denning's attack on the Bill as a serious erosion of the sovereignty of the Queen in Parliament. He singled out the ECJ for criticism, instancing *Marshall*[168] as an example of the ECJ according supremacy to a Community directive: 'She [Miss Marshall] said the [British] court should not take any notice of the 1975 [Sex Discrimination] Act. I am sorry to say that the European Court held her to be right . . . We talk of the sovereignty of Parliament, but it can be overruled in that way by a directive.'[169] He again criticized the *Conegate* judgment, pointing out that the Customs Act 1876 clearly instructed customs officers to prevent the importation of obscene articles. 'How are Customs officers to act? . . . The European Court says "You need not obey the Act". The supremacy of Parliament . . . is being overruled from Brussels or from that Court.'[170] He considered that the ECJ in these decisions had trespassed beyond its allotted task of Treaty interpretation.[171]

---

[165] Ibid, col 842, 16 June 1986.   [166] HC, 100, col 662, 27 June 1986.
[167] HL, 479, cols 1004–1034 and 1046–1088, 31 July 1986.
[168] Case 152/84 *Marshall v Southampton and South West Hampshire Area Health Authority (Teaching)* [1986] ECR 723.
[169] HL, 479, col 1057, 31 July 1986.   [170] Ibid, col 1058, 31 July 1986.
[171] Ibid, col 1059, 31 July 1986. Lord Denning suggested that such a departure from what he saw as the ECJ's proper role was a recent innovation. He ignores that, as far back as *Van Gend en Loos*, the ECJ made clear, in answer to the Belgian and Dutch governments, that questions as to the direct effect (and supremacy) of Community law were to be treated as questions of Treaty interpretation.

Lord Denning's attitude makes a bizarre contrast to his holding in *Macarthys*[172] that there could be no implied repeal of EC law by Parliament, and his doubts in *Blackburn*[173] over whether the UK could lawfully withdraw from the Community. Nor was his volte-face heralded in his writings. In his final book, *The Closing Chapter* (1993), Lord Denning in fact expressed the hope that the English courts would emulate the ECJ by adopting a 'gap-filling' approach to statutory interpretation.[174]

From SEA to Merchant Shipping Bill

Passage of the European Communities (Amendment) Act 1986 was followed by an upsurge in parliamentary interest in the ECJ. In the short 1986–7 Session[175] there were twelve written questions on the Court's judgments; in the longer 1987–8 Session[176] there were sixty-one. MPs tended to be preoccupied with enforcement actions, in particular a challenge by the Commission to the UK's VAT zero-rating of *inter alia* new house building, gas, and electricity. The questions tended to come either from seasoned anti-Marketeers (for instance Teddy Taylor asked a whole series of questions about VAT) or from MPs with highly specialized interests.

Conclusion

By the time Parliament debated the Merchant Shipping Bill on 28 January 1988 there had been a sea-change in MPs' attitudes to the ECJ. In the early years of membership ECJ judgments inspired virtually no interest. Little by little this situation changed. To be sure, even at the end of the period there was still widespread lack of understanding over the role which the ECJ intended for the national courts in the scheme of things. And in addition MPs tended to look too much at compliance with Commission enforcement actions as their yardstick for determining national obedience to EEC rules, an overemphasis which served to obscure the ECJ's recruitment of the national courts as the ordinary courts of Community law, a development

---

[172] [1979] 3 All ER 325.   [173] [1971] 2 All ER 1308.
[174] Denning (1993) 113–114.   [175] 12 November 1986–15 May 1987.
[176] 17 June 1987–15 November 1988.

which was at once both more effective and more supranational. But at least MPs were belatedly waking up to the fact 'that Acts of Parliament can be made subject to the superior jurisdiction of a written constitution and a court'.[177] It is clear that this gradual awakening to a new constitutional order, stimulated by the SEA and a series of controversial cases, started well in advance of the first direct clash in the domestic courts between an Act of Parliament and Community law.

[177] Coombes (1981) 256.

7

Factortame, *EOC*, and Maastricht

This chapter examines the interplay between courts and parliamentarians from the late 1980s until *United Kingdom v Council*, the *Working Time Directive* case,[1] in November 1996. This period witnessed the first two cases in which British courts set aside statutory provisions in favour of Community law. The chapter analyses the judicial reasoning in these landmark decisions along with academic critiques. With a view to assessing the evolution of legal thinking, the judgments before all the national instances will be examined, to dissect what was being said at each level about the sovereignty of Parliament in the context of Community membership. Considerations of space preclude a blow-by-blow account of the removal of Thatcher and incorporation of Maastricht, which in any case have been covered in depth by other commentators.[2] Instead this chapter adopts a thematic approach, concentrating on parliamentary sovereignty and the relationship of courts with Parliament, and analysing the extent to which consciousness of the new constitutional situation permeated the legislature.

Developments pre-*Factortame*

In two cases decided in the late 1980s, *Pickstone v Freemans plc*[3] and *Litster v Forth Dry Dock*,[4] the House of Lords eschewed any direct challenge to parliamentary sovereignty, choosing instead to resolve apparent contradictions

---

[1] Case C–84/94 *United Kingdom v Council* [1996] ECR I–5755, [1996] 3 CMLR 671.
[2] eg Rawlings (1994*a*) 254–278, Loveland (2000) 393–397, 399–403.
[3] [1989] AC 66, judgment of 30 June 1988.
[4] [1989] 1 All ER 1134, judgment of 16 March 1989.

between British and Community law by purposive statutory construction.[5] Nonetheless these cases raised questions of their own as to whether the courts were respecting the proper limits of their constitutional role. Indeed, *Pickstone* and *Litster* underscored how imaginative interpretation might give the judiciary an even greater power than disapplication, by permitting courts in effect to generate 'new' legal provisions rather than merely set aside existing ones.

Pickstone v Freemans plc concerned apparent incompatibility between Community law and the provisions of the Equal Pay Act 1970. The plain words of the British statute seemed to make it clear that it was not open to women, paid equally with male colleagues engaged in the same work as their own, to claim equality of pay with other male employees who did different work which was nonetheless of 'equal value' to their own. The British wording seemingly permitted employers to evade equal pay legislation by engaging one token male on the same work as a group of potential women claimants who could be deliberately paid less than a group of men employed on work of equal value with that of the women.

The Court of Appeal was inclined to let the women claimants sue under Article 119 EEC (the Treaty provision on equal pay between men and women), on the grounds that this article was directly effective in this particular context. Purchas LJ was sufficiently forthright to admit that this approach involved disapplying the British statutory provision, arguing that 'there is clear authority that in a case of conflict Community law must prevail'.[6] He did not spell out where precisely this 'clear authority' existed in English law whereby Community provisions prevailed over the doctrine of parliamentary sovereignty rather than vice versa.

By contrast, the House of Lords considered that it could achieve the same result merely by applying a purposive construction to the British legislation. This was the case despite the facts that the British provision seemed unambiguous, and that the purposive construction would basically involve *adding words in* to the statute. Their Lordships insisted that legislation passed to give effect to EEC obligations fell into a special category which justified recourse to a particularly strong creative approach to interpretation.

Their Lordships' approach surprised some academics. *Public Law* commented that 'for a time it might have seemed to a spectator that *Pickstone v Freemans plc* would be the long-awaited case in which the House of Lords

[5] cf *Duke v Reliance Systems* [1988] 1 AC 618, judgment of 11 February 1988.
[6] [1989] 1 QB 95H.

would have to choose between accepting allegiance to Community law or maintaining its loyalty to the will of the British legislature. But it was not to be, and those who believe that a sovereign Parliament, like a contemporary Canute, may turn back the incoming tide of Community law must wait patiently for confirmation of their faith.'[7] It is, however, arguable that their Lordships were undermining Parliament by usurping its legislative role through overly creative interpretation. Perhaps too the House's willingness in *Pickstone* to inspect *Hansard* to assess parliamentary intention might in the long term undermine the inviolability of statute. In earlier cases, attempts to secure judicial review of Acts of Parliament on the grounds of procedural defects during a Bill's passage had been met with judicial refusal to look beyond the text of the Act.[8]

Some eight months later the House confirmed its commitment to an ultra-purposive interpretative approach in the EEC context in *Litster v Forth Dry Dock*. The case involved apparent incompatibility between an EEC directive which protected workers' rights in the event of a change of employer, and the UK implementing regulations, which protected the rights only of those employed in the business *immediately* before the transfer. Here, employers sought to evade the legislation by arranging a one-hour gap between dismissing the staff and transferring the business. The issues of direct effect and supremacy did not actually arise here, since the ECJ had established in an earlier case that directives could not of themselves impose obligations on private concerns.[9] However, the House of Lords applied *Pickstone* and held that, even though the wording of the British legislation seemed clear and unambiguous, a purposive construction was appropriate. The regulations should be construed as applying not only to employees who were employed in the business immediately before the transfer but also to those who would have been so employed but for being unfairly dismissed before the transfer for a reason connected with the transfer. Both Lord Keith and Lord Oliver accepted that they were *implying words in* to the legislation. Were their Lordships violating the separation of powers by assuming a legislative role which properly belonged to the country's political institutions? Lord Slynn of Hadley argued extra-judicially that if national law conflicted with

---

[7] [1988] Public Law 485.

[8] See eg *Edinburgh and Dalkeith Rly Co v Wauchope* (1842) 8 Cl & Fin 710, 8 ER 279, *British Railways Board v Pickin* [1974] AC 765.

[9] Case 154/84 *Marshall v Southampton and South West Hampshire Area Health Authority* [1986] ECR 723, [1986] 1 CMLR 688.

Community law, the answer was not for judges to strain language but for governments to introduce new legislation.[10]

At the same time parliamentary awareness of the ECJ's importance was growing. Whilst the Labour Party became increasingly reconciled to the supremacy of Community law,[11] the Conservative government was becoming increasingly concerned about it. In March 1988 the House of Commons was asked to endorse the establishment of the Court of First Instance. According to Sir Nicholas Lyell SG this was necessitated by 'the increasing role played by Community law in the affairs of everybody in the Community'[12]—a stark contrast to the earlier views of Lord Chancellors Dilhorne, Gardiner, and Elwyn Jones that few ordinary people would ever feel the impact of Community law. In February and June 1988 the UK lost two enforcement actions relating to VAT. On both occasions Conservative backbenchers urged the government to defy the ECJ judgments. In February Terence Higgins (Conservative, Worthing) noted that if a British court made a ruling on the scope of VAT which the House[13] wished to change, the House had the power to do this. Peter Lilley replied that whilst Parliament could overrule decisions of British courts, Britain would have to obtain the consent of her European partners to overturn an ECJ decision.[14] In June, in response to a similar question, he said that parliamentary defiance of an ECJ judgment would lead to a constitutional impasse.[15] It is interesting that Lilley assumed that British courts would accept parliamentary reversal of their decisions, even those relating to directly effective Community law rights, and that he did not anticipate that any 'constitutional impasse' might be resolved by the British courts according supremacy to Community law. These issues became still more controversial in the context of *R v Secretary of State for Transport ex parte Factortame Ltd.*

---

[10]   Slynn (1992) 124.

[11]   The 1988 Labour Conference recognized that Britain was 'politically and economically integrated into the European Community' and that accordingly Labour had to 'seek to use and adapt Community institutions to promote democratic socialism' (Composite 58, 1988 Labour Party Annual Conference). In its Policy Review of 1987–9, Labour rejected proposals to repeal section 2 of the European Communities Act 1972 or amend it to allow Parliament to approve or reject Community secondary legislation. *Meet the Challenge, Make the Change: A New Agenda for Britain* (1989) 80.

[12]   HC, 130, cols 674–693, 25 March 1988.

[13]   Another instance of a parliamentarian muddling the 'House of Commons' with 'Parliament'.

[14]   HC, 128, cols 297–302, 24 February 1988.   [15]   HC, 135, col 984, 21 June 1988.

Factortame in Parliament and the courts

The facts of *Factortame* can be summarized briefly.[16] To protect the British fishing industry against 'quota-hopping', the practice whereby Spanish fishing companies circumvented the Community's imposition of national quotas for fish catches, Parliament passed the Merchant Shipping Act 1988 which *inter alia* imposed stringent nationality conditions on fishing companies wishing to register as British. Ironically in the House of Commons the quota-hopping issue had hardly featured at the Bill's Second Reading.[17] It was a non-contentious, wide-ranging piece of legislation, and the two dominant issues in debate were the Zeebrugge disaster and the decline of the British merchant navy. Transport Secretary Paul Channon devoted only seven sentences of his speech to quota-hopping; Robert Hughes for the Opposition just two. David Harris (Conservative, St Ives) was the only backbencher to devote his speech to quota-hopping. He noted that there was some suggestion that if the Bill became law, it would be challenged in the European Court, and asked whether this constituted a real threat.[18] Closing the debate, junior minister David Mitchell replied that the government were confident that their measures were wholly in accord with the Community's fishing quotas system.[19] The nationality conditions were not discussed in Committee.[20]

Some companies owned and controlled largely by Spanish nationals applied for judicial review, arguing that the provisions breached prohibitions on nationality discrimination in the EEC Treaty. The domestic courts were finally faced with a conflict between Community law and statute which could not be resolved by benevolent interpretation.

In the courts much of the argument revolved around the issue of interim relief, ie whether statutory provisions could be temporarily disapplied before the inconsistency of the Act of Parliament with Community law had been established. This analysis will not focus on this issue, which has been well covered elsewhere.[21] In any case it is arguable that although suspension of a statute is undoubtedly of constitutional importance, it is neither so belittling to the status of a Parliament, nor so obstructive to the will of a government, as permanent disapplication, which brings with it the knowledge of *future* permanent parliamentary impotence to enact similar provisions. The judg-

---

[16] For a fuller account see Gravells (1989).   [17] HC, 126, cols 506–558, 28 January 1988.
[18] Ibid, col 552, 28 January 1988.   [19] Ibid, col 553, 28 January 1988.
[20] HC, 130, cols 1164–1250, 30 March 1988.   [21] Gravells (1989).

ments will be analysed instead for what they tell us more generally about why the European Communities Act 1972 binds successor Parliaments and whether the supremacy of Community law is substantively or merely procedurally entrenched. In other words, has Parliament lost the right to legislate contrary to Community law completely, or can Parliament still do so provided that it manifests an express intention to that effect?

Significantly it was common ground between the parties that, had the incompatibility of the statute with Community law been established, the courts would have been obliged, in conformity with the ECJ's supremacy principle, to disapply the offending statutory provisions. Despite Prime Minister Thatcher's growing hostility to the Community, the government did not argue that the sovereignty of Parliament was 'inescapable and enduring', even in the face of section 2(4) of the 1972 Act. Yet despite the Crown's acceptance that *established*—as opposed to merely putative—Community law rights would prevail over statute, the courts at all instances felt the need to confirm and justify the principle of the primacy of Community law. This was doubtless due not only to the close connection between interim relief and parliamentary sovereignty, but also to the fact that if the ECJ resolved that the 1988 Act breached Community law, the courts would be obliged to disapply permanently provisions of this more recent Act in favour of 'enforceable Community rights' created by the earlier, 1972, Act. The 1972 Parliament would have bound its successors.

High Court: reasoning renounced?

In the High Court, Neill LJ explained that the courts' traditional approach to primary legislation failed to take sufficient account of

the new state of affairs which came into being when the United Kingdom became a Member State of the European Community in January 1973. Twenty years ago the idea that the High Court could question the validity of an Act of Parliament or fail, having construed it, to give effect to it would have been unthinkable. But the High Court now has a duty . . . where there is a conflict, to prefer the Community law to national law.[22]

He recited the familiar passage from *Simmenthal*, that national courts must disapply incompatible national measures.[23] However, rather than attribute

---

[22] [1989] 2 CMLR 353, 373.   [23] [1978] ECR 629, 644; [1978] 3 CMLR 263, 283.

this duty to entry into the Community *per se*, Neill LJ ascribed it to the combined effect of sections 2(1) and 2(4) of the 1972 Act, namely *'as I understand it*, that directly applicable Community provisions are to prevail not only over existing but also over future Acts of Parliament (that is, Acts subsequent to 1972) in so far as those provisions may be inconsistent with such enactments'.[24] Yet Neill LJ did not explain how this squared with the traditional doctrine that Parliament cannot bind its successors. He did not spell out why the 1972 Act was not to be treated like any other Act, subject to both express and implied repeal. Instead he merely relied on the dictum of Lord Denning MR in *Macarthys Ltd v Smith*:

It is important now to declare—and it must be made plain—that the provisions of Article 119 of the EEC Treaty take priority over anything in our English statute which is inconsistent with it. That priority is given by our own law. It is given by the European Communities Act 1972 itself. Community law is now part of our law: and whenever there is *any* inconsistency Community law has priority. It is not supplanting English law. It is part of our law which overrides *any other part* which is inconsistent with it.[25]

However handy this *obiter*[26] statement of Lord Denning, surely more is needed to justify overturning the fundamental principle that Parliament cannot bind its successors. After all, Lord Denning's dictum is merely an assertion. Like Neill LJ, Lord Denning made no attempt to furnish a normative justification for the supremacy of EC law based on arguments of principle.[27] The second judge, Hodgson LJ, stated that it used to be

unthinkable that there should be in an English court a higher authority than an Act of Parliament, but there is now in English law such a higher authority. My Lord Neill L.J. has cited the dictum of Lord Denning M.R. in *Macarthys v Smith* which explains the position with his habitual clarity.... Primary legislation is still inviolable, save that primacy over all other law is now given to the Treaty and Community law by the European Communities Act 1972.[28]

So, like Neill LJ, he ascribes the supremacy of Community law to the 1972 Act, without explaining why it should be immune from implied repeal.

---

[24] [1989] 2 CMLR 353, 374 (emphasis added).   [25] [1981] 1 QB 180, 200 (emphasis added).
[26] *Macarthys* involved the effect of Community law on a *pre*-accession statute, the Equal Pay Act 1970.
[27] cf Craig (1991).   [28] [1989] 2 CMLR 353, 381.

Court of Appeal: reasoning diverse?

The two High Court views, however inadequately reasoned, at least sat happily together. The same cannot be said for the three Court of Appeal judges, whose reasoning pointed in different directions.[29] Lord Donaldson MR stated that the courts could strike down legislation 'on a permanent basis founded upon Community law or on the British European Communities Act 1972'. His use of the word 'or' circumvents the fundamental question of whether the primacy of Community law springs from the UK's entry into the 'new legal order' or from a British statute.[30]

Bingham LJ in contrast argued that it was the 1972 Act which ensured that Community law prevailed in the event of inconsistency. He prayed in aid Lord Denning's familiar dictum in *Macarthys* and also an *obiter* statement of Lord Hailsham in *The Siskina*[31] to the effect that, in the case of Community law which 'directly applies' (*sic*), '[i]t is the duty of the courts here and in other Member States to give effect to Community law as they interpret it in preference to the municipal law of their own country over which *ex hypothesi* Community law prevails'.[32] Bingham reinforced his case with a review of the ECJ's supremacy jurisprudence—*Van Gend, Costa,* and *Simmenthal.* These ECJ authorities do not, however, deal with whether the ECJ's supremacy jurisprudence can be accepted by UK courts in the face of parliamentary sovereignty. This was a matter of national constitutional law for the national courts to resolve. Bingham also noted that the Crown was bound to accept, and indeed readily accepted, the legitimacy of permanent disapplication of an Act of Parliament proven to be incompatible with Community law.[33] Consequently Bingham had no doubt that '[a]ny rule of domestic law which prevented the court from, or inhibited it in giving effect to directly enforceable rights established in Community law would be bad. To that extent a United Kingdom statute is no longer inviolable as it once was.'[34] It had to be

---

[29] Ibid 393.

[30] Lord Donaldson later clarified his position in an address to the European Society on 22 November 1990. Here he fell into line with Lord Bridge's view in *Factortame (No 2)* (handed down eleven days earlier) that the supremacy of Community law in the United Kingdom derived entirely from the 1972 Act. Parliament was free not only to repeal that Act but to enact that specific provisions of Community law would not be applicable in the United Kingdom and to provide when enacting a new law that it should prevail over Community law. See Donaldson (1991).

[31] *Siskina (Cargo Owners) v Distos SA* [1979] AC 210.   [32] At 262G.

[33] Yet fundamental constitutional doctrines should surely not vanish due to concession by counsel.

[34] [1989] 2 CMLR 353, 404.

measured against, in Bingham's words, 'the higher law of the Community'. Thus for Bingham the 1972 Act seemingly serves as conduit to a higher form of law. Does this make the 1972 Act itself the highest form of law, since its repeal would restore the *status quo ante*, or does the higher nature of Community law render the 1972 Act unrepealable, since any repealing Act would be disapplied? If the latter is the case, the 1972 Act can be viewed as *a mere catalyst* leading to the new legal order. The third judge was Mann LJ, who, in a very short judgment, asserted that 'This court is obliged to defer to the Sovereignty of the Queen in Parliament. We can only not so defer where legislation is inconsistent with the United Kingdom's obligations under the Treaty of Rome.'[35] This mildly suggests that Mann was perhaps more sympathetic to the 'change in basic norm' argument. There is no mention at all of the 1972 Act. Rather, some special quality attaches to the Treaty of Rome itself which makes it prevail over the Queen in Parliament.

House of Lords 1: reasoning renounced again?

The House of Lords decided to make a preliminary reference on the question of interim relief. Lord Bridge delivered the only speech. On the issue of parliamentary sovereignty generally, he stated:

[b]y virtue of section 2(4) of the Act of 1972 Part II of the Act of 1988 is to be construed and take effect subject to directly enforceable Community rights and those rights are, by section 2(1) of the Act of 1972, to be 'recognised and available in law, and . . . enforced, allowed and followed accordingly . . .' This has precisely the same effect as if a section were incorporated in Part II of the Act of 1988 which in terms enacted that the provisions with respect to registration of British fishing vessels were to be without prejudice to the directly enforceable Community rights of the nationals of any Member States of the EEC. Thus it is common ground that, in so far as the appellants succeed before the ECJ in obtaining a ruling in support of the Community rights which they claim, those rights will prevail over the restrictions imposed on registration of British fishing vessels by Part II of the Act of 1988 and the Divisional Court will, in the final determination of the application for judicial review, be obliged to make appropriate declarations to give effect to those rights.[36]

Lord Bridge's approach is curious. First, he wanted the courts *in temporal terms* to assimilate the 1972 Act with more recent Acts through the fiction

---

[35] At 408.   [36] [1989] 3 CMLR 1, 10.

that every post-1972 Act includes an implicit rider that its provisions take effect without prejudice to Community law rights. (Thus Lord Bridge had accomplished by judicial implication what Wade had suggested eighteen years earlier needed to be done as standard legislative practice.) Secondly, the very nature of a rider dictates that the courts *in hierarchical terms* are to ensure that it prevails over incompatible express provisions of the Act into which it is impliedly incorporated. Lord Bridge did not reveal whether Parliament's newly discovered ability to self-bind can only relate to Community law.[37] Importantly, Lord Bridge faithfully follows *Simmenthal* in acknowledging that it is for the High Court as the first instance judicial review court to dis-apply offending statutory provisions. He also confirmed that a declaration is the appropriate remedy for permanent disapplication. But, like the judges below, Lord Bridge did not explain *why* parliamentary sovereignty should fall victim to the ECJ's supremacy principle rather than the other way round.

The more modest interpretation of Lord Bridge's position would be that Parliament can 'contract out' of the implied rider by legislating expressly 'notwithstanding any contrary provision of Community law' or some such formulation. However, if so, he should have surely explained why this is an exception to the long-standing nostrum that 'the Legislature cannot, accord-ing to our constitution, bind itself as to the *form* of subsequent legislation, and it is impossible for Parliament to enact that in a subsequent statute dealing with the same subject matter there can be no implied repeal'.[38]

Some commentators, however, have read a more expansive form of entrenchment into Lord Bridge's words. For instance Loveland argues that the inference appears to be that the courts would no longer obey an Act of Parliament which breached directly effective EC law even if the Act expressly stated it was intended to achieve that result.[39] If so, then a fortiori Lord Bridge's statement ought to have been more fully reasoned. After all, it was always common ground between the supporters of the rival 'continuing' and 'self-embracing' views of sovereignty that Parliament could not be bound as to the *substance* of future legislation.

---

[37] Wade (1991) speculates whether the ECHR could be entrenched in the same way.

[38] *Per* Maugham LJ, *Ellen Street Estates Ltd v Minister of Health* [1934] 1 KB 590 (emphasis added).

[39] Loveland (2000) 386.

House of Commons: debate stifled?

On 19 August 1990 the ECJ ruled that a national court was obliged to set aside any rule of domestic law which would prevent it granting interim relief in order to ensure the full effectiveness of a judgment to be given on the existence of Community law rights. There was no adequate discussion of this judgment in the House of Commons. On 20 August Teddy Taylor requested a debate under Standing Order 20[40] on 'the implications for parliamentary sovereignty of the decision of the European Court of Justice yesterday on interim relief', arguing that until the preceding day no court had ever told Parliament to suspend or nullify its Acts.[41] The Speaker decided that the matter should not take precedence over other business, but expressed the view that the ECJ's ruling constituted a vital issue affecting the sovereignty of Parliament and hoped the House would address it in due course.[42] Significantly, Taylor complained of an all-party conspiracy to prevent discussion of the judgment, and this appeared borne out by Business Questions the following day,[43] when the Shadow Leader of the House requested neither a debate nor an Attorney General's statement on *Factortame*. This starkly contrasted with bellicose demands for a debate from six backbenchers, two of whom had picked up on the implication that the judgment meant that the right to strike down Acts of Parliament was not restricted to the House of Lords but extended to 'any tuppenny ha'penny court in the land'.[44] Leader of the House Sir Geoffrey Howe assured MPs that he would bring the request for a statement to the attention of the Attorney General. He also argued that the issue could be raised in a debate on European legislation to be held the following Thursday.[45] In the event, that debate focused almost exclusively on scrutiny procedure.[46] At Prime Minister's Questions Mrs Thatcher

[40] This permits adjournment debate on 'a specific and important matter that should have urgent consideration'. The Speaker must be satisfied that the matter is proper to be so discussed.

[41] HC, 174, cols 923–924, 20 June 1990. Taylor should have limited this argument to the post-1688 revolution era. Moreover, to be accurate, it was not a question of the courts telling Parliament to do anything; rather, they were automatically suspending the statutory provision.

[42] The Speaker's ruling led to a flurry of points of order by disgruntled backbenchers—Derek Conway (col 925), Richard Shepherd (col 926), William Cash (col 927), Sir Dudley Smith (col 928)—but the Speaker was unmoved.

[43] HC, 174, cols 1107–1112, 21 June 1990.

[44] Nick Budgen (col 1115) and Tony Marlow (col 1117). The phrase was Marlow's. The other four MPs were Richard Shepherd (col 1115), Peter Shore (col 1116), Edward Leigh (col 1116), and Neil Hamilton (col 1121), 21 June 1990.

[45] Ibid, col 1116, 21 June 1990.   [46] HC, 175, cols 523–586, 28 June 1990.

expressed concern about the judgment,[47] but in a Written Answer she declined a request to review the operation of the ECJ in the light of it.[48]

Sir Patrick Mayhew AG issued his statement in the form of a Written Answer,[49] an unusual arrangement[50] which again prevented debate. The Attorney General told MPs that it was Parliament, by passing section 2(1) of the European Communities Act 1972, that had given effect to the Community law requirement that national courts must set aside any rule which even temporarily prevents the effective application of Community law.[51] Moreover it was Parliament, by enacting section 2(4), that had provided that Acts such as the 1988 Act should be construed and have effect subject to section 2(1). In effect the government seemed to be inviting the House of Lords to accept the ECJ ruling irrespective of the traditional doctrine that Parliament cannot bind its successors. It was also apparently inviting their Lordships to heap the 'blame' for the limitation of parliamentary sovereignty squarely on Parliament. It is curious that a government with a (by 1990) highly Eurosceptic Prime Minister should take such an attitude and seemingly discourage debate.

Press comment was remarkably one-sided, in favour of the *Factortame* decision. The *Independent* praised the ECJ judgment as 'logical, inevitable and right',[52] arguing that the real debate was not about elusive notions of sovereignty but about the national interest and agreeing with the Attorney General that the choice to surrender legislative supremacy had been made by Parliament itself in 1972.[53] The *Guardian* too argued that the ruling should come as no surprise and that since Luxembourg had now in effect created a UK Supreme Court to which Parliament was subordinate, the best way forward was to readjust the British constitution by adopting a Bill of Rights and written constitution.[54] *The Times* chose not to devote a leader to the decision, and even the *Daily Telegraph*'s hostility was muted, its editorial conceding that the primacy of Community law was logical since 'the Common Market has enough difficulties making laws, and especially enforcing them, without having them countermanded by national parliaments'.[55] As for the tabloids, the

---

[47] HC, 174, col 1108, 21 June 1990. [48] HC, 176, col 282w, 12 July 1990.

[49] HC, 175, cols 141–143w, 26 June 1990.

[50] Most controversial ECJ judgments involving the UK have been reported to the House by way of oral statement with questions.

[51] The Attorney General failed to mention that *Simmenthal*, in which this 'doctrine of immediacy' was established, post-dated the 1972 Act. (Case 106/77 *Amministrazione delle Finanze dello Stato v Simmenthal SpA* [1978] ECR 629, [1978] 3 CMLR 263, paras 21–23.)

[52] *Independent*, 20 June 1990. [53] Ibid, 23 June 1990.

[54] *Guardian*, 21 June 1990. [55] *Daily Telegraph*, 20 June 1990.

Sun, Daily Express, Daily Mirror, and *Daily Mail* neither reported nor commented on the case.

On 18 July 1990 the High Court decided *Stoke-on-Trent City Council v B&Q plc.*[56] Here the court had to decide whether provisions of the Shops Act 1951 contravened Article 30 EEC. While deciding that the British statute was compatible with Community law, on the level of general principle Hoffman J held that

> The Treaty of Rome is the supreme law of this country, taking precedence over Acts of Parliament. Our entry into the Community meant that (subject to our undoubted but probably theoretical right to withdraw from the Community altogether) Parliament surrendered its sovereign right to legislate contrary to the provisions of the Treaty on the matters of social and economic policy which it regulated. The entry into the Community was itself a high act of social and economic policy, but where the partial surrender of sovereignty was seen as more than compensated by the advantages of membership.[57]

Thus for Hoffman, Community law prevails not because of the European Communities Act 1972 but because of *entry* into the Community. Furthermore he characterized entry as *a high act of policy*, conceivably an act of the national polity tantamount to legal revolution.[58]

House of Lords 2: reasoning flawed?

When *Factortame* returned to the House of Lords, the House, applying the preliminary ruling, granted interim relief.[59] Although Lord Goff, delivering the leading speech, did not deal with the general question of sovereignty, he spoke of the case as being 'concerned with a challenge to the *lawfulness* of an Act of Parliament as being incompatible with European law'[60] and of the applicants having 'strong grounds for challenging the *validity* of the provisions'.[61] Lord Goff appears to go further than the supremacy doctrine requires, since the ECJ only directs courts to set aside national provisions to the extent to which they are incompatible with Community provisions,

---

[56] [1990] 3 CMLR 31.   [57] Ibid 34.

[58] However, like Lord Donaldson, Hoffman J fell into line with the more orthodox reasoning of Lord Bridge once *Factortame (No 2)* was decided by the House of Lords. See Hoffman (1991).

[59] [1991] AC 645.   [60] Ibid 664 C–D. Emphasis added.

[61] Ibid 674 G–H. Emphasis added.

which may fall short of total invalidity.[62] It is of interest that, in a lengthy speech, Lord Goff did not mention the 1972 Act at all. Lord Bridge was the only judge to talk generally about sovereignty, so his (uncontradicted) statement has been taken to be the House of Lords' position on parliamentary sovereignty in the context of Community membership. Lord Bridge stated:

Some public comments on the decision of the Court of Justice, affirming the jurisdiction of the courts of the Member States to override national legislation if necessary to enable interim relief to be granted in protection of rights under Community law, have suggested that this was a novel and dangerous invasion by a Community institution of the sovereignty of the United Kingdom Parliament. But such comments are based on a misconception. If the supremacy within the European Community of Community law over the national law of Member States was not always inherent in the EEC Treaty it was certainly well established in the jurisprudence of the Court of Justice long before the United Kingdom joined the Community. Thus, whatever limitation of its sovereignty Parliament accepted when it enacted the European Communities Act 1972 was entirely voluntary. Under the terms of the 1972 Act it has always been clear that it was the duty of a United Kingdom court, when delivering final judgment, to override any rule of national law found to be in conflict with any directly enforceable rule of Community law. Similarly, when decisions of the Court of Justice have exposed areas of United Kingdom statute law which failed to implement Council directives, Parliament has always loyally accepted the obligation to make appropriate and prompt amendments. Thus there is nothing in any way novel in according supremacy to rules of Community law in areas to which they apply and to insist that, in the protection of rights under Community law, national courts must not be prohibited by rules of national law from granting interim relief in appropriate cases is no more than a logical recognition of that supremacy.[63]

Academic critiques of *Factortame*

There has been much academic comment as to whether Lord Bridge's reasoning was sufficiently convincing to justify overturning the basic constitutional ground rule of the last three hundred years. Wade, for example, has accused the House of turning 'a blind eye to constitutional theory'.[64] This is unconvincing, because the notion that the courts can change the basic norm is essential to *Kelsenian* constitutional theory.[65] Rather superficially, Wade

---

[62] Case 106/77 *Amministrazione delle Finanze dello Stato v Simmenthal SpA* [1978] ECR 629, [1978] 3 CMLR 263, para 17. See Nicol (1996).
[63] [1991] 1 AC 603, 658.   [64] Wade (1996) at 575.   [65] McLeod (1999) 81–83.

argued that MPs in 1972 had been misled as to the 'prospect of [Parliament's] subservience during the period of membership', and that in *Factortame* 'Parliament discovered too late that it had been deceived'. Chapter 4 has shown that, as far as the House of Commons was concerned, ministerial statements on the post-accession fate of parliamentary sovereignty were equivocal. Only when the Bill had cleared the Commons and was proceeding effortlessly through the House of Lords did government spokesmen plainly insist that Community law would always give way to subsequent statute in the event of irreconcilable conflict. Here, the statements of Lord Hailsham LC and Viscount Colville may well have been inspired by a quite innocent over-estimation of the strength of parliamentary sovereignty on the part of lawyers immersed in Diceyan orthodoxy.

Wade also claims that the 1972 Act failed to explain how the supremacy of Community law would take effect. This is patently wrong. The combination of sections 2(4) and 3(1) make it clear that it was for *the British courts* to construe and give effect to future British statutes subject to the supremacy of Community law, something that was expressly stated by ministers such as Sir Geoffrey Howe at the time. Wade heaps the blame on government chicanery whilst turning a blind eye to parliamentary inability to comprehend the direct effect doctrine. In contrast to Wade, Eekelar argued that the House had really opted for *legal continuity* by basing its decision on the sovereignty of (the 1972) Parliament rather than on the jurisdiction's entry into the 'new legal order'. The decision merely reflected the widely held 'new view' of parliamentary sovereignty[66] and accordingly could not be regarded as revolutionary.[67]

Craig, in his influential article 'Sovereignty of the United Kingdom Parliament after *Factortame*', pointed to the vulnerability of the parliamentary sovereignty doctrine stemming from the failure of its latter-day adherents to furnish arguments of principle in support of parliamentary omnipotence.[68] He suggested that the willingness of the courts to countenance limitations of sovereignty in the context of Community law made it more likely that they would be prepared to relax the doctrine in other areas, for example in the context of a procedurally entrenched Bill of Rights. Craig observed that it remained open to the courts to choose between a change in

---

[66] ie parliamentary sovereignty means that the courts will accept the right of Parliament to change the allocation of legislative competence for as long as the European Communities Act 1972 remains in force. (But is this an example of substantive entrenchment masquerading under the thin disguise of procedural entrenchment?)

[67] Eekelaar (1997) 187.   [68] Craig (1991).

the ultimate legal principle and a less dramatic 'rule of interpretation' approach, whereby inconsistencies would be resolved in favour of Community law unless Parliament expressed a clear wish to legislate contrary to Community law. The latter option would serve 'to preserve the formal veneer of Diceyan orthodoxy while undermining its substance'.[69] Wade, however, argued that Lord Bridge's language did not suggest that he regarded the matter as one of interpretation. Wade noted that the decision could mean either that Parliament could 'voluntarily' limit its successors' sovereignty in any matter, or alternatively that accession to the Community was a unique constitutional event, setting no precedent for self-bindingness in other contexts.[70]

However, in addition, the following criticisms of Lord Bridge's *reasoning* could be advanced. First, the argument that 'whatever limitation of its sovereignty Parliament accepted when it enacted the European Communities Act 1972 was entirely voluntary' assumes too much. Earlier chapters of this book have uncovered little evidence that parliamentarians were aware of the way in which Community law would be enforced by *the national courts* setting aside Acts of Parliament. In interpreting sections 2(1) and 2(4), Lord Bridge—in a manner reminiscent of the ECJ's interpretative technique—focuses on what *ought to* have been in the minds of MPs in passing the 1972 Act rather than what *was* actually in MPs' minds. Whether such an interpretative approach is appropriate in the case of so fundamental a constitutional change is contestable. Secondly, in any event, it is one question whether parliamentarians should have been aware of the ECJ's case law on supremacy and quite another question whether they could safely assume that this jurisprudence could apply in the United Kingdom. After all, parliamentarians were told by the Solicitor General that the sovereignty of Parliament was 'inescapable and enduring' and unalterable by Parliament. In other words, the *terms* of the 1972 Act need to be distinguished from its *effects*. Irrespective of what it commanded British courts and tribunals to do, it was ultimately for the courts to determine whether the Act would fall victim—like every other—to implied repeal by future Acts, in conformity with the doctrine that Parliament cannot bind its successors. The central thrust of Lord Bridge's argument—that Parliament, rather than the courts, ultimately determined the fate of its own sovereignty—is therefore wholly misleading. The real issue is not what Parliament does, but *how the courts react thereto*. Thirdly, irrespective of the ECJ's supremacy jurisprudence, it was plainly 'novel' for a *British* court to

---

[69] Ibid 251.   [70] Wade (1996) 574–575.

accord supremacy to Community law over a British statute. In the United Kingdom the setting aside of primary legislation has traditionally been considered impermissible.[71] Fourthly, there is constitutionally nothing very 'similar' about Parliament loyally amending domestic law to comply with Community law. Such amendment—however habitual in practice—depends on Parliament's continuing and voluntary acceptance of Community obligations, whereas disapplication of Acts of Parliament by the domestic courts is automatic, taking place irrespective of the view of the legislature on any particular policy issue. In sum, the assertions that Parliament's surrender of its sovereignty was 'entirely voluntary' and that the disapplication of statute by British courts was 'nothing in any way novel' are highly questionable. The major criticism, however, is that the House of Lords did not sufficiently elucidate *why* the European Communities Act 1972 binds successor Parliaments. Merely to chant the mantra of the ECJ's supremacy jurisprudence does nothing to explain why in the United Kingdom it should prevail over the doctrine of parliamentary sovereignty rather than vice versa.

Craig has suggested that there are two foundations for Lord Bridge's reasoning:

One is essentially *contractarian*: the United Kingdom knew when it joined the EC that priority should be accorded to EC law, and it must have been taken to have contracted on those terms. If therefore, 'blame' was to be cast for a loss of sovereignty then this should be laid at the feet of Parliament and not the courts. The other conceptual base for Lord Bridge's reasoning is *a priori* and *functional*; it was always inherent in a regime such as the Community that it could only function adequately if EC law could indeed take precedence in the event of a clash with domestic legal norms.[72]

The 'contractarian' argument is certainly present in Lord Bridge's statement. However, Chapter 4 of this book shows that parliamentarians did not realize what they were letting themselves in for when they passed the 1972 Act. Therefore any contractarian justification for *Factortame* would need to be based on the classical rule of contract law that the terms of agreements are determined objectively rather than subjectively. But is it appropriate to transplant from private law doctrines which may not be appropriate in the context of fundamental constitutional changes? The objective principle in contract law has been attributed to the needs of commercial convenience.[73] In public law, however, there might perhaps be democratic arguments in favour of insisting that 'the people', at least in the form of their representative institu-

---

[71] See eg *British Railways Board v Pickin* [1974] AC 765; *Cheney v Conn* [1968] 1 All ER 779.
[72] Craig (1997*b*) 203.   [73] Treitel (1999) 1.

tions, broadly understand the implications of what they have agreed before the courts enforce the agreement. The 'functional' argument is more normatively acceptable but is dealt with so fleetingly in Lord Bridge's dictum ('if the supremacy within the European Community of Community law over the national law of Member States was not always inherent in the EEC Treaty . . .') that it might hardly be said to constitute an argument at all.

In a less well-known but insightful work, 'Report on the United Kingdom', Craig proffers a rationale for *Factortame* which is both plausible and normatively attractive.[74] He argues that political disagreements in Britain over the Community should not mask the facts of Britain's long-term membership, the increasing acceptance of Community law as part of our law, and the acceptance by the majority of the population of Britain's EEC membership as a political norm. Viewed against this backdrop *Factortame* can be seen as *an attempt by the courts to bring constitutional doctrine up to date with political reality*, a form of 'constitutional catch-up'. Thus their Lordships modified parliamentary sovereignty to reflect the political reality of Britain's EEC membership.

This reasoning furnishes a convincing explanation as to what really motivated their Lordships to decide *Factortame* in favour of the supremacy of EC law rather than in favour of the preservation of parliamentary omnipotence. It also constitutes a normatively attractive justificatory basis, casting the judiciary in an essentially secondary and reflective constitution-developing role. It is the people and their politicians (whom the people elect and eject) who are properly the primary instigators of constitutional change in a democratic society. Widespread, long-term acceptance by the British polity of EEC membership constituted a good reason to modify parliamentary sovereignty. It is at this point that the 'functional' argument—that, irrespective of the 1972 legislators' original intent, the Community requires the supremacy doctrine in order to work—might legitimately be brought into play. The legitimate exercise of the judicial duty of updating constitutional law in conformity with constitutional practice amounts in itself to a good reason of principle to justify the outcome of *Factortame*.

The *EOC* case

At this juncture it might be appropriate to depart from the strict chronology of this book, in order to examine the case which might be considered the

[74] Craig (1997*b*) 211–212.

natural follow-up to *Factortame*. This was *R v Secretary of State for Employment ex parte Equal Opportunities Commission*. The case involved a challenge to the 'threshold' provisions of the Employment Protection (Consolidation) Act 1978 for their compatibility with Community law. These stipulated that to acquire the right to bring a claim of unfair dismissal before the industrial tribunal, and to gain the right to redundancy pay, an employee working sixteen or more hours per week had to be with the same employer continuously for at least two years. However, the arrangements for employees working less than sixteen hours per week were considerably more onerous. Those who worked between eight and sixteen hours per week required five years' continuous employment. Those working less than eight hours per week never acquired these rights. The Equal Opportunities Commission considered that these statutory provisions constituted indirect discrimination against women and as such breached Community law. It wrote to the Employment Secretary to this effect. The Employment Secretary replied by letter, stating that Article 119 EC did not apply and in any case the current thresholds were entirely justifiable. The EOC brought an application for judicial review.

High Court and Court of Appeal: sovereignty respected?

The Divisional Court[75] considered that *Factortame* was authority for the proposition that it was the courts' duty to make appropriate declarations giving effect to directly enforceable Community law rights, in other words stating that employees who work less than sixteen hours per week were subject only to the 'two-year rule'. However, Nolan LJ distinguished this sort of declaration from a declaration that the Secretary of State was in breach of the UK's Community law obligations in failing to introduce legislation to amend the 1978 Act. It could not be right for the courts to tell the Secretary of State that he must introduce legislation amending the 1978 Act when it would equally be open to him as a Member of Parliament to introduce legislation amending or repealing the 1972 Act.[76]

As a matter of Community law, this is a distinction without substance. To maintain on the national statute book legislation which contravenes Community law constitutes in itself a breach of Community law, even if national authorities ignore it, since it 'gives rise to an ambiguous state of

---

[75] [1992] ICR 341 (Nolan LJ and Judge J).   [76] Ibid 358 C–E.

affairs'.[77] Thus from a Community law standpoint a declaration that national legislation is incompatible with Community law is tantamount to a declaration that the Member State is in breach of its Community obligations. Nolan LJ's statement indicates that, far from perceiving the Treaty of Rome as the supreme law of this country, he merely regarded it as protected from implied repeal. On the facts the Divisional Court held that the Secretary of State had in any case objectively justified the indirect discrimination involved.

The Court of Appeal[78] disposed of the case rather artificially, the majority holding that the Secretary of State's letter did not constitute a 'decision' or a 'challengeable expression of view' susceptible to judicial review. On the constitutional issue, the majority followed the Divisional Court's distinction. It was not for the courts to pronounce upon whether the UK was in breach of international obligations, although it was for the courts to apply directly effective Community law in preference to domestic law if the laws conflict. Again this seems based on a traditionalist view of parliamentary sovereignty, the premiss being that the Treaty of Rome is simply an international treaty, something that the ECJ has denied since the days of *Van Gend*.

House of Lords: sovereignty discarded?

The House of Lords[79] held that what was under attack was not any 'decision' or view in the Employment Secretary's letter but the legislation itself. The House dealt separately with the issue of redundancy pay and unfair dismissal rights, since it had difficulty deciding whether compensation for unfair dismissal constituted 'pay' within the meaning of Article 119 EC and the equal pay directive (Council Directive 75/117/EEC). It granted a declaration in the following terms:

1. in the context of redundancy pay, the statutory provisions were contrary to both Article 119 EC and the equal pay directive;
2. in the context of unfair dismissal, the statutory provisions were contrary to the equal treatment directive (Council Directive 76/207/EEC).

It also held that judicial review constituted the appropriate means of testing the compatibility of UK primary legislation with Community law.

---

[77] See Case 167/73 *Commission v France* (French Merchant Seamen) [1974] ECR 359.
[78] [1993] 1 All ER 1022 (Dillon, Kennedy, and Hirst LJJ).
[79] [1995] 1 AC 1 (Lords Keith, Jauncey, Lowry, Browne-Wilkinson, and Slynn).

What was remarkable was the self-confidence of the House of Lords. No longer did the United Kingdom's highest court feel compelled to refer statutory provisions to the ECJ whenever it believed them to be incompatible with Community law. Now it was prepared to override them itself. This innovation was greeted with howls of protest from sections of the press and government backbenchers. *The Times* commented in an editorial that

The House of Lords . . . has, in effect, struck down as 'unconstitutional' an Act of Parliament which is still believed—in some quarters more than others—to be 'sovereign' . . . [T]he issue of greatest constitutional significance is the role of the English courts. Until the revolutionary *Factortame* case—where the Divisional Court suspended the operation of an Act of Parliament while the ECJ ruled on the substantive question—the courts have always been faithful to the Diceyan approach. But by its methods in the *EOC* case, the House of Lords has given Britain its first taste of a constitutional court. The significance of its decision is great. . . . In any other society, such constitutional 'revision' would be a subject for heated debate. Its significance must not be lost on Britain's citizens and its Parliament.[80]

In fact there was no 'heated debate' in Parliament. The case received some attention in a Commons debate on sex discrimination a few days after the judgment. Clare Short on behalf of the Opposition said Labour were 'absolutely delighted' with the decision[81] whereas Eurosceptic MPs displayed a heightened awareness of the impact of Community membership on the power of *domestic* courts *vis-à-vis* Parliament. Bernard Jenkin said:

When we wanted to join the European Community, it was not explained that we would be setting up our own courts to compete with us in matters such as this. . . . Under that ruling, the Law Lords have treated Parliament no differently from an errant local authority that has passed some unreasonable bye-laws or an employment scheme run by a private company.[82]

Their Lordships' self-confidence also manifested itself in the narrow margin of appreciation they permitted the government when it came to objectively justifying the thresholds on the grounds that they boosted the availability of part-time employment. Lord Keith undertook a rigorous statistical comparison, examining the legislative provisions and employment figures of other Member States, and concluded that no objective justification had been established. This contrasts sharply with the attitude of Hoffmann J in *Stoke-on-*

---

[80] *The Times*, 5 March 1994.   [81] HC, 239, col 428, 10 March 1994.
[82] Ibid, col 479, 10 March 1994. See also Iain Duncan-Smith (ibid, cols 474–475, 10 March 1994).

Trent City Council v B&Q plc[83] where, on the question of whether the UK's Sunday trading rules were proportionate in their effect on the free movement of goods, he adopted a *Wednesbury*-style test[84] of whether the compromise adopted by Parliament, so far as it affected Community trade, was one which a reasonable legislature could have reached.

Originally some commentators assumed that there was a link between the House of Lords' decision not to request a preliminary ruling and the fact that, under Community law, it is for the national court to assess whether indirect discrimination has been objectively justified. Doubtless this had an influence. However, the House of Lords speeches do not indicate that this was the determining factor. Nowhere is it suggested that the granting of a declaration of incompatibility with Community law by the Divisional Court is restricted to contexts in which the ECJ has 'hived off' decision-making functions to the national courts. The better explanation is that, as far as the House of Lords was concerned, there was here no *question* of Community law which needed to be answered by the ECJ. The House considered that it merely had to *apply* Community law. This makes their Lordships' self-confidence even more striking.

Furthermore, Lord Keith went out of his way to emphasize that the power to disapply operates before *any* court to which a case comes; it is not the preserve of the House of Lords or the Court of Appeal. This was confirmed by his attitude to Mrs Day's claim. Mrs Patricia Day was a second applicant who was joined to the proceedings due to the EOC's concern that its own application might be dismissed for want of standing. She had been made redundant by a health authority, but, having worked only eleven hours a week for less than five years, was ineligible for a redundancy benefit. She sought judicial review of the Employment Secretary's policy of refusing to introduce amending legislation. It was held that she had a good *private law* claim for redundancy pay against her employers under Article 119, which would prevail over the discriminatory provisions of the 1978 Act. The appropriate forum for her was the industrial tribunal, which was likewise fully competent to disapply the British statute.

The choice of remedy, a declaration that the statutory thresholds were incompatible with Community law, warrants some reflection. Coupled with

---

[83] [1990] 3 CMLR 31. Mindful of his constitutional position, Hoffmann J noted at para 47 that '[t]hese questions involve compromises between competing interests which in a democratic society must be resolved by the legislature. . . . The function of the court is to review the acts of the legislature but not to substitute its own policies or values.'

[84] *Associated Provincial Picture Houses Ltd v Wednesbury Corpn* [1948] 1 KB 223.

the *Simmenthal* obligation resting on the lower courts, a declaration of incompatibility with Community law adds up to much the same thing as invalidation. It transmits a signal to the lower courts and tribunals: whenever they dealt with the statutory thresholds, they would now be obliged to disregard them to the extent laid down by the House of Lords. Lord Keith recognized this when he stated that there was no need for a declaration that the UK or the Secretary of State were in breach of Community obligations; a declaration that the thresholds were incompatible with Community law would suffice for the purposes sought to be achieved by the EOC.[85] Thus the compatibility of UK law with EC law would not depend on whether government or Parliament amended the law to conform with the House of Lords view of Community law.

From partial to total invalidity, courtesy of the industrial tribunal

As it was, the statutory amendment was tardy. The House of Lords delivered its judgment on 3 March 1994, but the legislation was not amended until 6 February 1995 when the Employment Secretary, using his power under section 2(2) of the European Communities Act 1972, made the necessary statutory instrument.[86] In between these two dates, it was for the industrial tribunals to apply the law whenever they were faced with an applicant who did not satisfy the thresholds currently on the statute books. The series of cases which followed revealed the readiness of courts and tribunals at the lowest level to set aside statutory provisions which contravened EC law. Indeed in certain respects the lower courts and tribunals surpassed the House of Lords in their enthusiasm to disapply statute.[87]

On 19 May 1994 the industrial tribunal in the unfair dismissal complaint of *Mediguard Services Ltd v Thame*[88] went further than the House of Lords, by holding that—despite the existence of crucial differences between redundancy payments and unfair dismissal compensation—it felt obliged to treat such compensation as 'pay' within the meaning of Article 119 EC. This is

[85] At 328D.
[86] Employment Protection (Part-Time Employees) Regulations 1995 (SI 1995 No 31).
[87] See Nicol (1996).
[88] Unreported. There is, however, an account of the IT's reasoning in the EAT decision, reported in [1994] ICR 751.

significant, for whereas a Court of Appeal majority believed the unfair dismissal thresholds were contrary to Community law, the House of Lords had declined to decide the matter and had intimated that, although compensation for unfair dismissal could well be 'pay' for the purposes of Article 119 EC, only a preliminary reference could resolve the question. Rather than make the order for reference as their Lordships suggested, the industrial tribunal in *Mediguard* boldly strode where the House of Lords feared to tread. The significance of holding that the unfair dismissal threshold violated Article 119 as well as the equal treatment directive is that Article 119 has 'horizontal' direct effect between private parties, whereas a directive is only effective against an employer who is part of the State or an emanation thereof.[89] Thus the thresholds were now ineffective for the purposes of unfair dismissal, not just redundancy payments. This is important, since the work of industrial tribunals overwhelmingly consists of hearing unfair dismissal claims. The Employment Appeal Tribunal upheld the industrial tribunal decision, reasoning that the matter was acte clair so there was no need for a preliminary ruling. This decision was followed in the IT and EAT decisions in *Methilhill Bowling Club v Hunter*.[90] For good measure, in *Warren v Wylie and Wylie*[91] the industrial tribunal decided that it was acte clair that the rule precluding those who worked less than eight hours from ever gaining unfair dismissal rights was contrary to EC law and agreed that unfair dismissal compensation fell within the definition of 'pay'. These conclusions were reinforced two months later by the EAT decision in *Clifford v Devon County Council*.[92] The question of law was not ultimately resolved until 1999 when the ECJ in *R v Secretary of State for Employment ex parte Seymour Smith and Perez* confirmed that a judicial award of unfair dismissal compensation constituted pay within the meaning of Article 119 EEC.[93]

Thus the lower courts and tribunals now felt comfortable disapplying statutory provisions in favour of Community rules. Furthermore they did so with striking terseness. Unlike the superior courts in *Factortame* and *EOC* they felt no need to refer to the 1972 Act to justify their actions. Rather the subordination of Acts of Parliament to Community law was simply taken as read.

---

[89] See Case 152/84 *Marshall v Southampton and South West Hampshire Area Health Authority (Teaching)* [1986] ECR 723, [1986] 1 CMLR 688.

[90] [1995] IRLR 232.   [91] [1994] IRLR 316.   [92] [1994] IRLR 628.

[93] Case C–167/97 [1999] IRLR 253. See also [1997] ICR 371 (House of Lords), [1995] IRLR 464 (Court of Appeal), and [1994] IRLR 448 (Divisional Court).

The Community, sovereignty, and the fall of Thatcher

In June 1989 the European Council had decided to convene an intergovernmental conference (IGC) on Economic and Monetary Union. The European
Parliament pressed for the reform process to go beyond EMU,[94] and in April
1990 Kohl and Mitterrand had written to their colleagues proposing a second
IGC on political union, an idea endorsed by the Dublin II European Council
in June 1990. Once again both IGCs were convened in the face of British
reluctance.[95] These developments, together with the House of Lords' acceptance of the supremacy of Community law in *Factortame*, set the stage for an
intensification of prime ministerial Euroscepticism. On 30 October, just
nineteen days after their Lordships delivered their *Factortame* speeches, Mrs
Thatcher famously opined

> The President of the Commission, Mr Delors, said at a press conference the other day
> that he wanted the European Parliament to be the democratic body of the
> Community, he wanted the Commission to be the Executive, he wanted the Council
> of Ministers to be the Senate. No. No. No.
>
> Perhaps the Labour Party would give all those things up easily. Perhaps it would
> agree to a single currency and the abolition of the pound sterling. The right hon.
> Gentleman would be glad to hand it over. What is the point of trying to get elected to
> Parliament only to hand over sterling and the powers of this House to Europe?[96]

This performance, poorly received in most newspapers,[97] prompted the
resignation from the Cabinet of Sir Geoffrey Howe on 1 November. In his
resignation letter Howe objected to Thatcher 'trying to draw an arbitrary
line under our engagement in the European process':

> As much as you, I have wanted to make the most of Britain's influence in the world, to
> deploy Britain's sovereignty to the best advantage of our people. Ever since our orig-
> inal application to join the European Community in 1962, that has clearly involved
> Britain's firm, practical commitment to the historic process of closer European part-
> nership.[98]

Thatcher replied that their differences over Europe had been exaggerated:
'We are at one in wishing to preserve the sovereignty of Parliament. We want

---

[94] Corbett (1992) 273–274.   [95] Thatcher (1993) 752, 761–762.

[96] HC, 178, col 873, 30 October 1990.

[97] *Daily Telegraph*, 2 November 1990; *Guardian*, 3 November 1990, 6 November 1990;
Independent, 14 November 1990.

[98] *Independent*, 2 November 1990.

Britain to play a leading part in Europe and be part of the further political, economic and monetary development of the European Community.'[99] It is ironic that the notion of sovereignty was being used in two different senses in the same exchange of letters. Howe saw it as the opportunity to bind future decision-making in the perceived best interests of the people; Thatcher saw it as the preservation of national choice. This merely replicated the two visions of sovereignty which have sat side by side since the debate on Community membership began.

In a personal statement to the House of Commons, Howe warned against drawing 'a false antithesis' between 'cooperation between individual sovereign states' and a 'centralised, federal super-state', as if there were no middle way. Accusing the Prime Minister of conjuring up a nightmare image, he quoted Churchill's view that European union would involve 'the gradual assumption by all the nations concerned of that larger sovereignty which can alone protect their diverse and distinctive customs and characteristics and their national traditions'.[100] Howe's speech set in motion the 1990 Conservative leadership contest. The sovereignty issue was not the only factor in Mrs Thatcher's downfall. Others were her dogged adherence to the community charge, her authoritarian style, her longevity as Premier, and above all the feeling among Conservative MPs that her continuation in office would guarantee electoral defeat. Nonetheless her views on the Community not only precipitated the leadership election but were a major contributory factor to her removal. Thus the issues of the Community and parliamentary sovereignty once again took centre-stage in the British political arena.

The Maastricht Treaty and the ECJ

In December 1990 the two IGCs, one on Economic and Monetary Union, the other on European Political Union, opened in Rome to devise a new set of Treaty amendments. Despite the change of Premier, the UK government took a minimalist position on a range of issues from legislative reform to extending Community competence.[101] Although the resulting Maastricht Treaty appeared to many British observers to lead to greater integration, the majority of Member States were profoundly dissatisfied with it since they saw the gradual extension of the *Community* as the basis of the future Union.[102]

[99] Ibid.   [100] HC, 180, col 463, 13 November 1990.   [101] Dinan (1994) 168–195.
[102] Pryce (1994) 40.

Reluctantly, they had to accept a strong element of intergovernmentalism,[103] in the form of the pillarized structure of the European Union, which excluded the Commission, European Parliament, and ECJ from any major role in Justice and Home Affairs and the Common Foreign and Security Policy. Furthermore, agreement was only possible because other Member States were willing to tolerate British opt-outs from the Social Protocol and the third stage of EMU.[104] The Treaty nonetheless involved a considerable increase in Community competence, in return for which the UK secured the principle of subsidiarity in the new Article 3b EC which it considered would claw back powers passed to Community institutions.[105]

Although largely excluded from the two intergovernmental 'pillars', the ECJ's jurisdiction was expanded by the revised Articles 173 and 175. Changes to the third paragraph of Article 165 allowed the ECJ to work more effectively, since whereas the ECJ had previously been obliged to sit in plenary session whenever Member States or other institutions brought cases before it, it was now obliged to do so only when asked.[106] Moreover the very expansion of Community competences enhanced the ECJ's institutional position. On the other hand, the IGC ignored the proposal of the Court of First Instance for the creation of a unitary and hierarchical system of Community courts.[107] It also eschewed academic suggestions that the Treaty be amended to introduce the principle that a Member State incurs liability towards the victim of its infringements of Community law.[108] Ironically just three weeks before the Treaty amendments were finalized at Maastricht the ECJ delivered its landmark *Francovich* judgment, which reinforced the *de facto* supremacy of Community law by making Member States liable to individuals for their breaches of Community law.[109] Thus the questions of *scope* of Community law inherent in the Maastricht Treaty were debated in the context of ever more effective *enforceability* of Community law.

---

[103] George (1996) 17.   [104] Baun (1996) 95–97, Lamont (1999) 122.

[105] Duff (1994) 57.

[106] Church and Phinnemore (1994) 280. Jeremy Lever QC in his Memorandum to the House of Commons Foreign Affairs Committee considered that, of all the reforms, this was the one which would have the greatest practical impact in strengthening the institutional position of the ECJ (Second Report from the Foreign Affairs Committee, *Europe after Maastricht*, Cm 223-I, Session 1991–2, 70–71).

[107] (1991) 28 CML Rev 5.   [108] Ibid 711.

[109] Joined Cases C–6/90 and C–9/60 *Andrea Francovich and another v The Republic of Italy* [1991] ECR I–5357, [1993] 2 CMLR 66 (judgment of 19 November 1991).

Government presentation and parliamentary perceptions

In the White Paper *Developments in the European Community July–December 1991*[110] Prime Minister John Major argued that Maastricht had been a success because (i) it established an extra-Community basis for European cooperation, (ii) subsidiarity would deter unnecessary action by Brussels in matters properly left to national governments, and (iii) it 'strengthened the Community as a Community of law' by empowering the ECJ to fine Member States who failed to remedy infringements established under Article 169. Thus the government's intention was that Community law should do less, but that which it *did* do should be uniformly enforced.

There was parliamentary scepticism as to whether the government had achieved all of this. The Select Committee on European Legislation observed that although subsidiarity was in theory justiciable, in practice it was difficult to visualize a successful legal challenge. It also suggested that *Francovich* liability would prove a greater deterrent to national defiance of Community law than the government's much-prized system of fining Member States laid down in the new Article 171(2) EC.[111]

The Foreign Affairs Committee considered that it could not be taken for granted that the Common Foreign and Security Policy and cooperation on interior and justice matters would continue to be handled intergovernmentally. Furthermore the application by the ECJ of the subsidiarity principle would need to be closely monitored.[112] The Committee took evidence from lawyers Jeremy Lever QC, Phillip Allott, and Professors Trevor Hartley and John Usher on 19 February 1992,[113] and again the academic view was that Maastricht would expand, not contract, the scope of Community law. Usher noted that the subsidiarity clause in Article 130r EEC (introduced by the SEA) had not eased the flow of environmental legislation. Hartley considered that whenever there was a question of the jurisdiction of the Community versus that of the Member States, the Community won. He thought the ECJ would only quash Community acts for breach of subsidiarity where institutions legislated in a glaringly excessive manner. There was disagreement over

---

[110] Cm 1857, March 1992.

[111] Fifteenth Report of the Select Committee on European Legislation, Session 1991–2, p xxxix.

[112] Second Report from the Foreign Affairs Committee, *Europe after Maastricht*, Cm 223-I, Session 1991–2.

[113] Ibid 78–80.

whether the UK could lawfully withdraw from the Community. Hartley asserted that if the UK Parliament passed an Act repealing the 1972 Act in whole or in part, the ECJ would hold it invalid to the extent that it conflicted with Community law, but the House of Lords would take the opposite view. In contrast Allott considered that parliamentary sovereignty had been terminated by Community membership, inasmuch as it was no longer legally possible to secede by Act of Parliament.[114]

When the Committee examined former Commissioner Sir Ralf Dahrendorf the ECJ was again remarkably central to MPs' questions. In answer to Ted Rowland's suggestion that ECJ judgments reflected the broad goal of European unity, Dahrendorf remarked: 'the European Court has certainly throughout the twenty-odd years I have followed it tended to interpret the institutional arrangements of the Community extensively rather than restrictively on all occasions . . . It raises a very interesting question about the quality of the whole institutional set-up.'[115]

Ratification of Maastricht

The European Communities (Amendment) Bill 1992 sought to carry the Treaty amendments into domestic law for the purposes of section 6 of the European Parliament Elections Act 1978. It also provided that a separate Act of Parliament would be required for the UK to join the single currency. The Bill was passed at Second Reading by 336 to 92, with Labour abstaining.[116]

Analysis of the Second Reading debate presents a wholly transformed picture compared to 1972. Of the eighty Members who spoke, only five criticized the Council of Ministers. The Commission was still a major target of criticism, with twenty-six MPs attacking it. The ECJ was attacked by eighteen Members. There were eleven criticisms of the European Central Bank (ECB). Only three MPs attacked the European Parliament, with ten

---

[114] See also Loveland (1996) 531–535; cf Radlett (1997).

[115] Second Report from the Foreign Affairs Committee, *Europe after Maastricht*, Cm 223-I, Session 1991–2, 83 (26 February 1992).

[116] The Labour leadership supported the Maastricht Treaty whilst pressing for the British opt-out from the Social Protocol to be removed. Labour's April 1992 election manifesto had pledged that a Labour government would play an active role in negotiations on Economic and Monetary Union (*It's Time to Get Britain Working Again*, 27). At its 1992 Conference the Party resolved that 'the Maastricht Treaty, while not perfect, is the best agreement that can currently be achieved' (Composite 69, 1992 Labour Party Annual Conference).

members commenting favourably upon it. (These figures may somewhat under-represent parliamentary hostilities, since the debate included a high proportion of maiden speeches, traditionally non-controversial.)

The Council was no longer the butt of significant criticism because it was now perceived as the less enthusiastic partner in European integration. It would have been difficult for Conservative MPs to target a body which preferred to operate by consensus[117] and on which members of the Thatcher/Major administrations had sat for the preceding thirteen years. The Commission was vulnerable to attack from Eurosceptics due to its leading role in the drive towards the single currency and its legislative activism during the single market programme. The ECB was criticized principally by Labour MPs for its prospective lack of accountability. The European Parliament largely escaped censure now that MPs had a more realistic perception of its limited powers. Indeed it received praise from some MPs who saw it as the only body that could make the Commission and ECB accountable.

For our purposes, the most significant finding is that the ECJ, having attracted no criticisms whatsoever in the 1972 Second Reading, now drew eighteen adverse comments. These criticisms suggest that MPs were finally grasping the ECJ's constitutional significance. A crucial lacuna, however, is that, as in 1972, the impact of direct effect was not fully understood, in that not one Member referred to the corresponding enhanced power of the *United Kingdom* courts and tribunals. Perhaps this was because it was still reasonably assumed, in the wake of *Factortame* and before *EOC*, that any disapplication by a British court would be preceded by a preliminary reference.

Apprehension about the ECJ's power on the part of several Members was heightened by anxiety that it would shortly declare Britain's frontier controls unlawful. Former Home Office Ministers Kenneth Baker[118] and Dame Angela Rumbold[119] expressed concern on this score, as did Chairman of the Home Affairs Select Committee Sir John Wheeler[120] and several backbenchers.[121]

Above all, the ECJ's teleological mode of interpretation was seen as illegitimate. Sir Trevor Skeet (Conservative, Bedfordshire North) complained that

---

[117] See eg Westlake (1995) 111, Nugent (1993) 121.

[118] HC, 208, cols 287 and 290, 20 May 1992.

[119] Ibid, col 299, 20 May 1992. [120] Ibid, col 552, 21 May 1992.

[121] eg Denzil Davies (ibid, col 303, 20 May 1992), Sir Teddy Taylor (ibid, col 561, 21 May 1992), Roger Knapman (ibid, col 396, 20 May 1992), Richard Alexander (ibid, col 411, 20 May 1992), Michael Colvin (ibid, col 431, 20 May 1992).

the ECJ was bound to 'put a European interpretation' on subsidiarity, entirely different from the conception of subsidiarity favoured by the UK.[122] Ian Paisley (DUP, Antrim North) considered that the ECJ 'always finds in favour of an extension of the powers of the Community'.[123] Iain Duncan Smith (Conservative, Chingford) wanted an impartial constitutional court set above it.[124] Even consummate diplomat Douglas Hurd admitted that ECJ decisions consistently reflected 'an integrationist approach'.[125]

In contrast to its vocal critics—and unlike in 1986—the ECJ's supporters in the Commons lay low. Only Sir Russell Johnston, Liberal Democrat Foreign Affairs spokesman, expressed regret at the ECJ's exclusion from the two intergovernmental 'pillars'.[126] A few Conservative backbenchers voiced satisfaction that, thanks to British efforts, the ECJ would have the power to fine Member States which refused to comply with Article 169 judgments.[127]

Significantly the government was at pains to calm MPs' misgivings regarding ECJ power under Maastricht. John Major extolled the EU's three-pillar structure, which would mean that decisions reached on foreign and security policy, and on justice and home affairs issues, would have 'no direct effect in United Kingdom law',[128] and that any disputes would go to the International Court of Justice, not the ECJ. Foreign Secretary Douglas Hurd argued that this, together with the subsidiarity test, would curb the ECJ's integrationist tendencies.[129] His Minister of State Tristan Garel-Jones reassured MPs that the ECJ, like the US Supreme Court, must ultimately be influenced by political opinion.[130]

Sovereignty: a redefinition?

The debate witnessed a paradigm shift in MPs' conception of sovereignty, in so far as national and parliamentary sovereignty were no longer discussed in absolute terms. It was no longer a question of whether the United Kingdom remained a sovereign country, or whether Parliament remained a sovereign

[122] HC, 208, col 422, 20 May 1992. [123] Ibid, col 547, 21 May 1992.
[124] Ibid, cols 354–355, 20 May 1992. [125] Ibid, col 514, 21 May 1992.
[126] Ibid, col 537, 21 May 1992.
[127] Stephen Milligan (ibid, col 325, 20 May 1992), Sir Giles Shaw (ibid, col 372, 20 May 1992), Nigel Evans (ibid, col 390, 20 May 1992).
[128] Ibid, col 265, 20 May 1992. [129] Ibid, cols 514–516, 21 May 1992.
[130] Ibid, col 463, 20 May 1992.

legislature, but rather *how much sovereignty* the country or Parliament retained. There was no talk of Parliament's right to 'make or unmake any law', surely reflecting growing consciousness post-*Factortame* of Parliament's demoted status as a legislature of limited competence. Thus Major spoke of Parliament clearly demonstrating its sovereignty by retaining for itself the right to decide whether to move to the third stage of EMU.[131] This tacitly assumed that Parliament would not retain 'sovereignty' to decide whether to move to preceding stages.

The debate therefore seemed to see a resurrection of the notion of 'essential' sovereignty so hastily jettisoned by the Heath government after publication of the 1971 White Paper. This trend was also apparent in backbench contributions. Thus Kenneth Baker considered that the ability to control one's frontiers was an essential element of sovereignty,[132] and Sir John Wheeler regarded the tasks performed by the Home Office and other agencies of justice as 'perhaps the most important manifestations of sovereignty'.[133] The question of whether Britain was giving up 'essential' sovereignty was linked to the pervasive theme of whether the contents of the Maastricht Treaty added up to federalism, something which again was treated as a matter of degree.[134] Naturally the government argued that the intergovernmental pillars and introduction of subsidiarity reversed federalizing trends, whilst its opponents countered that the single currency was a massive step towards a United States of Europe.

The paving motion: subsidiarity defended and denounced

On 4 November 1992 the Prime Minister proposed a motion that the House proceed with the Bill.[135] Although the ECJ itself appeared not to loom large as an issue in this debate, the scope of Community law did, and of course it is the ECJ which in the final analysis determines the Treaty's scope. Major claimed that

(a) the principle of subsidiarity, as a justiciable, legally binding rule, would restrain Community action;[136]

---

[131] Ibid, col 265, 20 May 1992.
[133] Ibid, col 552, 21 May 1992.
[135] HC, 213, cols 283–385, 4 November 1992.

[132] Ibid, col 287, 20 May 1992.
[134] See Hartley (1986) 229.
[136] Ibid, col 286, 4 November 1992.

(b) European integration through intergovernmentalism, rather than through the Treaty of Rome and ECJ jurisdiction, would prove 'much more amenable to the instincts of this country';[137]

(c) New Treaty articles on subjects such as health, education, culture, and vocational training had been carefully drafted to specify those powers retained by Member States and thereby counter the 'creeping competence' which came about by abuse of such articles or by ECJ judgments.[138]

The debate witnessed widespread scepticism from all shades of Commons opinion over government claims that subsidiarity would constitute a serious 'check in the Treaty of Rome'.[139] Opposition leader John Smith moved a Labour amendment suggesting that the principles of subsidiarity had yet to be worked out and that accordingly further consideration of the Bill should await the European Council's Edinburgh summit. Smith sought to cast doubt on the likely effectiveness of subsidiarity in the absence of decisions to make it an integral part of Community decision-making.[140] This suggests a lack of confidence in the ECJ's willingness to use the concept to rein in Community competences. Sir Edward Heath dismissed subsidiarity as irrelevant to the primary task of economic recovery in the Community.[141] Paddy Ashdown, whose Party's support for the government's motion proved highly controversial, cheerfully accepted that the Bill involved a shift in sovereignty to the European institutions and did not bother mentioning subsidiarity.[142] Numerous backbenchers, by no means just opponents of the Bill, also voiced scepticism.[143] Only two backbenchers—Tim Devlin and Michael Ancram[144]—lauded the subsidiarity principle. However, unlike in the case of the 'essential sovereignty' argument twenty-one years earlier, the Major government was not minded to abandon its fig leaf. The subsidiarity issue was intimately linked to the question of the ECJ's interpretative strategy. Clearly most MPs did not feel that Article 3b would make much impact on the Court's teleological decision-making. Labour's amendment was defeated,

---

[137] HC, col 288, 4 November 1992.   [138] Ibid, col 290, 4 November 1992.

[139] The phrase used by Douglas Hurd, Foreign Secretary, ibid, col 375, 4 November 1992.

[140] Ibid, cols 296–298, 4 November 1992.

[141] Ibid, col 312, 4 November 1992.   [142] Ibid, col 317, 4 November 1992.

[143] eg David Howell (ibid, col 331, 4 November 1992), Alan Howarth (Conservative, Stratford-upon-Avon) (ibid, col 352, 4 November 1992), Margaret Ewing (ibid, col 349, 4 November 1992).

[144] Ibid, col 335 and col 342 respectively, 4 November 1992. Both were subsequently appointed to ministerial office.

and the government's motion was carried by an uncomfortably close 319 to 316.[145]

Discussion of the ECJ in Committee

Academic narratives relating to the contentious amendments to the 1993 Bill may have obscured the strong element of bipartisanship between the three main parties which characterized the Committee proceedings. In sharp contrast to 1972 the vast majority of Opposition amendments were 'probing' amendments, intended to reveal government thinking, which Labour did not press to a vote.[146]

Opportunities for more detailed discussion of the ECJ's constitutional role arose in Committee in the context of amendments relating to the Social Policy protocol, the principle of subsidiarity, and the power to fine under Article 171(2) EC. While the former amendment was designed by the Opposition to force a general election,[147] the latter two were probing amendments. The very fact that there were three debates focusing on the ECJ contrasts with the single Committee debate during the incorporation of the SEA and none during the passage of the 1972 Act. All three amendments raised questions of the ECJ's interpretative strategy and institutional position. The debate on the Social Protocol involved discussion of whether the ECJ was likely to interpret Treaty of Rome provisions so broadly as to negate the British opt-out. The subsidiarity debate centred on whether the new Article 3(b) EC would decisively tone down the ECJ's project of promoting 'ever closer union'. Consideration of Article 171(2) enabled the House to discuss whether existing ECJ powers already went far enough.

The government's basic position was that the European Union's three-pillar structure, together with the introduction of subsidiarity, would clip the

---

[145] For an account of Conservative Party conduct on this vote, see Baker, Gamble, and Ludlam (1993) 151.

[146] This reflects Labour's transformation into a pro-Community party. None of the numerous Opposition-sponsored amendments to the 1972 Bill were of a merely probing nature. Amendments to the 1986 Bill came not from the official Opposition but from individual Eurosceptics.

[147] The government would not have permitted ratification of the Maastricht Treaty without the British opt-out from the Social Protocol, and had it been obliged to drop Maastricht ratification it would have resigned. This became clear with the vote on the Social Protocol which followed Third Reading. See HC, 229, cols 627–725, 23 July 1993.

ECJ's wings, and that indeed, in anticipation of Maastricht, the ECJ had already become more sympathetic to Member State freedom of action. Eurosceptics countered that the increase in Community competences, reflected in the revised Articles 2 and 3 EC, heralded a further expansion of ECJ power.

Three features are readily apparent from the Committee debates. First, the standard of legal argument—including from government spokesmen— was more sophisticated than in earlier years, with significant citation of authority. For example, Foreign Office Minister Tristan Garel-Jones made a statement of unprecedented detail on the government's attitude to the ECJ, pointing to the *Sunday Trading*[148] and *Walloon Waste*[149] judgments as evidence that the ECJ was not monolithically federalist but had grown more sensitive to Member State concerns.[150] On the other side of the argument, Iain Duncan Smith used *Van Gend*, *Van Duyn*,[151] and *Defrenne*[152] to show the consistency of the ECJ's approach, suggesting that, while the ECJ may pause at intervals to consolidate its position, its progress was always in the same— integrationist—direction. For example, he asserted that the 1978 *Defrenne*[153] decision, where the ECJ had held that Article 119 did not require identical retirement ages for men and women, had been reversed twelve years later in *Barber*.[154] (In fact Duncan Smith's account of *Barber* was inaccurate. The case merely established that a pension paid under a contracted-out private occupational scheme fell within the scope of Article 119 EEC. Thus it was unlawful for such a scheme to pay a deferred pension to a man made compulsorily redundant whereas a woman in the same position would be entitled to an immediate pension.)

Members who tried to make law-free speeches were given short shrift. Edward Garnier's attempt at a speech devoid of law was continually interrupted by interventions by MPs making legal points.[155] *Hansard* research by

---

[148]   Case 145/88 *Torfaen BC v B&Q plc* [1989] ECR 385, [1990] 1 CMLR 337; Cases C–306/88, 304/90, 169/91 *Stoke-on-Trent CC v B&Q plc* [1992] ECR I–6457, 6493, 6635, [1993] 1 CMLR 426.

[149]   Case C–2/90 *Commission v Belgium* [1992] ECR I–4431, [1993] 1 CMLR 365.

[150]   HC, 217, col 1057 (27 January 1993).

[151]   Case 41/74 *Van Duyn v Home Office* [1974] ECR 1337, [1975] 1 CMLR 1.

[152]   Case 43/75 *Defrenne v Société Anonyme Belge de Navigation Aérienne* [1976] ECR 455, [1976] 2 CMLR 98.

[153]   Case 149/77 *Defrenne v Sabena (No 3)* [1978] ECR 1365, [1978] 3 CMLR 312.

[154]   HC, 221, cols 937–938, 24 March 1993. Case C–262/88 *Barber v Guardian Royal Exchange Assurance Group* [1990] ECR I–1889, [1990] 2 CMLR 513.

[155]   Conservative MP for Harborough and, curiously, a barrister. HC, 217, cols 1045–1048, 27 January 1993. The interventions were from David Winnick (Labour, Walsall North), Sir Teddy Taylor (Conservative, Southend East), and Michael Spicer (Conservative, Worcestershire South)—all non-lawyers.

Garnett and Sherrington has suggested that the quality of parliamentary con-tributions in debates on the Community has declined since accession, and on a general level it is difficult to disagree that 'the front-bench spokesmen of 1993 would have been hard pressed by a selection from the best back-bench speakers of 1971'.[156] However, analysis of Committee proceedings relating to the ECJ indicates that a more impressive level of *legal* debate constitutes an exception to this deterioration.

The second feature is that it was the newer MPs who tended to be most familiar with the legal side of the Community constitution. The contribu-tions of Eurosceptics William Cash, Bernard Jenkin, Michael Spicer, and Iain Duncan-Smith, and Euro-enthusiasts Tristan Garel-Jones and Geoff Hoon, show far greater attention to, and understanding of, legal matters than sur-viving members of the 1970–4 Parliament who spoke during the Maastricht debates such as Edward Heath, Kenneth Clarke, Peter Shore, and Tony Benn. Legal education had little to do with this.[157] Rather it was an under-standable generational change. MPs of longer standing were conditioned to operating a politics-dominated rather than law-dominated constitution. The newer MPs were more attuned to the idea of Parliament as a legislature of limited competence. Although it might be considered disappointing that the 'Class of '72' made no greater effort to acclimatize to the more legal nature of the constitution, it is arguable that it took a generation before the British *judi-ciary* fully appreciated the opportunities opened up by Community law and that politicians, like judges, are creatures of habit.

The third feature was increased recognition—in contrast to the 1971–2 debates—that the ECJ enjoyed a status tantamount to that of a Supreme Court. Some Members thought that the ECJ would emulate the US Supreme Court's federalizing tendencies.[158] Others drew attention to the *Factortame* case in which the ECJ, from a British viewpoint, had earned its Supreme Court credentials.[159] This growing recognition of the ECJ as an immensely powerful institution led in turn to the questioning of its democ-ratic legitimacy, something conspicuously absent from both the 1971–2 and 1986 debates. For example Shadow Attorney General John Morris thought

---

[156] Garnett and Sherrington (1996) 400.

[157] The group of 'newer' MPs mentioned above contained only two lawyers—Cash (a solicitor) and Hoon (a law lecturer). Of the group of 'older' MPs, Clarke was a QC.

[158] eg Denzil Davies (HC, 225, col 428, 20 May 1993), Sir Richard Body (HC, 220, col 1185, 11 March 1993), Iain Duncan-Smith (HC, 221, col 941, 24 March 1993).

[159] eg Sir Teddy Taylor (HC, 221, col 936, 24 March 1993), Dr Norman Godman (HC, 220, col 783, 8 March 1993), Sir Trevor Skeet (ibid, col 680, 8 March 1993).

that careful consideration should be given before there was any transfer of power from elected representatives to the unelected European judiciary.[160] Bill Cash spoke of a 'new judocracy' in which decisions were taken by unelected political judges.[161] John Biffen (Chief Whip in 1986, since retired to the backbenches) was horrified at Garel-Jones's argument that Britain would rely on the changing sentiments of the ECJ, since normally 'it is the resolute certainties of the judicial system which are our guarantee'.[162] Euro-enthusiasts could have upheld the ECJ's democratic credentials on the grounds that it protects fundamental rights of individuals—the 'four free-doms' fortified by its own human rights doctrine—against the dictat of a popular majority, but this argument was not raised. Nor did they employ the argument that 'democracy requires the fair and equal application of laws that have been adopted'.[163] In the aftermath of *Factortame*, the ECJ's supporters were plainly on the defensive.[164]

Discussion of the ECJ and sovereignty in other Committee debates

Quite apart from debates which focused specifically on the ECJ, the issue of ECJ power was becoming so pervasive that it crept into Committee debates which superficially had little to do with the Court. So, for instance, in the debates on economic and monetary union, many Eurosceptics assumed that the ECJ would overturn the British 'opt-out' relating to the third stage of EMU on the grounds that Community law must apply uniformly.[165] Some even considered that the ECJ would force Britain back into the Exchange Rate

---

[160]   HC, 220, col 1170, 11 March 1993.   [161]   Ibid, col 510, 4 March 1993.

[162]   HC, 217, col 1067, 27 January 1993. The 'resolute certainties' would presumably include that courts accept as the supreme law of the land the latest expression of Parliament's will, which they interpret without judicial 'gap-filling' based on a purposive mode of interpretation.

[163]   Corbett (1994) 220.

[164]   This contrasts with the robust support given to the ECJ by pro-Marketeers during the passage of the 1986 Bill.

[165]   eg Christopher Gill (Conservative, Ludlow) (HC, 221, col 1273, 25 March 1993), Bill Walker (ibid, col 1276, 25 March 1993), Iain Duncan-Smith (ibid, col 1292, 25 March 1993). This neatly echoes the anti-Marketeer fear during the 1971–2 debates that the ECJ would declare the Luxembourg Compromise unlawful. The difference, however, is that here the ECJ would be over-turning a Treaty norm rather than a practice that was arguably contrary to the Treaty.

Mechanism.[166] In the debate on the Common Foreign and Security Policy, Douglas Hurd made play of the way in which Article L TEU removed foreign and security matters from ECJ jurisdiction.[167] Once again Eurosceptics simply did not believe that the ECJ would permit the text of Article L to oust its jurisdiction.[168] As for the Social Protocol opt-out, even Euro-enthusiasts (including Labour's European Affairs spokespersons George Robertson and Geoffrey Hoon) questioned whether it would survive a challenge before the ECJ.[169] On a Liberal Democrat amendment that Title I (Common Provisions) of the TEU be incorporated into UK law, one Member even flourished a copy of *Van Gend* to show that Title I might prove directly effective irrespective of Member State intentions.[170] (Had all these predictions proved accurate, they would have reinforced the view that the ECJ was prepared to *defy* the words of the Treaties to ensure that their 'spirit' was observed. Moreover it would have established the ECJ, rather than the High Contracting Parties, as 'master of the Treaties'.) Overall, the picture is one of acute consciousness of the ECJ's constitutional role permeating every aspect of Maastricht, as well as profound scepticism as to the IGC's ability to clip the ECJ's wings.

In addition the debates on substantive policies (particularly those on EMU) underlined the perception of sovereignty as relative rather than absolute. This was doubtless intensified by the fact that many supporters of the original EEC were among Maastricht's sternest critics.[171] Moreover questions of scope were

[166]   eg Austin Mitchell (HC, 224, cols 120–121, 4 May 1991), Barry Legg (Conservative, Milton Keynes SW), Bernard Jenkin and Iain Duncan-Smith (HC, 221, col 1292, 25 March 1993), Sir Trevor Skeet (Conservative, Bedfordshire North) (ibid, col 1304, 25 March 1993).

[167]   HC, 222, col 173, 30 March 1993. In contrast Dr John Cunningham for the Opposition did not mention the non-involvement of the ECJ, suggesting that preoccupation with it was a largely Conservative phenomenon (ibid, cols 181–193, 30 March 1993).

[168]   eg Sir Trevor Skeet (HC, 222, col 309, 30 March 1993), Sir Ivan Lawrence (ibid, col 307, 30 March 1993), Bill Walker (ibid, col 319, 30 March 1993), Nicholas Budgen (ibid, col 228, 30 March 1993).

[169]   eg George Robertson (HC, 223, col 533, 22 April 1993), Geoff Hoon (HC, 229, col 571, 22 July 1993), Giles Radice (HC, 225, col 424, 20 May 1993), Robert Maclennan (HC, 224, col 283, 5 May 1993), George Stevenson (Labour, Stoke-on-Trent South) (ibid, col 239, 5 May 1993), John Hutton (Labour, Barrow and Furness) (HC, 229, col 577, 22 July 1993). It is difficult to envisage how such a challenge could take place. The Protocol was not a Community act but an act of the High Contracting Parties. Like the Treaty itself it surely formed part of the supreme law of the Community, rendering it immune to challenge. Nor was it clear whether there was a mechanism whereby such a case could reach the ECJ. Since the Protocol did not constitute an act of the Community institutions it could not be subject to review under Articles 173 or 177.

[170]   John Butcher (Conservative, Coventry South West) HC, 215, col 336, 2 December 1992.

[171]   eg John Townend (Conservative, Bridlington) (HC, 223, cols 127–129, 19 April 1993), Sir Peter Tapsell (Conservative, Lindsey East) (HC, 221, cols 967–968, 24 March 1993), Dr Roger Berry (Labour, Kingswood) (HC, 221, col 998, 24 March 1993).

more significant now that *Factortame* had settled doubts about supremacy.[172] Several Members put forward the argument that EMU involved such a restriction of economic policy choice as to render national politics redundant.[173] This was intimately linked to the argument that the Maastricht convergence criteria bound future Parliaments too restrictively. Pro-Europeans retorted that price stability as an overriding priority was a desirable goal and therefore had no objection to its entrenchment as a governmental objective.[174] In other words, it was not 'essential' for the UK government and Parliament to maintain 'continuing sovereignty' on the choice of economic priorities. The aim of low inflation should be beyond the party battle.

No Eurosceptic argued for British withdrawal from the Community. Rather the substance of the dispute was about where to set the demarcation line between 'essential' and 'non-essential' sovereignty. Twenty-two years after the 'essential sovereignty' argument had sunk without trace, Maastricht had ensured its dramatic revival.

Legal practice, scholarship, and education in the wake of *Factortame* and Maastricht

The *Factortame*/Maastricht era was also characterized by increasing interest in Community law on the part of practitioners and academics. Already in 1988 the *Solicitors' Journal*, mindful of the potential inflow of continental lawyers resulting from completion of the internal market, featured numerous articles on Community law.[175] There was no dramatic rise in interest following *Factortame*, perhaps because practitioners were often concerned with areas where no issue of supremacy arises. However, in 1990 in the same journal Stephen Swabey, Factortame's solicitor, advised colleagues that if clients found themselves in dispute with the government in a Community law context, their rights might be more far-reaching than they might think.[176]

---

[172] This paradox corresponds loosely to the normative/decisional supranationalism divergence identified by Weiler. See Weiler (1981) 267.

[173] eg Tony Benn (HC, 221, col 984, 24 March 1993), Ron Leighton (HC, 223, col 134, 19 April 1993), Ted Rowlands (ibid, col 140, 19 April 1993).

[174] eg Malcolm Bruce (HC, 221, col 1008, 24 March 1993), Giles Radice (ibid, col 1014, 24 March 1993).

[175] eg Mackenzie, C, 'It'll Soon be 1992' (1988) 132 Sol Jo 769; Anon, '*1992*: What is All the Fuss About?' (1988) 132 Sol Jo 1220.

[176] (1990) 132 Sol Jo 1190.

In 1991 the legal professions in Scotland decided to require law under-graduates to study Community law[177] and in 1995 England and Wales followed suit,[178] some universities opting to integrate Community law into their Public Law courses rather than teaching the two subjects discretely.[179] There was also growing integration between domestic and Community constitutional studies in academic writings. As the 1990s progressed *Public Law* published several major pieces on Community law each year, new editor Dawn Oliver promising that the journal would chart the evolution of a 'developed system of European public law' and its impact on UK constitutional arrangements.[180] On the politics side, *Parliamentary Affairs* increased its coverage of both Community issues and domestic judicial review. In his 1995 review of constitutional developments, Shell linked the ECJ's importance post-*Factortame* with the growing prominence of the national courts in filling the vacuum resulting from Parliament's weakness in the face of executive power.[181] He noted that senior judicial figures were talking in terms of the courts striking down Acts of Parliament in the name of common law principles.

Intensification of anti-ECJ sentiment in the wake of Maastricht and *EOC*

The *EOC* case in 1994 underlined the subservience of Parliament to the Community legal order and the role of the British courts in policing the boundaries of Parliament's restricted legislative authority. *The Times* reported open murmurs in favour of withdrawal from the Community on the government backbenches, 'not just from those MPs who have always opposed membership, but also from those who feel that the club they joined in the 1970s is not the one they would willingly join today'.[182]

---

[177] (1991) 16 EL Rev 173.

[178] A growing number of clients were suing lawyers for professional negligence over failure to consider Community law in pursuit of cases. This led to pressure for law schools to increase their coverage of Community law on degree and professional updating courses. *Times Higher Educational Supplement*, 21 April 1995.

[179] eg Nottingham Trent University Common Professional Examination, London Guildhall University Common Professional Examination.

[180] [1993] Public Law 4.   [181] Shell (1996) 394.

[182] Leading article, *The Times*, 29 April 1994.

In the ensuing two years Eurosceptic campaigning focused increasingly on the ECJ and its impact on the national courts. Rather than demand withdrawal from the Community openly, Eurosceptics targeted the Community legal order as a backdoor means of disengagement with an unprecedented flurry of constitutional proposals. Thus William Cash promoted a European Communities (Reaffirmation of the Sovereignty of United Kingdom Parliament) Bill, aimed at ensuring that UK statutes prevailed over ECJ judgments.[183] Teresa Gorman put forward a Referendum Bill, which would offer voters a choice of whether to 'continue along the path to . . . a single body of law' or 'remain in the Union only on the basis of free trade with a very substantial repatriation of our national sovereignty'.[184] Tony Benn proffered a Commonwealth of Europe Bill, aimed at replacing the Community with a purely intergovernmental structure.[185] John Redwood suggested that Member States should be able to object to ECJ judgments on the grounds that they were 'redefining, stretching or altering' Community law, and then the Council would either 'uphold the objection or proceed to amend European law in the way recommended by the Court'.[186] This proposal seemingly transferred to the Council the task of interpreting the Treaty. Bernard Jenkin's European Communities (European Law) Bill sought to amend the 1972 Act so that 'the obligation to implement EC law should be transferred from our courts, which are making increasingly political judgments automatically, to the High Court of Parliament', which could 'deliberate and vote' on whether to accept an ECJ judgment.[187] Likewise Iain Duncan Smith proposed a Bill to permit disapplication of ECJ judgments by Order in Council.[188] In moving it he placed heavy emphasis on the way in which the ECJ had enabled British courts to 'overturn' Acts of Parliament. Although the Bill was defeated at Second Reading, sixty-six Conservatives, including four former Cabinet ministers, supported it.[189] Serving Cabinet members Michael Forsyth and Michael Portillo seemingly proffered tacit support by remaining in the chamber during the debate.[190]

Lady Thatcher threw her weight behind the campaign by stating that 'the sooner the initiative is wrested from the European Court so as to clarify British judicial thinking, the better'. She favoured amending the 1972 Act to

---

[183] HC, 255, col 591, 24 February 1995. The Bill was never debated.

[184] Ibid, cols 592–662, 24 February 1995. The Bill did not secure a sufficient majority at Second Reading to get any further.

[185] HC, 273, col 152, 5 March 1996.

[186] *The Times*, 21 August 1995.

[187] HC, 247, cols 195–199, 19 July 1994.

[188] HC, 276, col 198, 23 April 1996.

[189] *The Times*, 24 April 1996.

[190] Selsdon (1997) 646–647.

make clear that Parliament could *by express provision* override Community law as well as 'a procedure whereby an Act unintentionally in conflict with Community law can be suspended by Order in Council where necessary rather than by the court, so discouraging the drift in court decisions and judicial thinking towards narrowing the scope of parliamentary sovereignty'.[191] Lady Thatcher further proposed

a reserve list of protected matters where Parliament alone can legislate, to include our constitutional arrangements and defence. Finally, we should take reserve powers, exerciseable by Order in Council, to enable us in the last resort to prevent specific Community laws and decisions taking effect in the United Kingdom. These various powers would, one imagines, be used very sparingly; but their very existence would act as a disincentive to European encroachments. . . . [T]he debate about how rather than whether such actions should be taken is long overdue.[192]

War against the judges?

The war of attrition from the backbenches coincided with rising tensions between government and judiciary at Luxembourg, Strasbourg, and at home.[193] Governmental patience with the ECJ was wearing thin. In June 1994 the ECJ held that Britain had in various respects failed adequately to implement two Council directives, one relating to protection of employees in the event of a change of employer, the other relating to worker protection in the context of collective redundancies.[194] Most controversially the Court held that the UK had to establish a system for designating worker representatives, so that employers who refused to recognize such representatives could not frustrate the worker protection provided for in the directives.[195] *The Times* commented that, in comparison to the ECJ's decision-making, 'rows at Westminster seem little more than powerless bickering'.[196] In *Richardson*, decided in October 1995, the ECJ held that Britain's failure to equalize the ages at which men and women were entitled to free prescriptions was incompatible with the Treaty.[197] Health Minister Gerry Malone's announcement that the government would comply fully with the judgment

---

[191] Thatcher (1995) 504–505.   [192] Ibid 505.

[193] See generally Woodhouse (1996), Loveland (1997).

[194] Joined Cases C–382/92 and C–383/92 *Commission v United Kingdom* [1994] ICR 664.

[195] See paras 24–30.   [196] Leading article, *The Times*, 9 June 1994.

[197] Case C–437/94 *R v Secretary of State for Health ex parte Richardson* [1995] All ER (EC) 865, [1996] ICR 471.

by promulgating delegated legislation the very next day was met with Eurosceptic demands that the government defy the ECJ.[198] In November 1995 the ECJ decided in *Gallagher*[199] that the UK had breached Community law in expelling an Irish terrorist suspect from Britain without an independent hearing.[200] In the Commons the usual Eurosceptics were joined by Charles Wardle (Conservative, Bexhill & Battle) and John Greenway (Conservative, Ryedale) in condemning the judgment.[201] Doubtless this reflected the feeling that immigration controls, especially those relating to national security, constituted part of 'essential sovereignty'. The *Factortame III* judgment in March 1996 opened up the possibility that the government would have to compensate the Spanish fishermen.[202] Michael Heseltine, deputizing for John Major at Prime Minister's Questions, said that the government regretted the ECJ's decision and would press for 'changes' at the IGC.[203] When Agriculture Minister Douglas Hogg delivered a more detailed statement, the judgment was denounced by several new recruits to the ranks of the ECJ's critics[204] as well as by seasoned Eurosceptics who called for the judgment's disapplication in the United Kingdom[205] and for the overturning of the ECJ's supremacy doctrine generally.[206] Home Secretary Michael Howard accused the ECJ of extending the EU's jurisdiction without authority from the Member States.[207] In a debate on the impending IGC government ministers called for the IGC to show 'renewed determination that the European Union should stay out of areas where [cooperation] is not necessary'[208] and for ECJ judgments to be made 'more appropriate and more acceptable'.[209]

---

[198] HC, 264, cols 495–501, 19 October 1995. Those urging defiance were Nicholas Budgen, Sir Teddy Taylor, Patrick Nicholls.

[199] Case C–175/94 *R v Secretary of State for the Home Department ex parte Gallagher* [1995] CEC 667.

[200] *The Times*, 1 December 1995, *Guardian*, 1 December 1995.

[201] HC, 267, cols 1316–1318, 30 November 1995.

[202] Joined Cases C–46/93 and C–48/93 *Brasserie du Pêcheur SA v Germany* and *R v Secretary of State for Transport ex parte Factortame (No 4)* [1996] QB 404, [1996] 1 CMLR 889.

[203] HC, 273, cols 145–149, 5 March 1996, in answer to questions from Nicholas Budgen and John Wilkinson.

[204] Ibid, cols 345–355, 6 March 1996. The new faces were David Harris (Conservative, St Ives), Barry Field (Conservative, Isle of Wight), and Michael Stephen (Conservative, Shoreham).

[205] Ibid, col 354, 6 March 1996 (Iain Duncan-Smith).

[206] Ibid, col 348, 6 March 1996 (Sir Michael Spicer).   [207] *The Times*, 23 September 1996.

[208] Foreign Secretary Malcolm Rifkind, HC, 268, col 507, 7 December 1995.

[209] Minister of State, Foreign and Commonwealth Office, David Davis, ibid, col 588, 7 December 1995.

It was hardly surprising, therefore, that the government's White Paper on the 1996 IGC proposed 'appeals procedure [against ECJ judgments]; streamlined procedures for the rapid amendment of EC legislation which has been interpreted in a way which was never intended by the Council . . . and a Treaty provision clarifying the application of subsidiarity in the interpretation of EC law'.[210] The government also opposed the extension of Community competences and supported the existing intergovernmental basis for justice and home affairs.[211] The modesty of these proposals led to accusations of retreat.[212] For example the proposed appeals procedure was to be purely *within* the ECJ[213] and would not (as had been anticipated) give governments the right collectively to overrule court decisions.

In addition to conflicts with the ECJ, the decision of the European Court of Human Rights in *McCann*[214] led Deputy Prime Minister Michael Heseltine to moot British repudiation of the European Convention. Hand in hand with increasing animosity towards both European courts, a more general hostility towards the growth of judicial review had set in.[215] There was concern that national courts might emulate the judicial activism of the two European courts,[216] fuelled by the fact that British judges were happy to admit that European jurisprudence had pushed forward the boundaries of domestic judicial interventionism. Applications for judicial review had risen from 2,089 in 1991 to 2,886 in 1993, and this had been accompanied by a series of court defeats for the government, particularly in Home Office matters. By 1993 several Crown Office judges had acknowledged extra-judicially that a generational shift in opinion in the High Court, Court of Appeal, and House of Lords had led to a slow tilt in the constitutional balance in favour of the judiciary.[217] Although judicial review primarily concerns executive actions, there were suggestions that the executive might not in future be able

---

[210] *A Partnership of Nations: The British Approach to the European Union Intergovernmental Conference 1996* Cm 3181 (March 1996) paras 36–37.

[211] Ibid, paras 30 and 49.

[212] 'Major's Retreat on Euro Court: Tories Attack "Soft" Curbs' *Daily Telegraph*, 7 March 1996. 'Retreat on EU Curbs' *Guardian*, 23 July 1996.

[213] The proposal was that a ruling in chambers could be overturned on appeal to the plenary session of fifteen judges.

[214] *McCann & others v United Kingdom* Case No 17/1994/464/545 [1996] EHRR 97.

[215] See Woodhouse (1996).

[216] For example the leading article in *The Times*, 15 November 1993, made the important point that in the wake of *Francovich* the growing attractions of the copy-out approach (ie verbatim transposition) to the implementation of directives would militate in favour of a highly discretionary interpretative strategy by the British judiciary.

[217] eg Sir Thomas Bingham MR, Lord Woolf, and Farquharson LJ in *Observer*, 9 May 1993.

to render its decisions lawful by incorporating them into Acts of Parliament. Lord Woolf suggested that judicial power to disapply statute was not limited to the Community law context[218] and Sir John Laws wrote of a higher-order law which prevailed over Acts of Parliament.[219] Lord Mackay LC scorned this suggestion,[220] as did his Labour shadow Lord Irvine who warned judges against 'judicial supremacism'.[221]

During the same period, general anti-Community sentiment intensified as a result of the long-running saga of the Commission's worldwide export ban on British beef. On 21 May 1996 the Prime Minister announced a policy of non-cooperation with the Community,[222] warmly welcomed by most Conservative backbenchers[223] and the increasingly Eurosceptic tabloid press.[224] Asked whether the policy should extend to suspension of payments to the Community, Major showed considerable understanding of direct effect: 'it would not be a question of having to face the European Court of Justice: it would, within a matter of days, be a question of having to face the courts of this country. For that reason and others, I am not attracted to measures that are illegal.'[225]

The *Working Time Directive* case: Eurosceptics vindicated?

Back in November 1993 the Council, using as its legal base Article 118a on health and safety of workers, had issued Directive 93/104/EC on organization of working time. Originally presented as something of a triumph for Britain because of its many loopholes,[226] the government subsequently argued that the directive threatened UK employment. It therefore sought

---

[218] Woolf (1995) 67.   [219] Laws (1995).   [220] *Guardian*, 9 July 1996.

[221] *The Times*, 3 November 1995.

[222] The non-cooperation strategy consisted of the following measures: (1) the UK would not agree any matters requiring unanimity until the Community was able to agree on how to deal with the crisis; (2) there would be no progress at the IGC; (3) ministers would raise the matter at every meeting of the Council; (4) Britain would ensure that the matter dominated the forthcoming European Council.

[223] HC, 278, cols 99–112, 21 May 1996.

[224] A selection of tabloid headlines from the following day (22 May 1996) conveys the general mood: *Daily Express*: 'Major Speaks for Britain'; *Daily Mail*: 'Major Goes to War at Last'; *Sun*: 'Major Shows Bulls at Last'. In retaliation the *Daily Mirror* launched a 'Britain needs EU' campaign (*Daily Mirror*, 28 May 1996).

[225] HC, 278, col 106, 21 June 1996, in answer to a question from William Cash MP.

[226] The UK minister in Council had abstained rather than voted against the directive.

judicial review under Article 173 EC, on the grounds that the directive breached subsidiarity and should in any case have been issued by the other eleven Member States under the Social Protocol.[227] It also served notice that it did not intend to implement the directive until any legal challenge had been resolved.[228] The case neatly tested two key Eurosceptic arguments of the Maastricht debates, the efficacy of subsidiarity and the British opt-out.

The ECJ held that there was nothing in the wording of Article 118a to indicate that its concepts of 'working environment', 'safety', or 'health' should be interpreted restrictively.[229] This suggested that the British opt-out would not inhibit the ECJ from finding the requisite powers to legislate on employment matters within the main body of the Treaty.[230] Accordingly it would rarely be necessary for the other Member States to utilize the Social Protocol. On subsidiarity, the ECJ held that

Once the Council has found that it is necessary to improve the existing level of protection as regards the health and safety of workers, and to harmonise the conditions in this area while maintaining the improvements made, achievement of that objective through the imposition of minimum requirements necessarily presupposes Community-wide action, which otherwise, as in this case, leaves the enactment of the detailed implementing provisions required largely to the Member States.[231]

Thus the ECJ would generally leave questions of subsidiarity to the Council's discretion and would seemingly only invalidate Community legislation for breach of subsidiarity in the most exceptional circumstances. The ECJ's position on subsidiarity must have been a cruel blow to a government which had invested so much political capital in the concept.[232] For good measure, on the question of proportionality, the ECJ ruled that 'the Council must be allowed

---

[227] Case C–84/94 *United Kingdom v Council* [1996] ECR I–5755, [1996] CMLR 671.

[228] *Independent*, 7 March 1994. Since the time limit for implementation of the directive expired while the case was still being held, this position surely exposed the government to the risk of incurring liability under *Francovich*.

[229] Ibid, para 15.

[230] The *Financial Times* (13 November 1996) commented that ironically 'instead of having a piece of European Union social legislation knocked down by the court, the UK has opened the door for the Commission to introduce a raft of fresh social legislation under the pretext that it is safeguarding the health and safety of EU workers'.

[231] Ibid, para 47.

[232] The then Chancellor of the Exchequer Norman Lamont records: 'I pushed the idea of subsidiarity hard . . . But I could not have been more wrong about its effectiveness. It achieved absolutely nothing, but was endlessly used by the Government to illustrate they were winning the argument in Europe!' (Lamont (1999) 115).

a wide discretion in an area which, as here, involves the legislature in making social policy choices and requires it to carry out complex assessments'.[233]

Reporting the ECJ decision to the House of Commons, Industry Secretary Ian Lang argued that the use of Article 118A sanctioned by the ECJ was unacceptable and ran counter to the agreement reached at Maastricht.[234] His statement was met by a torrent of anti-ECJ invective by Conservative Eurosceptics.[235] Some—like Tony Marlow[236] and Bernard Jenkin[237]—called for outright defiance, Nicholas Budgen urged non-cooperation,[238] and John Wilkinson advocated cutting off contributions in addition to an 'empty chair' policy.[239] Labour's Andrew Mackinlay pointed out that industrial tribunals would now enforce the directive in the absence of implementing measures.[240] There was no concerted counter-argument from pro-EU MPs, either on the substantive or constitutional issue. The Speaker refused a request by Labour's Nigel Spearing for an adjournment debate on the effect of the decision on tribunals.[241]

In a frosty exchange of letters the following day, Major warned Commission President Jacques Santer that there would be 'no end' to the IGC negotiations unless Britain was granted an opt-out from the working time directive, arguing that the ECJ decision ran directly counter to the spirit of Maastricht. Santer replied that Britain was 'threatening to hold the IGC to ransom' and Social Affairs Commissioner Padraig Flynn warned that the UK demand would be unacceptable to the Commission and the other fourteen Member States since the UK did not have an opt-out from the Treaty proper.[242] Commissioner Sir Leon Brittan, perhaps more sensitive to UK feelings, observed that the government had either won or had its arguments

---

[233] Lamont (1999) 115, para 58.   [234] HC, 285, cols 155–156, 12 November 1996.

[235] For example, Sir Michael Spicer talked of the country being ruled by an unelected court rather than Parliament (ibid, col 160); Sir Ivan Lawrence argued that Parliament was being told what to do by a foreign court (ibid, col 162); Nicholas Winterton said that the country was 'sick to death of the decisions of the European court of political manipulation, which have nothing to do with justice at all or the strength of the case' (ibid, col 164); John Sykes (Scarborough) considered that Parliament found itself 'at the mercy and diktat of foreign courts' (ibid, col 165); Nigel Evans spoke of 'double dealing, cheating and twisting [by] faceless bureaucrats and their friends in the courts'.

[236] HC, 285, col 168, 12 November 1996.   [237] Ibid, col 169, 12 November 1996.

[238] Ibid, col 164, 12 November 1996.   [239] Ibid, col 168, 12 November 1996.

[240] Ibid, col 169, 12 November 1996. Ian Lang pointed out that this would only occur in the case of public sector employees. He should have added that in addition individual articles of the directive would need to satisfy the relevant tests for direct effect.

[241] Ibid, col 172, 12 November 1996.   [242] *Financial Times*, 13 November 1996.

taken on board in 75 per cent of ECJ cases involving the UK.[243] French President Jacques Chirac indicated that he sympathized with Britain inasmuch as he too sought a limitation of ECJ power.[244]

The pro-EU press chose not to focus on the constitutional but on the substantive issue.[245] In contrast the Eurosceptic press urged the reassertion of parliamentary sovereignty. For example the *Daily Telegraph* argued that

the single market need not require common social, environmental or monetary policies, let alone the control by Brussels of home affairs or defence. Obviously there will often be a case for co-operation on such matters between governments. But ultimate sovereignty over them should be reserved for Westminster, and the jurisdiction of the European Court limited strictly to issues that genuinely concern the single market.[246]

Since 'no formula of words can check that body's political ambitions', it suggested that the ECJ could only be restricted by the British Parliament 'ring-fencing' control of domestic matters by amending the 1972 Act.[247] *The Times*, denouncing the ECJ as a court 'which exists to advance integration', argued for 'a renegotiation of the Treaty which does not simply provide new opt-outs to be outflanked but throws the federalist ratchet into reverse'.[248] The *Daily Mail* wanted Britain governed by ministers answerable to 'our elected Parliament' rather than by 'the obscure lawyers and pernickety academics' who made up the 'over-mighty' ECJ.[249] The *Express* opined that Britain's opt-out had been 'contemptuously swept aside by a body whose overriding purpose is to prepare the ground for a European superstate, in which Britain will be reduced to the status of a subject province'.[250] The *Sun* denounced the decision of the 'unelected, politically-motivated socialist academics calling themselves a European Court' as 'an outrageous assault on 700 [sic] years of parliamentary sovereignty'.[251] Several columnists called for

[243] *Daily Telegraph*, 13 November 1996. Brittan was already familiar with the need to counteract the British government's attitude to the ECJ. Five months earlier he had warned the government not to 'play politics with the European Court of Justice' in the forthcoming general election, pointing to its crucial role in enforcing the single market. *Financial Times*, 5 July 1996.

[244] *Guardian*, 9 November 1996.

[245] For example, the *Daily Mirror* (13 November 1996) entitled its editorial 'Tories Don't Give a Damn for Workers'. The *Independent* (13 November 1996) also focused its leader on the reasonableness of the directive's provisions.

[246] *Daily Telegraph*, 14 November 1996.

[247] *Daily Telegraph*, 13 November 1996. The leader did not spell out the substance of the proposed amendment. Presumably certain policy areas would be reserved as areas of national competence.

[248] *The Times*, 13 November 1996.

[249] *Daily Mail*, 13 November 1996.

[250] *Express*, 13 November 1996.

[251] *Sun*, 13 November 1996.

Britain's withdrawal from the EU,[252] and Lady Thatcher let it be known that she believed Britain should review membership unless sweeping reductions in ECJ power were agreed by the IGC.[253]

The aftermath of the working time directive crisis saw a further intensification of anti-Community sentiment. Somewhat hamfistedly, John Major refused to permit a Commons debate on the single currency stability pact agreement. The Eurosceptic press presented the affair as an affront to Parliament.[254] Significantly, the press emphasized the likely effective enforceability of such rules,[255] and expressed scepticism as to the legal validity of the single currency opt-out.[256] Thus once again the power of the ECJ imbued the political debate.

Conclusion

Legally, the dismantling of parliamentary sovereignty advanced step by step in the early 1990s. In *Factortame* the House of Lords made it clear that it would uphold Community law over Acts of Parliament.[257] *EOC* showed that the House no longer felt the need for a reference to the ECJ before impugning an Act of Parliament; the supervisory jurisdiction of the Divisional Court now extends to declaring an Act of Parliament incompatible with Community law without recourse to Luxembourg. To that extent the Divisional Court was now a constitutional court. The post-*EOC* case law showed lower courts and tribunals joining the fray in setting primary legisla-

---

[252] eg Boris Johnson, 'This Ruling could Force us to Leave the EU' *Daily Telegraph*, 13 November 1996, Charles Moore, 'Tell us Why we should Stay' *Daily Telegraph*, 14 November 1996, Christopher Booker, 'Why our Leaders are Terrified of Coming Clean about Europe' *Sun*, 3 December 1996.

[253] *Sunday Times*, 22 December 1996.

[254] eg the *Daily Mail* (22 November 1996) considered that 'The issue cuts to the heart of Britain's sovereignty. In its efforts to stifle discussion, the Government is treating Parliament and the people with contempt.' *The Times* (22 November 1996) said that Major was 'treating the watchdog of Parliament as a poodle'.

[255] eg *The Times* (22 November 1996) suggested that 'under Articles 169 and 170 of the Treaty, the British government could be fined by the European Court of Justice for running an economy that was too competitive relative to the Continent'.

[256] eg Norman Tebbit in the *Sun* (22 November 1996) sneered at the suggestion that the opt-out from the third stage of EMU would save Britain from the consequences of the stability pact: 'An opt-out like the opt-out from the 48-hour week, I suppose. Pardon us while we laugh.'

[257] At least in the absence of express repeal. How the courts would react to Parliament expressly and intentionally legislating contrary to Community law remains a matter of conjecture.

tion aside. The *Working Time Directive* case indicated that the spheres in which the UK Parliament had transferred its sovereignty were not so limited as had been supposed.

Politically, this same period marked the final stage in the transformation from parliamentary ignorance to enlightenment. Consciousness of the ECJ's status and its effect on the British courts was no longer confined to a marginalized rump but increasingly permeated the highest reaches of government. For good or ill, the ECJ was at last exposed to a degree of political attention commensurate with its seminal role in the Community constitution.

The Human Rights Comparison

We have seen that prior to accession the constitutional understandings of MPs relating to Community membership were inadequate, and that even after the UK joined, these understandings were slow to develop. Although the constitutional consequences were beginning to dawn on MPs even before *Factortame* and *EOC*, it took the experience of British courts setting aside Acts of Parliament for MPs to grasp the full extent of judicial power under the Community constitution. Jurisdictional comparison with Ireland suggests that parliamentary ignorance may owe much to the predominantly political rather than legal character of the pre-1973 British constitution. This chapter explores a different comparison. It examines the history of attempts to incorporate a Bill of Rights into domestic law, culminating in the passage of the Human Rights Act 1998. It analyses whether parliamentary unawareness of legal aspects of Community membership was matched by a similar ignorance as to the likely constitutional impact of a Bill of Rights. If MPs were just as naïve about a Bill of Rights as they were about EC membership, this might confirm that the 'political constitution' precluded competent legal discourse by parliamentarians. If, on the other hand, parliamentarians enjoyed a greater comprehension of the likely constitutional impact of a Bill of Rights, one would need to look further for a plausible explanation of why the Community was a special case.

Bill of Rights and the European Community

There were remarkable parallels between the incorporation of EC law and the incorporation of the European Convention on Human Rights ('ECHR'). Politically, both represented different and complementary means of

European integration. Legally, depending on the terms of the incorporating legislation and the reaction of the courts thereto, it was possible that ECHR incorporation could bring about the direct effect, supremacy, and immediacy of Convention rights. In addition the European Court of Human Rights shared the ECJ's teleological and dynamic interpretative approach. Each Court treated its governing instrument as a constitutional charter, even though this may not have been the intention of the founding States.

Moreover ECHR incorporation raises much the same questions regarding parliamentary knowledge as those which we have investigated in the EC context. First, did parliamentarians realize that ECHR incorporation might not only invest the European Court of Human Rights with the status of a constitutional court, but also invite *British* courts to set aside statutory provisions deemed to violate fundamental rights? Secondly, how much awareness was there of the wide ambit of a Bill of Rights? Unlike Community law, limited in scope by the Treaty of Rome, any Bill of Rights would apply generally, to all areas of governmental activity. Did parliamentarians consider whether a Bill of Rights would impinge upon Parliament's 'essential' sovereignty? Thirdly, what degree of entrenchment was considered desirable? Fourthly, did parliamentarians consider Parliament *capable* of binding its successors and rendering future Acts subject to judicial review, or did they adopt the position that Sir Geoffrey Howe had taken during the passage of the 1972 Act, namely that the rules of parliamentary sovereignty lay beyond the reach of statute and were unalterable by Parliament? Did they consider that questions relating to the modification or abolition of parliamentary sovereignty were entirely for Parliament to decide—or did they appreciate that in the final analysis the choice lay with the courts?

From 1968 to the Human Rights Bill

The modern Bill of Rights debate[1] is considered to have started in 1968 with the publication by Anthony Lester of the pamphlet *Democracy and Individual Rights*.[2] Lester argued that Parliament could no longer be relied upon to safeguard individual freedom and that the ECHR should be incorporated into domestic law, albeit initially not enforceable in the courts.[3] After this,

[1] For a general account see Zander (1997) ch 1.   [2] Fabian Tract No 390.
[3] Lester at the time believed that 'some might use such a Bill to undermine radical social or economic legislation' and that the judiciary needed to prove to Parliament that they were capable of applying a Bill of Rights 'in a progressive and liberal fashion'. Ibid 15.

parliamentary debates on Bills of Rights snowballed as a result of numerous Private Members' Bills. This section will analyse thematically the debates that took place between 1968 and the introduction of the Human Rights Bill 1997/8.

The power of domestic courts *vis-à-vis* Parliament

In contrast to the debates over EEC membership, from the very start parliamentarians clearly understood that a Bill of Rights/ECHR incorporation would elevate the British judiciary to Supreme Court status. The first Bill of Rights debate following Lester's pamphlet was in April 1969 when Viscount Lambton (Conservative, Berwick) proposed a Bill modelled on the Canadian Charter in the Commons under the ten-minute rule.[4] His opponent Alex Lyon (Labour, York) focused on the issue of sovereignty and the courts, arguing that the Bill would fetter Parliament's right to change the law by instituting a British constitutional court. Instancing the US Supreme Court's *Dred Scott* decision, he argued that such a court, if it proved conservative, could block progressive change. Rather than adopt the 'American constitutional procedure through the Supreme Court', responsibility for safeguarding liberty in a changing economic and social climate should rest with Parliament. It is interesting that Lyons should have placed such emphasis on the role of the courts, because under the pre-1982 Canadian Charter, the courts were not given a mandate to nullify legislation. Perhaps this is an early indication that MPs were not prepared to take at face value arguments that specific Bill of Rights arrangements would keep the judicial role at a modest level. Rather they regarded any Bill of Rights, whatever its terms, as a 'thin end of the wedge' that would lead to judicial supremacism.

The second debate, the first of several initiated by Lord Wade, took place in the Lords in June 1969.[5] This time it was *supporters* of a Bill of Rights who drew the US comparison. The Earl of Cork argued that the judiciary should be able to declare Acts unconstitutional like the US Supreme Court, thereby, for example, saving the freedom of the subject from 'a party of the extreme Left, perhaps, dedicated to all the unreasoning and outmoded dogmas that the sacred Clause 4 could be made to spawn'.[6] Conversely Lord Chorley perceived a Bill of Rights as a way of liberalizing public opinion, praying in aid

---

[4] HC, 782, cols 474–478, 23 April 1969.   [5] HL, 302, cols 1026–1096, 18 June 1969.
[6] Ibid, cols 1076–1077, 18 June 1969.

the progressive influence of the US Supreme Court over the previous twenty years.[7] It is ironic that Bill of Rights supporters of both Left and Right saw such a reform as a way of promoting their own political values. There was disappointingly little analysis, however, of whether the track record of the *British* judiciary justified either prediction.

Since parliamentarians realized at once that a Bill of Rights would move the courts centre-stage, the *democratic legitimacy* of judicial decision-making was also hotly disputed from the start. Again this contrasts starkly with debates on the EC, where controversy over the democratic merits or demerits of ECJ decision-making only materialized in earnest during Maastricht ratification. Arguments calling into question the judicial role under a Bill of Rights frequently revolved around the lack of accountability of the courts compared to Parliaments and governments. Thus Enoch Powell argued that James Kilfedder's proposed Bill of Rights 1975 was 'incompatible with the responsibility of Government through this House to the electorate, a thing we call parliamentary democracy'. He emphasized that there was 'no means of calling a court of law to account for having annulled that which the Executive considered to be necessary in the public interest'.[8] Another long-standing 'democratic' argument against a Bill of Rights has been that it would undermine the separation of powers, since 'it is for Parliament to legislate and for the courts to interpret that legislation'.[9] Opponents often focused on the 'necessary in a democratic society' provisions in the ECHR, arguing that this involved political decisions, best made by a political body—Parliament.[10]

Opponents of a Bill of Rights repeatedly linked the legitimacy of judicial decision-making to the *generality* of Bill of Rights/ECHR provisions.[11] One of the best expositions of this argument was made by Lord Boston of Faversham in 1980:

[U]nder our constitution it has long been established and accepted that Parliament legislates in a specific form, and that it is then the job of the courts to interpret that legislation. But under those proposals we should be adopting a wide range of legislative policies in the most general terms, and then say to the judiciary, 'it is up to you to develop them in the way you think fit'. Thus, we should be giving them here not just an interpretative role but the task of developing the law on a wide range of subjects

---

[7] Ibid, col 1088, 18 June 1969.   [8] HC, 894, col 51, 7 July 1975.

[9] HC, 109, cols 1275–1276, 6 February 1987 (Nick Brown, Labour, Newcastle East).

[10] HL, 524, col 207, 5 December 1990 (Lord Mishcon).

[11] HC, 894, col 71, 7 July 1975 (Leon Brittan) HL, 369, col 793, 25 March 1976 (Lord Lloyd of Hampstead).

... freedom of speech, freedom of the press, privacy, race relations, education, forms of punishment and so on. What we have always tried to do in Parliament . . . is to pass laws which are as certain as possible and to seek to spell them out with precision, and that is after all what people have a right to expect.[12]

A couple of points might be noted about this line of argument, which was advanced throughout the Bill of Rights debates. First, the issue of generality was intimately linked to that of *scope*. Just as Eurosceptics in the Maastricht debates objected to the ECJ's teleological mode of interpretation because it enlarged (in their view illegitimately) the scope of Community law, similarly the broad terms of a Bill of Rights or of the ECHR were attacked for lending themselves to expansive construction, maximizing the judicial role in setting parameters to Parliament's legislative function. Thus, in the Bill of Rights context, the question of whether such a measure would impinge on Parliament's 'essential sovereignty' found expression in the form of objections to the generality of human rights provisions.

Secondly, rival definitions of the rule of law were at play here. To Lord Boston, a major objection to the generality of Convention rights was the uncertainty that would be created.[13] Likewise in 1969 Lord Gardiner LC had suggested that the terms of any Bill of Rights would be so general that it would be impossible to say what effect it would have.[14] For opponents of a Bill of Rights, therefore, the loss of legal certainty resulting from a Bill of Rights would *undermine* the rule of law in the United Kingdom. This is a sharp reminder of the flexible nature of the concept.[15]

Conversely, those who favoured a Bill of Rights have argued that it would promote both the rule of law and the separation of powers, since it would protect the citizen from the tyranny of the democratic majority[16] and could compensate for the lack of checks and balances in the modern constitution,[17] especially 'now the Executive and the law-making power are, to all intents and purposes, the same'.[18] They have also complained of the manipulation of Parliament by minorities[19] and the growth of an unbridled bureaucracy rush-

---

[12] HL, 415, col 538, 4 December 1980.   [13] Ibid.

[14] HL, 302, col 1046, 18 June 1969.

[15] As we have already seen, some parliamentarians perceived the rule of law as dependent upon the sovereignty of Parliament rather than in tension with it. See eg Enoch Powell in Ch 6 above.

[16] HL, 469, col 187, 10 December 1985 (Lord McGregor of Durris).

[17] HL, 402, cols 1031–1034, 8 November 1979 (Lord Carr of Hadley).

[18] HC, 4, col 431, 8 May 1981 (Geoffrey Rippon, Conservative, Hexham).

[19] Ibid, col 53, 7 July 1975 (David Lane, Conservative, Cambridge).

ing a mass of legislation through Parliament every year with minimal scrutiny.[20]

The durability of parliamentary sovereignty

During the pre-accession debates on EEC membership, successive governments presented parliamentary sovereignty as something that was 'inescapable and enduring'. Ostensibly the Heath government feared that the courts might continue to enforce the latest expression of Parliament's will, making British compliance with Community norms dependent on Parliament's ongoing cooperation. MPs had been reminded that no instruction issued by Parliament to the courts in the form of the 1972 Act could alter this situation, since Parliament could not change the fundamental ground rules of parliamentary sovereignty.

In contrast, and without any great apparent logic, *a Bill of Rights was consistently perceived as the exclusive means by which Parliament could abolish its own sovereignty*. Of course, much would depend on the nature of the Bill of Rights itself. Until 1990, many of the proposals put forward were relatively modest. Curiously the only 'manner and form' entrenchment ever proposed in the parliamentary debates was the prevention of implied repeal of human rights norms.[21] Formulations were repeatedly put forward that the Bill of Rights/ECHR provisions would prevail unless subsequent statute expressly stated otherwise. Nonetheless this would challenge the nostrum that Parliament cannot bind itself as to the form of subsequent legislation.[22] It also raised the question of just how 'express' Parliament would have to be in order to legislate contrary to a fundamental right. Even in the absence of a Bill of Rights, the *Anisminic* case suggested that judges would be most unwilling to accept restrictions to the citizen's right to recourse to the courts no matter how clearly Parliament legislated on the matter.

The House of Lords in 1977 established a Select Committee on a Bill of Rights which took the view that even this relatively modest change in the

[20] Ibid, col 32, 7 July 1975 (James Kilfedder, Ulster Unionist, Down North). See also Jonathan Aitken, col 63.

[21] eg Alan Beith's Bill of Rights (HC, 895, cols 1270–1273, 15 July 1975), Lord Wade's first Bill of Rights Bill (HL, 369, cols 775–817, 25 March 1976), Lord Wade's second Bill of Rights Bill (HL, 379, cols 973–1022, 3 February 1977), Lord Wade's fourth Bill of Rights Bill (HL, 415, cols 533–561, 4 December 1980).

[22] Maugham LJ in *Ellen Street Estates Ltd v Minister of Health* [1934] 1 KB 590 at 597.

sovereignty doctrine could not be accomplished. It took evidence from, *inter alia*, its Specialist Adviser, Mr D Rippengal, who advised that 'an Act can no more protect itself from implied derogation by a future Act than it can protect itself from express derogation'.[23] (For good measure Rippengal also doubted the efficacy of section 2(4) of the European Communities Act.[24]) This view was reinforced by evidence from Professor Hood Phillips, who rejected the idea that there could be 'manner and form' entrenchment, concluding that 'as our constitution now stands, Parliament would not be bound by an enacted Bill of Rights'.[25] Lord Diplock too saw no way in which the ECHR could be entrenched so that an Act of Parliament in breach of it could be void.[26] The Select Committee also interviewed members of the Executive of the National Council for Civil Liberties, who called for a reversal for Bill of Rights purposes of the position taken by Maugham LJ in *Ellen Street Estates*. Given the prevailing view, it was hardly surprising that their Lordships criticized this suggestion as 'a marked departure from the traditions of this country'[27] and considered that it would be 'very remarkable . . . for the courts to assume a power quite suddenly out of the blue to overrule the express words of Parliament, whether put in inadvertently or otherwise'.[28]

Accordingly in its Report the Select Committee was unanimous that 'there is no way in which a Bill of Rights could be made immune altogether from amendment or repeal by a subsequent Act. That follows from the principle of the sovereignty of Parliament which is the central feature of our constitution.'[29] More specifically, attempts to preclude implied repeal would prove useless since there was 'no way in which a Bill of Rights could protect itself from encroachment, whether express or implied, by later Acts'. A fortiori no attempt at entrenchment by a two-thirds majority or referendum requirement would be legally effective in the United Kingdom. A point of particular interest is that the Committee discussed whether section 2(4) of the European Communities Act supported the proposition that a Bill of Rights could effectively control future Acts. The Committee considered that it did not.

No cases as yet . . . have arisen in the United Kingdom courts in which the question whether section 2(4) could have this effect has been put to the test. Even if the United

---

[23] *Report of the Select Committee on a Bill of Rights* HL, 176 (1977–8) Minutes of Evidence Taken before the Select Committee on a Bill of Rights, 2, para 7.

[24] Ibid, 9, para 28.   [25] Ibid 277.   [26] Ibid 91.

[27] Ibid 170 (the Chairman).   [28] Ibid (Lord Lloyd of Hampstead).

[29] Report, ibid, para 14.

Kingdom courts ultimately hold that section 2(4) does indeed produce that result, it would not follow that a Bill of Rights could similarly control the contents of later Acts. If the courts ever arrived at this conclusion with respect to section 2(4) of the European Communities Act, it might be on the ground that that Act, coupled with our accession to the Communities, had in fact produced a structural change in the United Kingdom constitution, given that we had become part of an international Community having its own legislative, executive and judicial organs. The same could not be said of a Bill of a kind falling within the Committee's remit.[30]

At least the Committee appreciated that the fate of parliamentary sovereignty was ultimately a matter for the courts, and that judicial modification of the doctrine remained a distinct possibility. On the other hand it is surprising that the Committee did not consider that abandonment of parliamentary sovereignty in one particular area might make the judiciary more willing to consider limiting the doctrine in other spheres.[31]

The Committee's findings induced Lord Wade to tone down his third Bill of Rights Bill 1979. There would be no attempt to prevent implied repeal absolutely. Instead, without enthusiasm, he relied on benevolent statutory interpretation to check future parliamentary action. The relevant provision of his Bill stipulated that

in case of conflict . . . any . . . enactment passed after the passing of this Act shall be deemed to be subject to the provisions of the said Convention and Protocols and shall be so construed unless such subsequent enactment provides otherwise *or does not admit of any construction compatible with the provisions of this Act*.[32]

However, the influence of the Lords Committee was remarkably short-lived. By 1980 Lord Wade in his fourth Bill of Rights Bill 1980/1 reverted to his previous formula that the ECHR would prevail over subsequent statute unless such a statute specifically excepted itself therefrom.[33] Similar wording was also adopted by Robert Maclennan in his European Human Rights Convention Bill in 1983,[34] by Lord Broxbourne[35] in his Human Rights and Fundamental Freedoms Bill 1985/6,[36] and by Sir Edward Gardner in his Bill of Rights Bill 1987.[37] The astonishing speed with which Bill of Rights

---

[30] Ibid, para 19. It is noteworthy that the Committee's reasoning echoes that of the ECJ in *Van Gend en Loos*.

[31] cf Craig (1991) 253.   [32] HL, 402, col 1003, 8 November 1979 (emphasis added).

[33] House of Lords Public Bills (LSP) (1980–1), Bill 54 (Clause 3).

[34] HC, 50, cols 860–862, 13 December 1983.

[35] Formerly Sir Derek Walker-Smith QC MP, the prominent anti-Marketeer.

[36] HL, 469, cols 156–194, 10 December 1985.

[37] House of Commons Bills, vol 1–49 (1986–7), Bill 19 (Clause 4).

supporters jettisoned the conclusions of the Lords Committee suggests that they envisaged no difficulty in getting the courts to accept such reasonable modifications to the sovereignty doctrine as the Parliament of the day considered desirable. Parliamentarians clearly assumed that the courts would be prepared to be much more flexible with parliamentary sovereignty than the Committee thought would be the case.

The *Factortame* decision in 1990 emboldened proponents of a Bill of Rights to go much further. Now that Britain's highest judicial authority had permitted the 1972 Parliament to bind its successors, there was pressure to use similar provisions to entrench Convention rights. Thus Robert Maclennan in his Protection of Fundamental Rights and Freedoms Bill 1992 called for Convention rights to be given the same priority within the legal system as were accorded to enforceable Community rights under sections 2(1) and 2(4) of the European Communities Act 1972. He also proposed the establishment of a Human Rights Commission charged with challenging the validity of any Act of Parliament that in its opinion contravened fundamental rights.[38] In 1995 Lord Lester proposed a Human Rights Bill which sought to give similar effect to European Convention law as the 1972 Act gave to Community law.[39] He clearly saw no difficulty in Parliament generating a home-made supremacy doctrine which would enable the courts to override 'ordinary' statute in favour of Convention rights. It was for political, not legal, reasons that Lord Lester agreed in Committee to tone down this provision to seek the widest possible consensus. He substituted a provision whereby 'so far as the context permits, enactments (whenever passed or made) shall be construed consistently with' Convention rights and freedoms.[40]

Academic commentators broadly shared the parliamentary view that abolition of the sovereignty doctrine would pose no problem for the courts. As early as 1968, Gilmour argued that the institution of the right of individual petition to the European Court of Human Rights had in any case rendered parliamentary sovereignty meaningless since 'the realities of international politics' meant Parliament had to conform to ECHR requirements.[41] Again, around the time of the Lords Select Committee, Fazal questioned whether parliamentary sovereignty was unalterable,[42] Mann suggested that English judges could return to their pre-Revolution tradition of fundamental law,[43] and Dike proposed that the doctrine be abandoned, arguing that parliamen-

---

[38]　HC, 203, cols 991–993, 12 February 1992.
[39]　HL, 506, cols 1136–1174, 25 January 1995.　　[40]　See Lester (1995).
[41]　Gilmour (1968).　　　　　　　　　　[42]　Fazal (1974).　　　[43]　Mann (1978).

tary sovereignty was not a settled feature of the constitution and that there could be no guarantee that English courts would enforce legislation which contravened EC law.[44] It is striking that commentators on the Bill of Rights issue were substantially less cautious than academics who wrote contemporaneously purely on the effects of the 1972 Act.[45] There was curiously little academic cross-fertilization of ideas on these two inextricably linked issues. This perhaps serves as an extreme example of the tendency to pigeon-hole intimately connected issues in strictly separate compartments.

The trend in academic thinking which predicted a more flexible judicial approach to the future of parliamentary sovereignty became more pronounced in the 1980s and 1990s. Commentators emphasized that the courts' loyalty to parliamentary sovereignty was underpinned by the moral and political *reasons* justifying the doctrine, and that Community membership had already undermined it. Jaconelli considered judicial recognition of the unique nature of a Bill of Rights might lead in turn to abandonment of the 'old view' of parliamentary sovereignty.[46] Allan argued that the normative content of parliamentary sovereignty could shift in response to changing political morality. Thus if the Community came to replace the UK as the perceived fundamental political entity, this would be reflected in changes in the sovereignty doctrine.[47] Dworkin emphasized that law could change at great speed, and that, if a Bill of Rights were enacted, judges 'would have no legal or logical reason not to hold future Parliaments to the decision the nation had made'.[48] Indeed, the 'tradition' of parliamentary sovereignty was less appealing now that executive domination and party discipline had reduced backbench power.[49] Craig argued that any justification for parliamentary sovereignty had to be based on arguments of principle, and that, examined in this way, one might well conclude that right-based constraints were preferable to parliamentary omnipotence.[50]

Doubts over the durability of parliamentary sovereignty were reinforced by the extra-judicial writings of several prominent judges in the mid-1990s, raising the possibility that the courts might dispense with the doctrine without even parliamentary encouragement. Sir John Laws noted that, just as the House of Lords in *Anisminic* had overridden the apparently plain words of an ouster clause, so too the courts would presume against any statutory assertion of power to violate fundamental rights. Such a rule, he suggested, would possess as much force as that enjoyed by entrenched constitutional provisions in

---

[44] Dike (1976).

[45] See eg Wade (1972).

[46] Jaconelli (1980) 168.

[47] Allan (1985*b*).

[48] Dworkin (1990) 27.

[49] Ibid 30.

[50] Craig (1991) 254–255.

other countries.[51] He later argued that there was a 'higher order law' which both conferred and limited Parliament's sovereignty.[52] Laws's thesis rested on Kantian underpinnings,[53] emphasizing individual rights, and he did not believe that the legal ramifications of Community membership had any fundamental bearings on his arguments.[54] Lord Woolf argued that both Parliament and courts derived their authority from the rule of law, and that therefore statutes which fundamentally threatened the rule of law (such as one seeking to abolish judicial review) could be set aside.[55] Even Sir Stephen Sedley, who considered himself sceptical of notions of a higher-order law, argued that European developments cast doubt on the continued survival of parliamentary sovereignty.[56]

The undermining of parliamentary sovereignty by leading judges went hand in hand with their discarding of the *Wednesbury*[57] principle. The *Wednesbury* standard of review, as Craig has pointed out,[58] is founded upon contestable assumptions relating to parliamentary omnicompetence and parliamentary monopoly.[59] The judges in their academic articles welcomed the evolution of variable standards of substantive review, which would permit more intense scrutiny in cases involving fundamental rights.[60]

In sum, parliamentarians, judges, and academics alike took an increasingly uninhibited view of the future of parliamentary sovereignty. The strictures of the 1977–8 Lords Committee Report were swiftly abandoned. By the 1980s and 1990s it was increasingly assumed that if Parliament issued an invitation to the courts to do away with the doctrine, or at least to alter its content, the courts would comply without hesitation. Significantly this view was shared by opponents and supporters of parliamentary sovereignty alike.[61] The only argument was over the democratic merits and demerits of such a change.

---

[51] Laws (1993).   [52] Laws (1995).   [53] Laws (1996).

[54] Laws (1995) 89. For a critique of Laws's views, see Griffith (2000).

[55] Woolf (1995) 68.   [56] Sedley (1994).

[57] *Associated Provincial Picture Houses Ltd v Wednesbury Corporation* [1948] 1 KB 223.

[58] Craig (1990) 19–29.

[59] Both Laws and Woolf reject the *ultra vires* doctrine as the organizing principle of judicial review. For Laws, the grounds of review correspond to the virtuous conduct of the state's affairs. For Woolf, *ultra vires* is a fairy tale; the judges impose standards of fairness on public decision-makers. See further Craig (1998*b*).

[60] Woolf (1990) 121–122, Laws (1993) 69, Sedley (1995) 395, Steyn (1997) 94.

[61] See Ewing and Gearty (1994) 4–6.

Effect of Community membership on terms of the debate

Since *Factortame* had a major impact on the degree to which Bill of Rights supporters assumed that such a measure could be entrenched, one might expect the protagonists frequently to draw parallels between the Community and the ECHR. Despite the polarization of opinion on the Community (and ECJ) from the mid-1980s onwards, there was nonetheless a Commons majority for continued Community membership throughout the 1980s and 1990s. Supporters of the Community might have argued that if a limitation of sovereignty was tolerable in the Community context, it was also acceptable in other areas. Conversely opponents might argue that Parliament had lost enough of its legislative supremacy already. The connection between Community law and ECHR law was particularly strong in view of the ECJ's own fundamental rights jurisprudence and its propensity to utilize ECHR provisions in its judgments, leading to the argument that the UK already enjoyed a partial Bill of Rights.[62]

In fact few parliamentarians introduced a Community dimension into the Bill of Rights/ECHR debate. The 1987 debate on Sir Edward Gardner's Human Rights Bill provides a pre-*Factortame* example. Pro-EEC supporters of ECHR incorporation of the stature of Geoffrey Rippon[63] and Leon Brittan[64] made substantial speeches without any mention of the Community. Similarly anti-EEC and anti-incorporation backbencher William Cash spoke against the Bill without drawing any parallels between the Strasbourg and Community institutions. It is equally surprising that Nick Brown, for the Opposition, attacked the notion of judges striking down legislation and talked of the 'grave difficulties for judges in interpreting non-specific Articles', without any suggestion that this is what Community law involves.[65] The Second Reading of the 1995 Lester Bill furnishes a post-*Factortame* example.[66] Here there was somewhat more discussion of the Community, but largely because Lord Lester sought to introduce a provision akin to sections 2(2) and 2(4) of the 1972 Act. Moreover discussion of Community law parallels was mainly confined to the Law Lords.[67] Indeed Baroness Blatch,

---

[62] Bingham (1993), Browne-Wilkinson (1992), Grief (1991).
[63] HC, 109, cols 1243–1247, 6 February 1987.
[64] Ibid, cols 1262–1266, 6 February 1987.   [65] Ibid, cols 1275–1280, 6 February 1987.
[66] HL, 560, cols 1136–1174, 25 January 1995.
[67] For example Lord Taylor (ibid, col 1143) and Lord Lloyd of Berwick (ibid, col 1153).

winding up for the government, argued that EC obligations were 'narrow and well defined' whilst ECHR commitments were 'broad and general'.[68] This contention seems wholly unsustainable. It is hard to consider, for example, Article 28 EC as being either narrow or, in terms of the Treaty text, well defined.

Thus ECHR incorporation was perceived by parliamentarians as a discrete area of political debate. The similarities obvious to lawyers were not obvious to the politicians.

Passage of the Human Rights Bill 1997–8

The Blair government's introduction of a Human Rights Bill marked a departure from Labour's traditional distrust of judicial power. As an issue, the Bill of Rights did not attract sufficient political attention to merit a debate at Labour's Conference until 1985. On that occasion Jo Richardson, on behalf of the Party's National Executive Committee, argued that 'the best way to extend the rights and freedoms of ordinary people is not through courts packed with judges but through a Parliament packed with Labour MPs'.[69] Similarly at the 1988 Conference Roy Hattersley stated that a Bill of Rights would 'entrench the privileges of the already advantaged' and 'prejudice our chances of building a socialist society by requiring the courts and the judges to sit in judgment on the policies which the next Labour government will bring in'.[70] At the 1989 Conference a resolution calling for a Bill of Rights was rejected by 4,650,000 votes to 1,358,000 at the NEC's behest.[71] In 1990 the Conference voted down incorporation of the ECHR in favour of Hattersley's proposal of a comprehensive charter of rights.[72] The sea-change in Labour attitudes came with John Smith's statement of policy supporting a Bill of Rights in March 1993.[73] Smith favoured ECHR incorporation through a Human Rights Act protected by a provision that would require any intention to amend it to be expressly stated. Smith's views were reflected in

---

[68] HL, 560, col 1168, 25 January 1995.

[69] *Report of the Annual Conference of the Labour Party 1985*, 279, 4 October 1985.

[70] *Report of the Eighty-Seventh Annual Conference of the Labour Party 1988*, 124, 6 October 1988.

[71] *Report of the Eighty-Eighth Annual Conference of the Labour Party 1989*, 137, 5 October 1989.

[72] *Conference Report: Eighty-Ninth Annual Conference of the Labour Party 1990*, 299–300, 4 October 1990. For a critique of the 'charter of rights' proposal, see Loveland (1992).

[73] *Guardian*, 2 March 1993.

the NEC statement *A New Agenda for Democracy: Labour's Proposals for Constitutional Reform*, adopted by the 1993 Labour Conference.[74]

After Labour's 1997 election victory under Tony Blair, there was vigorous governmental debate as to what form the Human Rights Bill should take. Lord Irvine LC was anxious that the Bill should not 'disturb the supremacy of Parliament' and favoured the New Zealand model which gives no power to the courts to override statute.[75] In contrast the Home Secretary Jack Straw and his junior minister in the Lords, Lord Williams of Mostyn, were believed to have wanted a stronger model based on the Canadian Charter of Rights.[76] In the event Lord Irvine's (partial) victory may be attributed partly to the view taken by senior judges during the Lords debate on the 1995 Lester Bill— notably Lord Taylor LCJ,[77] Lord Browne-Wilkinson,[78] and Lord Donaldson[79]—that they did not seek the right to set aside Acts of Parliament, thereby dissociating themselves from the Woolf/Laws position.[80] Lord Irvine had made his own views clear when in 1996 as Shadow Lord Chancellor he had initiated a Lords debate on the relationship between judiciary and legislature. Having criticized Conservative attacks on judicial review, he also censured

equally unwise . . . extra-judicial statements by distinguished judges that in exceptional cases the courts may be entitled to hold invalid statutes duly passed by Parliament. This causes ordinary people not only to believe that judges may have got over and above themselves but that perhaps they are exercising a political function in judicial review cases instead of just upholding the rule of law.[81]

This view was endorsed in the debate by Lord Mackay LC, who declared that the supremacy of Acts of Parliament constituted the basis on which the courts exercised jurisdiction.[82]

The government's White Paper on the Bill broadly reflected this view. It affirmed that Parliament's authority to make decisions derived from a democratic mandate. To provide in the Bill for the courts to set aside Acts of Parliament would confer on the judiciary a power which would draw the

---

[74] *Conference Report: Ninety-Second Annual Conference of the Labour Party*, 214, 30 September 1993.

[75] *The Times*, 5 July 1998.   [76] *Guardian*, 5 July 1998.

[77] HL, 560, cols 1143–1144, 25 January 1995.   [78] Ibid, col 1150, 25 January 1995.

[79] Ibid, cols 1146–1148, 25 January 1995.

[80] All three opposed European Communities Act-style entrenchment. Lord Taylor seemed to favour the Canadian arrangement, Lord Browne-Wilkinson recommended the New Zealand model, and Lord Donaldson preferred the retention of full parliamentary sovereignty.

[81] HL, 572, col 1255, 5 June 1996.   [82] Ibid, col 1310, 5 June 1996.

judiciary into serious conflict with Parliament. There was no evidence they desired such power, nor that the public wished them to have it.[83]

To that end, the judiciary would only be able to grant 'declarations of incompatibility' which would flag up to government and Parliament that statutory provisions contravened Convention rights. It would then be for the executive and legislature to decide what—if anything—to do to remove the incompatibility. Even legislation pre-dating the Human Rights Act would not be subject to implied repeal by it. Rather, previous legislation—as in the case of legislation post-dating the Act—would merely be subject to declarations of incompatibility by the judiciary. The only *legal* effect of a declaration of incompatibility would be to trigger the power of a government minister to use what became known as the 'fast-track procedure' as a possible means of amending the offending statute. This would enable ministers to change primary legislation by means of delegated legislation—a so-called Henry VIII clause.

The government emphasized that the Bill was 'intended to provide a new basis for judicial interpretation of all legislation, not a basis for striking down any part of it'.[84] ECHR incorporation had to be distinguished from EC law, 'because it is a *requirement* of membership of the European Union that Member States give priority to directly effective EC law in their own legal systems. There is no such requirement in the Convention.'[85] (One might question, however, what purpose is served by incorporation if not to ensure that Convention norms prevail in the United Kingdom.) As for entrenchment, this 'could not be reconciled with our own constitutional traditions' and was neither necessary nor desirable.[86] It is notable that the government considered neither entrenchment nor the supremacy of ECHR norms over future Acts of Parliament to be impossible, merely undesirable.

The debates on the Human Rights Bill 1997–8 indicate that the issues of parliamentary sovereignty and the institutional position of Parliament *vis-à-vis* the courts remained central to political discourse surrounding ECHR incorporation. This is striking in view of the importance attached by the government to the Bill's preservation of parliamentary sovereignty. Indeed at Commons Second Reading Home Secretary Jack Straw described parliamentary sovereignty as 'paramount',[87] adding that, having decided on incorporation, 'the most fundamental question that we faced was how to do that in

---

[83] *Rights Brought Home: The Human Rights Bill* (Cm 3782, October 1997) para 2.13.
[84] Ibid, para 2.14. [85] Ibid, para 2.12 (original emphasis).
[86] Ibid, para 2.16. [87] HC, 306, col 772, 16 February 1998.

a manner that strengthened, and did not undermine, the sovereignty of Parliament'.[88]

One might have assumed that such robust defence of the traditional doctrine would have put paid to protracted argument about parliamentary sovereignty during the Bill's passage. In fact this was not the case. The Bill's opponents considered that the combination of declarations of incompatibility and the fast-track procedure (whereby ministers could amend statutory provisions by Order so as to make them compatible with the Convention) would undermine the *substance* of parliamentary sovereignty. If government or Parliament failed to act on a declaration of incompatibility, this would give the green light to the applicant to petition the European Court of Human Rights. Thus the Bill's vaunted preservation of parliamentary sovereignty was variously derided as 'a fiction',[89] 'a fig-leaf',[90] and even 'just the appearance of a fig-leaf, but no fig-leaf at all'.[91] As Lord McClusky put it,

Of course the judges will not possess quite the same power here as they do in the United States or in other places, but the effect will be exactly the same.... Parliament will at once move to bring the law into line with what judges say the convention says it is. In fact Parliament will have no option if the Strasbourg court so decides.[92]

Thus, in Lord Waddington's words, whatever the formal, legalistic, position, 'Parliament bows the knee and the judges' law prevails. That is the truth of the matter.'[93] This 'truth' was conceded by Jack Straw at Commons Second Reading, when he pointed out that since British governments invariably complied with Strasbourg judgments, Parliament could not sensibly ignore declarations of incompatibility from the British courts.[94] A Conservative amendment refusing the Bill a Second Reading on the grounds that it failed to respect the separation of powers and diminished the powers of Parliament was defeated by 335 votes to 144, and the Bill secured Second Reading by 332 votes to 144.

Conservative hostility to the system of the Act was underlined by a series of amendments tabled at the Committee and Report stages. Their amendment to

---

[88] Ibid, col 771, 16 February 1998.

[89] HC, 314, col 1123, 24 June 1998 (Robert Maclennan).

[90] Ibid, col 1125, 24 June 1998 (Edward Leigh).

[91] Ibid, col 1132, 24 June 1998 (Edward Garnier).   [92] Ibid, col 1267, 3 November 1997.

[93] HL, 582, col 1254, 3 November 1997. It is ironic that over the EEC issue in 1971, David Waddington had had no qualms in relation to Parliament giving up 'complete legal sovereignty'. See Ch 3 above.

[94] HC, 306, col 774, 16 February 1998. See also Lord Irvine LC HL, 582, col 1231, 3 November 1997.

Clause 4 of the Bill, which related to declarations of incompatibility, was mild, merely obliging judges to set out the 'nature and extent' of incompatibility in any such declaration.[95] The thinking behind the amendment was that Parliament would not be obliged to do 'one iota or scintilla more than is absolutely necessary' to meet ECHR obligations.[96] It is surprising that the Opposition did not consider that the terms of the declaration itself would almost invariably set down the nature and extent of incompatibility, and that any remaining ambiguities would probably be resolved by the accompanying judgment. The amendment was defeated by 320 votes to 128, and Clause 4 was then approved without division.

The Conservative amendment to Clause 10, which provided for the 'fast-track procedure', proposed that ministers should be able to issue certificates that declarations of incompatibility have no effect until the relevant issues were considered by the European Court of Human Rights. This would ensure that the Strasbourg Court's 'vital doctrine of margin of appreciation is given full and proper expression', thereby preventing the Convention being used by the British courts as a substitute constitution.[97] This amendment seemed based on the assumption that British courts would adopt a more rigorous intensity of scrutiny than the European Court of Human Rights. The Conservatives did not pursue this amendment to a vote in Committee but reintroduced it on Report as New Clause 2. In proposing it, Sir Nicholas Lyell argued that where a government disagreed with a declaration of incompatibility it would be better to force a case to continue on to Strasbourg, rather than to remain silent and leave the matter in limbo.[98] Jack Straw countered that the same result could be achieved simply by inaction accompanied by a statement that the government did not accept a declaration of incompatibility.[99] New Clause 2 was rejected by 372 votes to 132.

It should be noted that predictions that a British declaration of incompatibility would prove to be merely the speedy equivalent of a Strasbourg judgment were based on imponderables. It was possible that British court judgments might by and large mirror the standards of the European Court of Human Rights. Alternatively domestic courts, free of the inhibitions which afflict an international tribunal and imbued with the ethos of British life, might generally prove more assertive in deciding for themselves what was 'necessary in a democratic society' or what constituted a 'pressing social need'

---

[95] HC, 313, cols 437–464, 3 June 1998.
[96] Ibid, col 447, 3 June 1998 (John Selwyn Gummer).
[97] HC, 314, col 1116, 24 June 1998 (Edward Garnier).
[98] HL, 317, cols 1296–1297, 21 October 1998.   [99] Ibid, col 1303, 21 October 1998.

in the UK context.[100] Conversely it was conceivable that British judges, mindful of their constitutional position, might tend to permit the elected legislature a wider margin of appreciation and largely defer to Parliament's own assessment of the proportionality of its measures.[101]

The Opposition also proposed in Committee that, in the absence of 'exceptional reasons', any amending legislation should take the form of Acts of Parliament. This would ensure that changes to the law resulting from declarations of incompatibility would mainly be 'created and crafted by Parliament, with proper opportunity to debate and amend' rather than by the courts or government.[102] Jack Straw retorted that pressures on the legislative timetable precluded the exclusive use of statute to remedy incompatibilities, though he conceded that in the past primary legislation had sometimes been enacted very quickly.[103] He saw the merit of changes resulting from declarations of incompatibility being effected by primary legislation, since this allowed Parliament and judges to engage in a dialogue on human rights. Accordingly use of remedial orders would be 'limited and constrained'.[104] In Committee the government itself proposed an amendment to Clause 10 to require 'compelling reasons' for proceeding by Order.[105] Despite this, on Report the Opposition proposed outright deletion of Clause 10, arguing that the ECHR constituted a 'broad framework within which all our laws should be framed' and that therefore there was no justification for government to diminish Parliament's role.[106] Difficult issues on which the UK could exercise its margin of appreciation, such as the lawfully permissible degree of chastisement of children,[107] would benefit from full debate with proper opportunity for amendment and reflection in both Houses.[108] For the government, Mike O'Brien again emphasized the overcrowded legislative timetable and reiterated that under Clause 10(2) ministers would use the

---

[100] See eg Laws (1998).

[101] See Hoffman J in *Stoke-on-Trent City Council v B&Q plc* [1990] 3 CMLR 31. See also Hooper (1999).

[102] Ibid, col 1132, 24 June 1998 (Edward Garnier).

[103] Ibid, col 1137, 24 June 1998. Indeed, during the period of the Bill's passage, Parliament enacted the Criminal Justice Act 1998 in the course of a day (see HC, 317, cols 713–932, 2 September 1998).

[104] Ibid, col 1141, 24 June 1998.   [105] HC, 314, col 1138, 24 June 1998.

[106] HC, 317, cols 1326–1329, 21 October 1998 (Edward Garnier).

[107] This followed the European Court of Human Rights' holding in *A v United Kingdom* (1998) 27 EHRR 611, that by lawfully permitting a father to administer a severe beating to his son the United Kingdom had breached Article 3 ECHR. *Independent*, 8 November 1997, *Guardian*, 8 November 1997.

[108] Ibid, col 1328, 21 October 1998.

fast-track procedure only if there were 'compelling reasons' for so doing. The Opposition amendment was rejected by 362 votes to 110.

Defending parliamentary sovereignty: indirect means

Just as it could be argued that the system of enforcement under the Human Rights Act eroded parliamentary sovereignty *de facto*, it could also be contended that other provisions of the Act relating to access to the courts militated in the direction of *de facto* defence of the sovereignty doctrine. Thus ministers abandoned the proposal for a Human Rights Commission, according to the *Daily Telegraph*, out of fear that the 'creation of a new umbrella organisation will unleash a flood of legal claims against the Government and threaten the traditional supremacy of Parliament'.[109] The Act also adopted a restrictive 'victim' standing test, in place of the liberally interpreted 'sufficient interest' test applicable in English judicial review, virtually eliminating the prospect of non-governmental organizations being accorded representative standing.[110] The government may have been mindful that an increasing proportion of judicial review proceedings were being brought by pressure groups, trade unions, and other non-governmental organizations, and may have wished to discourage this trend in the context of the new Act. At the same time it made Convention rights challenges a riskier venture for individuals by abolishing civil legal aid for many of the types of proceedings in which many Convention rights would be enforced.[111] These measures would seriously restrict access to the courts for the purposes of securing declarations of incompatibility. Since it was generally considered that such declarations would rarely be granted, few private individuals would wish to bear the costs of an action. Even if the action were successful, the court would have no power to grant a remedy to the litigant: the Act provides that a declaration of incompatibility does not affect the validity, continuing operation, or enforcement of the provision in question, and that the declaration is not binding on the parties to the case.[112]

In addition, in Committee, the government moved new clauses relating to the two contentious substantive areas—the position of the churches and press freedom. These clauses can be seen in terms of Parliament to some extent binding judicial hands by predetermining the hierarchy of competing

---

[109] *Daily Telegraph*, 5 July 1998.   [110] Marriott and Nicol (1998).
[111] *The Times*, 28 October 1997.   [112] s 4 (6).

Convention norms. The first new clause provided that if any litigation might affect the exercise by a religious organization of the right to freedom of thought, conscience, and religion, the court must have particular regard to the importance of that right.[113] Curiously this was added to the Bill without debate, although there had previously been vigorous Lords debate as to whether churches constituted 'public authorities' for the purposes of Clause 6 of the Bill.[114] The second new clause instructed courts to have particular regard for freedom of expression. Furthermore where proceedings concerned journalistic, literary, or artistic material, courts had to consider the extent to which (i) the material would be available to the public and (ii) publication would be in the public interest. In addition *ex parte* injunctions were made more difficult to obtain.[115] These amendments were secured by the campaigning efforts of the churches and press respectively. In moving the new clause Jack Straw expressed the view that it was not strictly necessary since the Strasbourg court 'time and again has come down in favour of press freedom as opposed to privacy and family life'.[116] It is noteworthy that pro-Bill of Rights newspapers such as the *Guardian*[117] and the *Observer*[118] had called in their leader columns for Parliament, not the judiciary, to determine the balance between freedom of expression and the right to privacy.

The Conservatives wanted to go further in ensuring that Parliament dictated the ordering of judicial priorities. They moved amendments to the effect that (1) every time a court considered that Article 8 ECHR (right to privacy) had been breached, it should issue a report to Parliament and stay proceedings until Parliament had debated the matter; and (2) in any proceedings involving an adjudication between Article 8 and Article 10 (freedom of expression), the court should 'normally, and particularly where the right to impart or receive information about matters of public interest is at issue, give precedence to rights arising under Article 10'. Straw considered that these proposals breached the separation of powers by compromising the independence of the judiciary *vis-à-vis* Parliament, whereas the government's proposal struck the right balance.[119] The Conservative proposals were not pursued to a vote.

---

[113] HC, 315, col 534, 2 July 1998.

[114] See eg HL, 583, cols 790–799, 24 November 1997 and HL, 584, cols 1319–1351, 19 January 1998. See also Hunt (1998).

[115] Ibid, cols 534–563, 2 July 1998. [116] HC, 315, col 535, 2 July 1998.

[117] *Guardian*, 25 October 1997. [118] *Observer*, 27 July 1997.

[119] HC, 315, cols 542–543, 2 July 1998.

Nonetheless even the government's proposals meant that Parliament was intervening to push the courts as far as possible into giving priority to freedom of expression rather than allowing maximum scope for common law development. Significantly several MPs expressed the intention that Parliament should keep the position under ongoing review. One might say that they were asserting Parliament's 'continuing' sovereignty in the matter. Thus Clive Soley (Chair of the Parliamentary Labour Party) argued for a full statutory regime to safeguard individuals from press intrusion,[120] Dominic Greive (Conservative, Beaconsfield) warned that Parliament should 'keep the matter under review',[121] and Home Office Minister Mike O'Brien spoke of Parliament being 'at the beginning of a journey' in relation to this aspect of the law.[122] Thus far from the Human Rights Act forming something 'fundamental' in the British constitution, parliamentarians considered themselves entitled to reorder judicial prioritization and curtail judicial discretion, both during the Act's passage and thereafter. They appear to have recognized, however, that any such parliamentary intervention should not itself fall outside the margin of appreciation permitted to Contracting States by the European Court of Human Rights.

Connection with EC law

Once again parliamentarians did not highlight the connection between ECHR incorporation and the incorporation of EC law some twenty-six years earlier, even though the reach of the ECJ's fundamental rights doctrine had been expanded by ECJ case law. By now the doctrine was binding on Member States whenever they implemented Community rules[123] and indeed whenever national rules fell within the scope of Community law.[124] The importance of the link between EC law and ECHR law had been noted by academics[125] and judges.[126] One might have expected ECHR supporters in Parliament to argue that if human rights were enforceable within the

---

[120] Ibid, col 547, 2 July 1998.   [121] Ibid, col 557, 2 July 1998.

[122] Ibid, col 563, 2 July 1998.

[123] Case 5/88 *Wachauf (Hubert) v Federal Republic of Germany* [1989] ECR 2609, [1991] 1 CMLR 328.

[124] Case C–260/89 *Elliniki Radiophonia Tileorassi—Anonimi Etairia v Dimitiki Etairia Pliroforissis and Sotirios Kouvelas* [1991] ECR I–2925, [1994] 4 CMLR 540, Case C–368/95 *Vereinigte Familiapress Zeitungsverlags- und Vertriebs-GmbH v Heinrich Bauer Verlag* [1997] ECR I–3689.

[125] Grief (1991).   [126] Browne-Wilkinson (1992), Bingham (1993).

Community sphere, they ought to be enforceable outside it. One might also have expected the argument to be raised as to why Parliament should 'be willing to qualify its sovereignty in commercial and employment matters, while refusing to do so in relation to human rights'.[127] Conversely, with the dramas of Maastricht incorporation still fresh in the political consciousness, opponents might have asserted that enough power had already been transferred to the national courts in order to do the bidding of 'Europe'.

In fact allusion to the EC was rare and cursory. At Second Reading, Jack Straw and Mike O'Brien, who respectively introduced and wound up for the government, pointed to the contradiction of Conservatives voting for the 1972 Act whilst opposing the 1998 Bill that 'will not overrule our primary legislation'.[128] Their Conservative counterparts made no mention of the EC. Straw also argued that the much-maligned fast-track procedure offered more safeguards than the 1972 Act, under which 'Parliament cannot vote on any declaration of the European Court of Justice that our law is outwith the ECJ; the law must be changed'.[129] Apart from Robert Maclennan who merely repeated the argument advanced by Straw and O'Brien,[130] no backbencher mentioned the Community connection during Second Reading. This sidelining of the EC meant that MPs fell into error. For instance Jack Straw declared that to have allowed courts to set aside Acts of Parliament would have given the judiciary a power it neither possessed nor sought.[131] Yet courts currently enjoy this power within the scope of application of Community law. Such was the extent to which politicians placed the EC and ECHR in discrete, hermetically sealed compartments.

Conclusion

The Times expressed its misgivings about the Human Rights Bill on the grounds that it 'could shift the balance between Parliament and the courts, irreversibly and in ways that may not be evident for years'.[132] In fact what is remarkable about the entire Bill of Rights debate is the extent to which the constitutional implications were indeed evident to parliamentarians. The

---

[127] Ben Emmerson, *The Times*, 22 July 1997.

[128] HC, 306, col 771 (Straw), col 858 (O'Brien), 16 February 1998.

[129] Ibid, col 773, 16 February 1998. This is an understatement. By virtue of the doctrines of direct effect and supremacy there is no need for the law to be changed; it changes automatically.

[130] Ibid, col 806, 16 February 1998.   [131] Ibid, col 772, 16 February 1998.

[132] *The Times*, 25 October 1997.

picture which emerges from the parliamentary debates reinforces the isolation of the EC issue. The Bill of Rights was seen as the only way by which Parliament could abolish its own sovereignty. Community membership was presented as no threat to parliamentary sovereignty since the doctrine was 'inescapable and enduring'. The Bill of Rights was perceived as leading to judicial supremacism. The EC was not. The European Communities Act 1972 sought to give British courts power to set aside Acts of Parliament and yet this was not understood by MPs. The Human Rights Act 1998 sought to deny British courts this power and yet the leading parliamentary protagonists were sufficiently adept to see through the legal formalism and assess the diminution of Parliament's legislative discretion in practical terms. Thus, in contrast to Community membership, parliamentarians passed the Human Rights Act 'with their eyes open' as to the constitutional consequences.

The explanation for the difference might lie in the fact that in the early EEC debates MPs were bamboozled by the existence and acts of the Community's political institutions. As we have seen, in the run-up to EEC accession MPs hostile to membership were preoccupied by the status, power, and secondary legislation of the Commission and, to a lesser extent, the Council. This not merely diluted but concealed the importance of the ECJ and the national courts. In contrast the Strasbourg institutions were transparently court-dominated.[133] There were no political institutions endowed with legislative competence to distract attention from the power of the European Court of Human Rights. Furthermore instruments laying down classical political and civil human rights were traditionally court-enforced whereas the notion of an international trade agreement elevating the institutional position of the judiciary was novel. For example, MPs were familiar with the United States model of a Bill of Rights and were therefore able to relate that to their own situation, whereas there was no model with which the European Community could be compared, in the absence of parliamentary knowledge of the way in which Community membership had affected the constitutional make-up of the other Member States.

The debate on the Human Rights Bill also witnessed further evolution of the perception by politicians of parliamentary sovereignty as a relative rather than absolute concept. The hard-and-fast 'right to make or unmake any law

---

[133] It is ironic, however, that the European Court of Human Rights, unlike the ECJ, has only recently started to single out the national *courts* as its 'policemen' in the Contracting States to ensure that national executives and legislatures respect Convention rights. Traditionally the Strasbourg Court took a more international law, 'institution-neutral', approach than its Community counterpart. See Nicol (2001).

whatsoever' assumed less importance. Politicians had to contend with the issue of preserving parliamentary sovereignty *de facto* not just *de jure*, and this involved consideration of the complex interplay between judiciary and Parliament which would arise from the cocktail of declarations of incompatibility and the fast-track procedure. As the constitution's legal dimension became increasingly sophisticated, parliamentarians were becoming correspondingly more adept at dealing with it.

Conclusion

On the face of it, there seems no shortage of ammunition with which to berate the performance of British parliamentarians. We have seen that MPs in the 1960s and 1970s failed to familiarize themselves with the likely constitutional implications of Community membership in terms of the ECJ's importance and the role of the national courts. They ignored *Costa* and *Van Gend*, even though these cases sent out the clear message that national courts would be duty-bound to override the commands of their national Parliaments whenever these conflicted with Community law. They disregarded the United States comparison, despite the fact that the adoption of our own 'written constitution', the Treaty, together with the establishment of a court charged with ensuring that 'the law' was observed, was likely to invest the ECJ with a status akin to that of the Supreme Court. They ignored *Internationale Handelsgesellschaft*, despite its warning that domestic courts would have to ensure that Community law prevailed even over the 'principles of a national constitutional structure'. They disregarded the fact that by the time of UK accession the ECJ's supremacy doctrine had broadly managed to establish itself in the Member States. Lack of understanding of the role to be played by the national courts also generated an overemphasis on the importance of Commission enforcement proceedings and an underemphasis on the significance of preliminary references. Actions under Article 169 EEC had more of an international law flavour than involvement of the national courts via Article 177, and MPs seemed unaware of the way in which the ECJ and national courts could use preliminary rulings to monitor the compatibility of statute with Community law. Fundamentally, the question of the appropriate relationship between Parliament and the courts (ECJ and national) was never debated in the run-up to accession. In short, a revolution occurred without political debate.

The legal constitution and legitimacy

Explanation, however, is more constructive than castigation. Why was it that MPs stumbled unwittingly from a 'political constitution' to a much more legally orientated one? Why was this transformation in the balance of power between Britain's institutions not subjected to the detailed parliamentary deliberation which it undoubtedly merited?

It might be noted as a preliminary point that for a country to enter into a constitutional arrangement without its politicians understanding the implications is, in itself, hardly unprecedented. In this respect one might note the curious symmetry between the British situation and the state of knowledge of the six original Member States. According to Mitchell, Kuipers, and Gull, the Six only half comprehended the globally constitutional changes which membership would inevitably bring about.[1] Weiler agrees that the Six created the EEC first, but commenced the 'harkening', deliberative process of listening, debating, and understanding only after they had committed themselves 'to do'.[2] Weiler reasons that, because 'the alternative to the European dream was the recent European nightmare', the Six were happy to enter a legal order the constitutional theory of which had not been worked out. Similarly, in a Britain bereft of its Empire and unable to escape a mediocre economic performance, the political imperative was to join a larger unit. The force of this political imperative was such as to make politicians indifferent to the constitutional make-up of this new construct. The finer details of whether the European entity was international or supranational could be considered at some later date.

With this overriding explanation in mind, the following additional reasons might be advanced to explain why it was that so many British parliamentarians did not go into the EEC 'with their eyes open'. The first relates to the UK's non-legal constitutional culture, the second to the nature of the Community, and the third to the lack of information proffered by government to Parliament.

First, parliamentarians were operating in an environment in which the role of the courts was minimal. In pre-accession Britain the courts did not intervene much in the national political scene; political matters were settled politically, not by legal action. It never really entered the heads of the overwhelming majority of MPs that joining the EEC would make much

---

[1] Mitchell, Kuipers, and Gull (1972) 134–135.   [2] Weiler (1999) 7–8.

difference to this particular state of affairs. MPs thought EEC membership would change a great many things, but it seems not to have occurred to them that one of the things it would change would be the relationship between Parliament and the courts. There was a failure to perceive parliamentary sovereignty in terms of what the UK courts do in response to Acts of Parliament. Instead, parliamentary sovereignty was largely seen as a *political* phenomenon—a question of what Parliament would refrain from doing as a matter of self-denying ordinance. Government and Parliament would broadly tailor their measures to the constraints of the Treaty, and that would be that. MPs failed to appreciate that the frequent promptings of the courts would be necessary, not merely because the scope of Community law was by no means self-evident,[3] but also because Community law would exact more by way of effective protection than could be secured by parliamentary goodwill alone.

The perception of parliamentary sovereignty as politically enforced rather than judicially enforced served to camouflage the seminal role of the ECJ within the Community constitution. Since MPs were ignorant of the ECJ's importance, they were all the more oblivious to the role which the ECJ intended the national courts to play. Little did they realize that the ECJ would recruit the British courts as its policemen to ensure that Parliament kept within the confines of its new restricted role. MPs were so unfamiliar with a prominent judicial role that they were in no position to debate it until they had experienced it. Even those MPs who were previously barristers or solicitors seemingly divested themselves of their legal baggage once they entered the political arena. Their former profession was law, their new profession was politics, and never the twain would meet. One might have hoped that lawyer-MPs would display a deeper understanding of parliamentary sovereignty, be they for it or against it, but in the event this proved not to be the case.

Thus the world view of British parliamentarians was based on an autonomous political sphere in which legal considerations played little part. Accordingly they were unable to grasp the lessons of long-standing ECJ precedents and had to await homespun case law before the new constitutional reality gradually sunk in. In the case of anti-Market MPs, their unfamiliarity with the judicial element led the vast majority of them to neglect what might otherwise have been a powerful argument against membership—Parliament's subordination to the courts, national as well as European, under

---

[3] See eg the predictions of Lord Chancellors Dilhorne and Gardiner (Ch 2 above) that Community law would have no impact on the vast majority of British people, being related almost exclusively to industrial and agricultural sectors.

EEC arrangements. In the case of the pro-Marketeers, they tended to be scornful of 'detailed constitutional points' relating to parliamentary sovereignty—a neglect which some of them with hindsight came to rue.[4] In view of the fact that the European Communities Act was passed by only six votes, had there been a more widespread recognition of the constitutional implications, the outcome would in all likelihood have been different.

As it was, it took until the mid-1990s for the ECJ to be subjected to the parliamentary attention which its constitutional importance merited. Thus only belatedly have British parliamentarians come to terms with the fact that, as Rawlings puts it, the parliamentary process now operates in the shadow of law.[5] The comparison with Ireland in Chapter 5 shows that legislators there were far more aware (albeit imperfectly so) of the reality of ECJ power when immersed in a legislative environment in which the judiciary already played a pivotal role.

It is also worth bearing in mind that politicians were not the only ones to underestimate the effect of EEC membership in facilitating the transformation to the legal constitution. Even the judges took time to adapt to the possibilities arising from Community law—as the initial reaffirmations of parliamentary sovereignty by Lords Diplock and Denning illustrate.[6] Likewise academics, both before and after accession, adhered to different views on the likelihood of the courts modifying the sovereignty doctrine.[7] This makes it all the more excusable that the politicians too should fail initially to recognize the way in which membership might limit parliamentary sovereignty.

Secondly, the nature of the Community helped to conceal the importance of the ECJ and the national courts in the Community scheme of things. MPs were preoccupied by the Community's political institutions (especially the Commission) at the expense of the ECJ. The novelty of international organizations which could enact legislation distracted attention from the fact that

[4] eg Brian Walden has admitted to never having bothered to look at the evidence as to whether there would be a serious loss of sovereignty (*The Times*, 1 January 2001), Margaret Thatcher has conceded that 'most of us, including myself, paid insufficient regard to the issue of sovereignty in consideration of the case for joining the EEC at the beginning of the 1970s.... [T]here was a failure to grasp the true nature of the European Court and the relationship that would emerge between British law and Community law' (Thatcher (1995) 497).

[5] Rawlings (1994*a*) 255–256.

[6] Diplock (1972), and see Lord Denning MR's judgment in *Felixstowe Dock and Railway Company v British Transport Docks Board* [1976] CMLR 655.

[7] Contrast the orthodoxy of Wade (1972) and Hood Phillips (1979) with the radicalism of Mitchell et al (1972) and Allan (1982).

the ECJ's doctrines had given teeth to such legislation by making it directly effective and supreme over national law. In addition MPs were unable to appreciate that an 'economic' Community (as opposed to an institution promoting classical liberal human rights) could be driven by a powerful Court fashioning a federal-type constitution. It was proposals for Bills of Rights which tended to evoke comparisons with the US Supreme Court. But whereas MPs were able to relate the US model of a Bill of Rights to the UK situation, and envisage the way in which it would augment judicial power, there was no model with which the Community could be compared. Without knowledge of the way in which membership had affected other countries, they were unable to envisage how an international economic agreement would transform the balance between legislature and judiciary.

The fact that the bridgehead to the legal constitution was Community law, rather than a Bill of Rights, is significant. It would have been harder to have achieved the judicialization of the constitution by Parliament accepting a Bill of Rights first and EEC membership subsequently. Many MPs perceived a Bill of Rights as representing a naked usurpation by the courts of governmental and parliamentary power, whereas in the case of EEC membership MPs' ignorance as to the way in which they were altering the UK's internal institutional arrangements eased the constitutional transformation. Chapter 8 shows that, had this transformation been effected by a Bill of Rights rather than by Community law, there would have been considerably more debate on the subject of judicial empowerment. As it was, the constitutional shift was facilitated by the way in which the Community's economic orientation, and the controversy surrounding its political institutions, distracted MPs from the role the courts would play.

Thirdly, Parliament was ill served by government and by Whitehall's army of lawyers. Information from successive governments could have acted as a corrective to compensate to some extent for MPs' constitutional law illiteracy. However, when one considers the White Papers in tandem with the speeches of government spokespersons, the overall impression is that governments were more concerned to 'get their way' on EEC membership than to furnish MPs with a realistic assessment of the constitutional shape of things to come. A candid approach would have emphasized the possibility that the national courts might eventually choose to enforce the ECJ's supremacy doctrine in preference to parliamentary sovereignty. In the event, Lord Chancellors Dilhorne and Gardiner talked in terms of Parliament having to *refrain* from passing inconsistent measures, the 1971 White Paper pledged no erosion of 'essential national sovereignty', Lord Hailsham LC insisted that section 2(4) of the 1972 Act was a mere rule of construction, rebuttable whenever clear statutory wording could not be reconciled with Community law, and Sir Geoffrey Howe SG argued that Parliament had no need to insert into the Act a declaration of its own supremacy, since parliamentary sovereignty was 'inescapable and enduring'. In a fine display of executive arrogance ministers too often presented their mere predictions of how the courts would react to Community law as hard fact. The difference of opinion between the Heath government's Commons and Lords spokespersons over the effect of section 2(4) of the Act is particularly striking.

There are two possible explanations for the lamentable part played by the executive. The first is that the senior civil service and the major figures in both parties understood only too well the possible impact of supremacy and direct effect on parliamentary sovereignty, but adopted equivocal positions on the constitutional issues out of fear 'that candid recognition of the *Costa* and *Van Gend* principles would further harden internal opposition to accession'.[8] The second possibility is that they simply suffered from the same constitutional law naïveté as the legislature.

There is no doubt that the executive deliberately played down the potential *scope* of Community law. Government realized the revolutionary implications of economic and monetary union[9] but insisted there would be no erosion of essential national sovereignty. Civil servants had to defer to 'politicians' judgment how much you have to put in the shop window and how much you don't'.[10] However, on the major theme of this book—the *enforceability* of Community law—it is less clear that ministers and civil servants appreciated that accession might well eventually lead to the radical limitation of parliamentary sovereignty. For example, in view of the ease with which the European Communities Bill was likely to clear the House of Lords, there seems little reason to doubt Lord Hailsham's sincerity in insisting to their Lordships that parliamentary sovereignty would survive section 2(4) unscathed. Similarly, Mr D Rippengal's evidence to the Lords Select Committee on a Bill of Rights several years after accession furnishes a civil

---

[8] Loveland (2000) 357. Shell (1996) suggests that both parties conspired in misleading the British people over the constitutional consequences of membership.

[9] 'The plan for economic and monetary union has revolutionary long term implications . . . It could imply the ultimate creation of a European federal state . . . It will arouse strong feelings about sovereignty and provoke vigorous discussions. Until we are [asked] we do not want to give our reactions.' *Ministerial Briefing Paper FCO 30/7/89, Committee on Approach to Europe*, 9 November 1970, released under the 'thirty-year rule' on 1 January 2001.

[10] Roy Denman, Deputy Secretary, Department of Trade, at the time of EEC accession, recalling the negotiations. *UK Confidential, Leviathan Special*, BBC2, 1 January 2001.

service example of genuine overestimation of the resilience of parliamentary sovereignty. He considered it 'more than likely' that, in the event of an irreconcilable conflict between statute and Community law, British courts would enforce the Act of Parliament notwithstanding section 2(4).

Perhaps the most convincing explanation, then, is one of *wilful blindness*. It would have required considerable reflection for political actors immersed in the political constitution to have perceived how membership might effect a transformation into a judicialized constitution. Why dwell on these putative 'drawbacks' of membership when the overriding Establishment imperative was to secure British accession? To have bent over backwards to produce a warts-and-all analysis for MPs would only have served to alienate wavering backbenchers.

The changing constitution and legitimacy today

Where does this leave the legitimacy of Parliament as a lawmaking body? For all the explanations proffered above, MPs do not come out of this story well. On the positive side, one must be mindful that things have improved. Before EEC accession the political and legal spheres kept themselves to themselves. Politicians were not much interested in what went on in the courts; the courts limited their interventions through a steadfast adherence to parliamentary sovereignty and the *Wednesbury* principle.[11] Since the 1980s, however, the robust growth of judicial review, whether emanating from the ECJ, European Court of Human Rights, or the domestic courts, has obliged the courts to take an increasing number of decisions in politically controversial areas. Consequently politicians were obliged to become more familiar with the requirements imposed upon them by public law.

In the early years of the European debate the competing conceptions of sovereignty were flawed and unsophisticated. Anti-Marketeers adopted a skewed conception of parliamentary sovereignty based on a wholly illogical focus on the rights of Parliament in isolation, rather than the reactions of the courts to what Parliament does. The right of Parliament to enact any law whatsoever is meaningless without the corresponding duty on the part of the courts to enforce all Acts of Parliament as the supreme law of the land. Pro-Marketeers took no interest in *parliamentary* sovereignty and were blasé

---

[11] *Associated Provincial Picture Houses v Wednesbury Corporation* [1948] 1 KB 223.

about the rights of Parliament post-accession. Instead they adopted a view of national sovereignty which centred on Britain being able to 'do the things we want to do for our people', even if these things were entrenched or predetermined, either in the Treaty or by virtue of further European integration sometime in the future. There was little dialogue between proponents of these two rival conceptions.

By the 1990s the terms of the sovereignty debate had changed. *Factortame* helped shape British politics in a broader way than first impressions might suggest. Had *Factortame* been decided in favour of parliamentary sovereignty rather than in favour of EC law supremacy, then this would have provided a safety valve which would have made the expansion of the scope of EC law involved in Maastricht more acceptable. As it was, their Lordships' acceptance of the supremacy of Community law over statute helped the Eurosceptics break out of their isolation and gradually assume the leadership of the Conservative Party.

The Maastricht debates introduced an emphasis on questions of competence and subsidiarity, with sovereignty being viewed as a relative rather than absolute concept. MPs adapted to a situation in which, to borrow a quip from Lord Howe, sovereignty was not like virginity—now you have it, now you don't—but was rather more subtle than that.[12] Parliament would retain its legislative freedom on some matters but not others, and the dividing line between areas of EC and national competence formed the battle-line at which political struggle was engaged. Maastricht witnessed a coming-together of law and politics, with politicians, not merely the vociferous anti-EC minority, taking a considerable interest in legal aspects. Similarly the nuanced way in which the proponents and opponents of the Human Rights Bill dealt with the parliamentary sovereignty issue also testifies to a marked increase in legislators' understanding of constitutional law. The passage of the Bill saw discussion of whether the *de jure* preservation of parliamentary sovereignty was accompanied by its *de facto* erosion. A more sophisticated discourse over questions of sovereignty is taking place, which might call into question the present-day appropriateness of Dicey's emphasis on a rigid demarcation between legal and political sovereignty.

Legitimacy can vary over time. Certainly parliamentarians lacked legal competence in the run-up to accession and this must to some extent damage Parliament's claim to legitimacy as a lawmaking body. Nonetheless MPs

---

[12] Letter to the author, 10 March 1998.

eventually adjusted to the creeping hegemony of law in the British constitution. Unable to learn from previous ECJ jurisprudence, legislators eventually learnt from experience, in the form of 'adverse' ECJ and national court decisions. The finding that MPs are now far more adept at dealing with constitutional law issues can be seen as *enhancing* Parliament's legitimacy. The contrast between today's constitution and the 'political constitution' of the past is a stark one. Complex legal questions—relating, for example, to the dividing line between areas of Community and national competence—are becoming the staple fare of the diligent legislator. Parliamentarians are increasingly having to take on the role of constitutional lawyers—and Maastricht ratification showed that an increasing number are doing so to a high standard of proficiency. It could therefore be argued that the legal incompetence of MPs has been 'cured' by their increasing legal sophistication evidenced in the Maastricht debates. Furthermore, now that Parliament has finally experienced the limitations on its sovereignty wrought by Community law, parliamentary opinion on the legitimacy of these legal inroads has polarized, and this polarization has sharpened MPs' legal understanding by moving the courts centre-stage. The majority in the 1997 and 2001 Parliaments seem more willing to countenance the courts setting parameters for parliamentary action in areas unrelated to the EC. This doubtless reflects the Labour government's broad approval of the legislative fetters imposed by EC membership. Conversely the Conservatives, growing ever more hostile to the ECJ's supremacy principle, were unwilling to support the 'diminution of Parliament' which they believed implicit in the Human Rights Act. Thus Parliaments evolve: the legally incompetent Parliament of the 1960s and 1970s has matured into the far more legally aware Parliament of today.

As for the future, in all likelihood we will witness a growing capacity on the part of legislators to handle constitutional law issues. This will be aided by the fact that accelerating intrusion of law into the political domain has spilt over into fields other than those occupied by Community law. Under the Human Rights Act, the courts now issue 'declarations of incompatibility' whenever they consider that statutory provisions conflict with Convention rights, placing a powerful moral onus on government and Parliament to amend the offending law. This may lead to disputes between courts and legislators over the scope, interpretation, and application of fundamental rights. Parliament's adeptness at dealing with issues of constitutional law is likely to be further enhanced as legislators engage in a dialogue with the courts arising from the granting of declarations of incompatibility and Parliament's reaction thereto.

The judicial review provisions under the devolution Acts are also drawing the courts further into sensitive political areas.[13]

This is not to deny that there is room for improvement. The lesson of the European story is that Parliament and public could only benefit from a wider and deeper parliamentary understanding of the legal aspects of constitutional development. Arrangements could be made to facilitate parliamentary awareness of constitutional law issues and thereby help legislators deal with an increasingly complex picture. To this end the House of Lords has recently established a Constitution Committee to examine the constitutional implications of all public bills coming before the House, a useful corrective to governmental attempts to bamboozle Parliament into passing legislation without adequate reflection on constitutional questions.[14] It is an example which the Commons ought to follow. Another move in the right direction is that both Houses have set up a Joint Committee on Human Rights to examine proposals for remedial orders under section 10 of the Human Rights Act 1998 and to consider whether to draw the attention of the Houses to such measures.[15] Perhaps this may herald a proactive approach by Parliament in which MPs will not merely defer to judicial decisions about the need to change statute and executive decisions about the 'correct' response. It cannot be assumed that constitutional change is now a one-way street in which the powers of the courts are progressively strengthened and the powers of the politicians correspondingly diminished. My analysis of the Human Rights Bill debates shows that MPs and peers had no inhibitions about substituting their own conceptions of Convention rights for those of the Strasbourg court. Under a flexible constitution like Britain's there may be moves to restore the constitutional position of the politicians *vis-à-vis* the judges. There is a strong normative case for Parliament as a representative assembly to contest the boundaries of its authority rather than submit to a judicial monopoly on, say, the (eminently contestable) interpretation of human rights and an executive monopoly on the (equally contestable) content of corrective measures.[16] A lesson here can be learnt from Canada, where the federal

---

[13] Craig and Walters (1999).   [14] HL, 621, cols 1269–1270, 8 February 2001.

[15] HL, 615, cols 233–234, 12 July 2000; HC, 361, cols 146–167, 15 January 2001, and cols 482–490, 17 January 2001.

[16] See generally Cooper (1998) ch 8. This argument militates in favour of amending the Human Rights Act to enhance the role of Parliament in determining the conception of the Convention rights which should hold sway in the UK. This might involve doing away with the fast-track procedure so that all legal changes inspired by judicial declarations of incompatibility obtain the benefit of the full parliamentary process. It might also involve introducing a mechanism which would allow the legislature to express reasoned disagreement with a declaration of incompatibility.

Parliament has made it abundantly clear that elected representatives are not prepared to acquiesce to judicial interpretation of Canada's Charter of Rights. The Parliament uses legislative preambles to explain to the courts why its legislation constitutes a thoughtful and reasonable (and therefore lawful) balance between competing rights. This can be perceived as 'a stage in a conversation between elected and judicial officials on how the Charter should be interpreted and applied'.[17] Furthermore, in view of the difficulty in keeping constitutional trends in discrete watertight compartments, it is not beyond the bounds of possibility that the UK Parliament may one day start to flex its muscles even in relation to EC law.[18]

The reasoning in *Factortame No 2*

The history of the parliamentary debates also suggests that there are problems with Lord Bridge's statement in *Factortame (No 2)* that Parliament's limitation of sovereignty was 'entirely voluntary'. For Parliament to have restricted itself 'entirely voluntarily' suggests that its constituent members broadly understood the way in which the national courts would enforce Community norms even in the face of conflicting statute. But, as we have seen, legislators *en masse* simply did not appreciate that the relationship between Parliament and the British courts was at issue. In the course of 181½ hours of debate on the European Communities Act 1972, the role of national courts was highlighted by neither government nor opposition and was touched upon by only three backbenchers. Indeed, had Lord Bridge undertaken a *Pepper v Hart* analysis,[19] then his interpretation of the ambiguous section 2(4) of the European Communities Act 1972 would have been informed by the clear statements of Lord Hailsham LC and Viscount Colville that Community law gives way to subsequent UK statute in the event of an irreconcilable conflict, with the result that the Merchant Shipping Act 1988

---

[17] Heibert (1999) 18.

[18] Consider, for example, the prominence in the Shadow Cabinet of MPs who proposed or supported Bills in the 1990s to restrict the supremacy of EC law in the United Kingdom.

[19] In *Pepper v Hart* [1993] AC 593, [1993] 1 All ER 42, the House of Lords held that it was permissible for courts to refer to *Hansard* as an aid to statutory interpretation, where (*a*) legislation was ambiguous or obscure or led to uncertainty; (*b*) the material relied upon consisted of one or more statements by a minister or other promoter of the Bill together if necessary with such other parliamentary material as was necessary to understand such statements or their effect; and (*c*) the statements relied upon were clear. As it was, *Pepper* was decided after *Factortame*.

would have prevailed over EC law. At best, Lord Bridge's reasoning can be said to be based on what *should* have been in the minds of legislators rather than what actually *was* in their minds.

If, as this book has shown, 'original intent' reasoning cannot be used to justify *Factortame* and *EOC*, it is necessary to look for other reasons to legitimize these House of Lords decisions. I have argued that the most convincing ground on which to base the supremacy of Community law within the United Kingdom lies in *the role of the courts in keeping constitutional law up to date with constitutional practice*. This underlying rationale represents the most plausible explanation for the outcomes of *Factortame* and *EOC*. It is realistic because it accepts the close connection between law and politics in a world in which 'the very dichotomy of law and politics is questionable'.[20] The desperate search for pure 'good legal reasons' unsullied by political concerns to justify *Factortame* flies in the face of the reality that politics and law are inseparable. The 'constitutional catch-up' explanation is also normatively attractive since it casts the judiciary in the secondary constitutional role of distilling from the political landscape those principles which enjoy the broadest possible consensus, thereby preserving the relatively non-partisan nature of the British constitution. The role of the judge ought not to be to impose his or her personal constitutional views under the camouflage of 'the rule of law' or 'implicit existing constitutional theory'. Conceptions of democracy are too numerous, contestable, and partisan for this to be a legitimate judicial function. It is difficult to see why a legal background, coupled with a lack of accountability, equip the judiciary for a primary constitutional-mongering role rather than a secondary constitution-reflecting one. Instead our courts ought to amend the constitution only to the extent that a *widespread political consensus* exists for such amendment. As Goldsworthy has convincingly argued, fundamental constitutional change should be brought about by consensus rather than by judicial fiat: limits on parliamentary sovereignty 'should be possible only if Parliament and the people so choose, understanding and accepting the legal and political consequences'.[21] Whether the demos makes the 'correct' choice is contestable and open to academic criticism. Normative arguments in favour of *this* or *that* constitutional change are therefore of fundamental importance, but the *power of choice* as to whether to accept or reject such arguments ought not to be confined to the courts. The audience to be convinced should extend wider than the judiciary's upper

---

[20] Weiler (1999) 15. [21] Goldsworthy (1999) ch 10.

echelons.[22] The question of whether the courts in their constitutional adjudication accurately capture the 'broad consensus' should also be open for academic criticism. In *Factortame* and *EOC*, the fact of twenty years of Community membership and the acceptance of membership by all the major political parties justified the conclusion of according supremacy to Community law rather than the conflicting statute.

The 'constitutional catch-up' justification represents in itself a good normative reason of principle to legitimize judicial modification of constitutional ground rules. However, the use of this justification leaves it open to question whether British courts should accord unlimited supremacy to Community law, or whether, like other Member States, our courts' acceptance of the supremacy doctrine ought to be more limited, conceding, perhaps, the right of Parliament to legislate contrary to Community law by express, intentional enactment. The fact of EC membership may be uncontroversial, but the notion of a limitless, 'inescapable and enduring' EC law supremacy does not enjoy consensus support. Unqualified EC law supremacy is not the kind of constitutional change which is 'capable of appealing to a plurality of different people and types of institution motivated by often diverse principles and goals'.[23] Accordingly there may be no call to circumscribe parliamentary sovereignty and disable the legislature to that extent. We may be led to the conclusion that the compromise adopted by Lord Denning MR in *Macarthys v Smith*, namely that Community law prevails save where Parliament 'deliberately passes an Act with the intention of repudiating the Treaty or any provision in it or intentionally of acting inconsistently with it and says so in express terms',[24] might represent a more balanced settlement between competing constitutional considerations all of which command very wide support: on the one hand, the need to ensure the effectiveness of Community rules in the normal run of events, on the other,

---

[22] There would not appear to be a compelling normative reason as to why courts should enjoy a more powerful role in the sphere of constitutional development than the one suggested here. For a critique of the argument that judges are more likely to deliberate on grounds of principle, whereas the demos tends to decide on the basis of interests, see Bellamy (1995) 164–165. For a critique of the argument that the judges are politically impartial and are determining legal as opposed to political questions in their constitutional adjudication, see Mandel (1989). As for the sentiment that judges possess superior wisdom to legislators, it is worth bearing in mind the finding of this book that the predictions of successive Lord Chancellors and prominent judges as to the legal impact of EEC membership were no more accurate than those of the politicians.

[23] Bellamy (1995) 155. For example, it is reasonably clear that as things stand such a limitation of parliamentary sovereignty would be vigorously opposed by the main opposition party.

[24] [1979] 3 All ER 325, 329 c–e. In contrast Lord Bridge in *Factortame* (No 2) spoke in terms of the duty of UK courts to override 'any' rule of national law found to be incompatible with EC law.

the importance accorded to the present generation not to be bound by the decisions of the previous generation, in other words the 'continuing' right of our electorate voting at the general election[25] to change the state of things.[26]

The study of law and politics

Finally, a few words remain to be said about the impact of the judicialization of British politics for future legislative and constitutional law studies. This book has highlighted a marked narrowing of the gap between the political and legal spheres in British public life. These spheres are now more interdependent and less autonomous. Three decades of EC membership have elevated the courts into an undisputed estate of the British body politic. Just as lawyers now take more interest in what is said in Parliament,[27] so too politicians have to take more interest in what is said by the courts. Constitutional development, formerly the preserve of the political actors, increasingly involves the interplay of judiciary and legislature, and tensions between the politicians and the judges are being played out in a more public arena. Britain's traditionally non-legal constitutional culture makes it unlikely that legislators will necessarily accept court decisions meekly. Parliament's adaptation to its new role as a legislature of limited competence need not connote passivity in the face of those charged with policing the new boundaries of Parliament's lawmaking authority. We may well be at the beginning of a fascinating story.

The evolution from a political constitution to a more judicialized one necessarily has an impact on scholarship. The disciplines of politics and law were always intimately connected;[28] but as they become even more so in the

---

[25] The dismal turnout at the 2001 election underlines the need for the constitution to facilitate rather than inhibit voters' potential breadth of choice.

[26] See Waldron (1993) for a powerful normative justification for parliamentary sovereignty based on the right to democracy as a 'right to participate *on equal terms* in social decisions on issues of high principle' (emphasis added). Waldron argues that 'respect for such democratic rights is called seriously into question when proposals are made to shift decisions about the conception and revision of basic rights from the legislature to the courtroom, from the people and their admittedly imperfect representative institutions to a handful of men and women, supposedly of wisdom, learning, virtue and high principle who, it is thought, alone can be trusted to take seriously the great issues that they raise'.

[27] *Pepper v Hart* (n 19 above), Klug (1999), Nicol (1999*b*). A recent Guide to the Human Rights Act contains thirty pages of *Hansard* extracts (Wadham and Mountfield (2000)).

[28] Griffith (1995) 3, Weiler (1999) 100.

United Kingdom, efforts to preserve a rigid division of academic labour become increasingly pernicious. The heightened interaction between the political and legal spheres reinforces the case for an interdisciplinary approach to both law and politics. Constitutional scholars from both disciplines will need to monitor the dialogue between legislature and judiciary if they are to provide an accurate assessment of the increasingly legal framework in which Parliament now operates.

BIBLIOGRAPHY

A. Official publications

United Kingdom (in date order)

European Communities

Membership of the European Communities, Cmnd 3269 (1967).
Legal and Constitutional Implications of United Kingdom Membership of the European Communities, Cmnd 3301 (1967).
Ministerial Briefing Paper FCO 30/7/89, Committee on Approach to Europe (1970).
The United Kingdom and the European Communities, Cmnd 4715 (1971).
Membership of the European Community, Cmnd 5999 (1975).
Membership of the European Communities: Report on Renegotiation, Cmnd 6003 (1975).
Britain's New Deal in Europe, government pamphlet (1975).
Single European Act and Parliamentary Scrutiny, 12th Report of the House of Lords Select Committee on the European Communities (Session 1985–6) HL, 149, para 12.
The Single European Act and Parliamentary Scrutiny, First Special Report from the Select Committee on European Legislation (Session 1985–6) HC, 265, para 21.
Developments in the European Community July–December 1991, Cm 1857 (1992).
Europe after Maastricht, Second Report from the Foreign Affairs Committee, Cm 223-I (1991–2).
Fifteenth Report of the Select Committee on European Legislation (1991–2).
A Partnership of Nations: The British Approach to the European Union Intergovernmental Conference 1996, Cm 3181 (1996).

Bill of Rights/Human Rights Act 1998

Report of the Select Committee on a Bill of Rights, HL, 176 (1977–8).
Rights Brought Home: The Human Rights Bill, Cm 3782 (1997).

Ireland (in date order)

European Economic Community, Pr 6106 (1961).
European Communities, Pr 9283 (1967).
Membership of the European Communities: Implications for Ireland, Prl 1110 (1970).

B. Books and articles

ALLAN, T [1982], 'Parliamentary Sovereignty and the EEC' Public Law 563.

——(1983), 'Parliamentary Sovereignty: Lord Denning's Dexterous Revolution' 3 Oxford Journal of Legal Studies 22.

——(1985*a*), 'Legislative Supremacy and the Rule of Law: Democracy and Constitutionalism' 44 Cambridge Law Journal 111.

——[1985*b*], 'The Limits of Parliamentary Sovereignty' Public Law 614.

——(1997), 'Parliamentary Sovereignty: Law, Politics and Revolution' 113 LQR 443.

ARNULL, A (1986), 'The Single European Act' 11 European Law Review 358.

ATTLEE, C (1954), *As It Happened* (Windmill Press, London).

AUDRETSCH, H (1986), *Supervision in European Community Law* (North-Holland, Amsterdam).

BAGEHOT, W (1905), *The English Constitution* (Kegan Paul, London).

BAKER, D, GAMBLE, A, and LUDLAM, S (1993), 'Whips or Scorpions? The Maastricht Vote and the Conservative Party' 46 Parliamentary Affairs 151.

————(1994), 'The Parliamentary Siege of Maastricht 1993: Conservative Divisions and British Ratification' 47 Parliamentary Affairs 37.

BAKER, K (1993), *The Turbulent Years: My Life in Politics* (Faber & Faber, London).

BALDWIN, N (1985), 'Behavioural Changes: A New Professionalism and a More Independent House' in P Norton (ed), *Parliament in the 1980s* (Basil Blackwell, Oxford).

BALEN, M (1994), *Kenneth Clarke* (Fourth Estate, London).

BALL, S, and SELDON, A (eds) (1993), *The Heath Government 1970–74* (Longmans, London).

BARAV, A (1994), 'Omnipotent Courts' in D Curtin and T Heukels (eds), *Institutional Dynamics of European Integration: Essays in Honour of Henry G Schermers* (Martinus Nijhoff, Dordrecht).

BAUN, M (1996), *An Imperfect Union: The Maastricht Treaty and the New Politics of European Integration* (Westview Press, Boulder, Colo).

BEATSON, J, and TRIDIMAS, T (eds) (1998), *New Directions in European Public Law* (Hart Publishing, Oxford).

BEBR, G (1971), 'Law of the European Communities and Municipal Law' 34 Modern Law Review 481.

BEER, S (1982), *Britain against Itself* (Faber & Faber, London).

BEETHAM, D (1991), *The Legitimation of Power* (Macmillan, London).

BELLAMY, R (1995), 'The Constitution of Europe: Rights or Democracy?' in R Bellamy, V Bufacchi, and D Castiglione (eds), *Democracy and Constitutional Culture in the Union of Europe* (Lothian Foundation Press, London).

——BUFACCHI, V, and CASTIGLIONE, D (eds) (1995), *Democracy and Constitutional Culture in the Union of Europe* (Lothian Foundation Press, London).

BELOFF, N (1968), *What Happened in Britain after the General said No* (Penguin, London).

BENN, T (1987), *Out of the Wilderness: Diaries 1963–7* (Hutchinson, London).

BINGHAM, Sir T (1992), 'There is a World Elsewhere: The Changing Perspectives of English Law' International and Comparative Law Quarterly 513.

——(1993), 'The European Convention on Human Rights: Time to Incorporate' 109 Law Quarterly Review 390.

BLACK, C (1973), 'Is There Already a British Bill of Rights?' 89 Law Quarterly Review 178.

BLACKBURN, R (1995), *The Electoral System in Britain* (Macmillan, London).

BOGDANOR, V, and BUTLER, D (1982), *Democracy and Elections: Electoral Systems and their Political Consequences* (Cambridge University Press, Cambridge).

BRADLEY, K, and SUTTON, A (1994), 'European Union and the Rule of Law' in A Duff, J Pinder, and R Pryce (eds), *Maastricht and Beyond* (Routledge, London).

BREST, P (1980), 'The Misconceived Quest for the Original Understanding' 60 Boston University Law Review 131.

BRIVATI, J, and JONES, L (eds) (1993), *From Construction to Integration* (Leicester University Press, Leicester).

BROWN, G (1972), *In my Way* (Penguin Books, London).

BROWNE-WILKINSON, Lord [1992], 'The Infiltration of a Bill of Rights' Public Law 397.

BUTLER, D, and KING, A (1965), *The British General Election of 1964* (Macmillan, London).

————(1966), *The British General Election of 1966* (Macmillan, London).

——and KITZINGER, U (1996), *The 1975 Referendum* (Macmillan Press, London).

——and PINTO-DUSCHINSKY, M (1971), *The British General Election of 1970* (Macmillan, London).

——and ROSE, A (1960), *The British General Election of 1959* (Macmillan, London).

BUTT, R (1967), *The Power of Parliament* (Constable, London).

CAMPBELL, J (1983), *Roy Jenkins: A Biography* (Weidenfeld & Nicolson, London).

——(1993), *Edward Heath: A Biography* (Jonathan Cape, London).

CAMPS, M (1993), 'Missing the Boat at Messina and Other Times' in J Brivati and L Jones (eds), *From Construction to Integration* (Leicester University Press, Leicester).

CASEY, J (1987), *Constitutional Law in the Republic of Ireland* (Sweet & Maxwell, London).

——(1992), *Constitutional Law in Ireland* (2nd edn) (Sweet & Maxwell, London).

CASTLE, B (1984), *The Castle Diaries 1964–70* (Weidenfeld & Nicolson, London).

CHORUS, J, GERVER, P-H, HONDIUS, E, and KOEKKEOK, A (1991), *Introduction to Dutch Law* (3rd edn) (Kluwer Law International, The Hague).

CHUBB, B (ed) (1964), *A Source Book of Irish Government* (Institute of Public Administration, Dublin).

——(1978), *The Constitution and Constitutional Change in Ireland* (Institute of Public Administration, Dublin).

CHUBB, B (1991), *Politics of the Irish Constitution* (Institute of Public Administration, Dublin).

CHURCH, C, and PHINNEMORE, D (1994), *European Union and European Community* (Prentice Hall, Hemel Hempstead).

CLARKE, D, and SUFRIN, B (1983), 'Constitutional Conundrums: The Impact of the United Kingdom's Membership of the Communities on Constitutional Theory' in M Furmston, R Kerridge, and B Sufrin (eds), *The Effect on English Domestic Law of Membership of the European Communities and Ratification of the European Convention on Human Rights* (Martinus Nijhoff Publishers, The Hague).

COAKLEY, J (1983), 'The European Dimension in Irish Public Opinion' in D Coombes (ed), *Ireland and the European Communities: 10 Years of Membership* (Gill & Macmillan, Dublin).

COHAN, A (1972), *The Irish Political Élite* (Gill & Macmillan, Dublin).

COLLINS, L (1984), *European Community Law in the United Kingdom* (3rd edn) (Butterworths, London).

CONNOLLY, W (ed) (1984), *Legitimacy and the State* (Basil Blackwell, Oxford).

COOK, D (1984), *Charles de Gaulle: A Biography* (Secker & Warberg, New York).

COOMBES, D (1981), 'Parliament and the European Community' in S Walkland and M Ryle (eds), *The Commons Today* (William Collins & Sons, Glasgow).

——(ed) (1983), *Ireland and the European Communities: 10 Years of Membership* (Gill & Macmillan, Dublin).

COOPER, D (1998), *Governing Out of Order* (Rivers Oram Press, London).

CORBETT, R (1992), 'The Intergovernmental Conference on Political Union' 30 Journal of Common Market Studies 271.

——(1994), 'Representing the People' in A Duff, J Pinder, and R Pryce (eds), *Maastricht and Beyond* (Routledge, London).

COSTELLO, D (1987), 'Natural Law, the Constitution and the Courts' in P Lynch and J Meenan (eds), *Essays in Memory of Alexis FitzGerald* (The Incorporated Law Society of Ireland, Dublin).

COUGHLAN, A (1970), *The Common Market: Why Ireland Should Not Join!* (Common Market Study Group, Dublin).

——(1979), *The EEC: Ireland and the Making of a Superpower* (Irish Sovereignty Movement, Dublin).

CRAIG, P (1990), *Public Law and Democracy in the United Kingdom and the United States of America* (Clarendon Press, Oxford).

——(1991), 'Sovereignty of the United Kingdom Parliament after *Factortame*' 11 Yearbook of European Law 221.

——(1992), 'Once Upon a Time in the West: Direct Effect and the Federalisation of EEC Law' 12 Oxford Journal of Legal Studies 453.

——(1994), 'Legality, Standing and Substantive Review in Community Law' 14 Oxford Journal of Legal Studies 507.

——[1997a], 'Formal and Substantive Conceptions of the Rule of Law: An Analytical Framework' Public Law 467.

——(1997*b*), 'The Impact of Community Law on Domestic Public Law' in P Leyland and T Woods (eds), *Administrative Law Facing the Future: Old Constraints and New Horizons* (Blackstone Press Ltd, London).

——(1998*a*), 'Report on the United Kingdom' in A Slaughter, A Stone Sweet, and J Weiler (eds), *The European Court and National Courts: Doctrine and Jurisprudence* (Hart, Oxford).

——(1998*b*), 'Ultra Vires and the Foundations of Judicial Review' 57 Cambridge Law Journal 63.

——(1999*a*), 'The Nature of the Community: Integration, Democracy and Legitimacy' in P Craig and G de Búrca (eds), *The Evolution of EU Law* (Clarendon Press, Oxford).

——(1999*b*), *Administrative Law* (4th edn) (Sweet & Maxwell, London).

——and DE BÚRCA, G (1998), *EU Law: Text, Cases and Materials* (2nd edn) (Clarendon Press, Oxford).

————(eds) (1999), *The Evolution of EU Law* (Clarendon Press, Oxford).

——and WALTERS, M (1999), 'The Courts, Devolution and Judicial Review' Public Law 274.

CROSLAND, S (1982), *Tony Crosland* (Coronet Books, London).

CROSSMAN, R (1975), *The Diaries of a Cabinet Minister* (Book Club Associates, London).

CULLEN, P (1993), *The United Kingdom and the Ratification of the Maastricht Treaty: The Constitutional Position* (Edinburgh Europa Institute, Edinburgh).

DE BÚRCA, G (1996), 'The Quest for Legitimacy in the European Union' 59 Modern Law Review 347.

DENNING, Lord (1993), *The Closing Chapter* (Butterworths, London).

DE SMITH, S (1971), 'The Constitution and the Common Market: A Tentative Appraisal' 34 Modern Law Review 507.

——WOOLF, Lord, and JOWELL, J (1995), *Judicial Review of Administrative Action* (Sweet & Maxwell, London).

DE WITTE, B (1999), 'Direct Effect, Supremacy and the Nature of the Legal Order' in P Craig and G de Búrca (eds), *The Evolution of EU Law* (Clarendon Press, Oxford).

DE ZWAAN, J (1986), 'The Single European Act: Conclusion of a Unique Document' 23 Common Market Law Review 747.

DICEY, A (1959), *Introduction to the Study of the Law of the Constitution* (10th edn) (Macmillan, London).

DIKE, C [1976], 'The Case against Parliamentary Sovereignty' Public Law 283.

DINAN, D (1994), *Ever Closer Union?* (Macmillan, London).

DIPLOCK, Lord [1972], 'The Common Market and the Common Law' Law Teacher 3.

DONALDSON, Lord (1991), 'Can the Judiciary Control Acts of Parliament?' 25 Law Teacher 4.

DUFF, A (1994), 'Ratification' in A Duff, J Pinder, and R Pryce (eds), *Maastricht and Beyond* (Routledge, London).

DUFF, A, PINDER, J, and PRYCE, R (eds) (1994), *Maastricht and Beyond* (Routledge, London).

DUNCANSON, I [1978], 'Balloonists, Bills of Rights and Dinosaurs' Public Law 391.

DWORKIN, R (1990), *A Bill of Rights for Britain* (Chatto & Windus, London).

EDWARDS, D (1987), 'The Impact of the Single Act on the Institutions' 24 Common Market Law Review 19.

EEKELAAR, J (1997), 'The Death of Parliamentary Sovereignty: A Comment' 113 Law Quarterly Review 185.

ELLIS, E (1980), 'Supremacy of Parliament and European Law' 96 Law Quarterly Review 511.

EWING, K, and GEARTY, C (1994), *Democracy or a Bill of Rights?* (Society of Labour Lawyers, London).

FAZAL, M [1974], 'Entrenched Rights and Parliamentary Sovereignty' Public Law 295.

FINER, S (1975), *Adversarial Politics and Electoral Reform* (Wigram, London).

FISHER, N (1982), *Harold Macmillan* (Weidenfeld & Nicolson, London).

FITZGERALD, G (1970), *Towards A New Ireland* (Charles Knight, London).

FORDE, M (1987), *Constitutional Law of Ireland* (Mercier Press, Cork).

FORMAN, J (1973), 'The European Communities Act 1972: The Government's Position on the Meaning and Effect of its Constitutional Provisions' 10 Common Market Law Review 39.

FREDMAN, S (1998), 'Bringing Rights Home' 114 Law Quarterly Review 538.

FURMSTON, M, KERRIDGE, R, and SUFRIN, B (eds) (1983), *The Effect on English Domestic Law of Membership of the European Communities and Ratification of the European Convention on Human Rights* (Martinus Nijhoff Publishers, The Hague).

GANSHOF VAN DER MEERSCH, W (1983), 'Community Law and the Belgian Constitution' in S Bates et al (eds), *In Memoriam J.D.B. Mitchell* (Sweet & Maxwell, London).

GARNETT, M, and SHERRINGTON, P (1996), 'UK Parliamentary Perspectives on Europe 1971–93' 2 Journal of Legislative Studies 383.

GEORGE, S (1996), *Politics and Policy in the European Union* (Oxford University Press, Oxford).

GEORGE-BROWN, Lord (1971), *In my Way* (Victor Gollancz, London).

GIBSON, N, and SPENCER, J (eds) (1977), *Economic Activity in Ireland* (Gill & Macmillan, Dublin).

GILMOUR, D [1968], 'The Sovereignty of Parliament and the European Commission of Human Rights' Public Law 62.

GOLDSWORTHY, J (1999), *The Sovereignty of Parliament: History and Philosophy* (Oxford University Press, Oxford).

GRANT, C (1994), *Delors: Inside the House that Jacques Built* (Nicholas Brearly Publishing, London).

GRAVELLS, N [1989], 'Disapplying an Act of Parliament Pending a Preliminary Ruling: Constitutional Enormity or Community Law Right?' Public Law 568.

GRIEF, N [1991], 'The Domestic Impact of the European Convention on Human Rights as Mediated through Community Law' Public Law 555.

GRIFFITH, J (1974), *Parliamentary Scrutiny of Government Bills* (Allen & Unwin, London).

——(1979), 'The Political Constitution' 41 Modern Law Review 1.

——(1993), *Judicial Politics since 1920* (Blackwell, Oxford).

——(1995), 'The Study of Law and Politics' 1 Journal of Legislative Studies 3.

——(1997), *The Politics of the Judiciary* (Fontana Press, London).

——(2000), 'The Brave New World of Sir John Laws' 63 Modern Law Review 1.

HAAHR, J (1992), 'European Integration and the Left in Britain and Denmark' Journal of Common Market Studies 77.

HAAS, E (1958), *The Uniting of Europe* (Stanford University Press, Stanford, Calif).

HABERMAS, J (1973), *Legitimation Crisis* (Heinemann, London).

——(1979), *Communication and the Evolution of Society* (Heinemann Educational, London).

HAILSHAM, Lord (1978), *The Dilemma of Democracy: Diagnosis and Prescription* (Collins, London).

——(1990), *A Sparrow's Flight* (Collins, London).

HAIN, P (1986), *Proportional Misrepresentation* (Wildwood Press Ltd, Aldershot).

Hansard Society (1976), *Commission on Electoral Reform* (Hansard Society, London).

HARDEN, I, and LEWIS, N (1986), *The Noble Lie* (Hutchinson, London).

HARTLEY, T [1986], 'Federalism, Courts and Legal Systems' American Journal of Comparative Law 229.

HEALEY, D (1989), *The Time of my Life* (Penguin, London).

HEDERMAN, M (1983), *The Road to Europe: Irish Attitudes 1948–61* (Institute of Public Administration, Dublin).

HEIBERT, J (1999), 'Wrestling with Rights: Judges, Parliament and the Making of Social Policy' 5 Choices 18.

HENCHY, S (1977), 'The Irish Constitution and the EEC' 1 Dublin University Law Journal 20.

HERMAN, V (1972), 'Backbench and Opposition Amendments to Government Legislation' in D Leonard and V Herman (eds), *The Backbencher and Parliament: A Reader* (Macmillan, London).

HILLMAN, J, and CLARKE, P (1988), *Geoffrey Howe: A Quiet Revolutionary* (Weidenfeld & Nicolson, London).

HOFFMAN, L (1991), 'A Dog's Breakfast? The Supremacy of EC Law' 135 Solicitors Journal 1130.

HOGAN, G (1987), 'The Supreme Court and the Single European Act' 22 Irish Jurist 55.

——and WHELAN, A (1995), *Ireland and the European Union* (Sweet & Maxwell, London).

HOOD PHILLIPS, O (1979), 'Has the Incoming Tide Reached the Palace of Westminster?' 95 Law Quarterly Review 167.

Hood Phillips, O (1980), 'High Tide in the Strand? Post-1972 Acts and Community Law' 96 Law Quarterly Review 31.

Hooper, Sir A [1999], 'The Impact of the Human Rights Act' European Human Rights Law Review 676.

Horne, A (1988), *Macmillan: The Official Biography* (Macmillan, London).

Howe, G (1994), *Conflict of Loyalty* (Macmillan, London).

——(1996), 'Euro-Justice: Yes or No?' 21 European Law Review 187.

Hunt, M [1998], 'The "Horizontal Effect" of the Human Rights Act' Public Law 423.

Hyde, A [1983], 'The Concept of Legitimation in the Sociology of Law' Wisconsin Law Review 379.

Irvine, Lord [1996], 'Response to Sir John Laws 1996' Public Law 636.

Jacobs, F, Corbett, R, and Shackleton, M (1992), *The European Parliament* (Longman, Harlow).

Jaconelli, J [1976], 'The European Convention on Human Rights: The Text of a British Bill of Rights?' Public Law 226.

——(1980), *Enacting a Bill of Rights: The Legal Problems* (Clarendon Press, Oxford).

——[1985], 'Comment I' Public Law 629.

Janis, M (1992*a*), 'The European Court of Human Rights' in M Janis (ed), *International Courts for the 21st Century* (Martinus Nijhoff, Dordrecht).

——(ed) (1992*b*), *International Courts for the 21st Century* (Martinus Nijhoff, Dordrecht).

Jay, D (1980), *Change and Fortune: A Political Record* (Hutchinson, London).

Jenkins, R (1991), *A Life at the Centre* (Macmillan, London).

Jennings, I (1961), *The British Constitution* (Cambridge University Press, Cambridge).

Jones, M (1994), *Michael Foot* (Victor Gollancz, London).

Judge, D (1988), 'Incomplete Sovereignty: The British House of Commons and the Completion of the Internal Market in the European Communities' 41 Parliamentary Affairs 441.

Keatinge, P (1973), *A Place among the Nations: Issues of Irish Foreign Policy* (Institute of Public Administration, Dublin).

——(1978), *A Place among the Nations: Issues of Irish Foreign Policy* (Institute of Public Administration, Dublin).

——(ed) (1991), *Ireland and EC Membership Evaluated* (Pinter Publishers, London).

Keenan, P [1962], 'Some Legal Consequences of Britain's Entry into the European Common Market' Public Law 327.

Keeton, G, and Schwarzenberger, G (eds) (1963), *English Law and the Common Market* (Stevens & Sons, London).

Kelly, J (1967), *Fundamental Rights in the Irish Law and Constitution* (Allen Figgis & Co, Dublin).

——(1994), *The Irish Constitution* (3rd edn) (Butterworths, Dublin).

KENTRIDGE, S [1997], 'Parliamentary Supremacy and the Judiciary under a Bill of Rights: Some Lessons from the Commonwealth' Public Law 96.

KEOGH, D (1997), 'The Diplomacy of "Dignified Calm": An Analysis of Ireland's Application for Membership of the EEC 1961–1963' 3 Journal of European Integration History 83.

KILMUIR, Lord (1964), *Political Adventure* (Weidenfeld & Nicolson, London).

KITZINGER, U (1973), *Diplomacy and Persuasion: How Britain Joined the Common Market* (Thames & Hudson, London).

KLUG, F [1999], 'The Human Rights Act 1998, Pepper v Hart and All That' Public Law 246.

——and WADHAM, J [1993], 'The "Democratic" Entrenchment of a Bill of Rights: Liberty's Proposals' Public Law 179.

KOHN, L (1932), *The Constitution of the Irish Free State* (George Allen & Irwin, London).

KOOPMANS, T (1983), 'Receptivity and its Limits: the Dutch Case' in S Bates et al (eds), *In Memoriam J.D.B. Mitchell* (Sweet & Maxwell, London).

LACOUTURE, J (1985), *De Gaulle the Ruler: 1945–1970* (HarperCollins, London).

LAFFAN, B (1991), 'Sovereignty and National Identity' in P Keatinge (ed), *Ireland and EC Membership Evaluated* (Pinter Publishers, London).

LAMONT, N (1999), *In Office* (Little, Brown & Co, London).

LASOK, D (1972), 'The Introduction of European Community Law onto the Syllabus' 12 Journal of the Society of Public Teachers of Law 83.

——(1973), 'The Place of European Law in the Undergraduate Curricula' Law Teacher 154.

LAUTERPACHT, E (1997), 'Sovereignty—Myth or Reality?' 73/1 International Affairs 137.

LAWS, Sir J [1993], 'Is the High Court the Guardian of Fundamental Constitutional Rights?' Public Law 59.

——(1994), 'Judicial Remedies and the Constitution' 57 Modern Law Review 213.

——[1995], 'Law and Democracy' Public Law 72.

——[1996], 'The Constitution: Morals and Rights' Public Law 622.

——[1998], 'The Limitations of Human Rights' Public Law 254.

LAWSON, N (1993), *The View from No. 11* (Corgi Books, London).

LEE, S [1985], 'Comment II' Public Law 632.

LEMAY, G (1964), *British Government 1914–63* (Methuen, London).

LEONARD, D, and HERMAN, V (1972), *The Backbencher and Parliament: A Reader* (Macmillan, London).

LESTER, A (1968), 'Democracy and Individual Rights' (Fabian Tract No 390, London).

——[1984], 'Fundamental Rights: The United Kingdom Isolated?' Public Law 46.

LESTER, Lord [1995], 'The Mouse That Roared: The Human Rights Bill 1995' Public Law 198.

LEYLAND, P, and WOODS, T (eds) (1997), *Administrative Law Facing the Future: Old Constraints and New Horizons* (Blackstone Press Ltd, London).

Lipset, S (1960), *Political Man* (Heinemann, London).

Lodge, J (1985–6), 'The Single European Act' 24 Journal of Common Market Studies 203.

Lord, C (1990), 'British Entry to the European Community and the Cognitive Paradigm of Foreign Policy Change' (PhD thesis, British Library of Political and Economic Science).

——(1992), 'Sovereign or Confused? The "Great Debate" about British Entry to the European Community Twenty Years On' 30/4 Journal of Common Market Studies 419.

——(1993), *British Entry to the EC under the Heath Government of 1970–4* (Dartmouth, Aldershot).

——(1996), *Absent at the Creation: Britain and the Formation of the European Community* (Dartmouth, Aldershot).

Loveland, I (1992), 'Labour and the Constitution: The "Right" Approach to Reform?' 45 Parliamentary Affairs 173.

——(1996), 'Parliamentary Sovereignty and the European Community: The Unfinished Revolution?' 49 Parliamentary Affairs 517.

——[1997], 'The War against the Judges' 68 Political Quarterly 162.

——(2000), *Constitutional Law: A Critical Introduction* (2nd edn) (Butterworths, London).

Lynch, P, and Meenan, J (eds) (1987), *Essays in Memory of Alexis FitzGerald* (Incorporated Law Society of Ireland, Dublin).

Lynskey, J (1970), 'Role of the British Backbenchers in the Modification of Government Policy' 23 Western Political Quarterly 347.

McAleese, D (1977), 'The Foreign Sector' in N Gibson and I Spencer (eds), *Economic Activity in Ireland* (Gill & Macmillan, Dublin).

McCutcheon, P (1991), 'The Legal System' in P Keatinge (ed), *Ireland and EC Membership Evaluated* (Pinter Publishers, London).

McLeod, I (1992), 'The Use of Hansard in Statutory Interpretation' 156 Local Government Review 1021.

——(1999), *Legal Theory* (Macmillan, London).

——(2000), *Legal Method* (3rd edn) (Macmillan, London).

McMahon, B (1971), 'Ireland and the Right of Establishment under the Treaty of Rome' 6 Irish Jurist 271.

——(1976), 'Ireland: Constitutional Adjustments Necessitated by Community Membership' 1 European Law Review 86.

——(1977), 'Ireland: The Oireachtas and Community Legislation' 2 European Law Review 150.

——and Murphy, F (1989), *European Community Law in Ireland* (Butterworths, Dublin).

Mackintosh, J (1977), *The Government and Politics of Britain* (4th edn) (Hutchinson, London).

Macmillan, H (1971), *Riding the Storm* (Macmillan, London).

——(1973), *At the End of the Day* (Macmillan, London).

Major, J (2000), *The Autobiography* (HarperCollins Publishers, London).

Mancini, G (2000), *Democracy and Constitutionalism in the European Union* (Hart Publishing, Oxford).

Mandel, M (1989), *The Charter of Rights and the Legalization of Politics in Canada* (Wall & Thompson, Toronto).

Mann, F (1972), 'The United Kingdom's Bill of Rights' 122 New Law Journal 289.

——(1978), 'Britain's Bill of Rights' 94 Law Quarterly Review 512.

March Hunnings, N (1968–9), 'Constitutional Implications of Joining the Common Market' 6 Common Market Law Review 50.

Marriott, J, and Nicol, D (1998), 'The Human Rights Act, Representative Standing and the Victim Culture' 6 European Human Rights Law Review 730.

Marshall, G (1990), *Constitutional Conventions* (Clarendon Press, Oxford).

——[1997], 'Parliamentary Sovereignty: The New Horizons' Public Law 1.

Martin, A (1968–9), 'The Accession of the United Kingdom to the European Communities: Jurisdictional Problems' 6 Common Market Law Review 7.

Maudling, R (1978), *Memoirs* (Sidgwick & Jackson, London).

Mayne, R (1963), *The Community of Europe* (Victor Gollancz, London).

Miller, J (1974), *Survey of Commonwealth Affairs: Problems of Expansion and Attrition 1953–1969* (Oxford University Press, London).

Mitchell, J [1960–1], 'The Flexible Constitution' Public Law 332.

——(1967–8), 'What do you want to be inscrutable *for*, Marcia?' 5 Common Market Law Review 112.

——(1968), *Constitutional Law* (2nd edn) (W Green & Son, Edinburgh).

——Kuipers, S, and Gall, B (1972), 'Constitutional Aspects of the Treaty and Legislation Relating to British Membership' 9 Common Market Law Review 134.

Moon, J (1985), *European Integration in British Politics 1950–1963: A Study of Issue Change* (Gower, Aldershot).

Mount, F (1993), *The British Constitution Now* (Mandarin, London).

Mowat, R (1974), *Creating the European Community* (Blandford Press, London).

Muir, R (1930), *How Britain is Governed* (Constable and Co, London).

Mullender, R (1998), 'Parliamentary Sovereignty, the Constitution, and the Judiciary' 49 Northern Ireland Law Quarterly 138.

Munro, C (1987), *Studies in Constitutional Law* (Butterworths, London).

——(1999), *Studies in Constitutional Law* (2nd edn) (Butterworths, London).

Murphy, F (1983), 'The Irish Legal System' in D Coombes (ed), *Ireland and the European Communities: 10 Years of Membership* (Gill & Macmillan, Dublin).

Nicol, D [1996], 'Disapplying with Relish? The Industrial Tribunals and Acts of Parliament' Public Law 579.

——(1999a), 'Limitation Periods under the Human Rights Act 1998' 115 Law Quarterly Review 48.

——(1999b), 'The Legal Constitution: United Kingdom Parliament and European Court of Justice' 5 Journal of Legislative Studies 135.

Nicol, D (2001), 'Lessons from Luxembourg: Federalisation and the Court of Human Rights' 26 European Law Review 3.

Nolan, Lord, and Sedley, Sir S (1997), *The Making and Remaking of the British Constitution* (Blackstone Press, London).

Norton, P (1982), *The Constitution in Flux* (Martin Robertson, Oxford).

——(1985), *Parliament in the 1980s* (Basil Blackwell, Oxford).

——(1989), 'The Glorious Revolution of 1688: Its Continuing Relevance' 42 Parliamentary Affairs 135.

——(ed) (1990), *Legislatures* (Oxford University Press, Oxford).

——(1997), 'Roles and Behaviour of British MPs' 3 Journal of Legislative Studies 17.

Nugent, N (1993), *The Government and Politics of the European Union* (2nd edn) (Macmillan, London).

Oliver, D [1993*a*], 'Pepper v Hart: A Suitable Case for Reference to Hansard?' Public Law 5.

——[1993*b*], 'The Frontiers of Public Law' Public Law 4.

O'Mahony, T (1991), *Jack Lynch: A Biography* (Blackwater Press, Dublin).

O'Neill, C (2000), *Britain's Entry into the European Community: Report on the Negotiations of 1970–1972* (Whitehall History Publishing/Frank Cass, London).

O'Reilly, J, and Redmond, M (1980), *Cases & Materials on the Irish Constitution* (Incorporated Law Society of Ireland, Dublin).

Owen, D (1991), *Time to Declare* (Michael Joseph, London).

Parkinson, C (1992), *Right at the Centre* (Weidenfeld & Nicolson, London).

Pescatore, P (1970), 'International Law and Community Law: A Comparative Analysis' 7 Common Market Law Review 167.

Phelan, D (1997), *Revolt or Revolution: The Constitutional Boundaries of the European Community* (Round Hall, Sweet & Maxwell, Dublin).

Pimlott, B (1992), *Harold Wilson* (HarperCollins, London).

Pinder, J (1986), 'Is the Single European Act a Step towards a Federal Europe?' 7 Policy Studies 19.

——(1995), *European Community: The Building of a Union* (Oxford University Press, Oxford).

Polsby, N (1990), 'Legislatures' in P Norton (ed), *Legislatures* (Oxford University Press, Oxford).

Powell, E (1971), *The Common Market: The Case Against* (Elliot Right Way Books, Kingswood).

——(1973), *The Common Market: Renegotiate or Come Out* (Elliot Right Way Books, Kingswood).

——(1978), *A Nation or No Nation?* (Batsford, London).

——(1987), 'Rules for Originalists' 73 Virginia Law Review 659.

Prior, J (1986), *A Balance of Power* (Hamish Hamilton, London).

Pryce, R (1994), 'The Treaty Negotiations' in A Duff, J Pinder, and R Pryce (eds), *Maastricht and Beyond* (Routledge, London).

Radlett, D (1997), 'On Democracy' 4 European Journal 22.

RASMUSSEN, H (1986), *On Law and Policy in the European Court of Justice* (Martinus Nijhoff, Dordrecht).

RAWLINGS, R [1994*a*], 'Legal Politics: The United Kingdom and Ratification of the Treaty on European Union (Part One)' Public Law 214.

—— [1994*b*], 'Legal Politics: The United Kingdom and Ratification of the Treaty on European Union (Part Two)' Public Law 367.

REID, M (1990), *The Impact of Community Law on the Irish Constitution* (Irish Centre for European Law, Dublin).

RIDDELL, P (2000), *Parliament under Blair* (Politico's Publishing, London).

RIDLEY, N (1991), *'My Style of Government': The Thatcher Years* (Hutchinson, London).

RIPPON, G, et al (1971), *Europe: The Case for Going In* (George G Harrop, London).

ROBERTSON, A (1961), *The Council of Europe* (Stevens & Sons, London).

ROBINS, L (1979), *The Reluctant Party: Labour and the EEC 1961–75* (G W & A Hesketh, Ormskirk).

ROBINSON, M (1973*a*), 'Recent Developments in Ireland in Relation to the European Communities' 10 Common Market Law Review 467.

—— (1973*b*), 'The Irish European Communities Act 1972' 10 Common Market Law Review 352.

ROSSITER, C (ed) (1961), *The Federalist Papers* (Mentor, New York).

ROTH, A (1967), *The Business Background of MPs: The 1967 Edition* (Parliamentary Profiles, London).

—— and KERBY, J (1972), *The Business Background of MPs* (Parliamentary Profiles, London).

SCHAAR, J (1984), 'Legitimacy in the Modern State' in W Connolly (ed), *Legitimacy and the State* (Basil Blackwell, Oxford) (1st pub 1969).

SCHMIDTTHOFF, C (1973), 'The Effects of the Accession of the United Kingdom to the European Communities on Law Teaching in England' 7 Law Teacher 65.

SEARING, D (1994), *Westminster's World* (Harvard University Press, Cambridge, Mass).

SEATON, J, and WINETROBE, B (1998), 'The Passage of Constitutional Bills in Parliament' 4 Journal of Legislative Studies 33.

SEDLEY, Sir S (1994), 'The Sound of Silence: Constitutional Law without a Constitution' 110 Law Quarterly Review 270.

—— [1995], 'Human Rights: A 21st Century Agenda' Public Law 386.

SELSDON, A (1981), *Churchill's Indian Summer: The Conservative Government 1951–55* (Hodder & Stoughton, London).

—— (1997), *Major: A Political Life* (Weidenfeld & Nicolson, London).

SHAPIRO, M (1999), 'The European Court of Justice' in P Craig and G de Búrca (eds), *The Evolution of EU Law* (Clarendon Press, Oxford).

SHELL, D (1987), 'The British Constitution in 1986' 40 Parliamentary Affairs 279.

—— (1996), 'The British Constitution in 1995' 49 Parliamentary Affairs 243.

SHEPHERD, R (1994), *Iain Macleod: A Biography* (Pimlico, London).

SHEPHERD, R (1996), *Enoch Powell: A Biography* (Pimlico, London).

SLAUGHTER, A, STONE SWEET, A, and WEILER, J (eds) (1998), *The European Court and National Courts: Doctrine and Jurisprudence* (Hart, Oxford).

SLYNN, G (1992), *Introducing a European Legal Order* (Stevens & Sons/Sweet & Maxwell, London).

SPANIER, D (1972), *Europe, our Europe* (Secker & Warberg, London).

STEYN, Lord [1997], 'The Weakest and Least Dangerous Department of Government' Public Law 84.

STRAUSS, G (1972), 'The Influence of the Backbencher: A Labour View' in D Leonard and V Herman (eds), *The Backbencher and Parliament: A Reader* (Macmillan, London).

TEBBIT, N (1988), *Upwardly Mobile* (Weidenfeld & Nicolson, London).

——(1991), *Unfinished Business* (Weidenfeld & Nicolson, London).

TEMPLE LANG, J (1963), 'A Constitutional Aspect of Economic Integration: Ireland and the European Common Market' 12 International and Comparative Law Quarterly 552.

——(1966), *The Common Market and the Common Law* (University of Chicago Press, Chicago).

——(1972), 'Legal and Constitutional Implications for Ireland of Adhesion to the EEC Treaty' 9 Common Market Law Review 167.

THATCHER, M (1993), *The Downing Street Years* (HarperCollins, London).

——(1995), *The Path to Power* (HarperCollins, London).

THOMPSON, D, and MARSH, N (1962), 'The United Kingdom and the Treaty of Rome: Some Preliminary Observations' 11 International and Comparative Law Quarterly 73.

TREITEL, G (1999), *The Law of Contract* (10th edn) (Sweet & Maxwell, London).

TRIDIMAS, T (1998), 'Damages for Breach of Community Law' in J Beatson and T Tridimas (eds), *New Directions in European Public Law* (Hart Publishing, Oxford).

TRINDADE, F (1972), 'Parliamentary Sovereignty and the Primacy of European Community Law' 35 Modern Law Review 375.

VON PRONDZYNSKI, F (1977), 'Natural Law and the Constitution' 1 Dublin University Law Journal 32.

WADE, H [1955], 'The Basis of Legal Sovereignty' Cambridge Law Journal 172.

——(1972), 'Sovereignty and the European Communities' 88 Law Quarterly Review 1.

——(1979), 'Anisminic ad Infinitum' 95 Law Quarterly Review 163.

——(1980), *Constitutional Fundamentals* (Stevens, London).

——(1991), 'What has Happened to the Sovereignty of Parliament?' 107 Law Quarterly Review 1.

——(1996), 'Sovereignty—Revolution or Evolution?' 112 Law Quarterly Review 568.

——and FORSYTH, C (2000), *Administrative Law* (8th edn) (Clarendon Press, Oxford).

WADHAM, J, and MOUNTFIELD, H (2000), *Blackstone's Guide to the Human Rights Act 1998* (2nd edn) (Blackstone Press, London).

WALDRON, J (1993), 'A Right-Based Critique of Constitutional Rights' 13 Oxford Journal of Legal Studies 18.

WALKLAND, S (1969), *The Legislative Process in Great Britain* (George Allen & Unwin, London).

——and RYLE, M (eds) (1981), *The Commons Today* (William Collins & Sons, Glasgow).

WALL, E (1973), *European Communities Act 1972* (Butterworths, London).

WARD, I (1996), *A Critical Introduction to European Law* (Butterworths, London).

WEBER, M (1968), *Economy and Society* (Bedminster Press, London).

WEILER, J (1981), 'The Community System: The Dual Nature of Supranationalism' Yearbook of European Law 267.

——(1986), 'Eurocracy and Distrust' Washington Law Review 1103.

——(1999), *The Constitution of Europe: Do the New Clothes Have an Emperor? And Other Essays on European Integration* (Cambridge University Press, Cambridge).

WESTLAKE, M (1995), *The Council of the European Union* (Cartermill, London).

WHELAN, A (1992), 'Article 29.4.3 and the Meaning of "Necessity"' 2 Irish Student Law Review 60.

WHITAKER, T (1973), 'From Protection to Free Trade: The Irish Experience' 21 Administration 405.

WILLIAMS, M (1972), *Inside No. 10* (Weidenfeld & Nicolson, London).

WILLIAMS, P (1979), *Hugh Gaitskell* (Jonathan Cape, London).

WILSON, H (1964), *Purpose in Politics* (Weidenfeld & Nicolson, London).

——(1971), *The Labour Government 1964–70* (Penguin Books, London).

——(1979), *Final Term: The Labour Government 1974–1976* (Weidenfeld & Nicolson and Michael Joseph, London).

WINTER, J (1972), 'Direct Applicability and Direct Effect: Two Distinct and Different Concepts in Community Law' 9 Common Market Law Review 425.

WOODHOUSE, D (1996), 'Politicians and the Judges: A Conflict of Interest' 49 Parliamentary Affairs 423.

WOOLF, Sir H (1990), *Protection of the Public: A New Challenge* (Stevens & Sons, London).

WOOLF, Lord [1995], 'Droit Public—English Style' Public Law 57.

YOUNG, J (1993*a*), *British and European Unity 1945–92* (Macmillan, London).

——(1993*b*), 'The Heath Government and British Entry into the European Community' in S Ball and A Seldon (eds), *The Heath Government 1970–74* (Longmans, London).

YOUNG, Lord (1990), *The Enterprise Years* (Headline, London).

ZANDER, M (1997), *A Bill of Rights?* (4th edn) (Sweet & Maxwell, London).

ZIEGLER, P (1993), *Wilson: The Authorised Life* (Hutchinson, London).

INDEX